Word Parts Dictionary

Word Parts Dictionary

Standard and Reverse Listings of
Prefixes, Suffixes, Roots and
Combining Forms

by

MICHAEL J. SHEEHAN

McFarland & Company, Inc., Publishers
Jefferson, North Carolina, and London

Library of Congress Cataloguing-in-Publication Data

Sheehan, Michael, 1939–
    Word parts dictionary : standard and reverse listings of prefixes,
suffixes, and combining forms / by Michael Sheehan.
        p.   cm.
    Includes index.
    ISBN 0-7864-0819-7 (library binding : 50# alkaline paper) ∞
    1. English language — Suffixes and prefixes — Dictionaries.
2. English language — Word formation — Dictionaries.   3. English
language — Reverse dictionaries. I. Title.
PE1175.S45   2000
423'.1— dc21   00-37217

British Library cataloguing data are available

Manufactured in the United States of America

*McFarland & Company, Inc., Publishers
  Box 611, Jefferson, North Carolina 28640
  www.mcfarlandpub.com*

To Dona Sheehan,
salubrious wife and gift

Table of Contents

Preface

This dictionary is based on word parts — those prefixes, suffixes, combining forms and roots which show up repeatedly to form words — and is meant to be used in conjunction with a standard dictionary and a thesaurus. It can help to retrieve words only dimly remembered, or it can lead to specific new words which otherwise might never have been discovered. And since a single recurrent letter combination often unlocks the partial meaning of dozens of words, it can act as an efficient way to expand one's general vocabulary.

The *Word Parts Dictionary* is divided into three sections.

Part I, the standard Dictionary, allows a reader to find the meaning of word parts conveniently arranged in alphabetical order, together with an example. For instance, Part I would reveal that the word part -nov- can mean either "new" (for instance, *novelty*) or "nine" (for instance, *novenary*), so the user would then become alert to context clues. This section is particularly useful to the person who has set out to expand his or her vocabulary. It is also a convenient place to consult to find actual examples after using Part II. Generally, one example is provided for each meaning.

Part II, the Finder, allows a user to start with a meaning or concept and then find the word parts which express that meaning. It is a reverse dictionary. For instance, one would learn that the meaning "color" is carried by the word parts **chromato-, -chrome, chromo-, -chroous, -pigm-, -tinct-,** and **-ting-**. Armed with that information, a user could then consult his or her memory or turn to the appropriate pages of a standard dictionary to find a variety of words which a thesaurus would not have contained. The alternative to finding such word parts is endless paging through an unabridged dictionary.

Part III, Categories, is also a reverse dictionary, but this time with the word parts arranged in clusters of meaning. For example, Part III would enable a reader to find, in one convenient listing, word parts which express many specific colors. Each color would also appear in Part II, of course, but in an isolated, alphabetical fashion.

This dictionary focuses on four kinds of word parts.

Prefixes (*pre*): A prefix is a syllable, group of syllables, or word united with or joined to the beginning of another word to alter its meaning or create a new word. For example, **re-** is a prefix in the word "redevelop." The hyphen at the end of the prefix indicates that it usually starts a word.

Suffixes (*suf*): A suffix is a syllable, group of syllables, or word added at the end of a word or word base to change its meaning, give it grammatical form, or form a new word. For example, **-ette** is a suffix in the word "kitchenette." The hyphen at the start of the suffix indicates that it normally ends a word.

Combining forms (*comb*): A combining form is a word form that occurs only in compounds, or in compounds and derivatives, and that can combine with other such forms or with prefixes and suffixes to form a word. For example, **cryo-** is one of the combining forms in the word "cryogenic," and **-genic** is the other one. The hyphens indicate that **cryo-** usually starts the word in which it appears and that **-genic** usually ends the word in which it appears.

Bases (*base*): A base is a stem or a root, a generally short letter combination that conveys a recurrent meaning all by itself without being involved in a compound word. Prefixes and suffixes may be added to it. For example, **-dict-** is a base in the word "predictable." The two hyphens indicate that it may appear at any location in a word: front, back, or middle. Thus, we have "dictation," "contradict," and "predictable."

PART I
Dictionary

A

a-¹ *see* **ad-**

a-², **ab-**, **abs-** *pre* from; off; away; down (avert, abduct, abscond)

a-³, **an-** *pre* not; without (anoxia, anandrous)

-a⁴ **1.** *suf* singular feminine ending (Roberta); **2.** plural ending (phenomena)

abdomino- *comb* abdomen (abdominocentesis)

abiet- *base* fir (abietic)

-able **1.** *suf* able to (durable); **2.** capable of being (drinkable); **3.** worthy of being (lovable); **4.** having qualities of (comfortable); **5.** tending to (peaceable)

ablut- *base* bathe; wash away (ablution)

-ably *suf* adverb form of **-able** (affably). *See* **-ible**

ac-¹ *see* **ad-**

-ac² *suf* of; pertaining to (cardiac). *See* **-ic**

acantho- *comb* spiny; thorny (acanthocyte)

acar-, **acari-**, **acarin-**, **acaro-** *comb* mite; tick (acarine, acariasis, acarinosis, acarophobia)

accipit- *base* falcon; hawk (accipitrine)

-acea *suf* plural for names of animal classes or orders (Cetacea)

-aceae *suf* plural for names of plant families or orders (Rosaceae)

-acean, **-aceous** *suf* of the nature of; like; characterized by; belonging to (crustacean, crustaceous)

acer-¹ *base* sharp; needle-like (acerose)

acer-² *base* maple (aceric)

acerb- *base* harsh; bitter (acerbic)

acerv- *base* heap (acervate)

acet-, **aceto-**, **acetyl-** *comb* acetic; acetyl; vinegar (acetamid, acetometer, acetylcholine)

acetabul- *base* saucer (acetabuliform)

acetar- *base* salad (acetarious)

acheron- *base* hell; underworld (acherontical)

achlu- *base* darkness (achluophobia)

aci- *base* needle (acicular)

acid- *comb* sour (acidosis)

acinaci- *comb* scimitar (acinaciform)

acini- *comb* grape (aciniform)

-acious *suf* characterized by; full of (audacious)

acipenser- *base* sturgeon (acipenserine)

-acity *suf* quality of (tenacity)

acou-, **acoust-** *comb* hearing; sound (acouesthesia, acoustical)

acrid- *base* grasshopper (acridid)

acro- **1.** *comb* pointed (acrocephaly); **2.** highest (acrospire); **3.** extremity (acroataxia)

acromio- *comb* upper arm; shoulder (acromioclavicular)

actino- **1.** *comb* [zoology] possession of tentacles (actinomorphic); **2.** [physics/chemistry] presence of actinic rays (actinometry); **3.** light ray (actinotherapy)

acu-, **acul-** *comb* sharp (acumen, aculeate)

aculei- *base* spine (aculeiform)

acuti- *comb* sharp-pointed (acutifoliate)

-acy *suf* quality; position; condition (democracy)

ad-¹ **1.** *pre* motion toward (advance); **2.** addition to (admit);

3. nearness to (adjoin)   NOTE:
ad- can change to: a- (ascribe); ac-
(acclaim); af- (affirm); ag- (aggrade); al- (allege); an- (announce); ap- (approve); ar- (arrive); as- (assent); at- (attrition)

-ad[2] *suf* of or relating to; used to
form names of 1. collective numerals (monad); 2. some poems
(Iliad); 3. some plants (cycad)

-ad[3] *suf* [anatomy]: toward; in the
direction of (dorsad)

-ade 1. *suf* the act of (blockade);
2. product of (pomade); 3. participant (brigade); 4. drink made
from (lemonade)

adelph- *base* brother (Philadelphia)

aden-, adeni-, adeno- *comb* gland
or glands (adenalgia, adeniform,
adenography)

adip-, adipo- *comb* fat (adipose,
adipocellular)

adjut-, adjuv- *base* help (adjutant,
adjuvant)

adren-, adreno- *comb* adrenal gland
(adrenalitis, adrenotoxin)

adul- *base* flattery (adulation)

adular- *base* blue (adularescent)

-ae *suf* plural ending (antennae)

aed- *base* yellow fever mosquito
(Aedes)

-aede- *base* genitals (aedeagus). *Also*
aedoe- (aedoeomania)

aedi- *base* temple; shrine; habitat
(aedicule). *See* edi-

aegr- *base* illness (aegritude)

aei- *base* always; ever; continued
(aeipathy)

aeluro- *see* ailuro-

-aemia *comb* blood condition (hyperaemia). *See* -emia

aen- *base* metallic brown (aeneous)

-aenio- *base* brass (aeniolithic)

aequor- *base* sea; ocean (aequorial)

aer-, aeri-, aero- *comb* air; gas (aerate, aeriferous, aerobatics)

aerug- *base* green-blue; verdegris
(aeruginous)

aerumn- *base* toil; trouble (aerum-
nous)

aescul- *base* horse chestnut (aesculin)

aestiv- *base* summer (aestivate)

aestu- *base* boil up (exaestuating).
Also estu- (estuosity)

aet- *base* eagle (aetites)

aetheo- *base* unusual (aetheoga-
mous)

aetio- *base* cause (aetiology). *See*
etio-

aev- *base* time; age (mediaeval)

af- *see* ad-

afflat- *base* breathe on; inspiration
(afflatus)

Afro- *comb* African (Afroasiatic)

ag- *see* ad-

agalma- *base* image; statue (styla-
galmatic)

agap- *base* love (agape)

agar- *base* mushroom (agariciform)

agath- *base* good (agathism)

agati- *comb* agate (agatiferous)

-age 1. *suf* act; condition; result of
(marriage); 2. amount; number of
(acreage); 3. cost of (postage);
4. place of (steerage); 5. collection
of (peerage); 6. home of (her-
mitage); 7. to act (forage)

agglut- *base* stick to (agglutina-
tion)

agito- *comb* excited; restless (agi-
tophasia)

agmat- *base* fracture; break (catagmatic)

agn- *base* lamb (agnification)

-agnosia *comb* loss of knowledge
(prosopoagnosia)

-agogue 1. *comb* leading; directing

(pedagogue); **2.** inciting (demagogue); *adj.* **-agogic** (hemagogic)

agon- *base* contest; struggle (antagonist)

agora- *comb* open space (agoraphobic)

-agra *comb* sudden pain; seizure (pelagra)

agrest- *base* rural; field (agrestic)

agri- *comb* field; earth; soil (agriculture)

agrio- *base* wild; savage (agriologist)

agro- *comb* field; earth; soil (agronomy)

agrost- *base* grass (agrostography)

-agrypn- *base* sleeplessness (agrypnode)

-aholic *comb* person addicted to or obsessed with __ (workaholic)

aichm- *base* needle (aichmophobia)

aichur- *base* pointed (aichurophobia)

ailuro- *comb* cat (ailurophobia). *Also* **aeluro-** (aeluromania)

-aire *suf* person characterized by or occupied with (legionnaire)

aischro- *base* smut; obscenity (aischrolatria)

al-[1] *see* **ad-**

al-[2] *comb* the (alchemy)

-al[3] **1.** *suf* belonging to; like; of (theatrical); **2.** nouns from adj. (perennial); **3.** act or process of (acquittal); **4.** [chemistry] having aldehydes (chloral)

ala- *base* wing (alation)

alacr- *base* promptness (alacrity)

alaud- *base* skylark (alaudine)

-alb- *base* white (albino)

alcelaph- *base* antelope (alcelaphine)

alcid- *base* auk (alcidine)

alea- *base* dice; chance (aleatory)

alectoro-, alectryo- *comb* cock; rooster (alectoromachy, alectryomancy)

-ales *suf* ending for scientific Latin names of plants (Liliales)

aleth- *base* truth (alethiology)

aleuro- *base* flour (aleuromancy)

alex-, alexi-, alexo- *comb* to ward off; keep away (alexiteric, alexipyretic, alexocyte)

alg- *base* cold (algid)

alge-, algesi-, -algia, algo-, -algy *comb* pain (algetic, algesiometer, neuralgia, algophobia, coxalgy)

ali-[1] *comb* wing (aliform)

-ali-[2] *base* another; other (alien)

-alim- *base* nourishment; food (alimentation)

-aliph- *base* unguent; fat (aliphatic)

-alis *suf* ending for scientific Latin names (borealis)

-allac-, -allag- *base* exchange; mutually binding (synallactic, synallagmatic)

allant(o)- **1.** *comb* membrane: fetal (allanto-chorion); **2.** sausage-shaped (allantoid)

-allaxis- *base* exchange (morphallaxis)

allelo- *comb* of one another; reciprocal (allelomorph)

alli- *base* garlic (alliaceous)

allo- *comb* variation; reversal; departure from normal (allonym)

-ally *suf* to form certain adverbs (terrifically)

alog(o)- *base* unreasonable (alogotrophy)

alopec- *base* fox (alopecoid); baldness (alopecia)

alphito- *base* barley (alphitomorphous)

alter- *comb* another; other (alternate)

alti-, alto- *comb* high (altimeter, altocumulus)

alumino- *comb* aluminum (aluminosilicate)

alut- *base* leather (alutaceous)

alv- *base* belly (alvine)

alve- *base* beehive (alveary)

alveolo- 1. *comb* connected with alveolus (alveolodental); 2. small cavity; socket (alveolopalatal)

alyt- *base* police officer (alytarch)

-am- *base* love; friendship (amity)

amar- *base* sour (amarine)

amaranth- *base* purple (amaranthine)

amath- *base* dust (amathophobia)

amaur- *base* dim; dark (amaurosis)

amaxo- *base* automobile (amaxophobia)

ambag- *base* oblique; indirect (ambagious)

ambi-, ambo- *comb* both; around (ambience, amboceptor). *See* **amphi-**

ambig- *base* uncertain (ambiguity)

ambly- *comb* dullness; dimness (amblyopia)

ambul- *comb* walk (somnambulate)

amelo- *comb* enamel (amelogenesis)

amensi- *base* amnesia (amensiphobia)

ament-[1] *base* insanity (amentia)

ament-[2] *base* catkin (amentaceous)

amic-[1] *base* friend (amicable)

-amic[2] *suf* amide related (lactamic acid)

amido- *comb* amide radical (amidohydrolases)

-amine *comb* having one hydrogen atom (Dramamine)

amino- *comb* in the ammonia molecule replaced by an alkyl or other nonacid radical (aminophenol)

amita- *base* aunt (amitate)

ammino- *comb* containing ammines (ammino-chloride)

ammo- *comb* sand (ammochryse)

ammonio-, ammono- *comb* containing ammonia (ammonioferric, ammonotelic)

amn- *base* river (amnicolist)

amnes- *base* forgotten (paramnesia)

amnio- *comb* amniotic sac; membrane: fetal (amniocentesis)

amorpho- *comb* shapeless; irregularly shaped (amorphogranular)

-ampel- *base* vine (ampelopsis)

amphi-, ampho- *comb* on both sides; surrounding (amphibology, amphoteric). *See* **ambi-**

-ampl- *base* large (amplifier)

ampull- *base* bottle (ampule)

amycho- *base* scratch; irritate (amyctic)

amygdalo- *comb* almond-shaped (amygdalophenin)

amyl-, amylo- *comb* of starch (amylamine, amylometer)

an-[1] *pre* not; lacking (anarchy)

an-[2] *see* **ad-**

-an[3] 1. *suf* belonging to; of; characteristic of (diocesan); 2. born in; living in (American); 3. believing in; following (Mohammedan)

ana-[1] *pre* up; upon; back; again; anew; throughout (anabolism)

-ana[2] *suf* plural: collective (Americana)

anacard- *base* cashew (anacardiaceous)

anaps- *base* turtle (anapsid)

anat- *base* duck (anatine)

anathem- *base* curse (anathematize)

-ance 1. *suf* the act of (utterance); 2. quality or state of being (vigilance); 3. a thing that __ (conveyance); 4. a thing that is __ (dissonance); *adv.* **-ancy** (constancy)

ancip- *base* doubtful; two-edged (ancipitous)

-ancon- *base* elbow (anconitis)

ancry- *base* anchor (ancryoid)

ancylo- *comb* bent; crooked; stiff (ancylostomiasis). *Also* **ankylo-** (ankyloglossia)

ancylostom- *base* hookworm (Ancylostoma)

andro-, -andry *comb* man; male (androgenous, polyandry)

-androus 1. *comb* man; male (polyandrous); 2. *BOT:* having stamens (diandrous)

-ane *suf* denoting a hydrocarbon of the paraffin series (methane)

anemo- *comb* wind (anemometer)

anet- *base* soothing (anetic)

aneth- *base* dill (anethated)

angin- *base* strangulation; heart attack (angina)

angio- *comb* vessel; case; pot (angiocarp)

Anglo- *comb* English (Anglo-Irish)

angui- *base* snake (anguiform)

anguill- *base* eel (anguilliform)

angul- *base* angle (angularity)

angusti- *comb* narrow (angustifoliate)

anhydro- *comb* anhydride (anhydroglucose)

-anim- *base* spirit; life (animation)

aniso- *comb* unequal; dissimilar (anisometropia)

ankylo- *comb* bent; crooked; stiff (ankylosis). *Also* **ancylo-**

-ann-, -enn- *base* year (annual, biennial); yearly (anniversary)

annul- *comb* ring (annular)

ano-[1] *pre* upward; above (anotropia)

ano-[2] *comb* anal; ring-shaped (anorectal)

anom-, anomo- *comb* unusual; irregular; abnormal (anomalous, anomocarpous)

anomalo- *comb* irregular; uneven (anomalogonatous)

anophel- *base* mosquito (anopheline)

ansa- *base* handle (ansated)

anser- *base* goose (anserine)

-ant 1. *suf* performing an act (defiant); 2. person who performs (accountant); 3. impersonal physical agent (lubricant)

ante- *pre* before in time, order, or position (antedate)

antero- *comb* anterior; front (anterolateral)

-anthema *comb* rash; eruption (enanthema)

antho- *comb* of flowers (anthomania)

-anthous *comb* having flowers of a specified kind or number (monanthous)

anthraco- *comb* coal; carbuncle (anthracomancy)

anthropo- *comb* human (anthropology)

anti- 1. *pre* against; hostile (antilabor); 2. operating against (antiballistic); 3. preventing, curing, neutralizing (antitoxin); 4. opposite; reverse (antiperistalsis); 5. rivaling (antipope)

antio- *comb* set against (antiopelmus)

-antiq- *base* old; ancient (antiquated)

antlo- *base* flood (antlophobia)

antro- *comb* nearly closed cavity; antrum (antroscope)

anu- *base* circular; ring-shaped (anulus)

-anus *suf* scientific word ending (Platanus)

aorto- *comb* extremity (aortoclasia)

ap- *see* **ad-**

apat- *base* deceit (apatite)

apeir- *base* infinite; endless (apeirogon)

apert- *base* open (apertometer)

aphe-, -aphia *comb* sense of touch (aphephobia, dysaphia)

aphro- *base* foam (Aphrodite)

aphrodisio- *base* sexual (aphrodisiac)

api- *comb* bee (apiculture)

-apical, apico- *comb* apex; tip (periapical, apicotomy)

apio- *base* pear (apiocrinite)

apo- *pre* off; from; away from; separation (apocopate)

apocris- *base* to give or receive answers (apocrisiary)

apolaust- *base* enjoyment; self-indulgence (apolaustic)

aporet- *base* doubt (aporetic)

apostem- *base* abscess (apostematous)

appell- *base* call to; name (appellation)

appet- *base* craving (appetite)

apricat- *base* sunbathing (aprication)

-aps-, -apt-[1] *base* joining (synapse, synaptic)

-apsia *comb* touch (parapsia)

apt-[2] *base* ability (aptitude)

aqua-, aque-, aqui- *comb* water (aquatic, aqueduct, aquiclude)

aquil- *base* eagle (aquiline)

ar-[1] *see* **ad-**

-ar[2] 1. *suf* pertaining to (angular); 2. one who __ (burglar); 3. connected with __ (collar)

arach- *base* peanut; ground nut (arachidic)

arachn-, arachno- *comb* spider; cobweb (arachnephobia, arachnodactylia)

-araneo- *base* spider (araneology)

arat- *base* farming; tillage (aratory)

-arbor- *base* tree (arboretum)

arcan- *base* secret (arcane)

arch-[1] *pre* main; chief; principal (archbishop)

-arch[2] *comb* ruler (patriarch)

archaeo-, archeo- *comb* ancient; original (archaeology, Archeozoic)

archi- *pre* [biology] primitive (archiplasm)

-archy *comb* rule; government (monarchy)

arci- *base* arch (arciform)

arct- *base* moth (arctian)

arcto- *comb* bear (cynarctomachy)

arctoid- *base* raccoon; weasel (arctoidean)

ard-[1], ars- *base* burn (ardor, arson)

-ard[2], -art *suf* one who is or does too much (drunkard, braggart)

ard-[3] *base* erect; steep; laborious (arduous)

arde- *base* heron (ardeid)

ardu- *base* laborious; steep (arduous)

aren- *comb* sand (arenicolous)

arenaceo- *comb* sandy (arenaceo-argillaceous)

arene- *base* spider (areneiform)

areo-[1] *comb* Mars (areology)

areo-[2] *base* thin; rare (areometer)

argent-, argenti-, argento- *comb* silver (argentite, argentiferous, argento-cuprous)

argillaceo- *comb* clay (arenaceo-argillaceous)

argillo- *comb* clay (argillo-calcareous)

argyro- *comb* silver (argyrophyllus)

-aria *suf* [botany/zoology] used to form names of groups and names of genera (Planaria)

-arian *suf* age; sect; occupation; social belief (Unitarian)

arid- *base* dry (aridity)

ariet- *base* ram (arietine)

-arious *suf* relating to; connected with (vicarious)

-aris *suf* scientific word ending (Polaris)

aristo- *comb* best (aristotype)

arithm- *base* number (arithmetic)

-arium *suf* location; receptacle (solarium)

armo- *base* shoulder (armomancy)

arrheno- *comb* male (arrhenotoky)

arseno- *comb* having arsenic (arsenopyrite)

arterio- *comb* artery (arteriosclerosis)

arthr-, arthro- *comb* connected with a joint (arthrectomy, arthrodynia)

arthropod- *base* millipede (arthropodal)

arti- *comb* workmanship (artifact)

-articul- *base* joint (multiarticular)

artio- *comb* even number (artiodactyl)

artiodactyl- *base* giraffe (artiodactylous)

arto- *comb* bread (artophagous)

arundi- *base* reed (arundiferous)

-ary 1. *suf* relating to; like (legendary); 2. thing/person connected to __ (military)

as-¹ *see* ad-

as-², asin- *base* jackass (asinine)

ascari- *comb* intestinal worm (ascariasis)

asco- *comb* [botany] sac (ascocarp)

-ase *suf* that decomposes; names of enzymes (amylase)

-asis *suf* condition resembling; disease names (psoriasis)

-asm *suf* result of an action (orgasm)

asmato- *comb* song (asmatographer)

asper- *comb* rough (asperity)

aspido- *base* shield (aspidomancy)

assid- *base* unceasing (assiduity)

-ast *suf* one who is __ (enthusiast)

astac- *base* lobster (astacian)

aster-¹ *comb* star (asteraceous)

-aster² *suf* diminution; inferiority; worthlessness; slight resemblance (poetaster)

asteroid- *base* starfish (asteroidean)

asthen-, astheno- *comb* weakness (asthenopia, asthenobiosis). *See* -esthenia

astra- *comb* lightning (astraphobia)

astragalo- *comb* anklebone; dice (astragalonavicular, astragalomancy)

astro- *comb* star; celestial activity (astronomy)

at- *see* ad-

-ata *suf* result of; plural ending (stomata)

atax-, ataxi-, -ataxia, ataxio-, ataxo- *comb* confusion; disorder (ataxaphasia, ataxiamnesic, psychataxia, ataxiophemia, ataxophobia)

-ate¹ *v.* 1. *suf* to become (maturate); 2. cause to become (invalidate); 3. form or produce (salivate); 4. provide or treat with (refrigerate); 5. put in the form of; form by means of (delineate); 6. to arrange for (orchestrate); 7. to combine; infuse; treat with (chlorinate)

-ate² *adj.* 1. *suf* characteristic of (collegiate); 2. having; filled with (passionate); 3. [biology] having or characterized by (caudate)

-ate³ *n.* 1.*suf* office; function; agent; official (directorate); 2. person or thing that is the object of an action (legate); 3. [chemistry] a salt made from an acid ending in -ic (nitrate)

ate-⁴ *base* ruinous; reckless impulse (atephobia)

atelia-, atelo- *comb* incomplete; undeveloped (myelatelia, atelocardia)

ather- *base* smelt (atherine)

athero- *comb* deposit: soft materials (atherogenic)

-athlon, -athon *suf* event; contest (pentathlon, walkathon)

-atic *suf* of the kind of (chromatic)

-atile *suf* possibility; quality (volatile)

-ation 1. *suf* the act of (alteration); **2.** condition of being (gratification); **3.** the result of (compilation)

-ative *suf* relating to; tending to (correlative)

atlanto- *comb* [anatomy] pertaining to the atlas, top vertebra (atlantoaxial)

atlo- *comb* of the neck (atloid)

atmo- *comb* steam; vapor; air (atmosphere)

-ator *suf* doer; agent; actor (educator)

-atory *suf* of the nature of; pertaining to; produced by (accusatory)

atrament- *base* ink (atramental)

-atresia *comb* imperforate; lacking an opening (colpatresia)

atreto- *comb* imperforate; lacking an opening (atretocyst)

atrio- *comb* cavity, esp. a chamber of the heart (atrioventricular)

atro- *comb* black (atrorubent)

-atrophia, atrophic 1. *comb* malnutrition (metatrophia); **2.** progressive decline (neuratrophia, myotrophic)

atto- *pre* one-quintillionth (attogram)

atychi- *base* failure (atychiphobia)

-auchen- *base* neck (maerauchenia)

audac- *base* boldness (audacity)

audi-, audio- *comb* hearing (auditorium, audiology)

-aug- *base* grow; increase (augment)

augur- *base* soothsaying; divination (augury)

aulo- *comb* pipe; reed (aulophyte)

auranti- *base* orange (aurantiaceous)

aur(i)-[1] *comb* ear (auricle)

aur(i)-[2]**, auro-** *comb* gold (auriferous, aurous)

auricalc- *base* copper; gold (auricalceous)

auriculo- *comb* outer ear; lobe (auriculo-temporal)

-auror- *base* dawn (aurorean)

aurora- *comb* radiant emissions in both hemispheres (aurora borealis)

austro- 1. *comb* wind: south (austromancy); **2.** eastern (Austro-Hungarian)

auto- *comb* self; self-moving (autobiography)

autumn- *base* fall (autumnal)

auxano-, auxeto-, auxo- *comb* increase; growth (auxanogram, auxetophone, auxochrome)

auxil- *base* help; assistance (auxiliary)

avar- *base* greed (avarice)

aven- *base* oats (avenaceous)

avern- *base* hellish (avernal)

avia-, avio- 1. *comb* bird (aviary); **2.** flight (aviator)

avid- *base* eager (avidity)

av(in)- *base* grandmother (avitic)

aviono- *comb* flying (avionics)

-avunc- *base* uncle (avunculate)

av(us)- *base* grandfather (avital)

axi-, axio-[1]**, axo-** *comb* related to an axis (axial, axiomesial, axometer)

-axill- *base* armpit (periaxillary)

axin- *base* ax (axinomancy)

axio-[2] *comb* values (axiology)

azo- *comb* [chemistry] nitrogen (azobenzene)

-azur- *base* sky-blue (azureous)

B

baccato- *comb* bearing berries (baccato-tuberculous)

bacci- *comb* berry (baccivorous)

bacill-, bacilli-, bacillo- *comb* rod-shaped bacillus (bacillemia, baciliform, bacillotherapy)

back- 1. *comb* of the back (backache); 2. behind (backfield); 3. prior (backdate); 4. opposing (backlash)

-bacter, bacteri-, bacterio- *comb* of bacteria (aerobacter, bactericide, bacteriology)

bacul- *base* rod (baculine)

balaen- *base* whale (balaenoid)

balani-, balano- *comb* acorn; gland (balanitis, balanorrhagia)

balatro- *base* buffoon (balatrophobia)

balaust- *base* pomegranate (balaustine)

balbut- *base* stutter; stammer (balbutiate)

ballist- *base* projectile (ballistic)

balneo- *comb* baths; bathing (balneology)

banaus- *base* mechanical (banausic)

-bar *comb* atmospheric pressure; weight (isobar)

barb- *comb* beard; tufted (barbate)

bari-, baro- *comb* atmospheric pressure weight (baritone, barograph)

bary- *comb* heavy difficult (baryphonia)

basi-, baso- *comb* [biology] the base; at or near base (basidigitale, basocellular)

-basia *comb* [medicine] ability to walk (abasia)

basiat- *base* kiss (basiation)

basidio- *comb* base (basidiomycetes)

basil- *base* king (basilic)

-bat- *base* walk; go; pass (diabatic)

batho-, bathy- *comb* depth; deep (bathometer, bathysphere)

bato-[1] *comb* height (batophobia)

bato-[2] *comb* brambles (batology)

batracho- *comb* frog; toad (batrachophagous)

batto- *comb* repetition (battologize)

bdell- *base* leech (bdellatomy)

be- 1. *pre* around (beset); 2. completely (besmear); 3. away (bereave); 4. about (bemoan); 5. make (besot); 6. furnish with (befriend); 7. cover(ed) with (becloud)

beati- *base* happy; blessed (beatitude)

-bell- *base* war (bellicose)

-belo- *base* arrow (beloid)

-belon- *base* needle; pin; sharp object (belonoid)

bene- *pre* good; well (benefactor)

benzo- *comb* [chemistry] benzine (benzo-phenone)

benzoxy- *comb* [chemistry] benzoyl group (benzoxyacetanilide)

benzyloxy- *comb* [chemistry] benzyl group (benzyloxyamine)

beryl- *base* green (berylline)

betul- *base* birch (betulaceous)

bi- 1. *pre* having two (biangular); 2. on both sides in two ways (bilingual); 3. every two (biweekly); 4. using two (bilabial); 5. involving two (bipartisan); 6. [botany/zoology] twice; doubly; in pairs (bipinnate); 7. [chemistry] having twice as many atoms or chemical equivalents for a definite weight of

the other constituent of the compound (sodium bicarbonate);
8. organic compounds having a combination of two radicals of the same composition (biphenyl)
bib- *base* drink (bibulous)
biblio- 1. *comb* of books (bibliography); 2. of the Bible (bibliomancy)
bili- *comb* gall; bile (biligenic)
-bility *suf* power to do or be (responsibility)
bin- *pre* two (binaural)
bio- *comb* living; life (biography)
-biosis *comb* way of living (symbiosis)
-bis- *pre* two; twice (bisferious)
bland- *base* flattery (blandishment)
-blast, -blastic, blasto-, -blasty *comb* formative; germinal; embryonic; developing (mesoblast, osteoblastic, blastoderm)
blatt-[1] *base* cockroach (blatta)
blatt-[2] *base* purple (blattean)
-ble *see* **-able**
blenn-, blenno- *comb* mucus; slime (blennadenitis, blennostasis)
-blep- *base* sight (ablepsia)
blepharo- *comb* eyelid (blepharotomy)
blesi- *base* stammering (blesiloquent)
-bly *see* **-ably**
-bole *comb* thrown down/out/in/together/beyond (hyperbole)
bolet- *base* fungus; mushrooms (boletus)
-bolic, bolo-[1] **, -boly** *comb* thrown down/out/in/together/beyond (catabolic, bolometer, epiboly)
bolo-[2] *base* ray; radiant energy (bolometer)
-bomb- 1. *base* bee (bombilation); 2. silk; silkworm (bombycinous)
bon- *base* good (bonanza)
borea- *base* north (boreal)

borbor- *base* filthy talk (borborology)
boro- *comb* [chemistry] boron (boroflouride)
-bosc- *base* to feed (hippoboscid)
botano- *comb* plant (botanomancy)
botaur- *base* bittern (botaurus)
-bothr- *base* pitted; grooved (bothrenchyma)
-bothro- *base* pit; mine (bothrodendron)
botry(o)- *comb* grapes (botryose)
-botul- *base* sausage (botulism)
bou-, bu- *comb* ox; cow (boustrophedon, bulemia)
-bound 1. *comb* constrained (snowbound); 2. going toward (westbound)
-bov- *base* cow (bovine)
brachi-, brachio- *comb* arm; upper arm (brachialgia, brachiopod)
brachisto- *comb* short (brachistocephaly)
brachy- *comb* short (brachycardia)
bract- *base* leaf (bracteate)
brady- *comb* slow; delayed (bradyarthria)
-branchia, branchio- *comb* gills (pulmobranchia, branchiopod)
brassic- *base* broccoli; cabbage (brassicacious)
brepho- *comb* fetus (brephotrophic)
brevi- *comb* brief; little; short (breviloquence)
brom-, bromo- *comb* stench (bromidrosis, bromopnea)
bromato- *comb* food (bromatology)
bromel- *base* pineapple (bromeliaceous)
bromo- *comb* [chemistry] bromine (bromoderma)
bronch-, bronchi-, bronchio-, broncho- *comb* the windpipe (bronchadenitis, bronchiectasis, bronchiogenic, bronchoscope)

bronto- 1. *comb* thunder (brontograph); 2. [paleontology] hugeness (brontosaurus)

-brotic *comb* inclined to eat (scolecobrotic)

bruch- *base* caterpillar (bruchus)

brum-[1] *base* winter (brumal)

brum-[2] *base* foggy (brumous)

brun- *base* dark brown (brunneous)

brux- *base* grind (bruxism)

bryo- *comb* moss (bryophyte)

bu- *see* **bou-**

bubal- *base* antelope; buffalo (bubaline)

bubo- *base* groin (bubonocele)

buccin- *base* trumpet (buccinatory)

bucco- *comb* cheek (buccolabial)

bucerat-, bucorac- *base* hornbill (Buceratinae, Bucoracinae)

bufo- *comb* toad (bufotoxin)

bulbo- *comb* bulb; bulbous (bulbospinal)

-bulia *comb* will (dysbulia)

bullat- *base* bubble; blister (bullate)

-burg, -burgh *comb* city; town; village (Vicksburg, Pittsburgh)

-burger *comb* sandwich made on a roll or bun (cheeseburger)

burs-, burso- *comb* pouch; purse; sac (bursar, bursopathy)

buteo- *comb* hawk; buzzard (buteonine)

butyro- *comb* butter (butyrometer)

bux- *base* box-tree (buxiferous)

by- 1. *pre* near; close by (bystander); 2. side (bystreet); 3. secondary (by-product)

-byon- *base* plug; stuff (rhinobyon)

-byss- *base* depth (hyperbyssal)

byssi- *comb* flax (byssinosis)

C

caball- *base* horse (caballine)

cachex- *base* ill health (cachectic)

cachin- *base* laugh (cachinnate)

caco- *comb* bad; poor; harsh (cacophony). *Also* **kako-** (kakistocracy)

cacumin- *base* tip (cacuminate)

cad- *base* fall (cadence)

cadav- *base* corpse (cadaverous)

-cade *comb* procession; parade (motorcade)

caduc- *base* transitory; perishable (caducous)

caec- 1. *base* blind (caecilian); 2. intestinal pouch (caeciform)

caed- *see* **-cide**

cael- *base* heavens (caelometer). *See* **celest-**

caeno-[1]**, ceno-, coeno-** *comb* in common (Caenozoic, cenobite, coenobium)

caeno-[2] *comb* new (caenogenesis). *Also* **caino-** (cainophobia)

caes- *base* blue; gray; green (caesious)

-caine *comb* synthetic alkaloid in anesthetic drugs (novocaine)

cal-, cale- *base* heat (decalescence, caleficient)

calam- *base* reed (calamiform)

calar-, calat- *base* inserted (intercalary, intercalated)

calathi- *comb* cup; basket (calathiform)

calcaneo- *comb* heel-bone (calcaneo-fibular)

calcareo- *comb* of lime (calcareosulfurous)

-calce- *base* shoe (discalced)

calci- *comb* calcium; lime (calcify)

calcitr- *base* kick (recalcitrant)

-calcul- *base* count; pebble (calculator)

-cali- *base* nest; hut (caliology)

calig- *base* fog; mist (caliginous)

calli- *comb* beautiful (calligraphy)

callithri- *base* marmoset (callithricid)

callo- *base* beautiful (callomania)

calo-, calori- *comb* heat (caloreceptor, calorimeter)

calumn- *base* slander (calumniate)

calv- *base* bald (calvarium)

calyc- *base* cup-shaped (calycanthemy)

calypto- *comb* hidden; covered (calyptoblastic)

calyptri- *base* hood (calyptriform)

-camb- *base* change; exchange (excambition)

cameli- *base* camel (cameline)

-camp-[1] *base* field (campimeter)

-camp-[2] *base* caterpiller (campodeiform)

campan- *base* bell (campanology)

-campsis, campto- *comb* bent (phallocampsis, camptomelia)

campylo- *comb* crooked; bent (campylospermous)

can-[1] *base* dog (canine)

can-[2] *base* gray (canescent)

canalic- *base* groove (canaliculate)

cancell- *base* barrier; latticed (cancellate)

cancr- *base* crab (cancrine)

cand- *base* white (candescent)

cantho- *comb* eye: corner of (canthoplasty)

-cap- *base* take; hold; receive (recapture). *Also* cep/cip (receptacle, recipient)

capel- *base* shopkeeper (capelocracy)

capilli- *comb* hair (capilliform)

-capit- *base* head (decapitate)

-capnia, capno- *comb* smoke; vapor; carbon dioxide (acapnia, capnomancy)

capri- *base* goat (capriform)

capsuli-, capsulo- *comb* capsule (capsuliform, capsulolenticular)

carbo- *comb* [chemistry] carbon (carbohydrate)

carbol- *base* of phenol (carbolize)

carbon- *base* charcoal (carbonara)

carcer- *base* jail (incarcerate)

carcharin- *base* shark (carcharinid)

carcin(o)- *comb* cancer (carcinogenesis)

cardi-, -cardia, cardio-, -cardium *comb* heart (cardiagra, tachycardia, cardiology, myocardium)

-carin- *base* keel; ridge (carinula)

cario- *comb* tooth disease; caries (cariogenic)

carni- *comb* flesh (carnivore)

carnoso- *comb* fleshy (carnosofibrous)

carot- *base* stupefying; soporific (carotic)

-carp, -carpic, carpo-[1], -carpous *comb* fruit; seeds (endocarp, endocarpic, carpophore, monocarpous)

carpho- *comb* straw; dry (carphology)

carpo-[2] *comb* wrist (carpoptosis)

carto- *comb* map; card; piece of paper (cartographer). *Also* charto- (chartometer)

caryo- *comb* nucleus (caryopsis). *Also* karyo- (karyokinesis)

cas- *base* fall (cascade)

case- *base* cheese (caseation)

cassidi- *base* helmet (cassidiform)

cassiter- *base* tin (cassiterite)

-cast *comb* transmit (telecast)

castan- *base* brown; chestnut (castaneous, castanet)

castella- *base* fortification (incastellate)

castig- *base* chasten; reprove (castigate)

castor- *base* beaver (castoreum)

castr- *base* camp (castrensian)

casuar- *base* cassowary (casuarina)

cata-, cath- *pre* down; through; against; completely (catabolism, cathartic). *Also* kata- (katabatic)

catagelo- *base* ridicule (catagelophobia). *Also* katagelo-

cataglott- *base* tongue-kissing (cataglottism)

catagm- *base* fracture (catagmatic)

caten- *base* chain (catenation)

cathar- *base* clean; purge; purify (catharize)

cathart- *base* buzzard (cathartine)

-cathex- *base* retention (acathexis)

cathis- *base* sit; seat (cathisma)

catoptro- *comb* mirror (catoptromantic)

caudo- *comb* tail (caudo-femoral)

cauli-, caulo- *comb* stem; stalk (caulicolous, caulocarpic)

caum- *base* heat (caumesthesia)

caupon- *base* tavern; innkeeper (cauponate)

-caust- *base* burn (holocaust)

caut- *base* heed; carefulness (precautionary)

cauter- *comb* caustic; burning (cauterize)

cava- *comb* hollow (cavate)

caval- *base* horse (cavalry)

-cave, cavi-, cavo- *base* hollow (cavate)

-ce *suf* multiplicative suffix (twice)

cebo- *comb* monkey (cebocephalic)

cecid- *base* gall: tumorous plant tissue (cecidomylan)

ceco- *comb* intestinal pouch; cecum (cecostomy). *Also* caec- (caeciform)

-ced-, -cess- *base* move; go; give way (concede, procession)

cedr- *base* cedar (cedrine)

-cele *comb* tumor; swelling (cystocele); hernia (perineocele)

-celer- *base* speed (accelerate)

celest- *base* heavens (celestial)

celido- *comb* spot; surface marking (celidography)

celio- *comb* abdomen (celiomyositis)

celli- *comb* cell (celliferous)

cello- *comb* cellulose (cellophane)

celluli-, cellulo- *comb* cell; cell wall (celluliferous, cellulo-fibrous)

celo-[1] 1. *comb* celom (celomate); 2. hernia (celotomy); 3. abdomen (celoscope). *Also* coelo- (coeloscope)

-celo-[2] *base* dry; burnt (celosia)

celsi- *base* dignity; eminence; lofty position (celsitude)

Celto- *comb* Celt; Celtic (Celto-Germanic)

cen- *base* meal (cenatory)

-cene *comb* geological epoch (Miocene)

ceno-[1] *comb* new; recent (cenogenesis). *Also* caeno-, caino-, kaino- (Caenozoic, Cainozoic, Kainozoic)

ceno-[2] *comb* in common; common (cenobite). *Also* coeno- (coenobite)

ceno-[3] *comb* empty (cenotaphic). *Also* keno- (kenosis)

cenoto- *comb* new (cenotophobia)

-centered *comb* focused on (market-centered). *Also* cainoto-, kainoto- (cainotophobia, kainotophobia)

-centesis *comb* puncture (amniocentesis)

centi- 1. *comb* hundred-fold (centipede); 2. hundredth part (centigram)

centri-, centro- *comb* center (centripetal, centrobaric)

-centric 1. *comb* having __ center (polycentric); 2. focused around __ (ethno-centric)

-cep-[1] *base* take (receptor). See -cap-

-cep-[2] *base* onion; bulb (cepivorous)

cephal-, -cephalic, cephalo-, -cephalous, -cephaly *comb* head; skull (cephalitis, dolichocephalic, cephalopod, brachycephalous, dolichocephaly)

cephalopod- *base* squid (cephalopodal)

-ceptor *comb* taker; receiver (neuroreceptor)

ceras- *base* cherry (cerasin)

cerato- *comb* horn; hornlike (ceratophyllous). *Also* kerato- (keratoglobus)

cerator- *base* rhino (ceratorhine)

cerauno- *comb* thunder (ceraunoscope). *Also* kerauno- (keraunoscope)

-cerca, -cercal, cerco- *comb* having a __ tail (Schistocerca, heterocercal, Cercopithecus)

cerebri-, cerebro- *comb* brain (cerebritis, cerebrospinal)

-cern- *base* to sift (excernent)

cero- *comb* wax (cerograph)

cerr- *base* evergreen oak (cerrial)

cerul- *base* blue (cerulean)

cerumini- *comb* wax-like secretion (ceruminiferous)

ceruss- *base* white (cerussal)

-cerv- *base* deer; elk; moose (cervine)

cervico- *comb* cervical; of the neck (cervicodorsal)

cervis- *base* beer (cervisial)

cespitoso- *comb* growing in dense tufts or clumps (cespitosoramose)

-cess-, -ced- *comb* move; go; give way (procession, concede)

-cet- *base* whale (cetology)

-chaem- *base* low (chaemacephalic)

chaeti-, chaeto- *comb* hair; bristle; seta (chaetiferous, chaetophorous)

chalast- *base* laxative; relaxant (chalastic)

chalax- *base* hailstone (chalaxa)

chalco- *comb* copper; brass (chalcocite)

chalyb- *base* steel (chalybean). See iron

chamae- *comb* low-growing; dwarf-like (chamaedorea)

chao- 1. *base* abyss (chaotic); 2. atmosphere (chaomancy)

charadr- *base* sandpiper, snipe, plover, woodcock (charadrine)

charit- *base* love (charity)

charto- *comb* paper; map (chartomancy)

chasmo- *comb* fissure (chasmophobia)

cheilo- *comb* lip (cheiloplasty). See chilo-

cheima- *comb* cold (cheimaphilic)

cheir(o)- *comb* hand (macrocheiria). See chiro-

-chela, cheli- *comb* claw (isochela, cheliferous)

chelid- *base* a swallow (chelidonian)

-chelo(n)-, chelys *base* turtle (chelonian, Lepidochelys)

chemo- *comb* chemicals (chemotherapy)

cheno- *base* goose (chenopod)

chero-[1] *comb* happy (cherophobia)

chero-[2] *base* hyrax (cherogril)

cherso- *base* dry (chersonese)

-chezia *comb* defecation condition (hematochezia)

chili- *comb* one thousand (chiliasm)

chilo- *comb* lip (chiloplasty)

chilopod- *base* centipede (chilopodal)

chim- *base* transplant; tissues from foreign source (chimera)

Chino- *comb* Chinese (Chino-Tibetan)

-chion- *base* snow (chionodoxa). *See* **-chium**

chiro- *comb* hand (chiromancy). *Also* **cheiro-**

chirur- *base* surgeon (chirurgery)

-chium *base* snow (hedychium). *See* **-chion-**

chlamyd- *comb* cloak; sheath (chlamydeous)

chloro- 1. *comb* green (chlorophyll); 2. having chlorine (chloroform)

choano- *comb* funnel (choanocyte)

chol-, chole-,cholo- *comb* bile; gall; anger (cholagogue, cholecyst, chololith)

chondr-, chondrio-, chondro- *comb* cartilage (chondrify, chondriosome, chondroblast)

chord-, -chorda *comb* cord; sinew (chorditis, (Protochorda). *Also* **cord-** (cordotomy)

-chorea, choreo- *comb* involuntary movement; spasm; dance (labiochorea, choreophrasia)

chori- *comb* apart; separate (choripetalous)

chorio- *comb* membrane; skin (choriocele)

choristo- *comb* apart; separate (choristophyllus)

choro- *comb* region; land (chorology)

choroid- *comb* membrane; skinlike (choroideremia)

chrem-, chremat- *base* wealth; money (chrematistic)

chreo- *comb* useful (chreotechnics)

chresis- *base* used for doing (catachresis)

chresmo- *comb* oracle (chresmomancy)

chresto- *base* useful (chrestomathic)

chromato- *comb* color; chromatin (chromatogenous)

-chrome 1. *comb* color (monochrome); 2. chromium (ferrochrome)

chromo- *comb* color (chromosome)

chrono- *comb* time (chronometer)

-chroous *comb* colored (xanthocroous)

chrys(o)- *comb* yellow; golden (chrysocarpous)

chyl-, chyli-, chylo- *comb* connected with chyle; digestive fluid gastric juice (chylaqueous, chyliferous, chylocyst)

chymo- *comb* partially digested food (chymotrypsin)

-chys-, -chyt- *base* to pour (synchysis, synchytic)

-cib- *base* food (cibarious)

cica- *base* scar (cicatrix)

cichlo- *base* thrush (cichlomorphous)

cichor- *base* chicory (cichoraceous)

ciconi- *comb* stork (ciconiiform)

cicur- *base* tame (cicuration)

-cid- *base* fall (incident)

-cidal, -cide, -cidious, -cidism *comb* killing (homicidal, patricide, parricidious, suicidism)

cilii-, cilio- *comb* cilia; hairlike process (ciliiferous, cilioretinal)

cimic- *base* bug (cimicoid)

cimol- *base* chalk; light earth (cimolian)

-cinc- *base* ring; girdle (cincture)

cinchon- *base* quinine (cinchonism)

cincinn- *base* curl (cincinnal)

cine- *comb* movement; movie (cinematography). *Also* **kine-** (kinescope)

ciner- *base* ashes (incinerate)

-cing- *base* ring; girdle (cingulate)

cinque- *base* five (cinquefoil)

-cion *suf* variation of -tion (suspi-
cion)

-cip- *base* take (recipient). *See* -cap-

circin- *base* round (circinate)

circul- *base* circle (circulate)

circum- *suf* around; about; surrounding (circumscribe)

cirr(h)i-, cirr(h)o- *comb* curl;
ringlet; tendril (cirrigerous,
cirrocumulus)

cirso- *comb* enlarged vein (cirsotomy)

cis-¹ *suf* on this side of; near
(cisalpine). *See* citra-

-cis², -cise- *base* cut; cut off (inci-
sion, precise)

ciss- *base* ivy (cissoid)

-cisto- *base* chest; container
(cistophorous)

-cit- *base* arouse (incite)

citra- *comb* on this side of; near
(citramontane). *See* cis-

citro- *comb* citric (citromalic)

civ- *base* citizen (civic)

clad- *base* leaf (cladode)

clado- *comb* branch (cladophyll)

-claim, clam- *comb* say; speak; tell
(exclaim, exclamation)

clar- *base* clear (clarified)

-clasia, -clasis, -clastic *comb* break
fracture; fragment (osteoclasia,
onychoclasis, aclastic)

clasmato- *comb* fragment (clasma-
tocyte)

clathr- *base* lattice; bars (clathrate)

claud- *base* lame (claudication)

claustro- *comb* closed; shut (claustrophobia)

-clav- *base* nail (inclavate)

clavato- *comb* studded; knobbed
(clavototurbinate)

clavi-¹ *comb* key; collarbone (clavi-
chord)

clavi-² *base* club (clavicorn)

-cle **1.** *suf* diminutive spelling (par-

ticle); **2.** place; means (receptacle)

cleido- *see* clido-

-cleisis *comb* closure (colpocleisis)

cleisto- *comb* shut; closed (cleisto-
carp)

clem-¹ *base* vine (clematis)

clem-² *base* mercy; leniency (clem-
ency)

clepto- *comb* robber (cleptobiosis).
See klepto-

clerico- *comb* clerical and __
(clerico-political)

clero- *comb* chance; lot (cleromancy)

clido- **1.** *comb* key (clidomancy);
2. clavicle (clidomastoid). *Also*
cleido- (cleidomancy)

climac- *base* stairs; ladder rungs
(climacophobia)

clin- *base* bed (clinoid)

-clinal, -clinate, -cline, -clinic,
clino-, -clinous *comb* sloped;
bent; directed toward; inclined
(anticlinal, proclinate, incline,
matroclinic, clinodiagonal)

-clisis *comb* proneness; bending
(pathoclisis)

-clit- *base* bend; inflect; lean (heteroclital)

-clithr- **1.** *base* closed; shut (clith-
ral); **2.** keyhole (clithridiate)

-cliv- *base* slope (proclivity)

cloac- *base* sewer (cloacal)

-clonic, -clonus *comb* spasm;
twitching (synclonic, myoclonus)

-clud-, -clus- *base* closed; shut (exclude, reclusive)

clupe- *base* herring (clupeoid)

clype- *comb* like a shield
(clypeiform)

-clysis *comb* irrigation (peritoneoclysis)

clysm-, clyst- *base* enema (clysmic,
clysterize)

-cnem- *base* leg; tibia (gastro-cnemius)

cnido- *comb* nettle; stinging organ (cnidophore)

co-[1] **1.** *suf* together; with (co-operation); **2.** joint (co-owner); **3.** equally (coextensive); **4.** complement of (cosine). NOTE: **co-** can change to: **col-** (colleague); **com-**(commingle); **con-** (convulse); **cor-** (correlate)

-co[2] *suf* trade names (Pepsico)

cobalti-, cobalto- *comb* cobalt (cobalti-cyanide, cobalto-cyanide)

-coccal, -coccic, cocco-, -coccoid, -coccus *comb* of or like a bacterium; bacteria names; berrylike; grainlike (staphylococcal, staphylococcic, coccobacillus, staphylococcoid, staphylococcus)

cocci- *comb* berry (coccigerous)

coccy-, coccygo- *comb* coccyx (coccyalgia, coccygodynia)

cochle(a)- *base* snail (cochleiform)

cochleari- *base* spoon (cochleariform)

cochlio- *comb* spiral (cochliocarpous)

-coct- *base* cook; boil (decoction)

-coele *comb* cavity; chamber (blastocoele)

coeli- *comb* heaven; sky (coelicolist)

coelo- *comb* hollow (coelodont)

coen- *base* meal (coenaculous)

coeno- *comb* in common (coenobite). *Also* **ceno-** (cenobite)

cogit- *base* know; think (cogitation)

-cogn- *base* know; related by blood (recognize, cognation)

coimet- *base* cemetery (coimetrophobia). *Also* **coemet-**

coit- *base* intercourse; coming together (coition)

col-[1] *See* **co-**

col-[2] *base* strain; filter (colander)

colaco- *base* parasite (colacobiosis)

colar-, colat- *base* strain (colarin, colation)

-cole, -colent *comb* [botany] inhabit; habitat (arboricole, accolent). *See* **-colous**

coleo- *comb* sheath; scabbard (coleorhiza)

coleopter- *base* beetle (coleopterous)

coli-[1], colo- *comb* colon (coliform, coloenteritis)

coli-[2] *comb* sieve (coliform)

coll-[1] *base* neck; collar (decollate, colliform)

coll-[2] *base* glue (collenchyma)

coll-[3] *base* hill (colliculate)

-colleto- *base* one who glues or fastens (colletocystophore)

collodio- *comb* collodion (collodiochloride)

collut- *base* mouthwash (collution)

-colous *comb* growing in; living among (arenicolous). *See* **-cole**

colp(o)- *comb* vagina (colpocele)

colubri- *comb* snake (colubriform)

columb- *base* dove; pigeon (columbaceous)

columelli- *comb* small column (columelliform)

column- *base* pillar (columniferous)

-com- *base* treatment (gerocomy)

-coma, comi-, como- *comb* having hair or a hairlike structure (Abrocoma, comiferous, comophorous)

comest- *base* eat up (comestible)

comico- *comb* humorous (comicocynical)

comit- *base* affable; courteous (comity)

conat- *base* attempt; desire (conative)

concavo- *comb* concave (concavo-convex)

concess- *base* grant; yield (concession)

conchi- *comb* shell (conchiferous)

concinn- *base* adjusted; suitable; harmonious (inconcinnity)

-cond- *base* put together (incondite)

condyl- *comb* knob; protuberance (condyloid)

conger- *base* pile (congeries)

congru- *base* come together (congruency)

coni-[1], -conia, conio- *comb* dust; granules (coniosis, fibroconia, coniofibrosis). *Also* konio- (koniosis)

coni-[2], cono- *comb* cone (coniferous, conodont)

conico- *comb* conical (conico-cylindrical)

conist- *base* dusty place (conistery)

conjugato- *comb* coupled; paired (conjugato-palmate)

connict- *base* blink (connictation)

conniv- *base* blink (connivance)

connochaet- *base* gnu (connochaetes)

conoido- *comb* nearly conical (conoido-hemispherical)

consil- *base* in accord; agreeing (consilience)

contig- *base* adjacent (contiguous)

contin- *base* unceasing (continuous)

contorto- *comb* twisted (contortofoliaceous)

contra- *pre* against; contrary; opposite (contradiction)

contre- *pre* opposite (contrecoup)

contum- *base* insolence; stubbornness (contumely)

convexo- *comb* rounded; convex (convexo-concave)

-cop- *base* beat; strike (syncope)

coph- *base* deaf (cophosis)

copi- *base* abundance (copious)

copro- *comb* excrement; filth (coprolite); obscenity (coprology)

coraci-, coraco- 1. *comb* coracoid bone; beaklike (coraco-acromial); 2. crow; raven (coraciiform, coracomorphic)

coralli- *comb* coral (corallidomous)

corb- *base* basket (corbula)

cord- *comb* cord; sinew (cordotomy). *Also* chord (chorditis)

cordato- *comb* heart-shaped (cordato-ovate)

cordi- *comb* heart (cordiform)

core-[1], coreo-, -coria, coro- *comb* pupil of the eye (corelysis, coreoplasty, isocoria, coroplastic). *Also* -koria (leukokoria)

core-[2] *base* bug (coreopsis)

-cori- *base* leather (coriacious)

cormo- *comb* trunk; stem (cormophyly)

-corn, corni- *comb* horn (unicorn, corniform)

corneo- 1. *comb* with a horny admixture (corneo-silicious); 2. cornea of eye (corneoiritis)

cornic- *base* little tentacles; antennae (corniculate)

cornu- *base* horn (cornucopia)

corolli- *comb* crown; flower garland (corolliflorous)

coroni-, corono- *comb* crown (coroniform, coronofacial)

-corp- *base* body; bulk (incorporate)

corrugato- *comb* wrinkled (corrugato-striate)

cortici-, cortico- *comb* bark; cortex (corticiform, corticotropin)

corv- *base* crow; magpie, raven (corvine)

corymbi- *comb* cluster (corymbiferous)

coryn- *base* rod; club (coryniform)

-coryph- *base* top; summit (coryphodon)

coscino- *comb* sieve (coscinomancy)

-cosm, cosmo- *comb* world; universe (macrocosm, cosmotheism)

costi-, costo- *comb* rib (costiform, costotome)

coturn- *base* quail (coturnine)

cotyle-, cotyli-, cotylo- *comb* cup-shaped; hollow; hipjoint socket (cotyledonary, cotyliform, cotylosacral)

counter- 1. *comb* opposite; contrary to (counterclockwise); 2. in retaliation (counterplot); 3. complementary (counterpart)

coupho- *comb* frail; fragile; tender (coupholite). *Also* **koupho-** (koupholite)

coxo- *comb* hip (coxodynia)

-cracy *comb* form of government (theocracy)

-craft *comb* work; skill; art; practice of (woodcraft)

cranio- *comb* skull (craniofacial)

-cranter- *base* wisdom teeth (syncranterian)

crapul- *base* excessive eating and drinking (crapulence)

-crasia 1. *comb* mixture (spermacrasia); 2. loss of control (coprocrasia). *Also* -crasy (idiocrasy)

-crass- *base* thickened; condensed (incrassated)

crastin- *base* tomorrow (procrastinate)

-crat *comb* participant in government (democrat)

-crataeg- *base* hawthorn (crataegin)

crater- *base* bowl (crateriform)

crateri- *base* crater (crateriform)

cratic- *base* lattice (craticle)

-crease *comb* grow (decrease)

crebr- *base* frequent (crebrous)

crebri- *comb* ridged (crebrisulcate)

-cred- *base* belief; trust (incredible)

-crem- *base* burn (incremable)

cremno- *base* precipice (cremnophobia)

cremo- *comb* hanging (cremocarp)

cren-[1], crenato-, crenulato- *comb* notched; scalloped (crenellation, crenato-serrate, crenulato-dentate)

cren-[2] *base* fountain; spring (crenic)

creo- *comb* flesh (creophagous). *Also* **kreo-** (kreophagy)

-crep- *base* shoe (hippocrepian)

-crepit- *base* crack; creak; crackle (decrepit)

-crepus- *base* twilight (crepuscular)

-cresc- *base* grow; build up (crescitive)

crescenti- *base* crescent (crescentiform)

cretaceo- *comb* [geology] chalk formation (cretaceo-tertiary)

crev- *base* crack; rift (crevice)

cribri- *comb* sieve (cribriform)

cricet- *base* gerbil; muskrat (cricetine)

crico- *comb* ring; circle (cricothyroid)

-crin- *base* cup; calyx (crinoidal)

crini- *comb* hair (criniferous)

crino-, -crine *comb* secretion (crinogenic, endocrine)

crio- *comb* a ram (criocephalous)

-crisp- *base* curl; wrinkle (incrispated)

crist- *base* crested (cristate)

crit-[1] *base* judge; decide (criticism); *Also* krit- (kritarchy)

-crit[2] *comb* separate (hematocrit)

crith- *comb* barley (crithology)

critico- *comb* critical and (critico-historical)

croce- *base* saffron (croceal)

crocodil- *base* crocodile (crocodilian)

cromny- *base* onion (cromnyo-mancy)

cross- *suf* transverse; contrary (crossroads)

crosso- *suf* fringed; tasseled (Crossopterygian)

-crot- *base* beat; strike (catacrotic)

crotal- *base* rattlesnake (crotali-form)

cruci- *comb* cross (cruciferous)

-cruent- *base* bloody (incruent)

cruor- *base* blood (cruorin)

-crur- *base* leg (crural)

crymo-, cryo- *comb* cold; freezing (crymophilic, cryogenics)

crypto- *comb* secret; hidden; covered (cryptogram)

crystallo- *comb* crystal (crystallo-genic)

cteno- *comb* comb (ctenobranch)

-cub- *base* lie; recline (incubator)

cubi-, cubo- *comb* cube; dice (cubi-contravariant, cubo-octahedron)

cubito- *comb* [anatomy] ulna and __ (cubito-carpal)

cucul- *comb* cuckoo; roadrunner (cuculiform)

cuculli- *comb* hood; cowl (cuculli-form)

cucumi- *comb* cucumber (cucumi-form)

cucurbit- *base* gourd (cucurbitin)

-cula, -cule, *suf* diminutive (Auric-ula, molecule)

culici- *base* gnat; mosquito (culici-form)

culin- *base* kitchen (culinary)

culmi- *comb* plant stem; straw (cul-micolous)

culmin- *base* peak; top (culmina-tion)

culp- *base* fault; blame (exculpate)

cult- *base* worship (cultism)

cultel- *base* knife (cultellary)

cultri- *comb* knife (cultrirostral)

-culture *comb* tillage; raising (vini-culture)

-culum, -culus *suf* diminutive (cur-riculum, fasciculus)

cuma- *base* wave; surf (cuma-phytism)

-cumb- *base* lie; recline (recum-bent)

cumulo- *comb* heaplike; cumulus and __ (cumulonimbus)

cunct- *base* delay; tardy action (cunctation)

cuneo- *comb* wedge (cuneo-scaphoid)

cunic- *base* hare; rabbit (cunicu-lous)

cunicul- *base* underground (cunic-ular)

cup- *base* desire (cupidity)

cupreo-, cupri-, cupro-, cuproso- *comb* copper (cupreo-violaceous, cupriferous, cupromagnesite, cuproso-ferric)

cupress- *base* cypress (cupressi-neous)

cupuli- *comb* cup (cupuliform)

cur- *base* health; healing (curative)

curculion- *base* weevil (curculio-nid)

-cur(r)-, -curs- *base* run; go (recur-rent, cursory)

curt- *base* short; abbreviated (cur-tail)

curvi- *comb* curved; bent (curvilin-ear)

cusp- *base* point (cuspid)

cuss- *base* strike; shake (percussion)

custod- *base* watchman (custodial)

cuti- *comb* skin (cutisector)

-cy 1. *suf* quality; fact of being; state; condition (democracy); **2.** position; rank (captaincy)

-cyam- *base* bean (hyoscyamine)

cyano- 1. *comb* dark blue (cyanosis); **2.** cyanide (cyanohydrin) cyathi-, cyatho- *comb* cuplike (cyathiform, cyatholith)

cyber- *comb* relating to computers (cyberphobia)

cyclo- *comb* wheel; circle; cycle (cyclograph)

cyclorraph- *base* fly (cyclorraphous)

cyclostom- *base* eel (cyclostomatous)

-cyesis *comb* pregnancy (polycyesis)

cygn- *base* swan (cygnine). *Also* cycn- (cycnean)

cylico- *base* bowl (cylicomancy). *Also* kylixo-

cylindro- *comb* cylinder (cylindroconical)

cyma-, cymato-, cymo- *comb* wave; billow (cymagraph, cymatolite, cymoscope) *Also* kymo- (kymograph)

cymbi-, cymbo- *comb* boat (cymbiform, cymbocephalic)

cyn-, cyno- *comb* dog (cynanthropy, cynophobia). *Also* kyno-

cyo- *comb* fetus (cyogenic)

cypho- *comb* humped; bent; crooked (cyphonism). *Also* kypho- (kyphosis)

cypriani- *base* lewd; harlot (cyprianite)

cyprid- *base* sexual (cypridophobia)

cyprin- *base* carp; goldfish; minnow (cyprinid)

cypsel- *base* swift (cypseline)

cyrio- *base* regular; proper (cyriologic)

cyrto- *comb* curved; arched (cyrtometer)

cyst-, -cyst, cysti-, cysto- *comb* like a bladder; pouch; sac; cyst (cystalgia, statocyst, cystiform, cystocarp)

-cyte, cyto- *comb* cell (lymphocyte, cytology)

-cythemia *comb* blood cell condition (leukocythemia)

D

dacn- *base* bite; kill (Tridacna)

dacry(o)- *comb* tear (dacryocystitis)

dactyl-, dactylo-, -dactylous, -dactyly *comb* finger; toe (dactyliology, dactylology, tridactylous, brachydactyly)

dactylio- *comb* finger ring (dactylioglyphic)

daedal- *base* cunning (logodaedaly)

daemono- *see* demono-

Dano- *comb* Danish and ___ (Dano-Irish)

dapat- *base* sumptuous; costly (dapatical)

daphn- *base* laurel (daphnomancy)

dasy- *comb* hairy or wooly; thick or dense (dasyphyllous)

dasypod- *base* armadillo (Dasypodid)

dasyproct- *base* agouti (Dasyprocta)

dativo- *comb* dative (dativo-gerundial)

de- 1. *pre* away from; off (detrain); 2. down (decline); 3. entirely (defunct); 4. undo; reverse (defrost)

debil- *base* weakness (debility)

dec(a)- *comb* ten (decagon)

decem- *base* ten (decemcostate)

deci- *comb* one-tenth (decimeter)

-decker *comb* having __ decks or in layers (double-decker)

decresc- *base* wane; lessen (decrescent)

decuss- *base* divided crosswise; x-shaped (decussate)

degen- *base* decline (degenerative)

dehydro- *comb* dehydrogenated (dehydrochlorinate)

de(i)- *base* God (deification)

-deictic *comb* demonstrating (epideictic)

deipno- *comb* dinner (deipnophobia)

deka- *comb* ten (dekaliter)

delect- *base* please (delectation)

delinq- *base* fault (delinquency)

delphin- *base* porpoise; dolphin (delphine)

delto- *comb* triangular (deltohedron)

dement- *base* insane (dementia)

demi- 1. *pre* half (demivolt); 2. less than usual (demigod)

-demia *comb* fatty degeneration (myodemia)

demo- *comb* people (democracy)

demono- *comb* demon (demonology)

dendri-, dendro-, -dendron *comb* tree; treelike (dendriform, dendrology, rhododendron)

dentato- *comb* dentate and (dentato-serrate)

denti-, dento- *comb* tooth (dentiform, dentosurgical). *Also* dont- (pedodontics)

deoxy- *comb* oxygen removed (deoxyhemoglobin)

deris- *base* mockery; scorn (deristic)

derm-, -derm, derma, -derma, dermato-, -dermatous, -dermis, dermo- *comb* skin; covering (dermabrasion, endoderm, derma-therm, scleroderma, dermatology, xerodermatous, epidermis, dermoneural)

des-[1] *pre* missing; deprived of (desoxydation). *See* dis-

-des[2] *suf* plural ending (proboscides)

desid- *base* wish; desire (desiderative)

desmo- *comb* bond; band; ligament (desmogen)

desmodont- *base* bat (desmodontid)

deuter(o)-, deuto- *comb* second; secondary (deuterogamy, deutoplasm)

dexio- *comb* on the right side (dexiotropic)

dextr(o)- 1. *comb* on the right side (dextrocardia); 2. [chemistry] clockwise (dextrorotatory)

di-[1] 1. *pre* twice; double (dichroism); 2. having two (diacid)

di-[2] *pre* away; apart (divest). *See* dis-

dia- 1. *pre* through; across (diagonal); 2. apart; between (diaphony)

-diabol- *base* devil (diabolic)

dialy- *comb* separate; distinct (dialysepalous)

diamido- *comb* having two atoms of hydrogen replaced by two of the radical Amidogen NH2 (diamidobenzene)

diaphano- *comb* transparent (diaphanometer)

diazo- *comb* having a group of two nitrogen atoms combined directly with one hydrocarbon radical (diazoamino)

dibromo- *comb* having two atoms of bromine which have replaced two of hydrogen (dibromoaldehyde)

dicarbo- *comb* containing two

atoms or equivalents of carbon (dicarbopyridenic)

dichloro- *comb* two chlorine atoms substituting for hydrogen atoms (dichlorohydrin)

dicho- *comb* in two; split; separately (dichotomy)

dichro- *comb* two-colored (dichromatism)

-dict- *base* say; speak; tell (contradiction)

dictyo- *comb* net (dictyogen)

dicyano- *comb* combined with two equivalents of the radical cyanogen replacing two of hydrogen, chlorine, etc. (dicyanodiamide)

did- *base* dodo (didine)

didact- *base* teach (didactic)

didelph- *base* opossum (didelphine)

didym-, didymo- *comb* relating to the testis (didymalgia)

diethene *comb* combined with two equivalents of ethene (diethenediamine)

dif- *pre* away; apart (differ). *See* **dis-**

digitato- *comb* having fingerlike divisions (digitato-pinnate)

digiti- *comb* finger; toe (digitigrade)

digito- *comb* digitalis; foxglove (digitoleic acid)

dihydro- *comb* having two atoms of hydrogen in combination (dihydrobromide)

diiodo- *comb* having two atoms of iodine replacing two of hydrogen (diiodomethane)

dike- *comb* justice (dikephobia)

dilat- *base* expansion (dilation)

diluv- *base* flood (diluvial)

(di)mid- *base* half (dimidiation)

(di)min- *base* lessen (diminution)

dioxy *comb* having two atoms of oxygen (dioxybenzene)

dinitro- *comb* having two nitro

groups per molecule (dinitrobenzene)

dino-[1] *comb* terrible; mighty; huge (dinosaur)

dino-[2] *comb* whirling (dinoflagellate)

diomed- *base* albatross (diomedeidae)

dior- *base* distinction; definition (dioristic)

dioscorea- *base* yam (dioscoreaceous)

diphy- *comb* double; bipartite (diphycercal)

diplo- *comb* two; double; twin (diplocephaly)

diplopod- *base* millipede (diplopodal)

dipso- *comb* thirst (dipsomania)

diptero- *comb* having two wings (dipterology)

dis- 1. *pre* away; apart (dismiss); 2. deprive of (disbar); 3. cause to be the opposite of (disable); 4. fail; refuse to (disallow); 5. not (dishonest); 6. lack of (disunion) NOTE: **dis-** can change to **di-** (divest) or **dif-** (differ). *See* **des-**

discip- *base* follower; learner (disciple)

disco- *comb* disk-shaped (discocarp)

discophor- *base* jellyfish; leech (discophoran)

-disso- *base* double (dissoconch)

disto- *comb* remote; farther away (distolabial)

disulpho- *comb* acids derived from two molecules of sulphurous acid (disulphoanthraquinic)

diurn- *base* day (diurnal)

diuturn- *base* lasting; long duration (diuturnal)

divergenti-, divergi- *comb* divergent (divergentiflorous, divergivenate)

doc- *base* teach (indoctrinate)

dodeca- *comb* twelve (dodecagon)

dogmato- *comb* pertaining to dogma (dogmatopoeic)

dolabri- *comb* ax; cleaver (dolabriform)

dolero- *comb* deceptive (dolerophanite)

dolicho- *comb* long; narrow (dolichocephalic)

dolio- *base* barrel (dolioform)

-dolor- *base* pain; sorrow (dolorific)

-dom-[1] *base* house; dwelling (domestic)

-dom[2] **1.** *suf* rank of; position of; domain of (kingdom); **2.** state of being (wisdom); **3.** total of all who are (officialdom)

-don- *base* give (donation). *Also* -**dor-** gift (Dorothy)

-dont *comb* tooth (orthodontist). *Also* **dent-** (dentifrice)

dora- *base* fur; hide (doramania)

-dorm- *base* sleep (dormitive)

dorsi-, dorso- *comb* the back (dorsibranch, dorsoventral)

double- *comb* in combination (double-breasted)

draco-, draconi- *base* dragon (dracocephalum, draconiform)

drapeto- *comb* flee; fugitive (drapetomania)

drepani- *comb* sickle (drepaniform)

driri- *base* drip (dririmancy)

-drome, dromo-, -dromous *comb* running; moving; racecourse (hippodrome, dromomania, catadromous)

droso- *comb* dew (drosometer)

drosophyl- *base* fruitfly (Drosophylidae)

du- *pre* two (duplicate)

dub- *base* doubtful (indubitably)

-duc(e), -duct- *base* lead (induce, conductor)

ducen- *base* two hundred (ducenarious)

-dulc- *base* sweet (dulcify)

dulo- *comb* slave (dulocracy). *Also* **doulo-** (doulocracy)

duo- *comb* two; double (duograph)

duodec-, duodecim-, duoden- *base* twelve (duodecuple, duodecimfid, duodenary)

duodeviginti- *base* eighteen (duodevigintiangular)

duplicato- *comb* doubly (duplicatodentate)

duplici- *comb* duplex (duplicipennate)

dur-, duro- *base* hard; lasting (endurance, durometer)

dyna-, dynamo- *comb* power; strength; energy (dynameter, dynamogeny)

-dynia *comb* pain (inguinodynia)

dyo- *comb* two (Dyophysite)

dys- *pre* hard; ill; bad; difficult (dysentery)

-dyte- *base* to get or enter (troglodyte)

E

e- *see* **ex-**

-ea *suf* noun ending (cornea)

-eae *suf* plant tribes: plural ending (Gramineae)

-ean *suf* belonging to; like (European)

ebon- *base* black (ebony)

ebur- *base* ivory (eburnine)

ec- *see* ex-

ecclesiastico- *comb* of the church or clergy (ecclesiastico-military)

-echia *comb* have; retain (synechia)

echidno- *comb* viper (echidno-toxin)

echin- *base* hedgehog; sea urchin (echinate)

echinato-, echino- *comb* prickly; spiny (echinato-dentate, echino-coccus)

echinoderm- *base* starfish (echino-dermatous)

echinulato-, echinuli- *comb* prickly; spiny (echinulato-striate, echinuliform)

echo- *comb* repeated sound (echo-lalia)

eco- *comb* environment (ecosystem)

-ecoia *comb* hearing condition (dysecoia)

-ectasia, -ectasis *comb* dilation; expansion (colpectasia, anectasis)

ect(o)- *comb* outside; external (ectoderm)

-ectomy *comb* surgical operation; excision; cutting (appendectomy)

ectro- *comb* congenital absence of a part (ectrodactyly)

ed-¹ *base* eat (edible)

-ed² *suf* having; provided with; characterized by (pileated)

edaph- *base* floor; ground (edaphic)

-edema *comb* swelling (myoedema)

-edent- 1. *base* lacking teeth (edentulous); 2. order of New World mammals which includes armadillos, sloths, anteaters (edentate)

edi- *base* building (edifice). *Also* aedi-

-ee 1. *suf* recipient (appointee); 2. person (employee); 3. thing (goatee)

-een *suf* diminutive (colleen)

-eer 1. *suf* person who does (engineer); 2. person who writes (sonneteer)

ef- *see* ex-

efficac- *base* effective; competent (efficacious)

egagro- *base* wild goat (egagropile)

ego- *comb* self (egomania)

egress- depart; leave (egressive)

egro- *comb* dead (egromancy): corrupt form of **necro-**

Egypto- *comb* Egyptian and __ (Egypto-Arabic)

eico- *comb* twenty (eicosapentae-noic)

eid-, eido- *comb* shape; form; that which is seen (eidetic, eidoclast)

eiren- *base* peace (eirenarchy)

eis- *pre* into (eisegesis)

eisoptro- *comb* mirror (eisoptro-phobia)

-eity *suf* noun of quality or condition (spontaneity)

eka- *comb* one (ekaselenium)

ekist- *comb* settlement; house (ekistics)

-el *suf* diminutive (satchel)

elao-, elaeo- *comb* oil (elaolite, elaeometer)

elaph- *base* deer; stag (elaphine)

-elasmo- *base* metal plate (elasmo-saurus)

elat- *base* joy (elation)

electro- *comb* electrical (electro-magnetic)

eleo- *comb* oil (eleoma)

elephant- *base* elephant (elaphantine)

eleuthero- *comb* freedom (eleu-theromania)

-ella 1. *suf* diminutive (umbrella); 2. bacteria genus (salmonella)

elytri- *comb* wing case (elytriform)

elytr(o)- *comb* [medicine] vagina (eletroplasty)

em- 1. *pre* in (embed); 2. cause to be

(empower); **3.** to place (emplacement); **4.** to restrict (embrace)

emberiz- *base* bunting (emberizine)

embol-, emboli-, embolo- *comb* plug; obstruction; patch; stopper (embolism, emboliform, embololalia)

embryo- *comb* fetus (embryogeny)

-eme *suf* [linguistics] significant contrastive unit (phoneme)

-emesis, -emetic, emeto- *comb* vomiting (hematemesis, antiemetic, emetophobia)

-emia *comb* blood condition; blood disease (leukemia). *Also* **-aemia** (hyperaemia)

emmen- *comb* monthly; menstrual (emmeniopathy)

empor- *base* trade; merchant; merchandise (emporetic)

-empt- *base* buy; take (exempt)

emul- *base* jealous; rivalrous (emulate)

emunct- *base* nose blowing; excretory (emunctory)

emydo- *comb* tortoise (emydosaurian)

en-[1] **1.** *pre* in; within (energy); **2.** to place (entomb); **3.** to cause to be in (enshrine); **4.** to restrict (encircle) NOTE: en- becomes em- before B and P: (embed). *See* **eis-**

-en[2] **1.** *suf* plural form (oxen); **2.** cause to be (weaken); **3.** cause to have (strengthen); **4.** made of (wooden); **5.** female (vixen); **6.** diminutive (kitten)

enalio- *base* of the sea (enaliosaur)

enantio- *comb* opposite (enantiopathic)

-enarthra- *base* jointed (enarthrosis)

-ence *suf* action; state; quality (excellence). *See* **-ance**

encephalo- *comb* brain (encephalocele)

-enchyma[1] *comb* sinuous; wavy (colpenchyma)

-enchyma[2] *comb* infusion (protenchyma)

encom- *base* praise (encomium)

enerv- *base* weakness (enervated)

-ency *suf* act; fact; quality; degree; state; result (emergency)

endeca- *comb* eleven (endecagon). *Also* **hendeca-** (hendecasyllabic)

endo- *comb* inside; within (endocardium)

-ene *suf* hydrocarbons (benzene)

engraul- *base* anchovy (Engraulid)

enigmato- *comb* obscure; enigmatic (enigmatology)

enisso- *comb* reproach; criticism (enissophobia)

-enn- *base* year (biennial). *Also* **-ann-** (annual)

-enne *suf* feminine ending (comedienne)

ennea- *comb* nine (enneahedron)

enneacent- *base* nine hundred (enneacentenary)

enneaconta- *base* ninety (enneacontahedral)

enneakaideca- *comb* nineteen (enneakaidecahedron)

-enoic *suf* unsaturated acid (eicosatrienoic)

enoptro- *comb* mirror (enoptromancy)

enosi- *base* reproach (enosiophobia)

ensi- *comb* sword-shaped (ensiform)

-ensis *suf* scientific derivatives of place names (carolinensis)

-ent 1. *suf* having the quality of (insistent); **2.** person who (superintendent); **3.** material agent (emolient). *See* **-ant**

enter- *pre* between; among; mutually (entertain). *Usually* **inter-**

entero- *comb* intestines (enteropathy)

ento- *comb* within; inner (entophyte)

entomo- *comb* insect (entomogenous)

entostho- *comb* from within (entosthoblast)

entre- *base* in; undertaking (entrepeneur)

eo- *pre* early time period; dawn (eolithic)

eoso- *comb* dawn (eosophobia)

-eous *suf* having the nature of; like (beauteous)

epana- *comb* repetition (epanastrophe)

-epeiro- *base* mainland; continent (epeirogenic)

ephem- *base* lasting for a day (ephemeris)

ephipp- *base* saddle (ephippium)

epi- *pre* on; upon; up to; over; on the outside; among; beside; following (epicardium). NOTE: epi- can change to: **ep-** (epaxial) and **eph-** (ephedrine)

epicid- *base* pertaining to funeral rites (epicidial)

episcop- *base* bishop (episcopicide)

episio- *comb* vulva (episiotomy)

epistem- *base* knowledge (epistemology)

equ- *base* horse (equine)

equi- *comb* equal (equidistant)

equiset- *base* horsetail (equisetiform)

-er 1. *suf* person who (farmer) ; 2. person living in (New Yorker); 3. thing or action (doubleheader); 4. repeatedly (flicker); 5. comparative degree (cooler)

-erel *suf* pejorative (doggerel)

eremo- 1. *comb* alone; solitary (eremophobia); 2. of/in a desert (eremophyte)

-erethis- *base* irritate (erethistic)

-ergasia *comb* interfunctioning of mind and body; work; activity (hypoergasia). *Also* **ergasio-** (ergasiophobia)

ergo-, -ergic, -ergy *comb* work; activity; result (ergonomics, neurergic, allergy)

erinac- *base* hedgehog (erinaceous)

erio- *base* wood; fiber (eriometer)

eris- *base* controversy; strife (eristic)

-ern *suf* direction names (southern)

eroso- *comb* incised; indentated (erosodentate)

erot- *base* question (erotesis)

eroto- *comb* sexual desire (erotomania)

err- *base* wander (errant)

eruci- *base* caterpillar (eruciform)

-ery 1. *suf* a place to (brewery); 2. a place for (nunnery); 3. practice/act of (robbery); 4. product/goods of (pottery); 5. collection of (crockery); 6. condition/state of (slavery)

erysi- *comb* red; inflamed (erysipeloid)

erythro- *comb* red; erythrocyte (erythrocarpous)

es- *see* **ex-**

-es *suf* plural ending (dishes)

-esce *suf* incomplete action (incandesce)

-escence *suf* something becoming (convalescence)

-escent *suf* starting to be; becoming (obsolescent)

eschato- *base* last (eschatology)

escul- *base* food (esculent)

-ese 1. *suf* of a country (Portuguese); 2. of a language (Chinese); 3. in the style of (journalese)

-esis *suf* condition; process; action (enuresis)

-esmus *comb* spasm; contraction (tenesmus). *Also* **-ismus** (vaginismus)

eso- *comb* inner; within (esotropia)

esophag- *base* gullet (esophagus). *Also* **oesophag-** (oesophagalgia)

-esque 1. *suf* in the style of (Romanesque); 2. like (picturesque)

-ess *suf* female who (princess)

esse- *base* being; existence (essential)

-est *suf* superlative degree (coolest)

-esthesia-, -esthesio- *comb* sensation; perception (myesthesia, esthesiogenic)

estu- *base* 1. boil (estuant); 2. tide (estuary). *Also* **aestu-**

esur- *base* hunger; appetite (esurient)

-et *suf* diminutive (rivulet)

-eth *suf* ordinal numbers (fiftieth)

ethico- *comb* ethical and (ethico-political)

ethmo- *comb* sieve; ethmoid bone (ethmo-turbinal)

ethno- *comb* race; people; culture; nation (ethnology)

etho- *comb* character; behavior (ethology)

-etic *suf* adjective ending (pathetic)

etio- *comb* cause; origin (etiologist). *Also* **aetio-** (aetiology)

-ette 1. *suf* diminutive (dinette); 2. female (suffragette); 3. substitute (leatherette)

-etum *suf* a grove of the plant specified (pinetum)

eu- *pre* good; well (eulogy)

-eum *suf* scientific name ending (peritoneum)

-eur *suf* one who (voyeur)

euro- *comb* east (euroboreal)

Euro- *comb* European (Eurodollars)

Europaeo-, Europeo- *comb* European (Europaeo-Siberian, Europeo-Asiatic)

eury- *comb* [science] broad; wide (eurycephalic)

-eus *suf* scientific name ending (nucleus)

eusuch- *base* alligator (eusuchian)

even- *comb* smooth; consistent (even-tempered)

ever- *comb* always (ever-abiding)

ex- 1. *pre* from; out (expel); 2. beyond (excess); 3. away from; out of (expatriate); 4. thoroughly (exterminate); 5. upward (exalt); 6. not having (exanimate); 7. former (ex-husband). NOTE: ex- can change to: **e-** (eject); **ec-** (eccentric); **ef-** (efferent); **es-** (escape)

exa- *comb* quintillion (exameter)

exanim- *base* without life (exanimate)

excito- *comb* [anatomy] stimulating (excito-nutrient)

excub- *base* watchman (excubation)

-exia *See* **-orexia**

exig- 1. *base* demanding (exigency); 2. scanty (exiguous)

exo- *pre* without; outside; outer part (exocardia)

exousia- *comb* authority (exousiastic)

explanato- *comb* spread out in a plane or flat surface (explanato-foliaceous)

extero- *comb* outside (exteroceptive)

extra-, extro- *pre* outside; beyond; more than; besides (extraordinary, extrovert)

-ey *suf* characterized by; inclined to (gooey)

F

-faba-, -fabi- *base* bean (fabaceous, fabiform)

-fabr- *base* make; construct (fabrication)

fabul- *base* tale (fabulist)

-fac-, -fec-, -fic- *base* make; do (factory, efficient, fictitious)

-facient *comb* causing to become; making (liquefacient)

facil- *base* easy (facilitate)

facin- *base* wicked; vile (facinorous)

facio- *comb* face (facioplegia)

-faga- *base* beech (fagaceous)

-falc- *base* sickle (falciform)

falco-, falconi- *base* falcon; kestrel; hawk (falconry)

fan- *base* lighthouse; beacon (fanal)

farct- *base* to stuff; obstruct (infarction)

farin- *base* flour (farinaceous)

farr-, farrag- *base* mixed feed grains; spelt (confarreation, farraginous)

fasciculato- *comb* arranged in a bundle (fasciculato-glomerate)

fascio- *comb* fibrous tissue; fascia; bundle (fasciotomy)

fastid- *base* disgust (fastidious)

fastig- *base* gabled; pointed; tapered (fastigate)

fati- *base* prophet (fatidic)

fatisc- *base* cleft (fatiscent)

fatu- *base* foolish (fatuous)

fauc- *base* throat (faucal)

faust- *base* fortune; chance (faustity)

fav- *base* honeycomb (faviform)

favill- *base* ashes (favillous)

favon- *base* west wind (favonian)

favoso- *comb* honeycombed (favoso-dehiscent)

febri- *comb* fever (febrifuge)

-fec-[1] *base* make; do (effective). *See* fac-

-fec-[2] *base* filth; dregs (feculent)

fedi- *base* compact; covenant (fedifragous)

fel- *base* cat (feline)

felic- *base* happy (felicify)

femin- *base* woman (feminization)

femto- *pre* one-quadrillionth (femtometer)

fenest- *base* window (fenestrate)

-fer *comb* one that bears; one that produces (aquifer)

-fer- *base* wild animal (ferine)

ferment- *base* yeast (fermentareous)

feroc- *base* bold; fierce (ferocity)

-ferous *comb* bearing; producing; yielding (coniferous)

ferri-, ferro- *comb* containing ferric iron (ferricyanide, ferromagnetism)

ferul- *base* rod; stalk (ferulaceous)

ferv- *base* boil; glow (fervency)

fescinn- *base* obscene (fescinnine)

-fest *comb* assembly or celebration (songfest)

festin- *base* haste; speed (festination)

festuc- *base* stalk; straw (festucine)

fet- *base* stink (fetid)

fibri- *comb* fiber (fibriform)

fibrilloso- *comb* fibril-shaped (fibrilloso-striate)

fibrino- *comb* fibrin (fibrinogen)

fibro- *comb* fibrous matter (fibro-adipose)

fibroso- *comb* fibrous (fibroso-calcareus)

-fic *comb* making; creating (scientific). *See* fac-

-fication *comb* a making; a creating; a causing (calcification)

fici- *base* fig (ficiform)
fict- *base* made up (fiction)
-fid-[1] *base* faith; belief (confide)
-fid-[2] *comb* cleft; segment (multifid)
figur- *base* form; shape (disfiguration)
fil-[1], fili-, filo- *comb* threadlike (filament, filigrain, filoplume)
fil-[2] *base* child (filial)
filamento- *comb* threadlike (filamento-cribrate)
filari- *base* worm (filariform)
filic- *base* fern (filiciform)
fim-, fimi- *comb* dung (fimetic, fimicolous)
fimbr- *comb* fringe; border (fimbricate)
fimbriato- *comb* fringed with hairs (fimbriato-lacinate)
fimbrilli- *comb* small fringe (fimbrilliferous)
-fin- *base* end; limit (infinity)
Finno- *comb* Finnish (Finno-Ugric)
fissi- *comb* [anatomy] cleft (fissidactyl)
fissuri- *comb* fissure (fissuriform)
fistul- *base* reed; pipe; tube (fistuliform)
flabelli- *comb* fanlike (flabellifoliate)
flacc- *base* drooping; weak (flaccid)
-flagel- *base* whip; lash (flagelliferous)
flagit- *base* vicious; wicked (flagitious)
-flat- *base* wind (flatulent)
flavido- *comb* yellowish (flavidocinerascent)
-flavin *comb* natural derivatives of flavin (riboflavin)
flavo- 1. *comb* yellow (flavopurpurin); 2. flavin (flavoprotein)
fleb- *base* weeping; doleful (flebile)
-flect-, -flex- *base* bend (inflection, flexible)

-flet- *base* weep; cry (fletiferous)
flexuoso- *comb* winding; bending; undulating (flexuoso-convex)
-flocc- *base* wool; tuft (flocculent)
flori-, -florous *comb* flower; having flowers (floriferous, multiflorous)
-flu- *base* flowing (fluent)
flucti- *comb* undulation; wave (fluctifragous)
flum- *base* river (fluminal)
fluo-, fluor-, fluoro- *comb* fluorine; fluorescent (fluophosphate, fluorhydric, fluoroscope)
-fluv- *base* flowing (effluvia)
fluvio- *comb* [geology] river; stream (fluvio-terrestrial)
fod- *base* dig; burrow (fodient)
-fold 1. *suf* having parts (twofold); 2. larger; more (hundredfold)
foliato- *comb* leaf-like (foliato-explanate)
folii-, folio-, -folious *comb* leaf (foliiferous, foliolar, unifolious)
follic- *base* tube; small bag (follicular)
-foot(er) *comb* so many feet long (six-footer)
for- 1. *pre* away; apart; off (forgo); 2. very much (forladen)
foramin- *base* hole (foraminate)
-forc-, -fort- *base* strength (enforcement, fortification)
fore- 1. *pre* before (forecast); 2. front part of (forehead)
-forfic- *base* scissors (forficulate)
forficul- *base* earwig (forficulid)
-foris- *base* outside (forisfamiliate)
-form 1. *suf* shaped like (oviform); 2. having __forms (uniform)
-formic- *base* ant (formication)
formo- *comb* [chemistry] formic acid (formo-benzoic)
-fornic- *base* arch; vault (forniciform)
foss- *base* dig (fossorial)

fov- *base* pitted; pockmarked (foveate)

-fract- *base* break (fracture). *Also* -frag- and -frang-

fracto- *comb* ragged mass of cloud (fracto-stratus)

-frag- *base* break (fragmented). *Also* -fract- and -frang-

fragar- *base* strawberry (fragarol)

Franco- *comb* French (Franco-American)

-frang- *base* break (irrefrangible). *Also* -fract- and -frag-

frat- *base* brother (fratricide)

-frax- *base* ash tree (fraxetin)

-frem- *base* roar; murmur (fremescent)

frend- *base* grind; gnash (frendent)

frenet- *base* frenzied (frenetic)

-frig- *base* cold (frigorific)

-fringill- *base* finch (fringillaceous)

-frond- *base* leaf (frondivorous)

fronto- 1. *comb* frontal bone (fronto-parietal); 2. meteorological front (frontogenesis)

fructi-, fructo- *comb* fruit; fructose (fructiferous, fructosuria)

frug-¹ *base* fruit; fructose (frugivorous)

frug-² *base* sparing; thrifty (frugality)

-frument- *base* grain; cereal; corn (frumentaceous)

frust- *base* fragment; piece (frustulent)

fruticuloso- *comb* shrub-like (fruticuloso-ramose)

-fuc- *base* seawood (fucivorous)

-fuge *comb* driving out; driving away (febrifuge)

-ful 1. *suf* full of (painful); 2. having qualities of (masterful); 3. having ability to (forgetful); 4. amount that fills (handful)

fulic- *base* coot (fulicinae)

-fulg- *base* bright; flashing (fulgurant)

-fulig- *base* black; sooty (fuliginated)

fuligul- *base* duck (fuliguline)

-fulmin- *base* lightning; thunder (fulmination)

-fulv- *base* brown (fulvescent)

fulv- *base* yellow-brown; tan (fulvous)

-fum- *base* smoke (fumigate)

-fun- *base* rope (funambulist)

-fund- *base* bottom; base (fundamental)

-fundi- *base* sling (fundiform)

funest- *base* fatal; deadly; disastrous (funestous)

fungi- *comb* fungus (fungicide)

funi- *comb* cord; rope; fiber (funiform)

fur- *base* angry (furious)

-furc- *base* forked (bifurcation)

-furfur- *base* bran; dandruff (furfuraceous)

furt- *base* theft; stealth (furtive)

-fus- *base* flow; pour; melt (transfusion)

fusco- *comb* dark brown; dusky; gloomy (fusco-ferruginous)

fusi-, fuso- *comb* spindle; rod (fusiform, fusobacterium)

-fustig- *base* beat; cudgel (fustigation)

futil- *base* useless (futility)

-fy 1. *suf* make; cause to be (deify); 2. cause to have; imbue with (dignify); 3. become (putrefy)

G

-gaea *comb* earth (Paleogaea)

galact(o)- *comb* milk; milky (galactocele)

-gale[1] *base* weasel (potamogale)

-gale-[2] *base* shark (galeod)

-gale-[3] *base* cat (galeanthropy)

-galea- *base* helmet (galeated)

-gallinac-, -gallinag- *base* poultry: chicken, grouse, partridge, pheasant, quail, turkey, woodcock (gallinaceous, gallinaginous)

Gallo- *comb* French; Gallic (Gallophobia)

galvano- *comb* galvanic; electricity (galvanometer)

gambog- *base* yellow (gambogian)

gameto- *comb* gamete; union (gametophore)

-gammar- *base* sea crab; lobster (gammarolite)

gamo- 1. *comb* sexually united (gamogenesis); 2. joined (gamosepalous)

-gamous, -gamy *comb* marrying uniting sexually (polygamous, polygamy)

ganglio- *comb* nerve cells; swelling; ganglion (ganglioplexus)

-gano- *base* bright; shiny (ganoidal)

garrul- *base* chatter; magpie, jay (garrulous, garruline)

gaso- *comb* gas (gasohol)

gastero-, -gastria, gastro- *comb* stomach (gasteropod, microgastria, gastroenteritis)

gastropod- *base* snail (gastropodal)

-gate *comb* [journalism] concealed scandal (Watergate)

gato- *comb* cat (gatophobia)

gaud- *base* joy (gaudiloquence)

gavi- *base* gull (Gaviae)

gavial- *base* crocodile (gavialoid)

geitono- *base* neighbor (geitonogamy)

-gel-[1] *base* ice; frost; freeze (regelation)

-gel-[2] *base* laughter (gelastic)

gelatino- *comb* gelatin (gelatinoalbuminous)

-gemelli- *base* twins (gemelliparous)

-gemin- *base* double (geminiflorous)

gemm-[1] *base* leaf buds (gemmate)

gemm-[2] *base* jewel (gemmiferous)

-gen 1. *comb* something that produces; origin (oxygen); 2. something produced (endogen). *Also* -genic (endogenic); -genous (endogenous); -geny (endogeny)

-genesis *comb* origination; creation; formation; evolution(parthenogenesis)

-geneth- *base* birthday (genethliacon)

-genetic *suf* origin (phylogenetic)

-genia, genio-, geny-[1] *comb* jaw; cheek; chin (microgenia, genioplasty, genyplasty)

genic-, genu- *base* knee (geniculate, genuflect)

genito- *comb* genital (genitourinary)

geno- *comb* race; genetic makeup (genotype)

-geny[2] *comb* product of (phylogeny)

geo- *comb* earth (geocentric)

gephyr- *base* bridge (gephyrophobia)

ger-[1] *base* hold; manage (gerent)

ger-[2] *base* old age (geriatric)

gerasco- *comb* aging (gerascophobia)

Germano- *comb* German (Germanophile)

gero-, geronto- *comb* old; elderly (gerodontics, gerontology)

-gerous *comb* producing; bearing; carrying (dentigerous)

gestat- *base* carrying; pregnancy (gestation)

-geton *base* neighbor (potamogeton)

geum-, geumat- *base* taste (geumaphobia, geumatophobia)

-geusia *comb* taste (parageusia)

-gibboso- *base* rounded; humped; convex; protuberant (gibbosolobate)

giga- *pre* billion (gigabyte)

giganto- *comb* gigantic; large (gigantology)

gilv- *base* yellow (gilvous)

gingivo- *comb* gums (gingivoglossitis)

-gingly- *base* hinge (ginglyform)

glabello- *comb* space between the eyebrows (glabello-occipital)

-glabr- *base* smooth; bald (glabrous)

glacio- *comb* glacier; ice (glaciologist)

gladi- *comb* sword (gladiolus)

gland- 1. *base* acorn (glandiferous); 2. yellow-brown (glandaceous)

glare- *base* gravel; sand (glareous)

glauco- *comb* bluish-green; gray; silvery; opaque (glaucoma)

-glea *comb* glue; cement (mesoglea)

-gleb- *base* clod; lump; dirt (glebous)

gleno- *comb* shallow joint-socket (gleno-humeral)

-glia, glio- *comb* glue; gluelike (neuroglia, glioblastoma)

glico- *See* **gluco-**

-glir- *base* dormouse (gliriform)

globi-, globo- *comb* round; ball-shaped; spherical (globiferous, globosphaerite)

glom- *base* cluster; ball (glomerulus)

glosso- 1. *comb* of the tongue (glossoplegia); 2. the tongue plus (glossopharyngeal); 3. of words; of language (glossology). *Also* **glossia-** (macroglossia)

-glot, glotto- *comb* language, communication in; languages, knowledge of (polyglot, glottogony)

gluco- *comb* glycerin; glycerol; glycogen; sugar (glucokinase)

glut- *base* rump (gluteus)

-glutin- *base* glue (glutinize)

glutt- *base* eat; gulp (glutton)

glycero-, glyco- *comb* glycerin; glycerol; glycogen; sugar (glycerolysis, glycogenesis)

glycyr- *base* licorice (glycyrize)

-glyph *comb* carve; engrave (hieroglyph)

-glypha *comb* [zoology] snakes with grooved fangs (Opisthoglypha)

glypto- *comb* carve; engrave (glyptograph)

gnatho-, -gnathous *comb* [zoology] jaw (gnathodynamics, prognathous)

-gnomy, -gnosia, -gnosis, -gnostic *comb* judging; determining; knowledge (physiognomy, dysgnosia, diagnosis, diagnostic)

gnoto- *comb* known (gnotobiote)

gog-, -gogue *see* **-agogue**

-gomph- *base* bolt; socket; nail (gomphosis)

-gon, -gonal *comb* figure with __ angles (pentagon, polygonal)

gonado- *comb* gonad; sex gland (gonadopathy)

-gone, -gonium, gono-, -gony *comb* reproduction; generation; origin; formation (myelogone, sporogonium, gonothecal, cosmogony)

gonio- *comb* angle (goniometry)

-gracil- *base* slender; lean (gracilescent)

gracul- *base* jackdaw (graculine)

grad- *base* walk; move; go (gradation)

-grade *comb* a specified manner of walking or moving (plantigrade). *See* -gress-

Graeco- *comb* Greek (Graecomania). *Also* Greco- (Grecophile)

-grall- *base* wading bird (gralline)

grallator- *base* stork; heron (grallatorial)

-gram 1. *comb* written or drawn (telegram); 2. grams: x number of (kilograms); 3. gram: fraction of (centigram)

-gramen-, -gramin- *base* grass (gramenite, graminiferous)

grand- *comb* of the generation older than or younger than (grandfather)

grandi- *base* great; large (grandiloquent)

grandin- *base* hail (grandinous)

grani- *comb* grain; corn (granivorous)

graniti- *comb* granite (granitiform)

grano- 1. *comb* granite: like/of (granolithic); 2. granular (granophyre)

granulo- *comb* granular (granuloadipose)

grao- *comb* old woman (graocracy)

-graph 1. *comb* that which writes/draws/describes (telegraph); 2. that which is written/ drawn (autograph). *Also* -grapher (stenographer); -graphic (telegraphic); grapho- (graphology); -graphy (autobiography)

grapto- *comb* writing (graptomancy)

grat- *base* thankful (gratitude)

-graticul- *base* gridiron (graticulation)

-grav- *base* weight heavy; serious (gravimeter)

-gravid- *base* pregnant (multigravida)

Greco- *comb* Greek (Greco-Roman). *Also* Graeco- (Graecophile)

-greg- *base* herd; flock (congregation)

grem- *base* bosom; lap (gremial)

-gress- *base* walk move; go (aggressive). *See* -grad-

-gris- *base* gray (griseous)

-grui- *base* crane (gruiform)

-grum- *base* clot (grumous)

gryll- *base* cricket; grasshopper (gryllotalpa)

gubern- *base* ruler; guide (gubernatorial)

gulos- *base* gluttony; voracity (gulosity)

-gust- *base* taste; eat (gustatory)

gutti- *base* drop; gum-yielding (guttiferous)

gutturo- *comb* throat (gutturolabial)

gymno- *comb* naked; stripped; bare (gymnocarpous)

gyn-, gyno- 1. *comb* woman; female (gynarchy); 2. ovary; pistil (gynophore). *Also* -gynous (polygynous) and -gyny (monogyny)

gynandro- *comb* of uncertain sex (gynandromorphism)

gyne-, gyneco-, gyneo- *comb* woman; female (gynephobia, gynecocracy, gyneolatry)

-gypso- *base* chalk (gypsophila)

gyro- 1. *comb* gyrating (gyroscope); 2. spiral (gyroidal); 3. gyroscope (gyrocompass)

gyroso- *comb* marked with wavy lines (gyroso-rugose)

H

habil- 1. *base* ability; equipped (rehabilitate); 2. clothing (habiliments)

-habro- *base* graceful; delicate (habroreme)

-hadro- *base* thick (hadrosaur)

haema- *see* hema-

hagi-, hagio- *comb* saintly; holy (hagiheroical, hagiology)

halcyon- *base* kingfisher (halcyonine)

-hale *base* breath; vapor (exhale)

-halec- *base* herring (halecomorphic)

-halieut- *base* fishing (halieutics)

-halit- *base* breath; vapor (halitosis)

halluc- *base* toe (hallucar)

halo- 1. *comb* of the sea (halosaurian); 2. of salt (halophyte); 3. of halogen (halogenous)

-ham- *base* hook (hamated)

hama- *pre* together with; at the same time; united (hamarchy)

-hamart- 1. *base* sin (hamartiology); 2. corporal defect (hamartoma)

hamat- *base* barb; hook (hamate)

hand- *comb* hand: of/with/by/for (handcuff)

-hapal- *base* soft (hapalote)

haph- *base* touch (haphalgesia)

haplo- *comb* onefold; single (haplodont)

hapt-, hapto-[1] *comb* touch; sensation (haptics, haptotaxis)

-hapto-[2] *base* fasten; combine (haptophore)

harengi- *comb* herring (harrengiform)

hariol- *base* divination (hariolation). *Also see* "Divination" in Part III

harmat- *base* car; chariot (harmatian)

harpax- *base* robber (harpaxophobia)

-hastato-, hasti- *comb* spear (hastato-lanceolate; hastiform)

-haur-, -haust- *base* draw (forth); drain; suck (exhauriate, haustellum)

-headed 1. *comb* having a __ head (clearheaded); 2. having __ heads (two-headed)

heauto- *comb* of oneself (heautomorphism)

hebdom- *base* week; seven days (hebdomadal)

hebe- *comb* pubescent (hebegynous)

-hebet- *base* dull; blunt (hebetude)

Hebraico- *comb* Hebrew (Hebraico-Hibernian)

hecato-, hecto- *comb* one hundred (hecatophyllous, hectoliter). *Also* hekto- (hektograph)

hecatonicosa- *comb* one hundred twenty-four (hecatonicosachoron)

-heder- *base* ivy (hederaceous)

-hedon- *base* pleasure (anhedonia)

-hedral, -hedron *comb* geometric figure with x number of surfaces (hexahedral, hexahedron)

-hedy- *base* sweet (hedychium)

hegemon- *base* leader; chief (hegemonic)

-hekisto- *base* smallest (hekistotherm)

helco- *comb* festering wound; ulcer (helcoplasty)

helici-, helico- *comb* spiral-shaped (heliciform, helicopter)

helio- *comb* sun; bright; radiant (heliocentric)

helminth(o)- *comb* [botany] worm (helminthogogue)

helo-[1] *comb* nail; spike (helodont)
helo-[2] *comb* marsh (helobious)
helv- *base* yellow (helvenac)
Helvet- *base* Swiss (Helvetian)
hema-, hemato-, hemo- *comb* blood (hemachrome, hematogenic, hemophilia). *Also* haem- (haemachrome)
hemangio- *comb* blood vessels (hemangiosarcoma)
hemer- *base* day (monohemerous)
hemi- *pre* half (hemicardia)
hemispherico- *comb* hemispheric (hemispherico-conical)
hendeca- *comb* eleven (hendecahedron)
-heno- *base* one (henotheism)
heort- *base* feast day; festival (heortology
hepatic-, hepato- *comb* liver (hepaticostomy, hepatogastric)
hepta- *comb* seven (heptagon)
heptakaideca- *comb* seventeen (heptakaidecahedron)
-herbi- *base* plant (herbivorous)
-herco- *base* wall; barrier (hercogamy)
heredo- *comb* heredity (heredofamilial)
heresio- *base* heresy (heresiologist)
heri- *base* master (hericide)
-hermen- *base* interpretation (hermeneutical)
hernio- *comb* hernia (herniotomy)
herpeto- *comb* reptile (herpetology)
-hesper- *base* west (hesperian)
-hesperid- *base* the orange (hesperidine)
-hesson- *base* less; inferior (hessonite)
-hestern- *base* yesterday (hesternal)
hestho- *base* clothing; dress (hesthogenous)
hesy- *base* still; quiet (hesychastic)

hetaero- *base* companion; courtesan (hetaerocrasy)
hetero- *comb* other; another; different (heterosexual)
-heur- *base* discover; invent (heuristic)
hexa- *comb* six (hexameter)
hexaconta- *comb* sixty (hexacontahedron)
hexacosi- *comb* six hundred (hexacosichoron)
hexadeca-, hexakaideca- *comb* sixteen (hexadecachoron, hexakaidecahedron)
hexakis- *comb* six times (hexakisoctahedron)
hexametro- *comb* hexameter (hexametromania)
-hexi- *base* habit; behavior (hexiology)
hibern- *base* winter (hibernation)
Hiberno- *comb* Irish (Hiberno-Celtic)
-hidro- *base* sweat (anhidrosis)
hiem- *base* winter (hiemal)
hieraco- *comb* hawk (hieracosophic)
hiero- *comb* holy; consecrated; sacred (hierophobia)
hilasm- *base* propitiatory (hilasmic)
-himant- *base* strap; thong (himantopus)
hind- *comb* rear; following (hindbrain)
hippo-, -hippus *comb* horse (hippocrepian, eohippus)
hippocamp- *base* seahorse (hippocampine)
hippocrepi- *base* horseshoe (hippocrepiform)
hippogloss- *base* halibut (hippoglossoid)
-hirc- *base* goat (hircine)
-hirmo- *base* series; connection (hirmologion)

hirsuto- *comb* having hair of a certain color (hirsuto-rufus)

-hirudin- *base* leech (hirudiniculture)

-hirund- *base* swallow; martin (hirundine)

Hispano- *comb* Spanish (Hispano-American)

-hispid- *base* shaggy; hairy (hispidulous)

histio-, histo- *comb* tissue (histiocytoma, histology)

historico- *comb* historical (historico-geographical)

-histrion- *base* stage-player (histrionically)

-hodiern- *base* today (hodiernal)

hodo- *comb* way; road (hodograph). See odo-

-holco- *base* furrow (holcodont)

holo- *comb* complete; entire; whole (holocaust)

hom- *base* humankind (homicide)

homalo-, homolo- *comb* even; regular; level; ordinary (homalographic, homolographic)

-homar- *base* lobster (homarine)

homeo- *comb* similar; like (homeomorphism)

homichlo- *base* cloud; fog; dimness (homichlophobia)

homil- *base* sermon (homiletics)

homin- *base* humankind (hominiform)

homo- *comb* same; equal (homosexual)

homoeo-, homoio- *comb* similar; like (homoeodont, homoiothermal)

homolo- *comb* corresponding; assenting (homologous). See homalo-

-hood 1. *suf* quality; character; state; condition (childhood); 2. whole group of __ (brotherhood)

hoplo- *comb* weapon; armor (hoplophorous)

-hord- *base* barley (hordeaceous)

horm- *base* urge; impel (hormetic)

horo- *comb* hour time; season (horology)

-hort- *base* urge; encourage (exhortation)

-horti- *base* garden (horticulture)

hosp- *base* host (hospitality)

-hum- *base* ground (exhumation)

humano- *comb* human and (humano-taurine)

-humect- *base* moist; wet (humectant)

humero- *comb* shoulder; upper arm (humero-cubital)

hyalo- *comb* [chemistry] transparent; glassy (hyalophane)

-hybo- *base* hump (hybodont)

-hydno- *base* truffle (hydnocarpous)

hydraulico- *comb* hydraulic (hydraulico-pneumatical)

-hydric *comb* the presence of x number of hydroxyl radicals or replaceable hydrogen atoms (monohydric)

hydro- 1. *comb* water (hydrometer); 2. [chemistry] hydrogen (hydrocyanic)

hydroxy- *comb* hydroxyl group (hydroxy-benzene)

hyeto- *comb* rain; rainfall (hyetograph)

hygeio-, hygien- *comb* health; hygiene (hygeiolatry, hygienist)

hygro- *comb* wet; moisture (hygrometer)

hylac- *base* barking (hylactic)

hylaeo- *comb* forest (hylaeosaurus)

hyle-, hylo- 1. *comb* wood (hylephobia, hylophagous); 2. matter (hylozoism)

hylobat- *base* gibbon (hylobatine)

hymeno- *comb* membrane (hymenogeny)

hyo- *comb* hyoid bone (hyoglossal)

hyos- *base* hog (hyoscyamine)

hypegia- *base* responsibility (hypegiaphobia)

hypengy- *base* responsibility (hypengyophobia)

hyper- 1. *pre* over; above; excessive (hypercritical); 2. [chemistry] maximum (hyperoxide)

-hypho- *base* web (hyphomycetes)

hypno- *comb* sleep; hypnotism (hypnophobia)

hypo- 1. *pre* under; below (hypodermic); 2. less than (hypotaxis); 3. [chemistry] having a lower state of oxidation (hypophosphorous)

hypocrater- *base* tray (hypocrateriform)

hypsi-, hypso- *comb* high; height (hypsicephalic, hypsodont)

hyraci-, hyraco- *comb* hyrax: rabbit-like quadruped (hyraciform, hyracodont)

-hystat- *base* lowest (hystatite)

hystero-[1] 1. *comb* uterus; womb (hysterodynia); 2. hysteria (hysteroepilepsy)

hystero-[2] *comb* later; inferior (hystero-genetic)

-hystric- *base* porcupine (hystriciasis)

I

-i *suf* plural ending (foci)

-ia 1. *suf* country names (India); 2. disease names (pneumonia); 3. festival names (Lupercalia); 4. Gk/Lat. words (militia); 5. plurals >Gk/Lat. (genitalia); 6. [biology] class names (Reptilia); 7. [botany] some generic plant names (zinnia); 8. [chemistry] alkaloid names (strychnia)

-ial *suf* of; pertaining to (magisterial)

-ian/-iana *see* **-an/-ana**

ianth- *base* violet (ianthine)

-iasis 1. *comb* process; condition; 2. morbid condition (hypochondriasis)

-iatrics, iatro-, -iatry *comb* medical treatment (pediatrics, iatrophysical, psychiatry)

Ibero- *comb* Spanish (Iberian)

-ibility, -ible, -ibly *suf* capable of (sensibility, sensible, visibly)

-ic 1. *suf* having to do with; of (volcanic); 2. like; having the nature of; characteristic of (angelic); 3. produced by; caused by (symphonic); 4. made up of; containing; consisting of (dactylic); 5. [chemistry] higher valence than is indicated by the suffix **-ous** (nitric); 6. nouns from adjectives (magic)

-ical, -ically *suf* adjective/adverb forms parallel to **-ic** (angelical, magically)

-ice[1] *suf* condition; state; quality of; action (malice)

-ice[2] *suf* feminine ending (mediatrice)

-ichno *comb* [paleontology] track; trace; posture; position (ichnology) ichor- *comb* serous fluid (ichor-remia)

ichthyo- *comb* fish; fishlike (ichthyophagous)

-ician *suf* practitioner; specialist (beautician)

-icity *suf* nouns formed from -ic adjectives (publicity)

icono- *comb* figure; likeness; image (iconograph)

icosa-, icosi- *comb* [mathematics/botany] twenty (icosahedron, icositetrahedron: 24)

-ics 1. *suf* art; science (mathematics); 2. activities; practice properties; system (statistics)

icter-[1], ictero- *comb* yellow; jaundice (icteric, icteroanemia)

icter-[2] *base* blackbird; bobolink; meadowlark; oriole (icterine)

-id[1] 1. *suf* belonging to; connected with (Aeneid); 2. animal group name (arachnid); 3. meteor names (Perseid)

-id[2] *suf* filled with (vivid)

-ida *suf* [zoology] order/class names (Acarida)

-idae *suf* [zoology] family names (Felidae)

-idan *suf* [zoology] of or pertaining to (arachnidan)

-ide *suf* [chemistry] compound names (chloride)

ideo- *comb* idea; creation (ideology)

-ides *suf* [science] name endings (cantharides)

-idine *suf* chemical compound related to another (pyridine)

idio- *comb* one's own; distinct; personal (idiocrasy)

-idion *suf* diminutive (enchiridion)

-idium *suf* [science] diminutive (phyllidium)

idolo- *comb* idol (idolomancy)

-ie *suf* diminutive (doggie)

-ier *suf* person concerned with (glazier)

-iferous *see* -ferous

-ific *see* -fic

-ification *see* -fication

-iformes *suf* [zoology] names: having the form of (Passeriformes)

-ify *see* -fy

igneo- *comb* fire (igneo-aqueous)

igni- *base* fire (igniferous)

il- *see* in-

-il, -ile *suf* like; having to do with; suitable for (civil, docile)

ilast- *base* propitiatory (ilastic)

ileo-, ilio- 1. *comb* of the ileum (ileostomy); 2. ileac plus (iliosacral)

-ilia *suf* able to be __ (memorabilia)

ilic- *base* holly (ilicic)

-ility *suf* quality; condition (sensibility)

-illa *suf* diminutive (cedilla)

-illo *suf* diminutive (cigarillo)

illyngo- *base* vertigo (illyngophobia)

im- *see* in-

-im *suf* Hebrew plural ending (cherubim)

imbri- *base* rain; rain tile (imbriferous, imbricated)

imbricato- *comb* composed of parts which overlap like tiles (imbricato-granulous)

-imido *comb* NH in acid radicals (imidogen)

imino- *comb* NH in nonacid radicals (iminourea)

immuno- *comb* resistant to disease; immune (immunotherapy)

immut- *base* unalterable (immutable)

impari- *comb* odd-numbered; unpaired (imparisyllabic)

imped- *base* snare; delay (impedance)

imper- *base* power; authority (imperial)

impet- *base* rush; assault (impetious)

in-¹ 1. *pre* within; inside; into; toward (inbreed); 2. intensifier (instigate); 3. not; without (insane). NOTE: in- can change to: il- (illuminate); im- (impossible); ir- (irrigate)

-in² *suf* [chemistry] names of neutral substances (albumin)

-ina 1. *suf* feminine ending (ballerina); 2. characterized by (sonatina); 3. [biology] name endings (Nemertina)

-inae *suf* names of subfamilies of animals (felinae)

inan- *base* empty; foolish (inane)

inaug- *base* start (inaugurate)

incess- *base* unceasing (incessant)

incip- *base* take in hand; begin (incipient)

inciso- *comb* cut into (incisolobate)

increp- *base* scold; rebuke (increpatory)

-indag- *base* trace; search; investigate (indagation)

indi-, indo-¹ *comb* indigo; metallic violet-purple (indirubin, indophenol)

-indigen- *base* native (indigenous)

Indo-² *comb* India (Indo-Malayan)

inducto- *comb* electrical induction (inductoscope)

-ine 1. *suf* of; like; pertaining to; characterized by (canine); 2. feminine ending (heroine); 3. abstract noun ending (discipline); 4. commercial names (Vaseline); 5. [chemistry] names of: halogens (iodine); alkaloid/nitrogen bases (morphine); hydrides (stibine); 6. of the nature of (crystalline)

inebr- *base* drunk (inebriated)

inequi- *comb* unequal (inequidistant)

infern- *base* underworld; hell (infernal)

infero- *comb* underneath; low; below (inferolateral)

infra- *pre* below; beneath (infrastructure)

infundib- *base* funnel (infundibuliform)

-ing 1. *suf* belonging to; descended from (atheling); 2. present participle (shifting sand); 3. act of; process (talking); 4. produced by (painting); 5. material for (roofing)

ingen- *base* versatile; clever (ingenious)

ingress- *base* enter (ingressive)

inguino- *comb* inguinal; groin (inguinoscrotal)

-ini *suf* [zoology] group names (Acanthurini)

inimic- *base* hostile (inimical)

iniq- *base* bad; uneven (iniquity)

init- *base* begin; enter (initialize)

innato- *comb* inborn; natural (innato-sessile)

ino- *comb* fiber; fibrous growth (inolith)

inquis- *see* -quire

insecti-, insecto- *comb* bug (insecticide, insectology)

insul- *base* island (insularity)

integri- *comb* whole (integripallial)

inter- 1. *comb* between; among (interchange); 2. mutual; reciprocal; with each other (interact)

interno-, intero- *comb* internal; inside; within (internomedial, interoceptive)

intestino- *comb* intestine (intestino-vesical)

intra- *comb* within; inside (intramural)

intro- *comb* into; within; inward (introvert)

inund- *base* flood; overflow (inundate)

inutil- *base* useless (inutility)

-invid- *base* envy; resentment (invidious)

-involver- *base* wrapping; covering (involveriform)

iodo- *comb* iodine (iodoform)

-ion 1. *suf* act; process (solution); **2.** state; condition (ambition)

iono- *comb* ion (ionosphere)

-ior 1. *suf* one who __ (warrior); **2.** comparative form (inferior)

-ious *suf* characterized by; having (contentious)

ipse- *base* self (ipseity)

ir- *see* in-

-ira-, -irasc- *base* hatred; anger (irate, irascible)

-iren- *base* peace (irenic)

irid- *base* rainbow (iridial)

iridico-, iridio- *comb* iridium (iridico-potassic, iridio-cyanide)

irido- *comb* iris (iridomotor)

isch- *comb* restriction; deficiency (ischemia)

ischi-, ischio- *comb* hip; ischium (ischialgia, ischiocapsular)

-ise *suf* quality; condition; function (merchandise)

-ish 1. *suf* national connection (Irish); **2.** characteristic of; like (devilish); **3.** tending to (bookish); **4.** somewhat; rather (whitish); **5.** approximately (thirty-ish)

-isk *suf* diminutive (obelisk)

-ism 1. *suf* act; result of; practice (terrorism); **2.** condition of being (barbarism); **3.** qualities characteristic of; conduct characteristic of (patriotism); **4.** doctrine; theory; principle of (socialism); **5.** devotion to (nationalism);

6. instance of; example of; peculiarity of (Gallicism); **7.** abnormal condition caused by __ (alcoholism)

-ismus *suf* spasm; contraction (vaginismus). *See* -esmus

iso- *comb* equality; identity; similarity (isodactylous)

isoptero- *base* termite; white ant (isopteroous)

-ist *suf* practitioner; believer; person skilled in (theorist)

isthm- *base* narrow passage; neck of land (isthmian)

-istic, -istical *suf* tending towards; acting like (communistic, egotistical)

istiophor- *base* marlin; sailfish (istiophorid)

Italo- *comb* Italy (Italophile)

-ite 1. *suf* native; inhabitant; citizen of (Brooklynite); **2.** adherent; believer (Benthamite); **3.** manufactured product (dynamite); **4.** fossil (coprolite); **5.** bodily organ part (somite); **6.** salt or ester of an acid ending in **-ous** (nitrite); **7.** mineral or rock (anthracite)

itea- *comb* willow tree (iteatic)

-iter- *base* repeat (reiterate)

ithy- *comb* erect; straight (ithyphallic)

-itic *suf* relating to; of (syphilitic)

-itiner- *base* journey (itinerary)

-ition *see* -ation

-itious *suf* having the nature of; characterized by (fictitious)

-itis *suf* inflammation; disease (bronchitis)

-itive *see* -ative

-itol *suf* names of alcohols with more than 1 hydroxyl group (mannitol)

-ity *suf* state; character; condition (nobility)

-ium *suf* noun ending (opprobrium)

-ive **1.** *suf* related to; belonging to; (negative); **2.** tending to (creative)

-ivus *suf* [science] name endings (exfoliativus)

-ixo- *base* mistletoe; sticky or clammy like birdlime (ixolite)

ixobrych- *base* bittern (ixobrychus)

ixod- *base* tick (ixodicide)

-ization *suf* used to form noun from -ize verb (realization)

-ize **1.** *suf* cause to be or become; resemble; make (sterilize); **2.** become like (crystallize); **3.** subject to; treat with; combine with (oxidize); **4.** engage in; act (theorize)

J

-jact-, -jacula-, -ject- *base* hurl; throw (jactation, ejaculation, inject)

jaun- *base* yellow (jaundice)

jecor- *base* liver (jecorary)

-jejuno- *comb* of the jejunum (jejunocolostomy)

-jent- *base* breakfast (jentacular)

-joco(s)-, -jocu(l)- *base* joke; jest (jocosity, jocularity)

journ- *comb* day; daily (journalism)

jubat- *base* mane (jubate)

-jubil- *base* joy; elation (jubilation)

jud- *comb* wisdom; law; justice (judiciously)

Judaeo-, Judeo- *comb* Jewish (Judaeophobia, Judeo-Christian)

Judaico- *comb* Judaic (Judaico-Christian)

juglan- *base* walnut (juglandaceous)

jugo- *comb* neck; throat; yoke (jugo-maxillary)

-juli- *base* catkin (juliferous)

jun- *base* young (junior)

-junc- *base* a rush (juncaceous)

junct- *comb* join (conjunction)

jur-, juris- *comb* law (juridical, jurisprudence)

-juss- *base* command (jussive)

-jut-, -juv- *base* aid; help (adjutant, adjuvant)

juven- *comb* young; immature (juvenile)

juxta- *comb* near; beside; close by (juxtaposition)

K

kako- *comb* bad; evil (kakogenesis). *Also* caco- (cacophony)

kakorrhaph- *base* failure (kakorrhaphiophobia)

-kal- *base* beautiful (kaleidoscope)

kal(i)- *comb* potassium (kaliopenia)

karyo- *comb* [biology] nucleus (karyokinesis). *Also* caryo- (caryopsis)

kata-. *See* cata-

katheno- *comb* each; every; one by one (kathenotheism)

kathis- *base* sit; seat (kathisma)

kelyph- *base* shell; pod (kelyphite)

keno- *comb* empty (kenotic)

kephalo- *comb* head (kephalotomy). *Also* **cephalo-** (cephalopod)

kera-, kerato- 1. *comb* horn; horn-like; horny tissue (keracele, keratogenous); 2. cornea (keratotomy). *Also* **cerato-** (ceratosaur)

keraulo- *comb* hornblower (keraulophon)

kerauno- *comb* thunder (keraunograph). *Also* **cerauno-** (ceraunoscope)

kery- *base* proclamation; preaching (kerygma)

keto- *comb* ketone; organic chemical compound (ketogenesis)

-kibdelo- *base* adulterated; spurious (kibdelophane)

kil-, kill- *comb* cell; church; burying place (Kilpatrick, Kilkenny)

kilo- *comb* thousand (kilogram)

-kin *suf* diminutive (lambkin)

kinesi-, -kinesia, -kinesis, kineso- *comb* movement; muscular activity (kinesiology, hyperkinesia, telekinesis, kinesodic)

-kinetic, kineto- *comb* motion (hyperkinetic, kinetograph). *See* **cine-**

-kinin *suf* hormone names (cytokinin)

kino- *base* movement; muscular activity (kinocilium)

klepto- *comb* steal (kleptomaniac). *Also* **clepto-** (cleptobiosis)

klino- *comb* sloped; bent (klinocephalic). *Also* **clino-** (clinograph)

klope- *comb* steal (klopemania)

kniss- *base* incense (knissomancy)

koilo- *comb* hollow (koilonychia)

koin- *base* common (koine). *See* **ceno-**[2]

koll(o)- *comb* glue (kolloxylin). *Also* **coll-** (colloidal)

kolpo- *comb* vagina (kolpocele). *Also* **colpo-** (colposcope)

koly- *comb* inhibit; restrain (kolytic)

-kompo- *base* boasting (kompology)

koni(o)- *comb* dust (konimeter)

kopo- *base* exhaustion (kopophobia)

kopro- *comb* filth; excrement (koprophilia). *See* **copro-**

-koria *comb* pupil of the eye (leukokoria). *Also* **-coria** (leucocoria)

kreo- *comb* flesh (kreophagus)

-krio- *base* ram (krioboly). *Also* **crio-** (criocephalous)

krymo-, kryo- *see* **crymo-**

kryo- *comb* frost; cold (kryometer). *Also* **cryo-** (cryogen)

kyano- *see* **cyano-**

kylixo- *base* bowl (kylixomancy)

kymo- *comb* wave (kymograph). *Also* **cymo-** (cymophane)

kyno- *comb* dog (kynophagous)

kypho- *comb* hump (kyphosis). *Also* **cypho-** (cyphonism)

-kyrio- *base* authorized; proper (kyriolexy). *Also* **cyrio-** (cyriologic)

kyto- *comb* cell (kytometry). *Usually* **cyto-** (cytopathic)

L

-lab- *base* totter; shake; weaken (labefaction)

labar- *base* banner; standard (labarum)

-labido- *base* forceps (labidometer)

labio- *comb* lips (labiodental)

-labor- *base* work (laboriousness)

lac- *base* white (lacteous)

-lacco- *base* reservoir (laccolite)

-lacer- *base* mangle (laceration)

lacert- *base* lizard (lacertilian)

-lachan- *base* vegetable (lachanopolist)

-lacin- *base* fringed; jagged (laciniform)

lacrim-, lacrimo- *comb* tears; crying (lachrimation, lacrimonasal). *Also* lachrym- (lachrymose)

lacti-, lacto- 1. *comb* milk (lactiflorous); 2.[chemistry] lactic acid (lactophosphate)

lactuc- *base* lettuce (lactucarium)

-lacun- *base* cavity; hole (lacunose)

-lacus- *base* lake; pool (lacustrine)

ladron- *base* steal (ladronism)

laeo-, laevo- 1. *comb* on the left (laeotropic); 2. counterclockwise (laevorotation). *Also* levo- (levogyrate)

-lagen- *base* flask (lageniform)

-lagnia *comb* desire coition; lust (algolagnia)

lago- *comb* [zoology] hare (lagopodus)

-lalia *comb* speech disorder (coprolalia)

lalo- *comb* talking; speech defect (lalopathy)

lamb- *base* lick (lambent)

lamelli- *comb* plate; layer; scales (lamelliform)

lamini-, lamino- 1. *comb* plate; layer (laminiferous); 2. blade of the tongue (laminoalveolar)

-lampad- *base* torch; lamp (lampadomancy)

lampro- *comb* clear; distinct (lamprophony)

lampyr- *base* firefly (lampyrid)

-lana- *base* wool (lanate). *See* lani-

lanci- *base* lance (lanciform)

-land 1. *comb* a kind of land (highland); 2. territory or country (England); 3. place with a specified character (cloudland)

lani- *base* wool (laniferous). *See* lana-

-lania- *base* to tear; butcher (laniary)

laniar- *base* canine tooth (laniariform)

lanug- *base* hair (lanugo)

laparo- *comb* abdominal wall; flank; loins (laparotomy)

-lapid- *base* stone; gem (lapidary)

laps- *base* slip away; error; fall (elapsed)

lar- *base* gull (larine)

-largi- *base* abundant; copious (largiloquent)

larix- *base* larch (larixinic)

larvi- *comb* larva (larvigerous)

laryngo- *comb* windpipe larynx (laryngoscope)

-lass- *base* weary (lassitude)

-later- *base* brick (lateritious)

-later *comb* one who worships (gastrolater). *See* -latry

lateri-, latero- *comb* on the side (laterigrade, laterodeviation)

lati- *comb* wide; broad (latipennate)

latib- *base* hiding place (latibulate)

latici- *comb* latex (laticiferous)

-latra- *base* barking (latration)

latro- *base* robber (latronage)

latrodect- *base* black widow spider (latrodectus)

-latry *comb* excessive devotion; worship of (idolatry). *See* -later

-laud- *base* praise (applaud)

-lav- *base* wash (lavage)

lazul- *base* blue (lazuline)

-le 1. *suf* small (icicle); 2. person who does (beadle); 3. something used for doing (girdle); **4.** frequent (wriggle)

lecano- *comb* basin; pan; dish (lecanomancy)

lechrio- *comb* slanting (lechriodont)

lecith-, lecitho- *comb* egg yolk (lecithin, lecithoprotein)

-leco- *base* dish (lecotropal)

-lect- *base* read (lectionary)

-leg-¹ *base* read (legendary)

leg-² *base* law (legality)

-legia *comb* read (bradylegia)

leio- *comb* smooth (leiomyoma)

-lemma¹ *comb* assumption; proposition (dilemma)

-lemma² *comb* rind; peel; husk (neurolemma)

-lemnisc- *base* ribbon (lemniscus)

lemur- *base* tarsier (lemuroid)

-len- *base* gentle; mild; soothing (lenity)

leno- *base* entice; pander; wheedle (lenocinant)

-lenocin- *base* allure; entice (lenocinant)

-lent- *base* slow (lentitude)

lentig- *base* freckle (lentigo)

-lent *suf* full of (pestilent)

-leo- *base* lion (leonine)

lepido- *comb* [botany/zoology] scaly (lepidodendron)

lepidopter- *base* butterfly (lepidopterology)

-lepor- *base* hare (leporine)

-lepsia, -lepsis, -lepsy, lepti-, -leptic *comb* fit; attack; seizure (Epilepsia, catalepsis, catalepsy, epileptiform, narcoleptic)

lepto- *comb* narrow; thin; fine; frail (leptocephaly)

-less *suf* without; lacking; incapable of being (lawless)

lesto- *comb* thief; robber (lestobiosis)

-let 1. *suf* small (hamlet); **2.** band (anklet)

leth- *base* forgetfulness; drugged state (lethonomania)

leuco-, leuko- *comb* colorless; white (leucocyte, leukemia)

-levi- *base* airy; light (levitation)

-levig- *base* smooth; polished (levigated)

levo- 1. *comb* on the left (levogyrate); **2.** counterclockwise (levorotatory). *Also* **laevo-** (laevorotation)

levul- *base* sugar (levulose)

-lexia, -lexis, -lexy *comb* speech (dyslexia, catalexis, kyriolexy)

lexico- *comb* word; vocabulary (lexicographer)

-libano- *base* incense (libanomancy)

libell- *base* dragonfly (libelluloid)

-liber- *base* free (liberation)

libid- *base* desirous; lustful (libidinous)

-libr- *base* book (librarian)

-libra- *base* balance; scale (libration)

licheno- *comb* skin disease (licheno-lupoid)

lien(o)- *comb* spleen (lieno-gastric)

-liga- *base* tie; bind (ligament)

ligamenti-, ligamento- *comb* having ligaments (ligamentiferous, ligamento-muscular)

ligni-, ligno- *comb* wood (lignivorous, lignoceric)

liguli- *comb* tonguelike; strap (liguliflorate)

ligur- *base* lick (ligurition)

ligyr- *base* noise (ligyrophobia)

-like 1. *suf* characteristic of; suitable for (warlike); **2.** in the manner of (bird-like)

lilaps- *base* tornado; hurricane (lilapsophobia)

lili- *base* lily (liliform)

-lim- *base* mud (limicolous)
-limac- *base* snail; slug (limaceous)
limen- *base* harbor (limenarch)
-limin- *base* threshold (eliminate)
limno- *comb* lake; pond; pool (limnology)
limo-[1] *comb* clayey and (limo-cretaceous)
limo-[2] *comb* fasting; famine (limotherapy)
linar- *base* flax (linaria)
lineo- *comb* line (lineo-polar)
-ling[1] *suf* person or thing belonging to or concerned with (underling)
-ling[2] *suf* diminutive (duckling)
-ling[3] *suf* direction; extent; condition (darkling)
ling-[4] *base* lick (lingible)
lingui-, linguo- *comb* language; tongue (bi-lingual, linguopalatal)
linon- *base* string (linonophobia)
lipar- *base* grease; fat (liparocele)
lipo-[1] *comb* fatty (liposuction)
lipo-[2] *comb* lacking; without (lipostomosis)
lipsano- *comb* relics (lipsanographer)
-liqu- *base* melt; make liquid; dissolve (liquescent)
-lirio- *base* lily (liriodendron)
-liss(o)- *base* smooth (lissotrichous)
-litan- *base* prayer; entreaty (litaneutical)
-lite *suf* names of minerals; stone (chrysolite)
-lith *comb* stone (monolith)
-lithic *comb* stone-using stage (neolithic)
litho- *comb* stone; rock; calculus (lithosphere)
litig- *base* quarrel; lawsuit (litigation)
-littor- *base* shore (littoral)
-litu- *base* clarion (lituiform)
livid- *base* blue (lividity)

-lixiv- *base* lye; alkaline (lixivation)
lobulato- *comb* having small lobes (lobulato-glomerate)
lochio- *comb* childbirth (lochio-peritonitis)
loco- 1. *comb* from place to place (locomotive); 2. a particular place (locodescriptive)
-locu- *base* word; speech; discourse (interocutor). *Also* -loqu- (eloquence)
locust- *base* cricket; locust; grasshopper (locustarian)
lodic- *base* blanket; rug (lodicule)
-logic, -logical *comb* of a science (geologic, biological)
-logist *comb* one versed in __ (biologist)
logo- *comb* word; speech; discourse (logorrhea)
-logue *comb* kind of speaking; kind of writing (monologue)
-logy 1. *comb* kind of speaking (eulogy); 2. science; doctrine; theory/study of (geology)
-loimo- *base* pestilence (loimography). *Also* lœmo- (lœmology)
-lonch- *base* spearhead (lonchidite)
longi- *comb* long (longipennate)
lopho- *comb* [zoology/anatomy] crest; ridge (lophocercal)
-loqu- *base* talk; speech (grandiloquent). *See* locu-
-lor- *base* thong; strap (lorate)
lordo- *comb* hump (lordoscoliosis)
-lorica- *base* covering; hard shell (illoricated)
loxo- *comb* [medicine/zoology] slanting oblique (loxotomy)
-lubric- *base* smooth; slippery (lubricity)
luc-, luci *comb* light; clear; dawn (lucidity, lucifugal, antelucan)
lucern- *base* lamp (lucernal)

-lucr(i)- *base* profit; gain (luciferous)
-luct-[1] *base* sorrow (luctisonant)
luct-[2] *base* wrestle (luctation)
lucubr- *base* work; nocturnal study (lucubration)
-lude *comb* a play; to play with (prelude)
ludif- *base* hoax; deception (ludificatory)
-luetic *comb* syphilis (paraluetic)
-lum- *base* light (illumination). *See* -luc-
lumbo- *comb* loin; lumbar (lumbodorsal)
-lumbric- *base* worm (lumbriciform)
luni- *comb* moon (lunitidal)
lunu- *comb* crescent; moon-shaped (lunulite)
-lup- *base* wolf (lupine)
lupan- *base* brothel (lupanar)
lur- *base* yellow-brown (lurid)
lurido- *comb* yellow (lurido-cinerascent)
-lusc- *base* one-eyed (eluscate)
lustr- *base* shining; splendor (illustrious)
lut- *base* mud (lutulent)
luteo- *comb* yellow (luteo-fulvous)
lutjan- *base* snapper (lutjanid)
lutr- *base* otter (lutrine)

-ly 1. *suf* characteristic of; suitable to (earthly); 2. happening every __ (hourly); 3. in a specified way (harshly); 4. in some direction (outwardly); 5. in some order (thirdly)
lyc-, lyco- *comb* wolf (lycanthropy, lycomania)
-lych- *base* lamp (lychnic)
lyg- *base* dark; murky (lygaeid)
lymphaden(o)- *comb* lymph nodes (lymphadenopathy)
lymphangio- *comb* lymphatic vessels (lymphangioplasty)
lymphato- *comb* lymphatic (lymphatolysis)
lympho- *comb* of the lymph (lymphocyte)
lync- *base* lynx (lyncean)
lyo- *comb* dissolution (lyophilic)
lype- *comb* sadness; grief (lypemania)
lyri- *base* lyre (lyriform)
lyrico- *comb* lyric (lyrico-dramatic)
lysi-, -lysis, lyso-, -lyte, -lytic, -lyze *comb* freeing; relieving; breaking up; dissolving; destroying (lysimeter, lysogen, electrolysis, gazolyte, paralytic, paralyze)
-lysso- *base* rabies (lyssophobia)
-lyte *comb* decomposed substance; dissolved (hydrolyte)

M

-ma *suf* result of action (enigma)
macar- *base* happy; blessed (macarism)
macell- *base* meat market (macellarious)
-machaero- *base* sword (machaerodont)
macho-, -machy *comb* struggle; contest; battle; fight (machopolyp, hieromachy)
maci- *base* thin; lean (macilence)
macro- *comb* long; large (macrocosm)
macropod- *base* kangaroo (macropodine)
macrur- *base* shrimp (macruran)

-macul- *base* spot; stain (immaculate)

mad- *base* wet; moist (madefacient)

mageir- *base* cook (mageiricophobia). *Also* magir- (magiric)

-magist- *base* master; head; authority (magistrate)

magneto- *comb* magnetic force (magneto-electric)

magni- *comb* great; large (magniloquent)

mago- *comb* magic (mago-chemical)

maha- *base* mastery; control (maharanee)

maieusi- *base* bringing forth; midwifery (maieutic)

-maj- *base* great; large (majority)

mal- *comb* bad; wrong; ill (maladroit)

-malacia, malaco- 1. *comb* soft (gastromalacia); 2. mollusks (malacology)

-malax- *base* soften (malaxation)

Malayo- *comb* Malay (Malayo-Polynesian)

male- *comb* evil (malefaction)

-mali- *base* apple (maliform)

malleo- *comb* hammer (malleoincudal)

-mallo- *base* wool (mallophagous)

malneiro- *comb* nightmare (malneirophrenia)

mamilli- *comb* nipple (mamilliform)

mammato- *comb* rounded clouds (mammato-cumulus)

mammi-, mammo- *comb* breasts (mammiferous, mammogram)

-man *comb* human; male (anchorman)

-mancy, -mantic *comb* divination (necromancy, necromantic)

-mand- *base* command; oblige (mandatory)

mandibulo- *comb* jaw (mandibulomaxillary)

manduc- *comb* chew; eat (manducation)

mangan-, mangani-, mangano- *comb* manganese (manganbrucite, manganicyanide, manganosiderite)

mani-, manu- *comb* hand (manipulate, manuscript)

-mania 1. *comb* mental disorder (kleptomania); 2. excessive craving (bibliomania)

mano- *comb* thin; rare (manometer)

mansue- *base* tame; mild (mansuetude)

manubr- *base* handle (manubriated)

-marc- *base* faded; withered (marcescent)

mare- *comb* sea (mareography)

marg- *base* border; verge (marginal)

margarit- *base* pearl (margaritaceous)

-margy *base* raging mad (gastromargy)

mari- *comb* sea (mariculture)

marit- *base* spouse; marriage (marital)

-marm- *base* marble (marmoreal)

-marsup- *base* pouch (marsupial)

-mas *comb* feast day (Christmas)

masculo- *comb* male (masculo-nucleus)

-mastia, masto- *comb* [medicine/zoology] breast: of or like (macromastia, mastodynia)

mastic- *base* chew (mastication)

mastigo- *comb* whiplike; scourge bearing (mastigophore)

masto- *comb* breast (mastodynia)

mastoido- *comb* mastoid (mastoido-humeral)

-mataeo- *base* unprofitable; useless; vain (mataeology)

mater-, matri- *comb* mother (maternity, matriarchy)

matertera- *base* aunt on mother's side (materteral)

-math- *comb* learn (opsimath)

matur- *base* ripe (maturity)

-matut- *base* morning (matutinal)

maxi- *comb* very large; very long (maxicoat)

maxillo- *comb* of the maxilla; jaw (maxillo-palatine)

mazo-[1] *comb* placenta (mazolysis)

mazo-[2] *comb* breast (mazoplazia)

-meal *comb* measure (piecemeal)

meato- *comb* passage channel (meatoscopy)

mechanico- *comb* partly mechanical (mechanico-chemical)

mechano- *comb* machines (mechanotherapy)

-meco- *base* length (mecodont)

-mecon- *base* poppy; opium (meconidine)

-med- 1. *base s.* bladder (medorrhea); 2. *pl.* genitals (medorthophobia)

medi-, medio- *comb* middle (medicommisure, mediodorsal)

mediastino- *comb* membranous partition (mediastino-pericardial)

medico- *comb* medical; of healing (medico-legal)

mega- 1. *comb* large; powerful (megaphone); 2. a million of (megacycle)

megacheiropter- *base* bat (megacheiropteran)

megalo-, -megaly 1. *comb* large; powerful (megalomania); 2. abnormal enlargement (megalocardia, hepatomegaly)

meio- *comb* less (meiosis). *Also* **mio-** (Miolithic)

meizo- *comb* greater (meizoseismal)

melan-, melano- *comb* black; very dark (melanosis, melanocomous)

-mele *comb* limb; extremity (phocomele)

meleagr- *base* turkey (meleagrine)

melet- *base* meditation (meletetics)

-melia-[1] *comb* limb; extremity (macromelia)

-melia-[2] *base* ash tree (meliaceous)

melin- 1. *base* badger (meline); 2. tawny (meline)

-melior- *base* make better; improve (ameliorate)

melisso- *base* bee (melissean)

melitto- *base* bee (melittology)

mell(i)- *comb* honey; sweet (mellifluous)

melo-[1] *comb* song; music (melomania)

melo-[2] *comb* cheek (meloplasty)

melo-[3] *comb* limb; extremity (melorheostosis)

membrano- *comb* membrane plus (membranocartilaginous)

mendac- *base* falsehood (mendacious)

mendic- *base* beggar; poor (mendicant)

-menia *comb* [medicine] pertaining to the menses (paramenia)

meningo- *comb* [medicine/anatomy] related to the meninges (meningocele)

-menisc- *base* crescent-shaped (meniscoid)

meno- 1. *comb* [medicine] pertaining to the menses (menopause); 2. month (menology)

mens- *base* month (menses)

-ment[1] 1. *suf* result; product (pavement); 2. instrument; means (adornment); 3. process of doing (measurement); 4. state of being acted on (disappointment)

ment-² *base* mind; thought (mentation)

menth- *base* mint (menthaceous)

mento- *comb* chin (mentoplasty)

-mentul- *base* penis (mentulate)

mephit- *base* skunk (mephitic)

-mer, -meran *comb* part; unit (isomer, heteromeran). *Also* -mere (blastomere). *See* **mero-¹**

-merc- *base* goods (mercantile)

-merd- *base* dung (immerd)

-mere *comb* part; unit (blastomere). *See* **-mer** and **mero-¹**

meretric- *base* harlot (meretricious)

-merge, -merse *comb* plunge; dip (submerge, immerse)

merid- *base* noon (postmeridian)

merinth- *base* bind (merinthophobia)

mero-¹, -merous *comb* part; unit; partial; having __ parts (meroblast, heteromerous)

mero-² *comb* thigh (merocele)

merul- *base* blackbird (meruline)

mesati- *comb* medium (mesaticephaly)

mesmer- *base* hypnotism (mesmerism)

meso- 1. *comb* in the middle (mesocarp); 2. [anatomy] a mesentery (mesogastrium)

meta-¹ 1. *pre* changed (metamorphosis); 2. after (metaphysics); 3. behind; in back (metathorax); 4. beyond; higher (metapsychosis)

meta-² [chemistry] 1. *pre* polymer of (metaldehyde); 2. derivative of (metaprotein); 3. acid containing less water combined with the anhydride than other acids of the same non-metallic element (metaphosphoric); 4. characterized by substitutes in the 1,3 position in the benzene ring (metacoumarate)

metacarpo- *comb* metacarpus plus (metacarpophalangeal)

metalli-, metallo- *comb* metal (metalliferous, metallochrome)

metatarso- *comb* metatarsus plus (metatarso-phalangeal)

metax- *base* silk (metaxite)

-meter 1. *comb* device for measuring (barometer); 2. so many meters (kilometer); 3. fraction of a meter (centimeter); 4. having __ metrical feet (pentameter)

-meth- *base* intoxicated (methystic)

metho- *comb* methyl (methoxyl)

methoxy- *comb* methoxy group (methoxychlor)

methyl- *comb* methyl group (methyl-benzene)

methys- *base* drunk; intoxicated (methystic)

metopo- *comb* forehead (metoposcopy)

metr- *base* poem (metrical)

metra-, metro-¹ *comb* uterus (metratonia, metrorrhagia)

-metric, -metrics, metro-², -metry *comb* measure (geometric, econometrics, metrology, chronometry)

-metrio- *base* moderate (metriocephalic)

mezzo- *comb* middle; half (mezzotint)

micro- 1. *comb* little; small (microbarograph); 2. abnormally small (microcephalic); 3. enlarging what is small (microscope); 4. relation to microscopes (microchemistry); 5. one millionth part of (microgram)

microcheiropter- *base* bat (microcheiropteran)

-mict- *base* urine (micturient). *See* **-ming-**

mid- *comb* middle part (midbrain)

-milit- *base* soldier (militancy)

milli- 1. *comb* one thousandth part of (millimeter); 2. one thousand (millifold)

milv- *base* kite — the bird (milvine)

-mim- 1. *base* imitate (mimetic); 2. mockingbird (mimine)

min- *base* threat (minatory)

-ming- *base* urine (retromingent). *See* -mict-

mini- *comb* smaller; shorter; lesser than usual (miniskirt)

mio- *comb* less; diminished (miosis). *Also* **meio-** (meiosis)

-mir- *base* wonder (admiration)

mis- *pre* wrong; bad (miscalculate)

-misc- *base* mixed (immiscible)

miso- *comb* hated; hating (misogyny)

-miss-, -mit-¹ *base* send (dismiss, remit)

mit-², mito- *comb* thread (mitosis, mitochondria)

miti-¹ *base* mild; soothing (mitigate)

miti-² *base* mite (miticide)

mitri- *base* miter (mitriform)

mixo- *comb* mixed (mixogamy)

-mnem-, -mnesia, -mnesis *base* memory (mnemonics, amnesia, anamnesis)

-mo *suf* printing books: a suffix to the number designating one of the equal parts into which a sheet is divided, the size of a page varying with the size of the sheet folded (12mo)

-mob- *base* move (immobility)

-mobile *comb* special type of vehicle (bookmobile)

-mochl- *base* lever (hypomochlion)

mogi- *comb* with difficulty (mogigraphia)

mol- *base* grind (molar)

-molend- *base* mill (molendarious)

-moll- *base* soft (emollient)

mollusc- *base* mollusk (malluscous)

molybdo- *comb* lead (molybdocolic)

molys- *base* dirt (molysmophobia)

-mon- *base* warn (admonish)

monach- *base* monk (monachism)

-monil- *base* necklace (moniliform)

mono- 1. *comb* single; alone; one (monoclinal); 2. containing one atom (monochloride); 3. one molecule thick (monolayer)

monotrem- *base* platypus (monotremal)

-monstr- *base* show (demonstrate)

mont- *base* mountain (montane)

-mony *suf* resulting state (patrimony)

-mor-¹ *base* usage; custom (mores)

-mor-² *base* mulberry (moriform)

-mora- *base* delay (remorate)

-morb- *base* sickly; diseased (morbidity)

-mord- *base* sharp biting; acrid (mordant)

-moriger- *base* obedient; submissive (morigerous)

-morilli- *base* fungus; morel (moriliform)

moro- *base* foolish (morology)

moros- *base* surly (morosity)

-morph, -morphic, -morphism, morpho-, -morphous *comb* having a specified form (pseudomorph, anthropomorphic, monomorphism, morphology, isomorphous)

mort-, morti- *comb* death (immortality, mortify)

-mosch- *base* musk (moschiferous)

-most *suf* superlatives (foremost)

-motive *comb* moving (automotive)

moto- *comb* motor (moto-sensitive)

-mouthed *comb* having a __ mouth; having __ mouths (large-mouthed)

mov- *base* move (movable)

muci-, muco- *comb* snot; mucous membrane (muciparous, muco-protein)

mucid- *base* musty (mucidous)

mucoso- *comb* partly mucous (mu-coso-granular)

-mucro- *base* point (mucronulate)

-mug- *base* bellow (remugient)

mugil- *base* mullet (mugiloid)

muliebr- *base* woman (mulierbrity)

mult(i)- 1. *comb* having many (mul-ticolored); 2. more than two (mul-tilateral); 3. many times (multi-millionaire)

mummi- *base* mummy (mummi-form)

mun- *base* gift (munificent)

-mund-[1] *base* world (mundiciduous)

-mund-[2] *base* cleanse (mundation)

-mur-[1] *base* mouse (murine)

-mur-[2] *base* wall (immured)

-mur-[3] *base* mulberry (muriform)

muraen- *base* moray (muraenid)

-muri- *base* brine (muriatic)

-muric- *base* pointed; sharp (muri-cated)

musa- *base* banana (musaceous)

-musc-[1] base fly (musciform)

-musc-[2] base moss (emuscation)

muscar- *base* brush (muscariform)

muscicap- *base* flycatching bird; thrush (muscicapine)

musculo- *comb* muscle (musculo-phrenic)

musico- *comb* music (musicopho-bia)

muso- *base* poem (musophobia)

muss- *base* mutter; murmur (mus-sitation)

-mustel- 1. *base* weasel; badger; skunk; polecat; ermine; marten; mink; wolverine; ferret (muste-line); 2. tawny (musteline)

-mut- *base* change (immutable)

-mutil- *base* maim (mutilation)

-mutu- *base* reciprocal (mutuality)

-mycete, myceto- *comb* fungus of a specified group (schizomycete, mycetoma)

-mycin *comb* derivative of a specified substance from bacteria or fungi; antibiotic (streptomycin)

myco- *comb* mushroom; fungus (mycology)

mycter- *comb* sneer; scoff; nose (mycterism)

-myelia, myelo- *comb* spinal cord; marrow (micromyelia, myelo-genic)

myia- *base* fly (myiasis)

myo-[1] *comb* [medicine/anatomy] muscle (myocardium)

myo-[2] *base* mouse (myomancy)

myox- *base* dormouse (myoxine)

myria- 1. *comb* numerous; many (myriapod); 2. ten thousand (myriameter). *Also* myrio- (myriophyllus)

myringo- *base* tympanic (myringi-tis)

myrist- *base* nutmeg (myristic)

myrmeco-, myrmic- *comb* ant (myrmecology, myrmicine)

myrmecophag- *base* anteater (myrmecophagine)

myro- *comb* ointment; perfume (myropolist)

-myrti- *base* myrtle (myrtiform)

myso- *comb* dirt (mysophobia). *Also* miso- (misophobia)

mystico- *comb* partly mystical (mystico-religious)

mythico- *comb* partly mythical (mythico-romantic)

mytho- *comb* myth; story (mytho-clast)

-mytil- *base* mussel (mytiliform)

-myxia, myxo- *comb* slime; mucus (hypomyxia, myxomycete)

-myz- *base* suck (myzostoma)

N

-nacar- *base* orange-red (nacarine)

nano- 1. *comb* dwarfism (nano-cephalous); 2. one-billionth (nanosecond). *Also* nanno- (nan-nofossil)

-nao- *base* temple (naology)

-napi- *base* turnip (napiform)

narco- *comb* numbness; stupor (narcolepsy)

-nari- *base* nostrils (nariform)

narr- *base* relate; tell (narrative)

nasc- *base* born (nascent)

nasi-, naso- *comb* nose; nasal (nasi-cornous, nasolabial)

-nastic, -nasty *comb* plant growth: unequal by some specified means or in a specified direction (hypo-nastic, hyponasty)

-nata- *base* swim (natatorium)

-natal- *base* birth (neonatal)

-nati- *base* buttocks (natiform)

-natremia *comb* sodium (hypona-tremia)

-natured *comb* having a __ nature or temperament (good-natured)

naus- *base* sick; seasick (nausea)

-naut-, -nav- *base* ship; sea (nauti-cal, navigate)

navig- *base* voyage (navigable)

ne- *pre* not (nescience)

-nebul- *base* cloud; mist; vapor (nebulous)

necro- *comb* death; corpse; dead tis-sue (necrology)

necto- *comb* swimming (nectozooid)

necyo- *comb* demon; damned spirit (necyomancy)

-neg- *base* deny (negativist)

-negot- *base* business (negotiate)

-nema- *base* thread (hyalonema)

nemato- *comb* thread; threadlike (nematocyst)

nemor- *base* woods; forest (nemor-ous)

neo- 1. *comb* new; recent; latest (neo-classic); 2. [geology] chro-nologically last part of a period (Neocene)

nephal- *base* sober; abstinent (nephalism)

nephelo-, nepho- *comb* cloud (nephelometer, nephology)

nephro- *comb* kidney (nephrotomy)

-nepo- *base* nephew (nepotic)

-ner- *base* liquid (aneroid)

-nerter- *base* the dead (nerterology)

nerv-, nervi-, nervo- *comb* nerve (nervosity, nervifolious, nervo-vital)

-ness *suf* condition; quality of (greatness)

neuro- *comb* nervous system; nerve (neuropath)

neutro- *comb* neutral (neutropenia)

nev-, nevo- *base* birthmark; mole (nevoid, nevoxanthoendothe-lioma)

-nex- *base* connect; bind (annex)

nic- *base* victory (epinician)

-nict- *base* wink (nictitate)

nid-, nidi- *base* nest (nidal, nidification)

nidor- *base* smell (nidorous)

nigri-, nigro- *comb* black (nigri-cauline, nigrofuscous)

nihili- *comb* nothing (nihili-par-turient)

-nik *suf* one who is __ (beatnik)

nimb- *base* cloud; rainstorm (nimbification)

ning- *base* snow (ninguid)

nitid- *base* lustrous; bright (nitid-ity)

nitro- 1. *comb* presence of nitrogen

compounds made by the action of nitric or nitrous acid and other substances (nitro-cellulose); **2.** the presence of the NO^2 radical (nitrobenzene); **3.** niter (nitrobacteria)

nitroso- *comb* presence of the NO radical (nitrosamine)

-niv- *base* snow (niveous)

noci- *comb* hurt; pain; injury (nociceptor)

nocti- *comb* night (noctiferous)

noctilion- *base* bat (noctilionid)

-nod- *base* knot (nodulose)

-noe- *base* thought; intellect (noetic)

-noia *comb* thought (metanoia)

-nom-, -nym- *base* name (nomenclature, synonymous)

nomato- *see* **onomato-**

-nomia *comb* name (paranomia)

nomo- *comb* law; custom (nomology)

-nomy *comb* systematized knowledge of (astronomy)

non-[1] *pre* negative; not (nondescript)

non-[2] *base* ninth (nonan)

nona- *comb* nine (nonagenarian)

nonagen-, nonages- *base* ninety (nonagenarian, nonagesimal)

-noo- *base* mind (nooscopic)

Normano- *comb* Norman (Normano-Saxonic)

normo- *comb* usual; normal (normotensive)

noso- *comb* disease (nosophobia)

nosocom- *base* hospital (nosocomial)

nosto- *comb* a return home (nostomania)

nota-, noto- *comb* the back; dorsum (notancephalia, notochord)

-notho- *base* spurious; false (nothosaurus)

-noto- *base* south (notothere)

-nov-[1] *base* new (renovate)

-nov-[2] *base* nine (novenary)

-noverc- *base* stepmother (novercant)

-nox- *base* harmful (obnoxious)

-nub-, -nupt- *base* marry (connubial, nuptial)

-nubi- *base* cloud (nubiferous)

nuci- *comb* nut (nuciferous)

nucleo- *comb* nucleus: relation to; kernel (nucleoplasm)

nudi- *comb* naked; bare (nudibranchiate)

-nuga- *base* trifling (nugatory)

nulli- *comb* none (nullify)

-num- *base* count (enumerate)

-numisma- *base* coin (numismatist)

nummi- *comb* coin; disk (nummiform)

nundin- *base* market; commerce (nundinal)

-nupt- *base* wed (nuptial)

nur(us)- *base* daughter-in-law (nurine)

nuta- *base* sway; nod (nutation)

-nutr- *base* nourish (malnutrition)

-nychia *see* **onycho-**

nycta-, nycti-, nycto- *comb* night (nyctalopia, nyctitropic, nyctophobia)

-nym- *see* **-nom**

nympho- **1.** *comb* labia minora (nymphotomy); **2.** nymphs (nympholepsy)

O

-o 1. *suf* informal abbreviation (ammo); 2. person associated with (politico)

oario- *comb* ovary (oariopathy). *See* ovario-

ob- 1. *pre* to; toward; before (object); 2. opposed to; against (obnoxious); 3. upon; over (obfuscate); 4. completely; totally (objurgate). NOTE: ob- can change to: o- (omission); oc- (occur); of- (offer); op- (oppose

oben- *base* walrus (obenid)

obes- *base* fat; heavy (obesity)

obit- *base* death (obituary)

oblit- *base* erase (obliteration)

oblongo- *comb* with oblong extension (oblongo-elliptic)

obscur- *base* dark (obscurant)

obstin- *base* stubborn (obstinacy)

obtusi- *comb* obtuse; blunted (obtusi-pennate)

-occid- *base* west (occidental)

occipito- *comb* occipital; skull (occipito-axial)

occult- *base* hidden (occultation)

ocelli- *comb* spot; eyelet (ocelliform)

ochlo- *comb* crowd; mob (ochlophobia)

ocho-¹ *base* vehicle (ochophobia)

ocho-² *base* capacious; ample (ochopetalous)

ochreo- *comb* containing ochre; light brownish yellow (ochreoferrous)

ochro- *comb* pale yellow (ochrocarpous)

-ock *suf* diminutive: small (hillock)

-ocracy *comb* the rule of any class (tradeocracy)

octa-, octo- *comb* eight (octagon, octobrachiate)

octakaideca- *comb* eighteen (octakaidecahedron)

octan- *base* eighth (octant)

octocent- *base* eight hundred (octocentenary)

octogen-, octoges- *base* eighty (octogenarian, octogesimal)

oculi-, oculo- *comb* eye (oculiform, oculomotor)

ocy- *comb* swift (ocydrome)

-ode¹ *comb* way; path (cathode)

-ode² *suf* like (geode)

odi- *base* hatred (odious)

-odic *comb* smell (euodic)

odo- *comb* road; journey (odometer). *See* hodo-

-odont, odonto- *comb* tooth (macrodont, odontoblast)

odori-, odoro- *comb* smell; scent (odoriferant, odoroscope)

-odus *comb* having teeth; names of genera (ceratodus)

-odynia, odyno- *comb* pain in __ (osteodynia, odynophagia)

oeco- *comb* environment (oecology). *See* eco-

oego- *base* open (oegopsid). *Also* oigo- (oigopsid)

oeno- *comb* wine (oenophile)

oesophago- *see* esophag-

off-¹ *comb* away from (offbrand)

-off² *suf* a competition (bakeoff)

ogdo- *comb* eight (ogdoad)

-oid, -oidal *suf* shape; like; resembling (spheroid, trapezoidal)

-oidea *comb* names of zoological classes; names of entomological superfamilies (Molluscoidea)

-oigo- *base* open (oigopsid)

oiko- *comb* environment (oiko-fugic). *See* eco-

oino- *comb* wine (oinomania). *See* oeno-

-ol *suf* [chemistry] 1. alcohol or phenol (menthol); 2. same as -ole (anethol)

-ola *suf* diminutive (variola)

-ole[1] *suf* [chemistry] 1. compound: closed-chain with five members (pyrrole); 2. names of certain aldehydes and ethers (anethole)

-ole[2] *suf* diminutive (variole)

olea-, -oleic, oleo- *comb* oil; olein; oleic (oleaginous, palmitoleic, oleomargarine)

-olent *base* giving out a smell (redo-lent)

oler- *base* vegetables; potherbs (oleraceous)

olfacto- *comb* smell (olfactometer)

oligo- *comb* few; deficiency of (oligophrenia)

olit- *base* vegetables (olitory)

oliv-, olivaceo- *comb* dusky green (olivaceous, olivaceo-cinereous)

-ologist *comb* specialist (proctologist)

-oma, -ome *suf* morbid growth; tumor; neoplasm; formation (sarcoma, phyllome)

omalo- *see* homalo-

ombro- *comb* rain; shower (ombrometer)

ommat- *base* eye (ommatophore)

omni- *comb* all; everywhere (omniscient)

omo-[1] *base* shoulder (omodynia)

omo-[2] *base* raw (omophagia)

omphalo- *comb* navel; umbilicus (omphalitis)

-on *suf* [chemistry] 1. elementary particle (gluon); 2. inert gas (neon)

onco- *comb* tumor (oncologist)

-one *suf* [chemistry] a ketone (acetone)

oneiro- *comb* dream (oneirocritic)

-oner- *base* burden (onerous)

-onic *suf* names of acids (gluconic acid)

onio- *base* buy (oniomania)

-onisc- *base* woodlouse (onisciform)

ono- *base* donkey; beast of burden (onology)

-onocrot- *base* pelican (onocrotal)

onom-, onomato- *comb* name (onomastic, onomatopoeia)

onto- *comb* being; existence (ontology)

onych-, -onychia, onycho- *comb* claw; nail (onychosis, leukony-chia, onychophagy)

-onym *comb* name (pseudonym)

oo- *comb* egg; ovum (oogamous)

oophoro- *comb* ovary (oophoritis)

op- *comb* eye (opalgia)

-opac- *base* shade; dimness (opacity)

-oper-[1] *base* work; labor (operosity)

-oper-[2] *base* lid; cover (inoperculate)

ophio- *comb* snake (ophiolatry)

-ophidia, ophidio- *comb* [medicine] venemous snakes (Thanatophidia, ophidiophobia)

ophry- *base* eyebrow (ophryosis)

ophthalmo- *comb* eye (ophthalmoscope)

-opia *comb* eye defect; vision (diplopia)

opio- *comb* poppy juice (opiomania)

-opiso- *base* backwards (opisometer)

opistho- *comb* behind; dorsal (opisthodont)

opo- *comb* juice (opobalsam)

oppositi- *comb* opposite (oppositifolious)

opsi-[1] *comb* late (opsigamy)
opsi-[2] *comb* sight; eye (opsiometer)
-opsia *comb* sight; view (hemianopsia)
-opsis 1. *comb* see (synopsis);
  2. likeness; resembling (coreopsis)
opso- 1. *comb* eye (opsoclonus);
  2. cooked meat; relish; rich fare;
  provisions; sweets (opsomania)
-opsy *comb* examination (biopsy)
-opt-[1] *base* wish; choice (optional)
-opt-[2] *base* best (optimism)
optico- *comb* pertaining to sight
  (optico-ciliary)
opto- *comb* sight; eye (optometry)
opul- *base* riches (opulent)
opus- *base* work (opuscular)
or-[1] *base* mouth (orifice)
-or[2] *suf* person or thing that (inventor)
-or[3] *suf* quality; condition (horror)
orag- *base* storm (oragious)
-orama *comb* display; spectacle
  (georama)
-orat- *base* speak (oratorical)
orbiculato- *comb* partly rounded
  (orbiculato-cordate)
orbito- *comb* orbit; circle (orbito-nasal)
-orches- *base* dance (orchestic)
orchido-[1] *comb* orchid (orchidology)
orchido-[2] *comb* testicle (orchidotomy)
orchio- *comb* testicle (orchiocele)
orect-, -orexia *comb* appetite (orectic, dysorexia)
organo- *comb* organ; organic
  (organography)
-orial *suf* pertaining to an action
  (conspiratorial)
orient- *base* east; sunrise (orienteering)
-orious *suf* relating to; characterized by (meritorious)

orismo- *comb* definition; boundary
  (orismology)
-orium *suf* a place for __ (auditorium)
orneo-, orni-, ornitho-, orno- *comb*
  bird (orneoscopic, orniscopic, ornithology, ornomancy)
oro-[1] *comb* mouth (orolingual)
oro-[2] *comb* mountain (orogenic).
  Also **oreo-** (oreology)
orrho- *comb* serum (orrhocyst)
ortho- 1. *comb* straight; regular; upright (orthodontia); 2. right angle
  (orthorhombic); 3. proper; correct; standard (orthography);
  4. [chemistry] that acid of a group
  containing the same nonmetallic
  element that has the largest number of OH groups per atom of the
  nonmetal (orthophosphoric);
  5. [medicine] correction of deformities (orthopedics)
-ory 1. *suf* having the nature of
  (hortatory); 2. a place for __ (observatory)
orycto- *comb* dug up: fossil or mineral (oryctological)
-oryzi- *base* rice (oryzivorous)
oscheo- *comb* scrotum (oscheitis)
-oscill- *base* swing (oscillation)
oscin- *base* songbirds (oscine)
-oscit- *base* yawn (oscitation)
oscul- *base* kiss (osculation)
-ose[1] 1. *suf* carbohydrate (cellulose);
  2. protein hydrolysis: product of
  (proteose)
-ose[2] *suf* full of; containing; like
  (verbose). *See* **-osity**
-osis 1. *suf* state; condition; action
  (osmosis); 2. abnormal condition; diseased condition (neurosis)
-osity *suf* full of; containing; like
  (verbosity). *See* **-ose**[2]
-osmia *comb* smell; odor (anosmia)

osmio- *comb* osmium (osmio-chloride)

osmo-[1] *comb* smell; odor (osmodysphoria)

osmo-[2] *comb* osmosis (osmolarity)

osphresio- *comb* odor; sense of smell (osphresiophobia)

osphy-, osphyo- *comb* loins (osphyalgia, osphyocele)

-ossi, osseo-, osteo- *comb* bone (ossification, osseomucin, osteoplasty)

ossifrag- *base* osprey (ossifrage)

osti- *base* gate; opening (ostiole)

-ostraca, ostraco- *comb* shell (Leptostraca, ostracoderm)

ostre-, ostrei-, ostreo- *comb* oyster (ostreaceous, ostreiform, ostreophage)

ot-, oto- *comb* ear (othemorrhagia, otopyosis)

-ota *suf* plural ending of taxonomic names (biota)

-ote *suf* singular ending of taxonomic names (eukaryote)

oti- *base* idleness; leisure (otiose)

-otic 1. *suf* affected with; of (sclerotic); 2. producing (narcotic)

oulo- *comb* gums (oulorrhagy)

ourano- *comb* heavens (ouranomancy). *See* **urano-**

ouro- *comb* urine (ouromancy)

-ous 1. *suf* characterized by; having; full of (generous); 2. [chemistry] having a valence lower than in a compound whose name ends in -ic (sulfurous)

-ousia, -ousian *comb* essence; substance (homoousia, heteroousian)

out- 1. *comb* situated at; outside (outpatient); 2. going away; outward (outcast); 3. better; greater; more than (outsell)

ovario- *comb* ovary (ovariocentesis). *See* **oario-**

ovato- *comb* egg-shaped (ovato-deltoid)

over- 1. *comb* above; upper; superior; eminent (overbearing); 2. beyond normal; excessive (overrate); 3. passing across; passing beyond (overshoot); 4. moving lower (overwhelm)

ovi-[1] *comb* egg; ovum (oviduct)

ovi-[2] *comb* sheep (ovicide)

ovo- *comb* ovum; ovally (ovolecithin)

oxa- *pre* [chemistry] presence of oxygen, especially as replacing carbon in a ring (oxazine)

oxal-, oxalo- *comb* containing the radical ovalyl (oxalamide, oxalonitrate)

oxy-[1] *comb* sharp; pointed; acute; acid (oxycephalic)

oxy-[2] *comb* oxygen-containing (oxyacetylene)

oxyur- *base* worm (oxyuricide)

ozo- *comb* smell (ozostomia)

ozono- *comb* ozone (ozonolysis)

ozostom- *base* bad breath (ozostomia)

P

pac- *base* peace (pacific)

pachno- *comb* frost (pachnolite)

pachy- *comb* thick; large; massive (pachyderm)

pachyderm- *base* elephant; tapir (pachydermatous)

paedo-[1] *comb* dirt; soil (paedogenic). *Also* **pedo-** (pedocal)

paedo-[2] *comb* child; immature; doll (paedomorphic). *Usually* **pedo-** (pedophile)

-pagia *comb* conjoined twins (ecto-pagia)

pago- *comb* cold; frost (pagophagia)

pagur- *base* hermit crab (pagurian)

-pagus *comb* conjoined twins (diplopagus)

-paizo- *base* loveplay (paizogony)

palato- *comb* palate; roof of mouth (palatonasal)

palea- *base* chaff; chaff-like (pala-ceous)

paleo- 1. *comb* ancient; prehistoric (Paleozoic); 2. primitive (pale-olithic); 3. paleontological (paleo-zoology). *Also* **paeleo-** (paeleo-zoic)

-pali-, palil-, -palin- *base* over; again (paliphrasia, palilogy, palin-genesis)

pallio- *comb* pallium; mantle (pal-liopedal)

pallo- *comb* vibrations (pallometric)

palma- *base* palm tree (palmaceous)

palmati-, palmato- *comb* like the palm of the hand (palmatifid, palmatopeltate)

-palp- *base* touch; feel (palpable)

paludi-, palus- *base* marsh (paludi-cole, palustrine)

palumb- *base* pigeon (palumbine)

palyn- *base* pollen (palynology)

-pampin- *base* vine; tendril (pampiniform)

pan-[1] 1. *comb* all (pantheism); 2. common to all/every (Pan-Ameri-can); 3. belief in a unified group (Pan-Slavism)

pan-[2] *base* bread (panivorous)

pancreato-, pancreo- *comb* of the pancreas (pancreatotomy, pancre-opathy)

pandur- *base* fiddle (panduriform)

pann- *base* rag (pannose)

-pannychy *comb* lasting all night (psychpannychy)

pant-, panto- *comb* all; every (pan-talgia, pantograph)

-papaver- *base* poppy (papaverous)

papil- *base* butterfly (papiliona-ceous)

papilli-, papillo-, papilloso- *comb* papillary; nipple-like (papilliform, papillomatosis, papilloso-asper-ate)

papulo- *comb* papule; skin elevation (papulopustular)

papyro- *comb* papyrus (papyrology)

par-[1] *base* fraction; portion (parti-tion)

par-[2] *base* titmouse; chickadee (parine)

para-[1] 1. *comb* protecting from (parapet); 2. using a parachute (paratroop)

para-[2] 1. *pre* beside; beyond (paral-lel); 2. [chemistry] an isomer, modification, polymer, derivative of a specified substance (paradi-chlorobenzene); 3. [medicine] secondary capacity; accessory ca-pacity (paramedical); 4. [medi-cine] functionally disordered; ab-normal (parafunctional); 5. [medicine] like; resembling (paracholera)

-para[3] *comb* woman who has given birth; parturient (multipara)

paral- *base* seashore (paralian)

paralip- *base* neglect; omission (paralipomena)

paraphil- *base* unusual sexual prac-tices (paraphilia)

parasit- *base* parasite (parasitical)

pard- *base* leopard (pardine)

pari- *comb* equal (paripinnate)

-paria *comb* genera and order of trilobytes; cheeks (Opisthoparia)

parieto- *comb* forming a cavity; parietal; wall (parietomastoid)

pariso- *comb* evenly balanced; almost equal (parisology)

paroem- *base* proverb (paroemiology). *Also* **parem-** (paremiography)

-parous *comb* producing; bearing; bringing forth (viviparous)

pars- *base* spare; save (parsimony)

partheno- *comb* virgin (parthenogenesis)

parti- *base* division; part (partition)

-partur- *base* giving birth (parturition)

parvi-, parvo- *comb* small (parvifolious, parvoline)

pascu- *base* grazing (pascuant)

pasi- *comb* all; universal (pasigraphy). *See* **pan-**

-passeri- *base* perching bird; sparrow (passeriform)

-pated *comb* head: type of (baldpated)

-pater- *base* father (paternity)

-path, -pathic, patho-, -pathy *comb* suffering; disease; feeling (psychopath, telepathic, pathopoeia, antipathy)

patri- *comb* father (patrimony)

patroc- *base* support; defend (patrocinate)

patroio- *comb* ancestor (patroiophobia)

patru- *base* uncle (patruity)

patul- *base* open; spread out (patulent)

pauc-, pauci- *comb* few (paucity, pauciflorous)

paup- *base* poor (pauper)

-pavid- *base* fearful (impavidity)

-pavon- 1. *base* peacock (pavonine); 2. peacock blue (pavonine)

pax- *comb* peace (Pax Romana)

paxill- *base* pillarlike; stalklike (paxilla)

-pecca- *base* fault; sin; disease (impeccable)

pect- *base* breastbone (pectoral)

pectinato- *comb* like the teeth of a comb (pectinato-denticulate)

pecul- *base* embezzle (peculation)

-pecun- *base* money (impecunious)

ped-[1], -pede, pedi-, pedo-[1] *comb* foot (pedal, centipede, pedicure, pedopathy). *Also* **pod-** (tripod)

ped-[2] *comb* child (pedagogy)

pedati- *comb* pedately; like a foot (pedatifid)

-pedia *comb* teach (encyclopedia)

pedicul- *base* lice (pediculosis)

pedion- *base* flat surface; plain (pedionomite)

pedipalp- *base* scorpion (pedipalpous)

pedo-[2] *comb* child (pedodontia)

pedo-[3] *comb* dirt; soil (pedocal)

pegm- *base* framework; fastening (pegmatite)

pego- *base* spring; fountain (pegomancy)

peir- *base* try; experiment (peirastic)

pejor- *base* worse (pejorative)

-pel- *base* push; drive (propel). *Also* **-pul-** (propulsion)

pelad- *base* bald (peladic)

pelag- *base* sea (archipelago)

pelec- *base* hatchet (pelecypod)

pelecan- *base* pelican (pelecanid)

pell-, pelli- *base* skin; hide (pellagra, pellibranchiate)

pellarg- *base* stork (pellargic)

-pelm- *base* sole of the foot (antiopelmous)

pelo- *comb* mud; clay (pelophilous)

pelor- *base* monster (pelorization)

pelt-, pelti-, pelto- *comb* shield (peltate, peltiferous, peltogaster)

peltati-, peltato- *comb* shieldshaped (peltatifid, peltatodigitate)

pelvi- *comb* pelvis; pelvic; basin-shaped (pelvimeter)

-pend- 1. *base* hang (pendant); 2. pay; weigh (expend). *Also* **-pens-** (pension)

pendulin- *base* birds with hanging nests (penduline)

pen(e)- *comb* almost; nearly (penannular)

-penia *comb* poverty; deficiency; tightening (kaliopenia)

pennati- *comb* feather (pennatifid)

penni- *comb* feather; featherlike (penniform)

-penny *comb* monetary unit (half-penny)

peno- *base* punishment (penology)

penta- *comb* five (pentamerous)

pentacost- *base* fifty (pentacostal)

pentakaideca- *comb* fifteen (pentakaidecahedron)

penteconta- *comb* fifty (pentecontaglossal)

penther- *base* mother-in-law (pentheraphobia)

penur- *base* poverty; lack (penurious)

-peo- *base* penis (peotomy)

pepo- *base* pumpkin (pepon)

peps-, pept-, pepto- *comb* digest (pepsinogen, peptic, peptogenic)

per- 1. *pre* through; away (percolate); 2. completely; very (persuade); 3. [chemistry] containing a specified element or radical in its maximum or a relatively high valence (perchlorate)

percepto- *comb* perceived (percepto-motor)

perces- *base* barracuda (Percesocine)

percesoc-, -perci-, -perco- *base* barracuda; perch (percesocine, perciform, percomorph)

perchloro- *comb* indicates a compound in which there is the maximum replacement of hydrogen by chlorine (perchlorobenzine)

perd- *base* destroy; lose (perdition)

-perdic- *base* partridge (perdicine)

perdit- *base* wicked (perdition)

perdri- *base* partridge (perdricide)

peregrin- *base* journey (peregrination)

-peregrin- *base* travel; wander (peregrinate)

perenn- *base* lasting (perennial)

-pergamen- *base* parchment (pergameneous)

peri- 1. *pre* around; surrounding (periscope); 2. near (perigee)

pericardiaco-, pericardio- *comb* relating to the sac surrounding the heart; pericardial (pericardiacophrenic, pericardiostomy)

pericul- *base* danger (periculous)

perineo- *comb* perineum (perineocele)

periosteo- *comb* periosteum; bone membrane (periosteophyte)

perisso *comb* uneven; strange; redundant (perissodactyl)

-perister- *base* pigeon (peristeronic)

peritoneo- *comb* peritonium; abdominal sac (peritoneoclysis)

perm- *base* lasting; remaining (permanent)

pero- *comb* maimed; malformed (perodactyly)

peroneo- *comb* peroneal; fibula (peroneo-calcaneal)

peroxy- *comb* peroxy group (peroxyborate)

perpet- *base* unceasing (perpetual)

pers- *base* avocado (persea)

persic- *base* peach (persicaria)

-person *comb* person in a specialized activity (chairperson)

-pervic- *base* stubborn (pervicacious)

pesso- *comb* pebble (pessomancy)

-pessul- *base* bolt (pessular)

pesti- *comb* injurious plant or animal; pest; plague (pestiferous)

-pet- *base* seek; ask; require (compete)

peta- *comb* quadrillion (petameter)

-petal *comb* moving toward; seeking (centripetal)

petalo- *base* leaf (petalocerous)

petri-, petro- *comb* rock; stone (petrifaction, petroglyph)

petro- *comb* petroleum (petrodollars)

petrosel- *base* parsley (petroseline)

petuli- *base* petal (petuliform)

-peuce- *base* pine (peucedaneous)

-pexy *comb* fixation: surgical (nephropexy)

-phacell- *base* bundle (phacellate)

phaco- *comb* lens; lentil-shaped (phacolytic). *Also* phako- (phakocyst)

-phaein, phaeo- *comb* dusky; gray; muddy brown (haemophaein, phaeophyl). *Also* pheo- (pheochrome)

-phaeno- *base* showing (phaenogamous). *Also* pheno- (phenocryst)

-phage, phago-, -phagous, -phagy 1. *comb* eating destroying; 2. phagocyte (xylophage, phagocytosis, xylophagous, anthropophagy)

-phakia *comb* lens (microphakia). *Also* phaco- (phacolytic)

-phalacr- *base* bald (phalacrophobia)

phalacrocorac- *base* cormorant (phalacrocoracine)

-phalaen- *base* moth (phalaenoid)

-phalang- *base* spider (phalangium)

phall(o)- *comb* penis (phallocampsis)

-phane, -phanic, -phany *comb* appearance; resemblance (allophane, urophanic, epiphany)

phanero- *comb* visible; manifest (phanerogam)

phantas- *base* illusion (phantasmal)

-phar- *base* lighthouse (pharology)

pharmaco- *comb* drugs (pharmacotherapy)

pharyngo- *comb* the pharynx (pharyngology)

-phasco- *base* bag; purse (phascolome)

phascolom- *base* wombat (phascolomian)

-phaseol- *base* kidney bean (phaseolite)

-phasia, -phasic, -phasis, -phasy *comb* speech disorder (aphasia, dysphasic, emphasis, aphasy)

-phasian- *base* pheasant (phasianoid)

phasm- *base* apparition (phasmophobia)

phat- *base* speak (phatic)

-phein- *base* dusky (hemophein). *See* phaeo-

phello- *comb* cork (phellogen)

-phemia, -phemy *comb* speech disorder (paraphemia, heterophemy)

phenac-, phenakist- *base* imposter (phenacite, phenakistoscope)

phenanthro- *comb* [chemistry] phenanthrene (phenanthroline)

pheng(o)- *base* light; luster (phengite)

phenic- *base* purple (phenicine)

pheno- 1. *comb* appearance (phenomenon); 2. phenyl group (phenoxide)

pheo- *comb* dusky; gray (pheochrome). *Also* phæo- (phæophile)

-pher *comb* bearing; carrying (chronopher)

philatel- *base* postage stamp (philatelic)

-phile, -philic, -philism, philo-, -philous *comb* favorably disposed to; loving; liking (Anglophile, Francophilic, bibliophilism, philology, photophilous)

-philia, -philiac 1. *comb* tendency toward (hemophilia, hemophiliac); 2. abnormal attraction to (coprophilia)

philomel- *base* nightingale (philomelian)

philosophico- *comb* philosophical and (philosophico-historic)

-phim- *base* narrow (phimosis)

phlebo- *comb* vein (phlebotomy)

-phloem- *base* tree bark (epiphloem)

phlog-, phlogo- *comb* inflammation (phlogistic, phlogogenous)

phlyc- *base* blister (phlyctenous)

-phobe, -phobia, -phobic, phobo- *comb* fear; hatred; dread (Francophobe, claustrophobia, ailurophobic, phobophobia)

phoco- *comb* seal: sea mammal (phocomelia)

phoecaen- *base* porpoise (Phoecaenoides)

phœnicopt- *base* flamingo (phœnicopterous)

pholid- *base* scales (pholidosis)

-phone, phono-, -phony *comb* sound; tone; speech; voice (megaphone, phonology, cacophony)

phonetico- *comb* phonetic and (phonetico-grammatical)

-phor, -phore, -phorous *comb* bearer; producer (phosphor, carpophore, gonophorous)

phos- *base* light (phosphor)

phospho-, phosphoro- *comb* phosphorus (phosphoprotein, phosphoroscope)

photo- 1. *comb* of light (photodynamics); 2. of photography (photomontage)

-phragma, phragmo- *comb* barrier; wall; fence (diaphragma, phragmophorous)

phraseo- *comb* phrase; verbal expression (phraseology)

-phrastic *comb* word choice (periphrastic)

-phrat- *base* clan (phratric)

phreato- *base* well (phreatic)

-phrenia *comb* mental disorder (schizophrenia)

-phrenic, phrenico-, phreno- 1. *comb* diaphragm; midriff (gastrophrenic); 2. mental condition; mind (schizophrenic, phrenicotomy, phrenogastric)

phryno- *comb* toad (phrynoderma)

phthart- *base* destructive; deadly (phthartic)

phthino- *comb* wasting away; decay (phthinoplasm)

-phthir- *base* louse (phthirophagous). *Also* **phthyr-**

phthisi-, phthisio-, -phthisis, -phthysis *comb* wasting away; decay; tuberculosis (phthisiology, phthisiogenesis, myelophthisis, panmyelophthysis)

-phthong *comb* voice; sound (diphthong)

-phthor- *base* corruption (thelyphthoric)

-phyceae, -phyceous, phyco- *comb* seaweed (Rhodophyceae, Rhodophyceous, phycology)

-phygo- *base* shun; flee (phygogalactic)

-phylactic, phylacto-, -phylax, -phylaxis *comb* protection; defense; guard (prophylactic, phylactocarp, chartophylax, tachyphylaxis)

-phyletic *comb* origin (monophyletic)

-phyll, phyllo-, -phyllous *comb* leaf

(sporophyll, phyllophagous, monophyllous)

phylo- *comb* tribe; race; phylum (phylogenesis)

phym-, -phyma *comb* tumor; swelling; outgrowth (phymatosis, osteophyma)

-phyr- *base* mix; mingle (haunophyr)

-phyre *comb* porphyritic rock (granophyre)

physa- *base* flatulence (physagogue)

physali- *comb* bladder; bubble (physaliphore)

physc- *base* swelling; potbelly (physcony)

physi-, physico-, physio- *comb* nature natural; physical bodily (physitheism, physicochemical, physiography)

-physis *comb* growth (prophysis)

physo- 1. *comb* tendency to swell (physocele); 2. relating to air or gas (physometra); 3. bladder (physogastric)

-phyte, phyto- *comb* plant; flora; vegetation (microphyte, phytogenesis)

-piceo- *comb* reddish-black (piceoferruginous)

-pici- *base* woodpecker (piciform)

pico- *comb* one-trillionth (picogram)

picro- *comb* bitter (picroerythrin)

-pict- *base* paint (depiction)

-piesis *comb* pressure (anisopiesis)

piezo- *comb* pressure; strain (piezometer)

pigm- *base* paint; color (pigmentation)

-pign- *base* pledge; pawn; mortgage (impignorate)

-pigr- *base* slow; sluggish; slothful (impigrity)

pil-, pili-, pilo- *comb* hair (depilatory, piliform, piloerection)

-pile- *base* cap (pileolus)

piloso- *comb* hairy (piloso-fimbriate)

pimel-, pimelo- *comb* fat; fatty (pimelitis, pimelosis)

pin- *base* pine (pinaceous)

-pinac- *base* tablet; slab (pinacoid). *Also* **-pinak-** (pinakoid)

-pingu- *base* fat (pinguescence)

pinnati-, pinnato- *comb* like a feather; pinnately (pinnatifid, pinnato-pectinate)

pinni- *comb* fin; flipper (pinnigrade)

pino- *comb* drink (pinocytosis)

pio- *comb* fat (pioscope)

-piper- *base* pepper (piperic)

-piq- *base* stinging; sharp (piquant)

piri-, piro- *comb* pear (piriform, piroplasmosis). *See* **pyri-**

pisci- *comb* fish (piscivorous)

pisi- *comb* pea (pisiform)

pist-, pisti- *base* faith (pistology, pistiology)

pithec-, -pithecus *comb* primate; apelike (pithecoid, Australopithecus)

-pityr- *base* bran (pityriasis)

-plac- *base* please; appease (placidity)

placenti- *comb* placenta (placentiform)

placo- *comb* flat plate (placodermal)

plag- *base* kidnap; seize (plagiarize)

plagio- *comb* slanting; oblique (plagiotropic)

-plakia *comb* [medicine] patch (leukoplakia)

-plang- *base* strike; beat (plangency)

plani-, plano-[1] *comb* level; plane; flat (planimeter, plano-concave)

-plania, plano-[2] *comb* wandering moving (uroplania, planogamete)

-plant- *base* sole of the foot (plantigrade)

-plasia, -plasis *comb* development; growth; change (hypoplasia, cataplasis)

-plasm, plasmo- *comb* fluid cell substances of an animal or vegetable (endoplasm, plasmolysis)

-plast, -plastic, plasto- *comb* molded; formed (protoplast, protoplastic, plastotype)

-plasty 1. *comb* forming: act or means (genioplasty); 2. plastic surgery: specific part of the body (thoracoplasty); 3. plastic surgery: tissue from specified source (autoplasty); 4. plastic surgery: for a specific purpose (kineplasty)

plat-¹ *base* flat (platen)

plat-² *base* silver (plateresque)

platini-, platino- *comb* platinum (plantiniferous, platinocyanide)

platy- *comb* broad; flat (platypus)

plaustr- *base* cart; wagon (plaustrary)

-pleb- *base* common people (plebiscite)

pleco-, plecto- *comb* twist; twine; plait (plecopteran, plectognath)

-plegia, -plegy *comb* paralysis (paraplegia)

-pleisto- *comb* most (Pleistocene)

plemyr- *base* flood-tide (plemyrameter). *Also* plemmir- (plemmirrulate)

-plen-, -pler-, -plet- *base* fill; full (replenish, plerocercoid, complete)

pleo-, pleon-, plio- *comb* more; increased (pleomorphic, pleonasm, Pliosaurus. *Also* pleio- (pleomorphy)

pleonec-, pleonex- *base* greed; avarice (pleonectic, pleonexia)

-plero- *base* full (pleroma)

plesio- *comb* near (plesiosaurus)

pless(i)- *comb* striking; percussion (plessimeter)

plethys- *comb* increase; large number (plethysmometry)

pleuro- 1. *comb* side: on or near (pleurodont); 2. pleura: of or near (pleurotomy); 3. pleural (pleuropneumonia)

-plex *comb* network; folds; layers (cerviplex)

-plexia *comb* stroke (apoplexia)

plicato-, plici- *comb* folded (plicatolobate, pliciform)

plinthi- *comb* brick; squared stone (plinthiform)

plio- *see* pleo-

-ploid *comb* chromosones: of a specified multiple of (diploid)

plor- *base* cry (ploration)

plum-, plumi- *comb* feather (plumage, plumiform)

plumb-, plumbo- *comb* lead (plumbism, plumbocalcite)

pluri- *comb* several; many (pluriflorous)

pluto- *comb* wealth (plutocracy)

pluvial- *base* plover (pluvialine)

pluvio- *comb* rain (pluviograph)

-pnea, pneo- *comb* breath; respiration (dyspnea, pneograph)

pneum-, pneumato- 1. *comb* air vapor (pneumatophore); 2. breathing (pneumatometer); 3. spirits (pneumatology)

pneumo-, pneumono- *comb* lungs; air; gas (pneumobacillus, pneumonophorous)

pneusio- *comb* breathing (pneusiobiognosis)

-pnig- *base* choke; suffocate (pnigophobia)

-pocul- *base* drink; cup (poculiform)

-pod, -poda, -pode, podo-, -podous

1. *comb* foot (pleopod, Cephalopoda, pseudopode, podomere, cephalopodous); 2. having __ feet (tripod)

podic- *base* rump (podical)

-podium *comb* supporting part; footstalk (monopodium)

poecilo- *comb* irregular; many-colored (poecilomere). *Also* **poicilo-**

pogon-, pogono- *comb* beard (pogoniasis, pogonotrophy)

-poiesis, -poietic *comb* making; forming; producing (leukopoiesis, onomatopoietic)

poikilo- *comb* irregular; varied (poikiloderma)

poimen- *base* pastoral (poimenic)

poine- *base* punishment (poinephobia)

polari- *comb* polar (polari-guttulate)

-polem- *base* war (polemic)

polio- *comb* gray; gray matter (poliomyelitis)

-polis *comb* city (metropolitan)

politico- *comb* political (politicoreligious)

pollaki- *comb* many times (pollakiuria)

pollic- *base* thumb (pollicate)

pollin(i)- *comb* pollen (pollinosis)

poly- 1. *comb* more than one (polychromatic); 2. more than usual; excessive (polyphagia); 3. many kinds or parts (polymorphous)

polymorpho- *comb* multiform (polymorphocellular)

polyped- *base* frog (polypedatid)

pomerid- *base* afternoon (pomeridian)

pomi-, pomo- *comb* fruit; apple (pomiform, pomology)

-pomp- 1. *base* release; sending away (hypnopompic); 2. conductor; guide (psychopomp)

-pon-, -pos- *base* to place (opponent, opposition)

-pond- *base* weight (ponderous)

ponero- *comb* evil; wicked (ponerology)

pong- *base* gorilla; orangutan (pongid)

-ponic *base* cultivation (geoponic)

pono-^{1} *comb* pain; fatigue (ponograph)

pono-^{2} *comb* work (ponophobia)

pont- *base* bridge (pontal)

poplit- *base* back of knee (popliteal)

-popul- *base* people (depopulate)

porcin- *base* pork (porcine)

pori-, poro- *comb* pore; channel (poriferous, porencephalia)

porno- *comb* harlot (pornography)

poroso- *comb* filled with pores (poroso-punctate)

porphyro- *comb* purple (porphyrogenite)

porrac- *base* leek; green (porraceous)

-porrig- *base* dandruff (porriginous)

-port- *base* carry (portable)

porto- *comb* portal; entrance (portosystemic)

portulac- *base* purslain (portulaceous)

-pos- *see* -pon-

poso- *comb* dose (posology)

post- 1. *pre* after in time; following; later (postgraduate); 2. after in space; behind (postaxial)

postero- *comb* posterior; behind (postero-lateral)

pot-, poto- *comb* drink (potable, potomania)

potamo- *comb* river (potamologist)

-poten- *base* power; ability (impotency)

pothiri- *base* parasite (pothiriophobia)

poticho- *comb* porcelain (poticho-
mania)

pov- *base* poor (impoverished)

-pragia *comb* a quality of action
(bradypragia)

-prand- *base* dinner (postprandial)

-pras- *base* leek-green (prasine)

praso- *comb* leek (prasophagous)

-prat- *base* meadow (pratal)

-prav- *base* crooked; wrong; bad
(impravable)

-praxia, -praxis *comb* movement;
action (hyperpraxia, parapraxis)

pre- 1. *pre* before in time; earlier;
prior to (presuppose); 2. before in
place; anterior; in front of (preaxial); 3. before in rank; superior;
surpassing (preeminent); 4. in
preparation for (preschool). *Also*
prae- (praenomen)

-preca- *base* entreat; pray (impreca-
tion)

precip- *base* steep; headlong
(precipice)

pred- *base* robbery (predation)

-prehend, -prehens- *base* hold;
seize (apprehend, apprehensive)

presby- *comb* old age (presbyacusis)

presbyter- *comb* elder; priest (pres-
byteral)

preter- *pre* past; beyond; outside the
bounds (preternatural)

pri-, prion- *base* a saw (priodont,
prionodont)

prid- *base* yesterday (pridian)

prim-, primi-, primo- *comb* first;
original; early (primacy, primi-
gravida, primogenitor)

primaver- *base* spring (primaveral)

princip- *base* chief; first; main
(principal)

prisc- *base* ancient; primitive
(priscan)

-priv- *base* lack; absence (deprivation)

privign- *base* stepchild (privignal)

pro-[1] 1. *pre* moving forward; moving ahead of (proclivity); 2. forth
(produce); 3. substituting for; acting for (pronoun); 4. defending;
supporting (prolabor)

pro-[2] *pre* before in place or time
(prologue)

prob- *base* good; upright (probity)

-probosc- *base* long flexible snout
(proboscidiform)

procac- *base* bully; insolent (proca-
cious)

procell- *base* storm (procellous)

procellar- *base* albatross (procellar-
ine)

procer- *base* tall; long (procerity)

procto- *comb* rectum (proctology)

procyon- *base* raccoon (procyonine)

-prodit- *base* traitor (proditomania)

-profund- *base* deep (profundiplan-
tar)

prohib- *base* hold back; forbid
(prohibit)

proli- *comb* offspring (proliferous)

-proof 1. *suf* impervious to (water-
proof); 2. protected against
(weatherproof); 3. as strong as
(armorproof); 4. resistive to;
unaffected by (womanproof)

proprio- *comb* one's own (proprio-
ceptor)

pros- *comb* to; toward (prosody)

proso- *comb* forward; anterior
(prosopyle)

prosop(o)- *comb* face (prosopagnosia)

prostato- *comb* of the prostate
(prostatectomy)

proteo- *comb* protein (proteolysis)

protero- *comb* earlier; before; former; anterior (proterogyny)

proterv- *base* stubborn; insolent
(protervity)

proto- 1. *comb* first in time; original

(protocol); **2.** first in importance; principal; chief (protagonist); **3.** primitive (proto-Arabic); **4.** [chemistry] being that member of a series of compounds having the lowest proportion of the specified element or radical; being the parent form of a specified substance (protoactinium)

protother- *base* platypus (Prototheria)

prox-, proximo- *comb* near (proxemics, proximocephalic)

prozym- *base* yeast (prozymite)

-pruin- *base* frost (pruinose)

-prur- *base* itch (pruritic)

-psalid- *base* shears; scissors (psalidodect)

psamm(o)- *comb* sand (psammophilous)

-psar- **1.** *base* speckled; **2.** starling (psarolite)

-pselaph *base* grope (pselaphognath)

psell- *base* stuttering (psellism)

pseph(o)- *comb* pebble; counter (psephology)

psett- *base* turbot (psettaceous)

pseudo- **1.** *comb* fictitious; sham (pseudonym); **2.** counterfeit; spurious (pseudepigrapha); **3.** closely similar or deceptively similar (pseudomorph); **4.** illusory (pseudacusis); **5.** [chemistry] an isomer or related form (pseudocholinesterase)

psil-, psilo- *comb* bare; smooth; mere (psilanthropy, psilodermatous)

-psithur- *base* whisper (psithurism)

-psittac- *base* parrot; macaw; parakeet (psittacoid)

psor- *comb* itch (psoriasis)

psycho- *comb* mind; mental processes (psychology)

psychro- *comb* cold (psychrometer)

psyll- *base* **1.** snake charming (psyllic); **2.** flea (psylly)

ptarm- *base* sneeze (ptarmic)

pteno- *comb* feathered (ptenoglossate)

-pter, ptero- *comb* wing; wing-shaped; feather; fin (hymenopter, pterodactyl)

pterido- *comb* fern (pteridology)

ptern- *base* heel bone (pterna)

pterocl- *base* sand grouse (pteroclid)

pterono- *comb* wing; feather; fin (pteronophobia)

pterop- *base* bat (pteropine)

pterophyll- *base* angelfish (pterophyllous)

-pterous, pterygo- *comb* wing; wing-shaped; feather; fin (homopterous, pterygoblast)

-pteryl- *base* feather (pterylosis)

ptib- *base* wing (ptiboid)

ptilo- *comb* wing; soft feather (ptilogenesis)

ptis- *base* barley (ptisan)

ptocho- *comb* poor; beggar (ptochocracy)

-ptosia, -ptosis *comb* falling; drooping (phrenoptosia, nephroptosis)

ptyal-, ptyalo- *comb* saliva (ptyalagogue, ptyalogenic)

-ptych- *base* folded (ptychodont)

-ptysis *base* spitting (hemoptysis)

pubio-, pubo- *comb* pubic (pubiotomy, pubofemoral)

-puden- *base* shame; modesty (impudent)

-puer- *base* child (puerile)

puerper- *base* childbirth (puerperal)

pug- *base* attack; fight; fist (pugilistic)

-pugn- *base* fight; oppose (impugn)

-pul- *base* push; drive (propulsion).
  Also -pel- (repel)
pulchr- *base* beautiful (pulchritude)
-puli- *base* flea (pulicosity)
pull- *base* chicken (pullet)
pullastr- *base* pigeon (pullastrine)
pulmo-, pulmoni-, pulmono-
  1. *comb* lung (pulmonate); 2. pulmonary (pulmocutaneous, pulmonigrade, pulmonogastropod)
-puls- *base* beating; knocking (pul-
  sation)
pulver- *base* dust; ash (pulverize)
-pulvin- *base* cushion (pulvinate)
-pun-[1] *base* punish (impunity)
-pun-[2] *base* purple (puniceous)
-punct-, pung- *base* point; sharp
  (punctiform, pungent)
punctato- *comb* with points or dots
  (punctato-striate)
pupa- *base* puppet (pupaphobia)
pupillo- *comb* pupil of the eye
  (pupillometer)
-pur- *base* pus (suppuration)
-purg- *base* cleanse (purgative)
purpureo- *comb* [chemistry] purple
  compounds (purpureo-cobaltic)
purulo- *comb* pus (purulo-gangrenous)
pusill- *base* petty; very small (pusil-
  lanimous)
pustulo- *comb* pimple (pustulocrus-
  taceous)
-put- *base* think (reputed)
putamin- *base* husk (putaminous)
putea- *base* a well (puteal)
putre-, putri- *comb* rotten (putre-
  faction, putriform)

pycno- *comb* thick; compact; dense
  (pycnometer). *Also* pykn(o)-
  (pyknic)
pyelo- *comb* pelvis; kidney (pyelo-
  cystitis)
-pygia, pygo- *comb* rump; buttocks
  (steatopygia, pygopod)
pygm- *base* fist (pygmachy)
-pyle *comb* gate; aperture (mi-
  cropyle)
pylo- *base* gate; aperture (pylon)
pyloro- *comb* pylorus: stomach
  opening (pylorodiosis)
pyo- 1. *comb* pus (pyogenic); 2. suppurative (pyosis)
pyreto-, -pyrexia *comb* fever (pyre-
  tology, eupyrexia)
-pyrgo- *base* tower (pyrgocephalic)
-pyri- *base* pear (pyriform). *Also*
  piro- (piroplasm)
pyrito- *comb* pyrites (pyritohedron)
pyro- 1. *comb* fire; heat (pyromania); 2. [chemistry] a substance
  derived from the specified substance by or as if by the action of
  heat (pryrogallol); 3. [geology]
  formed by heat (pyroxenite)
pyrrho- *comb* reddish (pyrrhoco-
  rax)
pyrrhul- *base* bullfinch; bunting
  (pyrrhuline)
pyrrhulox- *base* cardinal (pyrrhuloxine)
pytho- *comb* corrupt; decomposed
  (pythogenesis)
pyx- *comb* box (pyxidate)

Q

quadr- *base* four; fourfold; square
  (quadrangle)

quadragen- *base* forty (quadragenarian)

quadrages- *base* forty (quadragesimal)

quadrato- *comb* four fourfold (quadratocubic)

quadri- *base* four; fourfold (quadrilateral)

quadricent- *base* four hundred (quadricentennial)

quadru- *base* four; fourfold (quadrumanous)

quaest- *base* gain; money-making (quaestuary)

quali- *base* characteristics; competence (qualitative)

quanti- *comb* amount; extent (quantitative)

quart-, quarter-, quarti- *base* one-fourth (quartile, quartering, quartisect)

quasi- *comb* seemingly; as if; resembling (quasi-judicial)

quass- *base* shake; beat (quassation)

quat-, quater-, quatr- *comb* four (quatrain, quaternion, quatrefoil)

quattuordec- *base* fourteen (quattuordecillion)

-quer- *base* complain (querimonious)

querc-, querci- *comb* oak (quercine, quercivorous)

querul- *base* complain (querulousness)

quid- *base* nature; essence (quiddity)

quiesc- *base* quiet (quiescent)

quin- *base* five; multiple of five (quinary)

quincent- *base* five hundred (quincentennial)

quindec(em)- *base* fifteen (quindecemvirate)

quinquagen- *base* fifty (quinquagenarian)

quinquages- *base* fifty (quinquagesimal)

quinque- *comb* five (quinquevalent)

quint-[1], quinti- *comb* five; multiple of five (quintuplets, quintilateral)

quint-[2] *comb* one-fifth (quintile)

-quire, -quiry *comb* seek; search for (require, inquiry)

-quis- *base* seek; search for (inquisition)

quot- *base* how many (quotient)

quotid- *base* daily (quotidian)

R

-racem- *base* cluster (racemiform)

rachi-, rachio- *comb* relating to the spine (rachicentesis, rachiometer). See -rrhachia

-rad- *base* ray; rod; spoke (irradiate)

radiato- *comb* ray-like (radiato-striate)

radici- *comb* root (radicicolous)

radiculo *comb* radicle; rootlike part (radiculoganglionitis)

radio- 1. *comb* ray; raylike (radiolarian); 2. by radio (radiotelegram); 3. [anatomy] radius and (radiobicipital); 4. [medicine] by radiant energy (radiotherapy); 5. [physics] radioactive (radiothorium)

rami- *comb* branch (ramification)

ramoso- *comb* protuberance (ramoso-palmate)

ramul- *base* twig (ramulose)

rani- *comb* frog (raniverous)

rap- *base* snatch; seize (rapture)

-raphan- *base* radish (raphania)

raptor- *base* falcon (raptorial)

rat- *base* emu; ostrich (ratite)

-rater *comb* specified rate or class (second-rater)

-ratio- *base* reasoning; thought (irrational)

re- 1. *pre* back (restore); 2. again; anew (retell)

recti- *comb* straight; right (rectirostral)

recto- *comb* rectal (rectoscope)

recurvo- *comb* bent back (recurvoternate)

-red *suf* condition; state (hatred)

regin- *base* queen (reginal)

-regn- *base* royal; ruling (interregnum)

regul- *base* standard pattern (regulations)

-rel *suf* diminutive (wastrel)

religio- *comb* religion (religio-educational)

relinq- *base* leave; jilt; abandon (relinquish)

reliq- *base* remains; relic (reliquary)

-reme, -remi- *base* oar (trireme, remiform)

reni-, reno- *comb* kidney (reniform, renovascular)

rep- *base* snatch; seize (surreptitious)

repando- *comb* bent back (repandodentate)

-rept- *base* creep; crawl (reptation)

reptil- *base* reptile (reptilian)

repud- *base* jilt; reject (repudiate)

resino- *comb* resin (resino-vitreous)

respirato- *comb* respiratory (respirato-prehensory)

-resti- *base* cord; cordlike (restiform)

reti- *base* net (retiform)

reticulato-, reticulo- *comb* net; network (reticulato-venose, reticulo-ramose)

retino- *comb* of the retina (retinoschisis)

retro- *comb* backward; back; behind (retroflex)

rhabdo- *comb* rod; wand (rhabdocoele)

-rhachia *see* -rrhachia

-rhag- *base* grape (rhagite)

-rhage *see* -rrhage

-rhamn- *base* buckthorn (rhamneous)

rhampho- *comb* beak (rhamphotheca)

-rhaphy *see* -rrhaphy

-rhaps- *base* stitch; poem (rhapsody)

-rhea *see* -rrhea

rhegma- *comb* fracture; break (rhegmatogenous)

rhema- *base* word; verb (rhematic)

rheo- *comb* flow; current (rheoscope)

rhet- *base* say; speak (rhetorical)

-rheum- *base* flow; stream (rheumatic)

-rhexis *see* -rrhexis

rhigo- *comb* cold; frost (rhigosis)

rhino- *comb* nose (rhinology)

rhipi-, rhipido- *comb* fan (rhipidate, rhipidoglossate)

rhizo- *comb* root (rhizomorph). *See* -(r)rhiza

rhodo- *comb* rose; rose-red (rhodolite)

-rhoeica *see* -rrhoeica

rhombo- *comb* rhombus (rhombohedral)

-rhonch- *base* snoring (rhonchal)

-rhopal- *base* club; cudgel (rhopalocerous)

-rhopo- *base* petty; restricted (rhopography)

rhyncho- *comb* snout; beak (rhynchophore). *See* -rrhyncha

rhyparo-, rhypo- *comb* dirt; filth (rhyparographer, rhypophagy). *Also* rypo- (rypophagy)

rhyti- *comb* wrinkle (rhytidectomy)

-ric *comb* jurisdiction; realm (bishopric)

ricinol- *comb* castor oil (ricinolamide)

-ridden *comb* obsessed or burdened with (guilt-ridden)

-rig- *base* wet (rigation)

rigesc- *base* stiff; rigid (rigescence)

-rim- *base* opening; crack (rimose)

-rip- *base* river; water (riparian)

-ris- *base* laugh (risible)

riv- *base* fishing (riviation)

-rix- *base* quarrel (rixation)

rizi- *base* rice (riziform)

-robor- *base* strength (roborant)

roentgeno- *comb* X-rays (roentgenology)

-rog- *base* ask; question (interrogate)

Romano- *comb* Roman and (Romano-Lombardic)

romantico- *comb* romantic (romantico-heroic)

-ror- *base* dew (roriferous)

roseo- *comb* [chemistry] reddish salts (roseo-cobaltic)

-rostell- *base* snout; radicle (rastelliform)

rostrato-, rostri-, rostro- *comb* beak (rostrato-nariform, rostriform, rostrocarinate)

rot-, roti- *comb* turn; wheel (rotation, rotiform)

rotundi-, rotundo- *comb* round (rotundifoliate, rotundo-tetragonal)

-rrhachia *comb* spine (glycorrhachia). *See* rachio-

-rrhage, -rrhagia *comb* abnormal discharge; excessive flow (hemorrhage, menorrhagia)

-rrhaphy *comb* suture (cystorrhaphy)

-rrhea *comb* flow; discharge (diarrhea). *Also* -rrhœa (diarrhœa). *See* rheo-

-rrhexis *comb* rupture; bursting (myorrhexis). *See* rhegma-

rrhexo- *base* pinch (rrhexophobia)

-rrhiza *comb* root (mycorrhiza). *See* rhizo-

-rrhoeica *comb* flow (seborrhoeica)

-rrhyncha *comb* snout; beak (oxyrryncha). *See* rhyncho-

-rub- *base* red (rubescent)

rubig- *base* rust (rubiginous)

-ruct- *base* belch; emit (eructation)

-rud- *base* rough; elementary (rudiments)

ruder- *base* stone fragments; rubble; rubbish (ruderal)

rufi-, rufo- *comb* red (ruficaudate, rufo-fulvous)

-rug- *base* wrinkle (erugate)

runc- *base* weed (runcation)

runcin- *base* saw-toothed (runcinate)

runo- *comb* rune (runographic)

rupes-, rupic- *base* rock (rupestrine, rupicolous)

rupicap- *base* chamois (rupicaprine)

rupo- *base* filth (rupophobia). *See* rhypo-

-rupt- *base* burst; break (disruption)

rur- *base* the country (rural)

Russo- 1. *comb* Russia (Russophobe); 2. Russian and (Russo-Japanese)

rut- *base* rue (rutaceous)

-rutil- *base* shining; reddish (rutilant)

-ry *see* -ery

rypo- *base* filth (rypophagy). *Also* rupo-

S

-s *suf* plural ending (dogs)

sabul- *base* sand; grit (sabulosity)

saburr- *base* sand (saburration)

-sacc- *base* pouch; bag; cyst (sacculation)

saccharo- 1. *comb* sugar (saccharometer); 2. saccharin and (saccharo-mucilaginous)

sacerdot- *base* priest (sacerdotal)

-sacr- *base* holy; set apart (sacrament)

sacro- 1. *comb* the sacrum (sacroiliac); 2. sacral and (sacrovertebral)

safran- *base* yellow (saffranin)

-sagitt- *base* arrow (sagittate)

-salebr- *base* rough; uneven (salebrosity)

-sali- *base* salt (desalination)

-salic- *base* willow (salicaceous)

salino- *comb* salt and (salinosulphureous)

salmoni- *base* salmon (salmoniform)

salpingo- 1. *comb* of a fallopian tube (salpingotomy); 2. of a eustachian tube (salpingitis)

sals- *base* salt (salsamentarious)

-salta- *base* leap; dance (saltatory)

saltu- *base* woods (saltuary)

-salub- *base* healthy (salubrious)

-salv- *base* save (salvage)

-san- *base* health; healing (unsanitary)

sanct-, sancti- *comb* holy (sanctuary, sancticolist)

sangui-, sanguineo-, sanguino- *comb* blood (sanguicolous, sanguineo-vascular, sanguino-purulent)

sanguisug- *base* leech (sanguisugous)

-sapien- *base* wise (sapiently)

sapon-, saponi- *comb* soap (saponaceous, saponification)

sapor- *base* taste (saporific)

sapro- *comb* [biology] dead; putrefying; decaying (saprogenic)

-sarc-, sarco- *comb* flesh; tissue (ectosarc, sarcology)

sarcin- *base* bundle (sarcina)

-sarmass- *base* loveplay (sarmassation)

sarment- *base* stem (sarmentaceous)

sartor- *base* tailor (sartorial)

sativ- *base* sown; planted (sativous)

sator- *base* sow (satorious)

sauciat- *base* wound (sauciate)

-saur, sauro-, -saurus *comb* lizard (dinosaur, sauropod, icthyosaurus)

sax-, saxi- *comb* rock; stone (saxatile, saxicoline)

scabi- *base* itch (scabiosity)

scaev- *base* leftsided; unlucky (scaevity)

-scal- *base* climb; ladder (escalation)

-scalpri- *base* chisel (scalpriform)

-scan- *base* climb (scansorial)

-scape *comb* view; scenery (seascape)

scapho- *comb* boat-shaped (scaphoid)

scapi- *comb* stalk; shaft (scapiform)

scapuli-, scapulo- *comb* scapula and; shoulder blade (scapulimancy, scapuloclavicular)

scarab- *base* beetle (scaraboid)

scato- *comb* excrement; feces (scatology)

scatur- *base* spring of water (scaturient)

-scel- *base* leg (isosceles)

sceler- *base* wicked (scelerous)

-scelia *comb* [medicine] condition of the legs (macroscelia)

-schem- *base* appearance; form (schematism)

schisto- *comb* split; cleft (schisto-cephalus)

schizo- *comb* split; cleavage; division (schizocarp)

-schœno- *base* rope (schœnobatic)

schol- *base* school (scholar)

-sci- *base* know (omniscient)

-scia- *base* shadow (macroscian). *Also* scio- (sciomancy). *See* skia-

-scintill- *base* spark (scintillation)

-scio-[1] *base* shadow (sciomancy). *Also* -scia- (macroscian)

scio-[2] *comb* knowledge (sciolism)

sciss- *base* cut; divide (scission)

-sciur- *base* squirrel; marmot (sci-urine)

sclero- 1. *comb* hard (sclerometer); 2. of the sclera (sclerotomy)

-scob- *base* sawdust (scobiform)

scoleci-, scoleco- *comb* worm (scoleciform, scolecobrotic)

scoli(o)- *comb* bent; crooked (scoli-osis)

scolo- *comb* spike (scolophore)

scolopac- *base* snipe; woodcock (scolopacine)

scolopendri- *base* centipede (scolopendriform)

scombr- *base* mackerel (scombroid)

scopa-, scopi- *base* twigs; broom; brush (scoparious, scopiform)

-scope, -scopic, scopo-, -scopy *comb* sight; observation; examination (telescope, microscopic, scopophilia, bioscopy)

scopeli- *base* bony fish; Scopelidae (scopeliform)

scophthalm- *base* turbot (scoph-thalmus)

scopi- *base* twig; broom (scopiform)

scopul- *base* crag; cliff (scopulous)

-scorb- *base* scurvy (scorbutigenic)

-scoria- *base* slag (scoriaceous)

-scoro- *base* garlic (scorodite)

-scort- *base* fornication; harlot (scortatory)

Scoto- *comb* Scottish and (Scoto-Irish)

scoto- *base* darkness; dimness (scotophobia)

-scrib-, -script- *base* write (scrib-bler, manuscript)

-scrobic- *base* furrowed; pitted (scrobiculous)

-scrot- *base* scrotum; testicular sac (scrotocele)

-scrut- *base* examine; search (scru-tinize)

-scut- *base* shield; scale (scutiform)

scutel- *base* dish (scutelliform)

scyphi-, scypho- *comb* cup; [botany] cup-shaped part (scyphi-form, scyphomancy)

Scytho- *comb* Scythian and (Scytho-Aryan)

se- *pre* away from (seclude)

-seb- *base* tallow; grease (sebaceous)

sebo- *comb* sebum; suetlike; tallow (seborrhea)

-sec-, -sect- *base* cut (secant, inter-section)

-secul- *base* worldly; temporal (sec-ularize)

securi- *comb* ax; hatchet (securi-form)

-secut- *base* follow (consecutive). *See* -seq-

-sed- *base* sit (sedentary)

sedat- *base* allay; calm (sedation)

sedecim- *base* sixteen (sedecimal)

segn- *base* sloth; sluggishness (seg-nity)

seismo- *comb* earthquake (seismo-graph)

sela- *comb* flash (selaphobia)

selach- *base* shark (selachoid)
seleno- *comb* moon (selenography)
self- *comb* oneself (self-denial)
sema-, -seme, semeio-, semio-
  comb sign; signal; symbol; index;
  symptom (semaphore, micro-
  seme, semeiology, semiotics)
semi- **1.** *pre* half (semidiameter);
  2. partly; imperfectly (semicivi-
  lized); **3.** twice per __ (semi-
  annual)
semin- *base* seedbed (seminal)
semper- *base* always (semper-
  vivum)
-sen- *base* old (seniority)
seni- *base* six (senary)
-sens-, -sent- *base* feel (sensitive,
  sentimental)
sensori- *comb* pertaining to the
  senses or to sensations (sensori-
  motor)
-sepalous *comb* having a specific
  kind or number of sepals (trisepalous)
sepi- *base* cuttlefish (sepiacean)
sept- *base* seven (September)
septem- *comb* seven (septempartite)
septen- *base* north (septentrion)
septendecim- *base* seventeen (sep-
  tendecimal)
septi-¹ *comb* seven (septilateral)
septi-², septico- *comb* decomposed;
  vitiated (septicemia, septico-
  pyaemia)
septim- *base* seventh (septimal)
septingenti- *base* seven hundred
  (septingentenary)
septo-¹ *comb* decomposed; vitiated
  (septogenic)
septo-² *comb* dividing wall (septo-
  cephalic)
septuagen- *base* seventy (septuagenarian)
septuages- *base* seventy (septagesi-
  mal)

septuagint- *base* seventy (septuag-
  intal)
sepul- *base* grave; tomb; burial
  (sepulcher)
-seq- *base* follow (consequence). *See*
  -secut-
-ser- *base* bar; bolt (reseration)
Serbo- *comb* Serbia (Serbo-Croa-
  tian)
seri-, sericeo-, serico- *comb* silk
  (serigraph, sericeo-tomentose,
  sericostoma)
serio- *comb* partly serious (serio-
  comic)
sero- *comb* serum (serology)
serot- *base* late in occurrence or development (serotine)
serpen- *base* snake (serpentine)
serrato- *comb* saw-toothed (serrato-
  crennate)
serri- *comb* [entomology/zoology] a
  saw (serrirostrate)
serv- *base* slave (servitude)
-serve *comb* keep; attend to (reser-
  vation)
sesqui- *comb* one and one half
  (sesquicentennial)
sesquipedal- *base* long words
  (sesquipedalophobia)
-sess- *base* sit; perch (insessorial)
setaceo- *comb* bristles and (setaceo-
  rostrate)
seti- *base* bristle (setiferous)
sexagen- *base* sixty (sexagenarian)
sexages- *base* sixty (sexagesimal)
sexcent- *base* six hundred (sexcentenary)
sexi- *comb* six (sexipolar)
sext- *comb* sixth (sextant)
sexti- *comb* six (sextisection)
she- *comb* female (she-bear)
-ship **1.** *suf* quality; condition; state
  of (friendship); **2.** rank; office;
  status (kingship); **3.** ability; skill
  (leadership); **4.** collective: all

individuals of a specified class (readership)

-siagon- *base* jawbone (siagonology)

sial-[1] *base* saliva (sialorrhea)

sial-[2] *base* bluebird (Sialia)

-sibil- *base* hiss; whistle (sibilant)

sica- *base* knife; dagger (sicarian)

-sicc- *base* dry (desiccate)

Siculo- *comb* Sicilian (Siculo-Punic)

-sid- *base* inhere; sit in (insident)

-sidere *comb* star (hagiosidere)

sidero-[1] *comb* iron (siderolite)

sidero-[2] *comb* star (siderostat)

siderodromo- *comb* railroad (siderodromophobia)

-sigil- *base* seal; signet (sigillation)

siliceo-, silici-, silico- *comb* [chemistry] silica: containing or relating to (siliceo-calcareous, siliciferous, silico-alkaline)

silig- *base* winter wheat (siliginous)

siliqu- *base* pod (siliquiferous)

-silur- *base* catfish (silurid)

Siluro- *comb* Silurian (Siluro-Cambrian)

silvi- *comb* tree; forest (silviculture)

sim- *base* ape; chimp (simian)

-simil- *base* like; resembling (dissimilarity)

-simo- *base* snub-nosed (simosaurus)

-simul- 1. *base* at the same time (simultaneous); 2. feign; pretend (simulate)

sinap- *base* mustard (sinapism)

sindon- *base* shroud (sindonology)

singult- *base* hiccup; sob (singultous, singultient)

sinistro- *comb* left: of, at, using (sinistro-cerebral)

sino- *comb* sinus (sinorespiratory)

Sino- *comb* Chinese: people/language (Sinology)

-sinu- *base* bending; winding (insinuate)

sinuato-, sinuoso- *comb* wavy; uneven (sinuato-dentate, simuoso-lobate)

-sion *see* -ion

siphoni-, siphono- *comb* tube; pipe (siphoniform, siphonostele)

-sis *suf* action; condition (stasis)

-siti- *base* thirst (insitiency)

-sitia, sitio-, sito- *comb* food; eating; appetite (asitia, sitiophobia, sitology)

sitt- *base* nuthatch (sittine)

situ- *base* located; inherent (situation)

-size, -sized *comb* having a specified size (life-size, small-sized)

skeleto- *comb* skeleton (skeletotrophic)

-skeuo- *base* vessel; utensil (skeuomorphic)

skia- *comb* shadow (skiascopy). *See* scia-

Slavo- *comb* Slav (Slavophile)

smaragd- *base* emerald (smaragdine)

socer- *base* father-in-law (soceraphobia)

socio- *comb* society; social (sociobiological)

sodio- *comb* sodium (sodio-hydric)

-soever *comb* any __ of those possible (whosoever)

sol- *comb* sun (solarium)

solen-, soleno- *base* [zoology] channel; pipe (solenite, solenoglypha)

soli- *comb* alone (solitude)

-solu-, -solv- *base* melt; dissolve (soluble, solvant)

-soma *comb* [zoology] names of genera (Schistosoma)

somato- *comb* body (somatology)

-some[1] *comb* body (chromosome)

-some[2] *suf* like; tending to be (tiresome)

-some³ *suf* number: in a specified (threesome)

somni- *comb* sleep (somniferous)

son-, soni-, sono-, sonoro- *comb* sound (sonancy, soniferous, sonogram, sonoro-sibilant)

-sophy *comb* knowledge; thought (philosophy)

-sopor- *base* sleep (soporific)

-sor- *base* heap (sorotrochous)

-sorb-¹ *base* soak up (absorbent)

-sorb-² *base* mountain ash (sorbic)

-sord- *base* dirt; filth (insordescent)

soric- *base* shrew (soricine)

-soror- *base* sister (sorority)

-sote *comb* preserver (creosote)

-soter- *base* salvation (soteriology)

spad- *base* brown (spadiceous)

spadici- *comb* succulent spike (spadicifloral)

spano- *comb* scarce (spanopnea)

sparasso-, sparax- *comb* laceration; tearing (sparassodont, sparaxis)

sparg- *base* sprinkle; scatter (spargefication)

spasmo- *comb* spasm; contraction (spasmolysis)

spathi- *base* spatula; broad blade (spathiform)

spatilo- *comb* excrement (spatilomancy)

spatul- *base* shoulder (spatulamancy)

spatuli- *comb* spatula (spatuliform)

-spec(t)-, -spic- *base* look; see (spectator, conspicuous)

-specific *comb* applied or limited to the particular item named (culture-specific)

specio- *comb* specific (speciographic)

spectr- *base* ghost (spectral)

spectro- 1. *comb* radiant energy as exhibited in a spectrum (spectrogram); 2. of/by a spectroscope (spectro-heliogram); 3. mirror (spectrophobia)

speleo-, spelunc- *base* cave (speleologist, speluncar)

sper- *base* hope (sperable)

-sperg-, -spers- *base* sprinkle (insperge, inspersion)

-sperm, sperma-, -spermal, spermatio-, spermato, spermi-, -spermic, spermo-, -spermous *comb* seed; germ; beginning (gymnosperm, spermaphore, gymnospermal, spermatiogenous, spermatocyte, spermiducal, endospermic, spermogonium, monospermous)

sphacel- *base* gangrene (sphaceloderma)

-sphagn- *base* moss (sphagnologist)

-sphair- *base* tennis (sphairistic)

-sphal- *base* error (sphalma)

-sphec- *base* wasp; hornet (sphecoid)

sphenisc- *base* penguin (spheniscan)

spheno- 1. *comb* wedge-shaped (sphenogram); 2. sphenoid bone (sphenoccipital)

-sphere, spherico-, sphero- *comb* sphere (stratosphere, sphericocylindrical, spherocyte). *Also* sphaero- (sphaeroblast)

-sphingo- *base* bound tightly (sphingometer)

-sphrag- *base* seal; signet (sphragistic)

sphygmo- *comb* pulse (sphygmograph)

sphyr- *base* hammer (sphyrelaton)

sphyraen- *base* barracuda (sphyraenoid)

sphyrn- *base* shark (Sphyrna)

-spici- *base* ear of corn (spiciferous)

spicul-, spiculi-, spiculo- *comb* spiky; pointed (spicular, spiculiferous, spiculofibrous)

-spil- *base* spot; speck (spilosite)

spini-, spino-, spinoso-, spinuloso-
comb spine (spini-acute, spino-
cerebellar, spinoso-dentate,
spinuloso-serrate)

-spinthar- *base* spark
(spinthariscope)

spiri- *comb* coil; spiral (spiriform)

spiro-[1] *comb* respiration; breath
(spirograph)

spiro-[2] *comb* spiral; coil (spirochete)

-spiss- *base* thick; dense (inspissa-
tion)

-splachn- *base* moss (splachnoid)

splanchno- *comb* viscera (splanch-
nology)

splenico-, splen(o)- *comb* spleen
(splenico-phrenic, splenocele)

spodo- *base* ashes (spodogenous)

spondylo- *comb* vertebra (spondylitis)

spongi-, spongio-, spongo- *comb*
sponge-like (spongiculture, spon-
giocyte, spongolith)

spor- *base* scatter (sporadic)

-spore, spori-, sporo-, -sporous
1. *comb* spore; seed (teliospore,
sporiferous, sporocarp); 2. specific
number/kind of spores (mono-
sporous)

-spum- *base* foam; froth (spumes-
cence)

-spurc- *base* dirty; foul (spurcity)

-squal- *base* shark (squaloid)

squamato-, squamo-, squamoso-,
squaroso- *comb* squama; scalelike
(squamato-granulous, squamo-
cellular, squamoso-dentated,
squaroso-laciniate)

stabil- *base* lasting; fixed (stability)

-stact- *base* drop (stactometer)

-stagm- *base* drop (stagmoid)

-stagn- *base* pool (stagnicolous)

-stal- *base* motion; contraction
(peristalsis)

-stalac(ti)-, -stalag- *base* dropping;
dripping (stalactite, stalagmite)

stamini- *comb* stamen (staminifer-
ous)

-stann- *base* tin (stanniferous)

-stap- *base* stirrup; stapes (stape-
dectomy)

staphylo- 1. *comb* uvula; grapelike
(staphylorrhaphy); 2. staphylococcus (staphylodermatitis)

stasi-, -stasis *comb* standing still;
balance; arrest; halt (stasimetry,
phlebostasis)

-stat *comb* scientific instrument
(thermostat)

stato- *comb* stationary; stabilized
(statocyst)

stauro- *comb* cross (staurophobia)

-stead *comb* place (homestead)

stearo-, steato- *comb* fatty substance (stearoglucose, steatopygia)

-stegano- *base* covered (stegano-
podous)

stegno- *comb* constriction (thecostegnosis)

stego- *comb* covered; closed (stego-
saur)

-stell- *base* star (interstellar)

stellio- *base* lizard (stellion)

-stema- *base* filament (stemapod)

sten(o)- *comb* small; thin; narrow;
abbreviated (stenographer)

step- *comb* relationship not by
blood (stepfather)

-ster 1. *suf* person who is/does/
creates __ (punster); 2. person associated with __ (gangster)

sterco- *comb* dung; feces (stercoraceous)

stereo- *comb* three-dimensional;
solid (stereoscope)

-sterigm- *base* prop; support
(sterigmatic)

stern- *base* tern (sternine)

sterno- *comb* sternum and; breast-bone (sternoclavicular)

-sternut- *base* sneeze (sternutation)

-sterquil- *base* dunghill (sterquilinious)

-stert- *base* snore (stertorous)

stetho- *comb* chest; breast (stethoscope)

-sthenia, sthen(o)- *comb* strength; force; power (hypersthenia, hyposthenuria)

stibio- *comb* [chemistry] black antimony (stibiotrimethyl)

stibo- *comb* footprint (stibogram)

-stichia, sticho-, -stichous *comb* row; line; verse (tristichia, stichometry, tristichous)

-stict- *base* spotted (laparostict)

-stig- *base* a point; to punctuate; to goad; stimulate (instigate)

-stigm- *base* mark; point; dot; puncture; tattoo (stigmatized)

stigno- *comb* writing (stignomancy)

-still- *base* drop (stillatitious)

-stilpno- *base* glittering (stilpnomelane)

-stip-¹ *base* stalk; support (stipitate)

-stip-² *base* press together; pack (constipation)

-stiri- *base* icicle (stiriated)

-stirp- *base* stem; stock (exstirpate)

-stoch- *base* guess (stochastic)

-stoicheio- *base* element (stoicheiometry)

stomato-, -stome, -stomous *comb* [medicine/botany] mouth (stomatalgia, cyclostome, megastomous)

-stomy *comb* surgical opening into __ (colostomy)

stone- *comb* very; completely (stone-broke)

-storgy *base* affection (philostorgy)

-stori- *base* tales; legends (storiology)

-strab-, strabism- *base* squinting (strabotomy, strabismometer)

-stragul- *base* covering (stragulum)

-strain *comb* restrict; bind (constrain)

-stramin- *base* straw (stramineous)

-strat- *base* a general; an army (strategic)

strati-, strato- *comb* layer; stratum (stratification, stratosphere)

-stren- *base* difficult (strenuous)

strep-, strepi- *base* noisy (obstreperous, strepitous)

strepho-, strepsi-, strepto- *comb* turned; twisted (strephosymbolia, strepsipterous, streptococcal)

-stress *suf* female (seamstress)

stria-, striato-, strio- *comb* furrow; groove (striaform, striatocrenulate, striomuscular)

-strict *comb* tightly drawn; limited (restriction)

-strid-, stridul- *base* creak; harsh noise (strident, stridulation)

-strig- *base* furrow; channel (strigated)

strigi- *base* owl (strigiform)

-string- *base* constricted (astringent)

-strob- *base* twisting; spinning (strobilation)

strobil- *base* pine cone (strobiliform)

-strom- *base* fibrous structure (stromatiform)

-stromb- *base* spiral; twisted (strombiform)

stromboli- *base* top (stromboliform)

strongyl- *base* round (strongylate)

-stroph- *base* turn; twist (strophiole)

struct- *comb* arrange; put together (constructive)

strum-, strumi- *base* goiter; swollen gland (strumitis, strumiferous)

-struma- *base* tumor (strumectomy)

-struthio- *base* ostrich (struthious)

-stult- *base* foolish (stultiloquy)

-stup- *base* senseless (stupefaction)

stupr- *base* fornicate; rape (stuprate)

-sturim- *base* sturgeon (sturionic)

-sturn- *base* starling; swallow (sturnine)

styg- *base* hellish (Stygian)

styl- *base* pen (styliform)

stylo-[1] 1. *comb* pointed; sharp (stylograph); 2. styloid: bony process (stylohyoid)

stylo-[2] *comb* column; pillar (stylolite)

-stypt- *base* astringent (stypticity)

-suad-, -suas- *base* urge (dissuade, persuasion)

suav- *base* sweet (suaveolent)

sub- 1. *pre* under; below (submarine); 2. lower in rank; inferior to (subaltern); 3. to a lesser degree; slightly (subtropical); 4. division (sublet); 5. [chemistry] less than the normal amount of __ ; basic (subchloride); 6. [mathematics] ratio inverse to a given ratio (subduplicate). NOTE: sub- can change to: su- (suspect); suc- (succeed); suf-(suffocate); sug- (suggest); sum- (summon); sup- (support); sur- (surrogate); sus- (suspend)

subagit- *base* sexual intercourse (subagitation)

-suber- *base* cork (suberose)

subero- *comb* suberic acid (suberopyroxylic)

subig- *base* knead (subigate)

subit- *base* sudden; hasty (subitaneous)

subsesqui- *pre* [chemistry] elements combined in the proportion of 2 to 3 (subsesquiacetate)

subter- *pre* below; under; less than; secretly (subterfuge)

-subul- *base* awl (subuliform)

suc- *base* juice (succulent)

-succino- *comb* amber (succino-sulphuric)

sucr- *base* sugar (sucrose)

sud-, sudori- *comb* sweat; perspiration (sudatory, sudorific)

-suet- *base* custom (conseutude)

suffrag- *base* voting (suffragette)

-suge *base* suck (potisuge)

sui- *base* oneself (suicide)

sui-, suid- *base* pig; boar (suilline, suidian)

sulc- *base* groove (sulcus)

sulcato- *comb* furrowed; grooved; cleft (sulcato-areolate)

sulfato- *comb* sulfate (sulfatidates). *Also* sulphato- (sulphato-acetic)

sulfo- *comb* sulfur; sulfonate sulfonic acid (sulfocyanogen). *Also* sulpho- (sulpho-indigotic)

sulfureo *comb* sulfureous (sulfureonitrous)

super- 1. *pre* over; above; on top (superstructure); 2. higher in rank/position; superior to (superintendent); 3. greater in quality/amount/degree; surpassing (superabundance); 4. greater or better (supermarket); 5. greater than normal (supersaturate); 6. extra; additional (supertax); 7. to a secondary degree (superparasite); 8. [chemistry] large amount of __ (superphosphate)

supero- *comb* [anatomy] on the upper side (supero-dorsal)

supin- *base* lying down (supine)

supra- *pre* above; over; beyond (supraliminal)

sur- *pre* over; upon; above; beyond (surface)

sura- *base* calf of the leg (sural)

surcul- *base* grafting; twig (surculose)

-surd- *base* deaf (surdity)

-surg- *base* rise (resurgent)

-susurr- *base* whisper; murmur (in-
susurration)

-sutil- *base* stitch; sew (inconsutile)

-syc- *base* fig (sycoma)

-sychno- *base* many (sychnocar-
pous)

symmetr- *base* symmetry (asym-
mertrical)

symphyo- *comb* growing together
(symphyogenesis)

syn- *pre* with; together; at the same
time; by means of (synagogue).
NOTE: syn- can change to: sy-
(syzygy); syl- (syllogism); sym-
(symbiosis); sys- (system)

synchro- *comb* synchronized (syn-
chromesh)

syndesmo- *comb* ligament; binding
together (syndesmoplasty)

-synœc- *base* community (synœcol-
ogy)

syphili-, syphilo- *comb* siphylis
(syphilitic, syphilophobia)

-syr- *base* reed; pipe; tube (syringe)

syringo- *comb* tube-shaped cavity
(syringocarcinoma)

Syro- *comb* Syrian and (Syro-Ara-
bian)

-syrt- *base* quicksand (syrtic)

T

-tab- *base* emaciated; wasted away
(tabescent)

taban- *base* horsefly (tabanid)

tabell- *base* tablet; ballot (tabellary)

tacho- *comb* speed (tachometer)

tachy- *comb* rapid; swift; fast
(tachycardia)

tacit- *base* quiet (taciturn)

-tact- *base* touch (contact)

-tactic, -tactous *comb* order; arrangement (heterotactous, syntac-
tic)

taeni-, taenio- *comb* ribbon or
band; tapeworm (taeniafuge, tae-
niosomous). *Also* teni- (teniacide)

-tain *comb* hold (maintain). *See*
-ten-

tali-, talo- *comb* ankle (taligrade,
talocalcaneal)

talpi- *base* mole (talpicide)

-tang- *base* touch (intangible)

tantalo- *base* tease (tantalize)

-taph, tapho-, taphro- *comb* tomb;
pit (cenotaph, taphophobia,
taphrenchyma)

tapin- *base* contagious (tapinophobia)

-tapino- *base* low (tapinocephalic)

-tard- *base* slow; delay (retardation)

tarso- 1. *comb* instep (tarso-meta-
tarsus); 2. eyelid cartilage (tarsoplasty)

tartr(o)- *comb* tartar; tartaric acid
(tartromethylates)

-taseo-, -tasi- *base* tension
(taseometer, tasimetric)

tauri-, tauro- 1. *comb* of/like a bull
(tauricide, tauromachy);
2. [chemistry] taurine (tauro-
cholate)

taurotrag- *base* eland (taurotragus)

tauto- *comb* the same; identical
(tautology)

tax- *base* yew (taxaceous)

taxi-, -taxia, -taxis, taxo-, -taxy *comb* arrangement; order (taxidermy, heterotaxia, parataxis, taxonomy, homotaxy)

techno-, -techny 1. *comb* art; science; skill (technocracy); 2. technical; technological (technochemistry, pyrotechny)

tecno- *comb* child (tecnonymy)

-tect- *base* roof; cover (tectiform)

-teen *suf* ten and numbers: cardinal (sixteen)

teg-, tegu- *base* cover (tegmental, tegument)

tegul- *base* tile (tegular)

-teicho- *base* wall (teichopsia)

tek- *base* child (ateknia)

tel- *base* dart (teliferous)

tele- 1. *comb* at a distance; far (telegraph); 2. television (telecast)

teleo-, telo- *comb* end; purpose; final stage (teleology, telophase)

tellur- *base* earth (intratelluric)

-telmat- *base* a bog (telamatology)

-temerat- *base* violate (intemerate)

temno- *comb* cut (temnospondylous)

-temp- *base* regulate; mix (temperament)

-tempor- *base* time (contemporary)

temporo- *comb* temple of the head (temporo-maxillary)

-temul- *base* drunkenness (temulency)

-ten- *base* hold (tenacious). *See* -tain

tend- *base* stretch (distend)

-tene *comb* [biology] ribbon-shaped (pachytene)

-tenebr- *base* darkness (tenebrosity)

-teni- *base* tapeworm; ribbon-like (teniacide). *Also* taeni(i)- (taeniiphobia)

teno-, tenonto- *comb* tendon (tenotomy, tenontodynia)

tensio- *comb* stretch; strain (tensiometer)

tentaculi- *comb* tentacle (tentaculiform)

tentig- *base* bore; penetrate (tentiginous)

tenui- *comb* slender; thin; narrow (tenuifolious)

tephro- 1. *comb* ashes (tephromancy); 2. gray (tephroite)

ter- *comb* thrice (tercentennial)

tera- *comb* one trillion (terahertz)

terato- *comb* monster; monstrosity (teratology)

terebinth- *base* turpentine (terebinthinate)

terebr- *base* bore; penetrate (terebration)

tered- *base* worm (teredines)

tereti-, tereto- *comb* rounded (tereticaudate, teretosetaceous)

tergi-, tergo- *comb* the back (tergiversation, tergolateral)

-termin- *base* end; limit (termination)

termit- *base* termite (termitophagous)

-tern- *base* three; triple (ternion)

-terr- *base* earth (territorial)

-tert- *base* third (tertiary)

tessera- *comb* four (tesseraglot)

tesseradeca- *comb* fourteen (tesseradecasyllabon)

testac- *base* reddish-brown (testaceous)

testaceo- *comb* shell (testaceology)

testud- *base* turtle (testudinal)

tetano- *comb* tetanus stiff (tetanospasmin)

tetarto- *comb* one fourth (tetartohedral)

tetra- *comb* four (tetragamy)

tetracyclo- *comb* with four circles; with four atomic rings (tetracycline) tetradeca- *comb* fourteen (tetradecapod). *Also* tetrakaideca- (tetrakaidecahedron)

tetrakis- *comb* four times (tetrakisdodecahedron)

tetraon- *base* grouse; ptarmigan (tetraonid)

tetrazo- [chemistry] 1. *comb* compound with 4 atoms of nitrogen (tetrazone); 2. presence of four azo groups (tetrazolyl)

teuth- *base* cuttlefish; squid (teuthologist)

teuto- *comb* German (teutophobia)

tex- *base* weave (textile)

-th 1. *suf* act of (stealth); 2. state of being/having; quality of being/having (wealth)

-th *suf* numbers: ordinal (sixteenth)

thalamo- *comb* thalamus (thalamocortical)

thalasso-, thalatto- *comb* sea; marine (thalassocracy, thalattology)

thalero- *comb* blooming; fresh (thalerophagous)

thall-, thallas- *base* green (thallium, thallasine)

thallo- *comb* thallium (thallophyte)

thamn- *base* shrub (thamnium)

thanato- *comb* death (thanatology)

thaumato- *comb* wonder; miracle (thaumatology)

theatro- *comb* theater (theatromania)

-theca, theci-, theco- *comb* sheath; container; case; cover (sarcotheca, theciform, thecostegnosis)

-thei- *base* tea (theiform)

thelo- *comb* nipple (perithelium)

thely- *comb* female (thelytoky)

theo- *comb* god (theocentric)

-thera- *base* catcher; trap (oenothera)

theraphos- *base* tarantula (theraphosid)

-there, therio-, thero- 1. *comb* extinct mammalian form (megathere); 2. beast (theriomorphic, theropod)

-therm, thermo-, -thermy *comb* heat; hot (isotherm, thermodynamics, diathermy)

-thesis, -thetic *comb* set; put; place (hypothesis, antithetic)

-thesmo- *base* law (thesmothete)

thesp- *base* actor (thespian)

thia-, thio- *comb* sulfur (thiabendazole, thioaldehyde)

thigmo- *comb* touch (thigmotropism)

thino- *base* beach; seashore (thinolite)

thio- *comb* [chemistry] sulfur (thiobacillus)

-thlips- *base* pressure (thlipsencephalus)

thneto- *comb* mortal (thnetopsychism)

thoracico-, thoraco- 1. *comb* thorax and (thoracico-abdominal); 2. thorax; chest (thoracoplasty)

thras- *base* brag; boast (thrasonical)

thremm- *base* breed; propagate (thremmatology)

thren- *base* lamentation (threnody)

thrept- *base* nourish; nurse (threpterophilia)

thripto- *base* mortal (thriptophobia)

-thrix- *base* hair (streptothrix)

-throated *comb* throat: specific kind (ruby-throated)

thrombo- *comb* blood clot (thrombo-phlebitis)

thumo- *comb* soul (thumomancy)

-thur- *base* incense (thurifer)

-thy- *base* offering; sacrifice (idolothyus)

-thylac- *base* pouch (thylacine)

-thymia[1] *comb* mental disorder (dysthymia)

-thymia-[2] *base* perfume; incense (thymiatechny)

thymo- 1. *comb* thymus (thymokinetic); 2. mind; soul; mood; emotions (thymogenic)

-thyrea, thyreo-, thyro- *comb* thyroid (hypothyrea, thyreotomy, thyromegaly)

thyrsi-, thyrso- *comb* stalk; stem; inflorescence (thyrsiflorous, thyrsocephalic)

-thysan- *base* fringe; tassel (thysanopter)

tibio- *comb* tibia and (tibiotarsal)

-tic *See* -ic

ticho- *base* wall (tichorhine)

-tight *comb* impervious to (watertight)

tigr- *base* tiger (tigrine)

tilia- *comb* lime; linden (tiliaceous)

-till- *base* to pluck (peotillomania)

-tim- *base* fear; dread (timorous)

timbro- *comb* postage stamp (timbrophilic)

-timo- *base* honor (timocracy)

timor- *base* fear (timorous)

-tinct-, -ting- *base* stain; color (intinction, tingible)

tinea- *base* moth; bookworm (tineid)

tinn-, tintinn- *base* jingling; ringing; bell (tinnitus, tintinnabular)

-tion, -tious 1. *suf* act of (correction); 2. state of being (elation, ambitious); 3. thing that is (creation)

titano-[1] *comb* titan (titanosaur)

titano-[2] *comb* titanium (titanocyanide)

titillo- *base* scratch; tickle (titillation)

-titub- *base* stagger (titubation)

-tmesis *comb* cutting (neurotmesis)

-tocia, toco- *comb* childbirth; labor (dystocia, tocolytic). *Also* toko- (tokogony)

-toky *comb* childbearing (thelytoky)

-tolypeut- *base* armadillo (tolypeutine)

-tome *comb* [medicine] cutting instrument (osteotome)

tomo-, -tomous, -tomy *comb* cutting; dividing; surgery (tomography, dichotomous, appendectomy)

-ton *comb* town (Washington)

-tonia 1. *comb* tone; muscle tension (isotonia); 2. personality disorder (catatonia)

-tonic 1. *comb* notes in a musical scale (pentatonic); 2. musical intervals (diatonic); 3. phonetic units of stress (pretonic); 4. muscle contraction (myatonic); 5. pathological spasms (vagatonic); 6. restorative substance (hematonic); 7. solution (isotonic)

-tonitru- *base* thunder (tonitrual)

tono- *comb* tension; pressure (tonometer)

tonsillo- *comb* tonsil (tonsillotomy)

tonsor- *base* shave; barber (tonsorial)

-toothed *comb* specific number/kind of teeth (big-toothed)

topo-, -topy *comb* place; topical (topology, somatotopy)

toreut- *base* embossing metal or ivory (toreutics)

torp- *base* numbness (torporific)

-tors-, -tort- *base* twist (torsion, distorted)

-tory *see* -ory

toti- *comb* whole entire (totipalmate)

tox-, toxi-, toxico-, toxo-[1] *comb* poison; infection (toxemia, toxituberculide, toxicogenic, toxoplasma) toxo-² *comb* archery (toxophily)

-trab- *base* beam (trabeation)

trachelo- *comb* neck (trachelodynia)

tracheo- 1. *comb* windpipe (tracheotomy); 2. trachea and (tracheobronchial)

trachy- *comb* rough (trachyspermous)

-tract- *base* draw; pull (detract)

tragelaph- *base* kudu (tragelaphus)

trago- *comb* goat (tragopogon)

trans- 1. *pre* across; over; on the other side; to the other side (transatlantic); 2. change thoroughly (transliterate); 3. transcending; above and beyond (trans-sonic)

transverso- *comb* transverse; crosswise (transversomedial)

trapezi- *base* trapezoid (trapezoid)

traumato- *comb* wound; injury (traumatopnea)

trecent- *comb* three hundred (trecentene)

tredecim- *base* thirteen (tredecimal)

tremo- *base* shaking; tremble (tremogram)

-trepid- *base* scared; agitated (intrepid)

-tresia *comb* perforation (proctotresia)

-tress *suf* feminine ending (actress)

tri- 1. *comb* three; three parts (triplane); 2. three times; into three (trisect); 3. every three; every third (triannual); 4. [chemistry] having three atoms; having three equivalents of; having three groups (tribasic)

triaconta- *comb* thirty (triacontahedral)

triakis- *comb* three (triakisoctahedron)

triangulato- *comb* triangulate (triangulato-subovate)

tribo- *comb* friction (tribology)

-trice *suf* feminine ending (genetrice). NOTE: -trix is now preferred

triceni- *base* thirty (tricenary)

-trich, -tricha *comb* [zoology] creature with hairlike structures (hypotrich, Gastrotricha)

trichec- *base* manatee (trichechine)

tricho- *comb* hair (trichogenous)

trient- *base* third (triental)

triethyl- *comb* [chemistry] three ethyl groups (triethylamine)

triges- *base* thirty (trigesimal)

trigint- *base* thirty (trigintal)

trigono- *comb* three-cornered; triangular (trigonocephalic)

tring- *base* sandpiper (tringoid)

trinitro- *comb* [chemistry] three atoms of nitrogen (trinitroglycerin)

-trione *comb* [chemistry] three ketone groups (Indantrione)

trioxy- *comb* having 3 atoms of oxygen (trioxynaphthalene)

triplicato- *comb* triplicate (triplicato-pinnate)

-triplo- *base* threefold; triple (triploblastic)

-tripsy *comb* crushing; friction (neurotripsy)

tripud- *base* dance; exult (tripudiate)

triquadr- *base* three-fourths (triquadrantal)

triskaideka- *comb* thirteen (triskaidekaphobia)

trist- *base* grief; sadness (tristful)

trit- *base* friction; threshing (triturate)

-tritic- *base* wheat (triticeous)

trito- *comb* third (tritocere)

-trix *suf* female agent (executrix)

troch-, trochi-, trocho- *comb* wheel; pulley rounded (trochlear, trochiferous, trochocardia)

-trocha *comb* [zoology] having a band (cephalotrocha)

trochalo- *comb* rolling; rotary (trochalopod)

trochil- *base* hummingbird (trochiline)

-trocto- *base* trout (troctolite)

-trog- *base* to gnaw (trogonine)

-troglo- *base* hole; cave (troglodyte)

troglodyt- *base* wren (troglodytine)

-tromo- *base* earth tremor (tromometry)

-tron *comb* names of devices used in electronic or subatomic experiments (cyclotron)

-trope, -tropic, -tropism, tropo-, -tropous, -tropy *comb* responding to a specific stimulus; turning; changing (heliotrope, phototropic, thermotropism, trophophilous, phototropous, entropy)

-troph, -trophic, tropho-, -trophy *comb* nutrition; food; nourishment (heterotroph, autotrophic, trophoplasm, atrophy)

trucid- *base* kill; slaughter (trucidation)

-trude, -trus- *base* push; thrust (protrude, intrusion)

-trutt- *base* trout (truttaceous)

trypano- 1. *comb* parasite; borer (trypanosome); 2. injection (trypanophobia)

trypet- *base* fruitfly (Trypetidae)

tuberculo- 1. *comb* tuberculous (tubercular); 2. tubercle bacillus (tuberculoid); 3. tuberculosis (tuberculocidin)

tubi-, tubo- *comb* tube (tubiflorous, tubotorsion)

tubuli-, tubulo- *comb* tubule; small tube (tubulidentate, tubulocyst)

-tude *suf* state of being quality of being (solitude)

-tum- *base* swelling (tumescent)

tupai- *base* shrew (tupaiid)

-turb- *base* confuse; disturb (perturbation)

-turbar- *base* peat bog (turbarian)

turbinato- *comb* top-shaped (turbinato-cylindrical)

turbo- *comb* consisting of or driven by a turbine (turbogenerator)

turd- *base* thrush; robin; bluebird (turdine)

-ture *comb* action (caricature)

-turg- *base* swelling (turgescent)

Turko- *comb* Turkey (Turko-Russian). *Also* Turco- (Turcophobe)

-turp- *base* pollute; disgrace (turpitude)

-turri- *base* tower (turriferous)

turtura- *base* turtle (turturring)

tus- *base* strike; bruise (contusion)

-tuss- *base* cough (antitussive)

twi- *comb* double (twi-arched)

-ty[1] *suf* quality of; condition of (novelty)

-ty[2] *suf* times ten; tens (sixty)

-tych-, tycho- *comb* chance; occasional accident (tychastics, tychopotamic). *Also* tich- (dystichiphobia)

-tyl-, tylo- *comb* knot; knob; callus; cushion (tylosis, tylopod)

tympano- *comb* drum tympanum (tympanoplasty)

-type 1. *comb* type; representative form; example (prototype); 2. stamp; printing type; print (monotype)

typhlo- 1. *comb* cecum; intestinal pouch (typhlostomy); 2. blindness (typhlosis)

typho- *comb* typhus; typhoid (typhogenic)

typo- *comb* type (typography)

tyro- *base* cheese (tyroleucin)

tyto- *base* owl (Tytonidae)

U

-ubi- *base* place; position; location (ubiquitous)

udo- *comb* wet; damp (udometer)

Ugro- *comb* Ugrian (Ugro-Slavonic)

-ula *suf* diminutive (fibula)

-ular *suf* having the form or character of (circular)

-ule *suf* diminutive (pustule)

-ulent *suf* full of (virulent)

-ulig- *base* full of moisture (uliginous)

ulm- *base* elm (ulmaceous)

ulno- *comb* ulna and (ulnoradial)

ulo-[1] *comb* scar (ulodermatitis)

ulo-[2] *comb* gums (uloglossitis)

ulo-[3] *comb* curly; crisp (ulotrichous)

-ulose *suf* characterized by; marked by (granulose)

-ulous *suf* characterized by; full of; tending to (populous)

ultim-, ultimo- *base* final; last (ultimatum, ultimogeniture)

ultra- 1. *pre* on the further side of; beyond (ultraviolet); 2. to an extreme degree; excessive (ultramodern); 3. beyond the range of (ultramicroscopic)

ultro- *comb* voluntary; spontaneous (ultroneous)

ulul-[1] *base* wail; howl (ululation)

ulul-[2] *base* owl (ululant)

-ulum *suf* diminutive (speculum)

-ulus *suf* diminutive (homunculus)

umbell-, umbelli- *base* sunshade; parasol (umbellated, umbellifer)

umbilici- *base* navel (umbiliciform)

umbo- *base* knob; nipple (umbonulate)

-umbr- *base* shadow (umbriphilous)

umbraculi- *comb* sunshade (umbraculiferous)

umbrelli- *base* umbrella (umbrelliform)

Umbro- *comb* Umbrian (Umbro-Etruscan)

un- 1. *pre* not; opposite of; lack of (unhappy); 2. back; reversal (unlock)

unci- *comb* hook (unciform)

-unct- *base* ointment; oil (unctuous)

-unda- *base* wave (exundant)

undec- *comb* eleven (undecagon)

under- 1. *pre* lower place: in/on/to; beneath; below (undershirt); 2. inferior rank/position; subordinate (undergraduate); 3. amount below standard; inadequate (underdevelop)

undeviginti- *comb* nineteen (undevigintiangular)

-undul- *base* wave (undulations)

ungu- *base* ointment; grease (unguent)

-ungui, -ungul- *base* claw; nail (unguiform, exungulate)

uni- *comb* having one only (unicellular)

-uous *suf* of the nature of; consisting of (strenuous)

-ura- *base* tail (gastruran)

uranisco- *comb* hard palate (uraniscoplasty)

urano- 1. *comb* hard palate (uranoschisis); 2. the heavens (uranography)

uranoso- *comb* [chemistry] containing uranium (uranosopotassic)

-urb- *base* city (suburban)

urcei-, urceo- *base* urn; pitcher (urceiform, urceolate)

-**ure** 1. *suf* act/result of being (expo-sure); 2. agent of; instrument of; scope of (legislature); 3. state of being (composure)

urea-, ureo- *comb* urine; urea (ure-apoiesis, ureometer)

uredo- *base* blight; fungus (uredo-spore)

uretero- *comb* urethra and (ureter-ostomy)

urethro- *comb* ureter and (urethro-scopy)

-**uretic** *comb* urine (diuretic)

-**urgy** *comb* working of; fabricating (zymurgy)

uri-, urico- *base* uric acid (uridro-sis, uricometer)

-**uria** *comb* diseased condition of urine (glycosuria)

-**urient** *suf* desiring (parturient)

urini-, urino- *comb* urinary tract; urine (uriniparous, urinometer)

uro-[1] *comb* tail (uropod)

uro-[2] *comb* urine (urolith)

-**urs-** *base* bear (ursine)

-**urtic-** *base* nettle (urticaceous)

-**ury-** *base* urination (strangury)

-**ust-** *base* burn (ustulation)

utero- *comb* uterus and (uterovagi-nal)

-**util-** *base* useful (inutile)

utrei-, utri-[1] *comb* leather bottle (utreiform, utriform)

utri-[2]**, utric-** *base* sac; baglike part (utriform, utricular)

-**uvi-, -uvu-** *base* grape (uviform, uvula)

uvulo- *comb* uvula (uvulectomy)

uxori- *base* wife (uxoricide)

V

-**vac-, -vacu-** *base* empty; free (va-cancy, vacuity)

vacci- *comb* cow (vaccimulgence)

vaccin- *base* blueberry (vaccinium)

vaccino- *comb* vaccine (vaccinopho-bia)

-**vacil-** *base* sway (vacillation)

-**vad-, -vas-** *base* rush; go (invade, invasion)

-**vag-, -vagr-** *base* wander (vagary, vagrant)

vagini-, vagino- *comb* sheath; vagina and (vaginipennous, vaginotomy)

vago- *comb* vagus nerve (vagotropic)

vagu- *base* uncertain (vagueness)

vale- *base* farewell (valediction)

valetud- *base* ill (valetudinary)

-**valent** 1. *comb* having a specified valence (monovalent); 2. specified number of valences (univalent); 3. having antibodies (multivalent)

vall- *base* wall (vallation)

valvi- *comb* valve; opening (valvi-form)

valvulo- *comb* valve, esp. of the heart (valvulotomy)

vapo-, vapori- *comb* emanation; vapor (vapography, vaporimeter)

-**vapul-** *base* beat; flog (vapulatory)

vari- *comb* changed; diverse (invari-able)

varic-, varici-, varico- *base* en-larged vein (varication, varici-form, varicocele)

-**variol-** *base* spotted; speckled (var-ioloid)

vasculo- *comb* blood vessel (vasculitis)

vasi- *comb* vessel; tube (vasifactive)

vaso- 1. *comb* blood vessels (vasoconstrictor); 2. vas deferens (vasectomy); 3. vasomotor (vasoinhibitor)

-vast- *base* destroy (devastation)

vati- *comb* prophet (vaticide)

-vect- *base* carry (provect)

vegeti-, vegeto- *comb* vegetable; plant (vegetivorous, vegeto-alkaline)

vel-, veli- *comb* cover; veil; sail (velated, veliferous)

-velar *comb* soft palate (labiovelar)

velit- *base* skirmish; dispute (velitation)

vell- *base* wish; desire (velleity)

-vellic- *base* pluck; twitch; nip (vellicative)

veloci- *base* speed (velocimeter)

-velut- *base* velvet (velutinous)

-ven- *base* come (convention)

-venat- *base* hunt (venatorial)

vene- *comb* vein (venesection)

-venefic- *base* sorcery; witchcraft (veneficious)

veneno- *comb* poison (veneno-salivary)

-vener-[1] *base* sexual desire; Venus (venereal)

-vener-[2], **-venerat-** *base* worship (venerable, veneration)

veni-, veno-, venoso-, -venous *comb* veins (venipuncture, venostomy, venoso-reticulated, intravenous)

-vent- *base* wind; air (ventilation)

ventri-, ventro- 1. *comb* abdomen; belly (ventricumbent); 2. ventral and (ventrodorsal)

ventricoso- *comb* distended abdomen (ventricoso-globose)

ventriculo- *comb* ventricle (ventriculoatrial)

-ver- *base* truth (verification)

-verber- *base* beat (reverberate)

verbi-, verbo- *comb* word; talk (verbification, verbotomy)

-verd- *base* green (verdant)

verecund- *base* shame; modesty (verecund)

-verge *comb* turn; bend (converge). *See* -vers-

vergi- *comb* rod-like (vergiform). *See* -virgul-

vermi- *comb* worm (vermicide)

vermin- *comb* vermin (verminous)

vermivor- *base* warbler (Vermivora); worm-eating (vermivorous)

-vern- *base* spring (vernal)

verruci- *comb* wart; growth (verruciform)

vers-, -verse, vert- *comb* turn; direct (reversal, transverse, revert). *See* -verge

vertebro- *comb* vertebra (vertebroiliac)

vertig- *base* dizziness (vertiginous)

-verv- *base* sheep (vervecine)

vesica- *comb* blister (vesicatory)

vesico- 1. *comb* bladder (vesicotomy); 2. bladder and (vesicoprostatic)

vesiculi-, vesiculo- *comb* vesicle; bladder-like vessel (vesiculigerous, vesiculo-pustular)

-vesper- *base* evening (vespertilionine)

-vespertil- *base* bat; vampire (vespertilionine)

vespi- *comb* wasp; hornet (vespiform)

vest- *comb* clothing (divest)

vestibulo- *comb* vestibule; small cavity (vestibulocochlear)

-vet- *base* old; experienced (veteran)

vex- *base* bother; irritate (vexatious)

vexill- *comb* flag; banner (vexillology)

vi-, via- *comb* journey; way (multivious, viaduct)

vibro- *comb* vibration; shaking (vibrograph)

vice- *comb* deputy; assistant (vice-chancellor)

-vicesim- *base* twentieth (vicesimal)

vicin- *base* neighborhood; proximity (vicinage)

-vid-, -vis- *base* see (video, invisible)

video- *comb* televised (videoconference)

vidu- *base* widowed; destitute (viduated)

-viges- *base* twenty (vigesimal)

vigil- *base* watchful (vigilant)

viginti- *comb* twenty (vigintiangular)

-vili- *base* worthless; base (viliorate)

vill- *base* shaggy (villose)

villoso- *comb* covered with hairlike material (villoso-scabrous). *See* piloso-

vimin- *base* wicker (vimineous)

-vinc- *base* conquer; bind (invincible)

vini-, vino- *comb* wine; grapes (viniculture, vinometer). *See* viti-

viol- *base* violet (violaceous)

viper- *base* snake (viperous)

vir- *base* green (virescence)

virgul- *base* rod; twig (virgulate)

-virid- *base* green (viridescent)

-viridae *comb* virus family (Picornaviridae)

-viril- *base* masculine (virility)

-virinae *comb* virus subfamily (Spumavirinae)

-virus *comb* virus genus (Flavivirus)

-vis-, -vid- *base* look; see (invisible)

-visaged *comb* having a specific kind of face (round-visaged)

visc-, visco- *base* sticky; thick (viscous, viscometer)

viscero- *comb* viscera (visceroptosis)

visuo- *comb* sight (visuo-auditory)

-vit- *base* alive (vitality). *See* vivi-

vitelli-, vitello- *comb* yolk; germinative contents (vitelligerous, vitellogenous)

viti- *comb* vine (viticulture)

vitia- *base* corrupt (vitiated)

vitreo-, vitri-, vitro- *comb* glass; glassy (vitreodentin, vitriform, vitrotype)

vitric- *base* stepfather (vitricophobia)

vitriolico- *comb* vitriol (vitriolico-muriated)

-vitul- *base* calf (vituline)

vituper- *base* blame; revile (vituperative)

viverr- *base* civet; ferret; mongoose (viverrine)

vivi- *comb* living; alive (viviparous)

voc-, voci-, -voke *comb* say; speak (invocation, vociferous, revoke)

vocif- *base* shout (vociferate)

-vol- *base* wish; will (involuntary)

volta- *comb* [electricity] voltaic (volta-electric)

volucr- *base* bird (volucrine)

volupt- *base* pleasure (voluptuary)

-volut-, -volv- *base* turn (revolution, revolve)

vomic- *base* abscess (vomicose)

-vora, -vore, -vorous *comb* feeding on; eating (Carnivora, herbivore, omnivorous)

-vorag- *base* chasm; whirlpool (voraginous)

vortici- *comb* whirling motion; vortex (vorticiform)

vulcan- *comb* volcanoes (vulcanology)

-vulg- *base* common; the public (divulge)

-vuln- *base* wound (invulnerable)
vulpi- *base* fox (vulpicide)
vult- *base* likeness; visage (invultuation)

vultur- *base* vulture (vulturine)
vulvi-, vulvo- 1. *comb* vulva (vulviform); 2. vulva and (vulvovaginal)

W

-ward *suf* having a specified direction (westward)
-ways *suf* in a specified direction, manner, or position (sideways)
-wheeler *comb* having a specified kind or number of wheels (eighteen-wheeler)
-wide *comb* throughout a given space (worldwide)
-wife *comb* traditional female role (midwife)
-wise 1. *suf* in a specified direction, manner, or position (sidewise); 2. characteristic manner (clockwise); 3. with regard to; in connection with (weatherwise)
with- 1. *comb* away; back (withdraw); 2. against; from (withhold)
-witted *comb* having a specified kind of intelligence (quick-witted)
-woman *comb* female (congresswoman)
-worthy *comb* deserving of; fit for (newsworthy)

X

xantho- *comb* yellow (xanthoderma)
-xen- *base* host (metoxeny)
xenarth- *base* sloth (xenarthral)
xeno- *comb* stranger; foreigner (xenophobia)
xero- *comb* dry (xerophyte)
xest- *base* polish (xesturgy)

xilin- *base* cotton (xilinous)
xiph(i)-, xipho- *comb* swordlike; xiphoid process; swordfish (xiphioid, xyphophyllous)
xylo-, -xylous *comb* wood (xylograph, epixylous)
xyr- *base* sharp-edged; razorlike (xyridaceous)

Y

-y[1] 1. *suf* characterized by; full of (healthy); 2. somewhat; rather (chilly); 3. tending to; inclined (drowsy); 4. suggestive of; somewhat like (wavy)
-y[2] 1. *suf* condition of; quality (jealousy); 2. action of (inquiry)
-y[3] *suf* diminutives; terms of endearment; nicknames (Billy)

-yer *suf* person concerned with (lawyer)

yester- *comb* previous time (yester-year)

-yl *suf* [chemistry] names of radicals (butyl)

-ylene *suf* [chemistry] bivalent hydrocarbon radical; possessing a double bond (piperylene)

ylo- *see* hylo-

yocto- *comb* heptillionth (yoctogram)

yotta- *comb* heptillion (yottameter)

-ysis *suf* action; process (electrolysis)

yttro- *comb* yttrium (yttrocerite)

Z

za- *pre* intensifier (zalambdodont)

zebr- *base* zebra (zebrine)

zelo- *base* zeal; emulation (zelotypia)

zemni- *base* mole rat (zemniphobia)

-zephyr- *base* west wind (zephyranth)

zepto- *comb* hexillionth (zeptovolt)

zetta- *comb* hexillion (zettabyte)

-zeug-, -zeux- *base* yoke (zeuglodont, zeuxite)

zibel- *base* sable (zibeline)

zinco- *comb* zinc as an element in specific double compounds (zincolysis)

-zingiber- *base* ginger (zingiberaceous)

zirconio- *comb* zirconium (zirconioflouride)

-zo- *base* animal (zoanthropy)

-zoa, -zoon *comb* [zoology] name of group (protozoa, protozoon)

-zoic 1. *suf* relating to animal life (celozoic); 2. relating to geologic ages (Mesozoic)

zon-, zoni- *comb* girdle; band; encircling structure (zonesthesia, zonifugal)

zono- *comb* zone (zonochlorite)

zoo- 1. *comb* animal; animal body (zoology); 2. zoology and (zoochemical)

-zooid *comb* distinct animal (Antherozooid)

zoster- *base* girdle; band; belt (zosterops)

zyga-, zygo- *comb* yoke; pair; articulation (zygapophysis, zygodactyl)

zygomatico-, zygomato- *comb* [anatomy] related to the zygoma (zygomatico-auricular, zygomatotemporal)

zym-, zymo- *comb* fermentation; enzymes; yeast (zymurgy, zymophoric)

PART II
Finder
(Reverse Dictionary)

A

aardvark *base* -edent-

abandon *base* relinq-

abbreviated *comb* brachisto-, brachy-, brevi-, micro-, mini-, parvi-, parvo, steno-; *base* -cort-, -curt-; *suf* -cle, -cula, -cule, -culum, -culus, -een, -el, -ella, -en, -et, -ette, -idion, -idium, -ie, -illa, -illo, -isk, -le, -let, -ling, -ock, -ola, -ole, -rel, -ula, -ule, -ulum, -ulus, -y

abdomen *comb* abdomino-, celio-, celo-[1], coelo-, laparo-, ventri-, ventro-; ***distended~:*** ventricoso-

abdominal sac *comb* peritoneo-

abet *base* auxil-, jut-, juv-

abhorrence *comb* miso-, -phobe, -phobia, -phobic; *base* -invid-, -ira(sc)-, odi-

ability *base* -apt-[2], -habil-, -poten-, -qual-; *suf* -bility, -ful, -ship

able to *comb* -potent; *suf* -able, -ible, -ile; ***in an ~way:*** -bly

abnormal *comb* anom(o)-, poecilo-, poikilo-; ***~attraction:*** *comb* -lagnia, -philia, -philiac; ***~condition:*** *pre* para-; *suf* -ism, -osis, -otic; ***~discharge:*** *comb* -(r)rhage, -(r)rhagy, -(r)rhagia; ***~enlargement:*** *comb* megalo-, -megaly; ***~smallness:*** *comb* micro-

abode *comb* -cole, -colent, -colous, eco-, oiko-; *base* -aed-, -dom-, -edi-

abolish *base* fin-, perd-, termin-, vast-; *suf* -ate-[4]

about *pre* be-, circum-, peri-; *comb* amphi-; *base* -zon-, -cing-, -cinct-

above *pre* ano-[1], epi-, hyper-, ob-, super-, supra-, sur-, ultra-; *comb* over-, poly-

abscess *base* apostem-, vomic-

abscond *base* drapeto-, phygo-

absence *pre* a-, an-, dis-, ex-, il-, im-, in-, ir-, un-; *comb* lipo-; *base* -priv-; *suf* -less; ***~of an opening:*** *comb* -atresia, atreto-; ***~of a part:*** *comb* ectro-

absorb *comb* -sorb; *base* bib-

absurd *base* fatu-, inan-, moro-, stult-

abundance *base* ampl-, copi-, larg-

abusive *comb* noci-, pesti-; *base* -nox-, pericul-

abyss *comb* batho-, bathy-; *base* -byss-

accept *base* -cap-, -cep-, -cip-, -dyte-

accessory *pre* co-, para-[2], syn; *comb* inter-

accidents *base* -tich-, -tych(o)-

accumulation *comb* cumulo-; *base* acerv-, -sor-

accurate *comb* ortho-, recti-

acetic *comb* acet-

acetyl *comb* aceto-, acetyl-

acid *comb* ortho-, oxy-[1]; *-base* -acerb-, -oxal-

acorn *comb* balani-, balano-; *base* -gland-

acquire *base* -cap-, -cep-, -cip-, -dyte-

acrid *comb* picro-; *base* -acerb-, -mord-

acrimonious *base* acerb-, mord-

across *pre* dia-, per-, trans-; *comb* transverso-

act (to) *base* -fac-, -fec-, -fic-; *suf* -age, -ate, -ize

act of *comb* -craft; *suf* -ade, -age, -al, -ance, -ancy, -asis, -asm, -ation, -cy, -ence, -ency, -ery, -esis, -iasis, -ice-[1], -ics, -ing, -ion, -ism, -ment, -osis, -otic, -sion,

-sis, -th, -tion, -tious, -ture, -ure, -y², -ysis

actinic rays *comb* actino-

activity *comb* -ergasia, ergasio-, -ergic, ergo-, -ergy, -orial, -pragia, -praxia, -praxis; *suf* -esce, -escence, -escent, -esis; *quality of~: comb* -pragia

actor *base* histrion-, thesp-

actual *base* ver-

acute *comb* oxy-¹; *base* acer-, -grav-, vehem-

adamant *base* contum-, obstin-, pervic-, proterv-

adder *base* colub-

addicted to *comb* -aholic

addition *pre* a-, ac-, ad-, af-, ag-, al-, an-, ap-, ar-, as-, at-, extra-, super-. *See* **more**

adherent *suf* -ist, ite

adjacent *base* contig-, -tang-, vicin-. *See* **near**

adjusted *base* concinn-

admirable *pre* bene-, eu-; *base* agath-, bon-, prob-

adrenal gland *comb* adren(o)-

adroit *base* agil-, facil-, ingen-

adulterated *base* kibdelo-

advance *pre* pro-; *base* ced-, cess-

adversarial *base* hostil-, inimic-

affected with *suf* -otic

affecting *comb* -tropic

affection *base* -storgy

affinity *comb* -trope. *See* **attracted**

affluence *comb* chryso-, pluto-; *base* chrem-, -opul-, pecun-

afraid *base* pavid-, tim-, trepid-. *See* **fear**

African *comb* Afro-

after *pre* meta-, post-; *comb* hystero-, opistho-, postero-, retro-

aftereffect *suf* -age, -asm, -ata, -ation, -ency, -ism, -ma, -ment, -mony, -sion, -ure

afternoon *base* pomerid-

again *pre* ana-, re-; *base* -pali(n)-

against *pre* anti-, cata-, cath-, contra-, contre-, ob-, with-; *comb* antio-, counter-, enantio-

agate *base* agati-

age *pre* eo-; *comb* chrono-; *base* -temp-; *suf* -arian. *See* **old**

agent *suf* -ant, -ate³, -ator, -ent, -ure

agitate *base* agit-, mov-, trepid-, turb-

agouti *base* dasyproct-

agree(ment) *pre* co-; *base* concinn-, congru-, consil-, unanim-

aid *base* -auxil-, -jut-, -juv-

ailment *pre* dys-, mal-; *comb* noso-, path, -pathic, patho-, -pathy; *base* aegr-, cachex-, -morb-, -pecca-, valetud-

air *comb* aer-, aeri-, aero-, anemo-, atmo-, physo-, -pnea, pneo-, pneumato-, pneumo-, pneumono-; *base* -flat-, -vent-

albatross *base* diomed-, -procellar-

alcohol *suf* -ol

aldehydes *suf* -al, -ole

alike *pre* co-; *comb* equi-, homo-, iso-, pari-, tauto-

alive *comb* bio-, -biosis, quick-, vivi-, -zoic, zoo-, -zooid; *base* -anim-, vita-

alkaline *base* lixiv-

alkaloid names *suf* -ia;~*with nitrogen bases:* -ine

all *pre* be-, cata-, cath-, de-, kata-, ob-, per-; *comb* holo-, omni-, pan-¹, panto-, pasi-, toti-

alligator *base* -eusuch-

allow *base* conced-, concess-

allure *base* lenocin-

almond *comb* amygdal(o)-

almost *comb* pene-

alone *pre* mono-; *comb* eremo-, soli-, uni-

alteration *pre* meta-, trans-; *comb*

-plasia, -plasis, -tropic; *base* -
mut-, -vari-, -vert-. *See* **change**
altitude *comb* acro-, alti-, alto-,
bato-, hypsi-, hypso-; *base* pro-
cer-
aluminum *comb* alumino-
alveolus *comb* alveolo-
always *comb* ever-; *base* aei-, etern-,
semper-
amber *comb* succino-
ambiguous *base* ambig, ancip-,
dub-, pariso-
amend *pre* be-, em-, en-, meta-,
trans-; *comb* aetio-, -blast, -blas-
tic, blasto-, -craft, ergo-, etio-,
-facient, -fic, -fication, -gen,
-genesis, -genic, -genous, -geny,
-parous, -plasia, -plasis, plasmo-,
-plast, -plastic, plasto-, -plasty,
-poiesis, -poietic, -trope, -tropic,
-tropism, tropo-, -tropous, -tropy,
-urgy; *base* camb-, -fabr-, -fec-,
-mut-, -vari-, -vert-; *suf* -ate, en,
-fy, -ize, -otic
amide *comb* -amic[2];~*radical:*
amido-
ammonia *comb* ammonio-, am-
mono-
amnesia *base* amensi-, amnesi-
amniotic sac *comb* amnio-
among *pre* dia-, epi-; *comb* enter-,
inter-
amount *comb* quanti-; *suf* -age,
-ful, -ling
ample *base* ocho-[2]
amplify *pre* ad-, extra-, hyper-,
super-; *comb* auxano-, auxo-,
multi-, myria-, myrio-, out-,
over-, -plasia, pleni-, pleo-, pleio-,
pleon-, plethys-, plio-, pluri-, pol-
laki-, poly-; *base* ampl-, -aug-,
-cresc-, dilat-, -fold-, pler-,
-plet-
anal *comb* ano-[2], podic-
ancestors *comb* patroio-

anchor- *base* ancry-
anchovy *base* -engraul-
ancient *comb* archaeo-, archeo-,
palaeo-, paleo-, proto-; *base*
-antiq-, prisc-, -vet-
anesthetic *comb* -caine
anew *pre* ana-, re-; *base* -palin-
angelfish *base* pterophyll-
anger *base* chol-, -invid-, -ira-,
-margy
angle *comb* -angle, -gon, -gonal,
gonio-; *base* -angul-
anguish *comb* lype-; *base* dolor-,
fleb-, flet-, luct-, trist-
animal *comb* therio-, thero-, zoo-,
-zooid; *base* -fer-, zo-;~*classes:*
suf -acea; *early* ~*form: comb*
larvi-; ~*group name: suf* -id[1],
-ida, -idae, -iformes, -zoa, -zoic,
-zoon; **wild~:** fer-. *Also see* "Animals" in Part III
animation *comb* bio-, -biosis, vita-,
vivi-, zoo-, -zoic, -zooid; *base* -
anim-
ankle (bone) *comb* astragalo-, tali-,
talo-
annoy *base* vex-
another *comb* allelo-, allo-, alter-,
hetero-; *base* -ali-[2]
answer *base* apocris-. *See* **say**
ant *comb* myrmec-, myrmeco-,
myrmic-; *base* -formic-
anteater *base* myrmecophag-
antelope *base* -alcelaph-, -bubal-
anterior *pre* fore-; *comb* antero-,
proso-
antibiotic *comb* -mycin
antibodies, having *comb* -valent
antimony *comb* stibio-
antrum *comb* antro-
any __ of those possible *comb*
-soever
apart *pre* de-, des-, di-[2], dia-, dis-,
for-, se-; *comb* chori-, choristo-,
dialy-

ape *comb* pithec-, -pithecus; *base* -sim-

aperture *base* -pylo-. *See* **hole**

apex *comb* -apical, apico-

apparel *base* habil-, hesto-, -vest-

apparent *comb* lampro, luc-, luci-; *base* -clar-

apparition *base* phantas-, phasm-

appearance *comb* -phane, phanero-, -phanic, -phany, pheno-; *base* -schem-, -spec-, -spic-

appease *base* -plac-

appetite *comb* -orexia, -sitia, sitio-, sito-; *base* esur-

apple *base* mali-, pomi-

approximately *suf* -ish

arched *comb* arci, cyrto-; *base* -fornic-

archery *comb* toxo-[2]

ardor *base* ard-, alacr-, -ferv-, zelo-

arduous *pre* dys-; *comb* -bar, bary-, mogi-; *base* ardu-, stren-

argument *comb* -machy; *base* litig-, pugil-, -pugn-, -rix-

arid *comb* carpho-, xero-; *base* arid-, -celo-, -sicc-

arm *limb: comb* acromio-, brachio-

armadillo *base* dasypod-, -tolypeut-

armor *comb* hoplo-

armpit *base* -axill-

aroma *comb* brom(o)-, odori-, odoro-, olfacto-,-osmia, osmo-, osphresio-, ozo-, ozono-

around *pre* be-, circum-, peri-; *comb* ambi-, ambo-, amphi-; *base* -cing-, -cinct-, -zon-

arouse *comb* agito-; *base* -cit-

arrange(ment) *comb* -tactic, -tactous, -taxis, taxo-, -taxy; *base* -pos-, -struct-; *suf* -ate

arrest *stop: comb* stasi-, -stasis, -stat, stato-

arrow *base* belo-, -sagitt-

arsenic *comb* arseno-

art *comb* craft-, -ship, techno-, -techny

artery *comb* arterio-, -venous

articulation *comb* zyga-, zygo-

as if *comb* pseudo-, quasi-

ash tree *base* -frax(in)-, -melia-[2]; *mountain~:* sorb-[2]

ashes *comb* ciner-, pulver-, spodo-, tephro-; *base* favill-

ask *base* -pet-, -quir-, -quis-, -rog-

ass *base* as-, ono-

assemblage *suf* -ad, -age, -ery, -hood, -ship

assemble *base* -fabr-, -fac-, -fec-, -fic-, -struct-

assist *base* -auxil-, -jut-, -juv-

assistance *base* -(ad)jut-, -(ad)juv-, auxil-

assumption *comb* -lemma[1]

astragalus *comb* astragalo-, talo-

astringent *base* stypt-

at *pre* ad-, juxta-; *~the same time: pre* co-, syn-; *comb* -simul-

atlas *map: comb* carto-; *vertebra: comb* atlanto-, atlo-

atmosphere *comb* -bar, baro-

atrophy *base* -tabe-

attack *fight: base* -pugil-, -pugn-; *seizure: comb* -agra, -lepsia, -lepsis, -lepsy, -leptic

attempt *base* conat-, peir-

attend to *comb* -serve

attracted to *comb* -phile, -philia, -philiac, -philic, -philism, philo-, -philous, -trope, -tropic, -tropism, -tropous, -tropy; *base* -urient

augmented *pre* ad-, extra-, hyper-, super-; *comb* auxano-, auxo-, multi-, myria-, myrio-, out-, over-, -plasia, pleni-, pleo-, pleio-, pleon-, plethys-, plio-, pluri-, pollaki-, poly-; *base* ampl-, -aug-, -cresc-, dilat-, -fold-, pler-, -plet-

auk *base* alcid-

aunt *base* -amita-, -matertera-
auricle *comb* atrio-
authority *comb* exousia-; *base*
 imper-, magist-
authorized *comb* cyrio-, kyrio-
automobile *comb* amaxo-, -mobile;
 base harmat-, -ocho-
avarice *base* avar-, avid-, cup(id)-,
 edac-, gulos-, pleonec-, pleonex-
avocado *base* pers-

avoid *base* avers-, drapeto-, fug-,
 phygo-
away (from) *pre* ab-, abs-, apo-, be-,
 de-, des-, di-², dia-, dif-, dis-, e-,
 ec-, ef-, ex-, for-, off-¹, se, with-;
 comb ectro-
awl *base* subul-
ax *base* axin-, dolabri-, securi-,
 pelec-
axis *comb* axi-, axio-¹, axo-

B

bacillus *comb* bacill-, bacilli-, bacillo-
back *pre* ana-, re-, un-, with-; *comb*
 retro-; *the~: comb* back-, dorsi-,
 dorso-, nota-, noto-; *base* -terg-
backbone *comb* rachi-, rachio-,
 rhach-, rhachio-
backward *comb* opiso-, retro-
bacteria *comb* bacter-, bacteri-, bac-
 terio-, coccal, -coccic, cocco-,
 coccoid, -coccus, mycin; *base* -ella
badger *base* -melin-, -mustel-
bad(ly) *pre* dys-, mis-; *comb* caco-,
 -iniq-, kak-, kako-, mal-, male-,
 perv-, ponero-, -prav-, -turp-,
 vitia-
bag(like) *comb* angio-, asco-, bursi-,
 burso-, ceco-, chlamyd-, chrysali-,
 coleo-, cyst, -cyst, cysti-, cysto-,
 follic-, pericardiaco-, pericardio-,
 peritoneo-, phasco- physa-,
 physali, physo-, -theca, theco-,
 typhlo-, utri-², utric-, vesico-; *base*
 -sacc-, -thylac-
balance *comb* counter-, libra-,
 pariso-, stasi-, -stasis, stat, stato-
bald *base* -calv-, glabr-, -pelad-,
 -phalacr-
ball-shaped *comb* globi-, globo-,
 -sphere, sphero-; *base* -glom-. *See*
 circle

ballot *base* tabell-, suffrag-
ban *pre* anti-; *base* imped-, prohib-
banana *base* musa-
band *comb* desmo-, syndesmo-,
 taeni-, teni-, -trocha , zon-, zoni-;
 base -lemnisc-, liga-, zoster-; *suf*
 -let
bang *comb* plessi-, -cuss-; *base*
 -cop-, -crot-, plang-, -puls-, -tus-,
 -vapul-, -verber-
banner *comb* labar-, vexill-
bar *base* clathr-, -ser-
barbed *base* hamat-
barber *base* tonsor-
bare *comb* gymno-, nudi-, psilo-.
 See bald
bark *dog: base* hylac-, latr-; *tree:*
 base cortici-, phloem-
barley *comb* alphito-; *base* crith-,
 horde-, ptis-
barracuda *base* -perces-, sphyraen-
barrel *base* dolio-
barrier *comb* herco-, septo-, pari-
 eto-, -phragma, phragmo-; *base*
 cancell-, claustr-, -mur-
base *foundation: comb* basi-, basio-,
 baso-, fund-; *base* -radic-; *evil:*
 pre dys-, mis-; *comb* caco-, iniq-,
 kak(o)-, mal(e)-, ponero-; *base*
 -prav-, sceler-, turp-

basic *base* prim-, -rud-; [chemistry] *pre* sub-
basin (shaped) *comb* cylico-, kylixo-, lecano-, pelvi-
basket *base* calath-, -corb-
bat *base* desmodont-, megacheiropter-, microcheiropter, noctilion-, -pterop-, -vespertil-
bath(ing) *comb* balneo-; *base* -ablut-, -lav-
battle *comb* macho-, -machy; *base* -bell-, -pugil-, -pugn-
beach *base* littor-, thino-; *See* **sand**
beak *comb* coraco-, rhampho-, rhyncho-, rostrato-, rostri-, rostro-, -rrhyncha; *base* -aquil-. *See* **nose**
beam *base* trab-
bean *base* cyam-, fab-, phaseol-
bear ***animal:*** *comb* arcto-; *base* -urs-; ***carry:*** *comb* -fer, -ferous, -gerous, -parous, -pher, -phore, -phorous; *base* -port-, -vect-
beard *comb* pogon(o)-; *base* -barba-
bearing *comb* -fer, -ferous, -gerous, -parous, -pher, phor-, -phore, -phorous; *base* -port-
beast *comb* -there, therio-, thero-; *base* fer-
beat *comb* -cuss-, plessi-, rhabdo-; *base* -cop-, -crot-, fustig-, plang-, puls-, quass-, vapul-, -verber-
beautiful *comb* calli-, callo-; *base* kal-, pulchr-
beaver *base* -castor-
become *suf* -ate[1], -en, -fy; ***~like:*** -ize
becoming *suf* -esce, -escence, -escent
bed *base* clin-
bee *comb* api(o)-, melisso-; *base* -bomb-; ***~hive:*** -alve-
beech *base* faga-
beer *base* cervis-
beetle *base* coleopter-, scarab-

before *pre* ante-, fore-, ob-, pre-, pro-[2]; *comb* antero-, protero-, proto-, retro-; *base* prior-
beggar *comb* ptocho-; *base* mendic-
begin(ning) *comb* -phyletic, spermato-; *base* incip-, -init-; *suf* -esce, -escence, -escent. *See* **origin**
behavior *comb* etho-; *base* hexi-
behind *pre* meta-, post-; *comb* after-, back-, hind-, opistho, postero, retro-; *base* terg-
being *comb* onto-; *base* -esse-
belch *base* -ruct-
belief *comb* -ousia; *base* -cred-, -fid-[1]; *suf* -ism
believer *suf* -ist, -ite
believing in *suf* -an
bell *base* campan-, -tintinn-
belligerence *base* chol-, -invid-, -ira-, -margy
bellow *base* -mug-
belly *comb* abdomino-, celio-, celo-, coelo-, laparo-, ventri-, ventro-; *base* -alv-. *See* **stomach**
belonging to *suf* -acean, -aceous, -ad,- al[3], -an[3], -ar, -arious, -ary, -atic, -ative, -atory, -eae, -ean, -eous, -ery, -etic, -ial, -ian, -ic, -id[1], -il, -ile, -ina, -inae, -ine, -ing, -ious, -istic, -ite, -itic, -itious, -itive, -ive, -oidea, -ory, -otic, -tious, -tive, -ular. *See* **characteristic of**
below *pre* hypo-, infra-, sub-, subter-; *comb* infero-, under-
bend, bent *comb* ancylo-, ankylo-, -campsis, campto-, campylo-, -clinal, -clinate, -cline, -clinic, clino-, -clinous, -clisis, curvi, cyrto-, -flect, flex-, flexuouso-, lechrio-, loxo-, recurvo-, repando-, scolio-, -tort, -verge; *base* -clit-, cliv- -sinu-
benefit *base* -auxil-, -jut-, -juv-

benzine *pre* meta-; *comb* benzo-, phen-

bereavement *comb* lype-; *base* dolor-, fleb-, flet-, luct-, trist-

berry *comb* baccato-, bacci-, cocci-; *base* -acin-

beside *pre* a-, ac-, ad-, af-, ag-, al-, an-, ap-, ar-, as-, at-, by-, epi-, para-², peri-; *comb* juxta-, citra-, pene-, proximo-

besides *pre* extra-

best *comb* aristo-; *base* -opt-²

bestow *base* -don-

better *comb* melior-, out-

between *pre* dia-, epi-; *comb* enter-, inter-

beyond *pre* ex-, extra-, meta-, para-², preter-, super-, supra-, sur-, ultra-; *comb* over-

Bible *comb* biblio-

big *base* grand-, magn-. *See* large

bile *comb* bili-, chole-, cholo-, gall-

billion *comb* giga-. *Also see* "Numbers" in Part III

billionth *comb* nanno-, nano-

bind *comb* sphingo-, -strain, -strict, syndesmo-; *base* liga-, -merinth-, nex-, -string-, -vinc-

bipartite *comb* diphy-. *See* two

birch *base* betul-

bird *comb* orneo-, orni-, ornitho-, orno-; *base* -avi-, grall-, muscicap-, oscin-, passer-, pendulin-, volucr-

birth *comb* -genic, -natal, -para, -tocia, -toky; *base* geneth-, -nasc-, -partur-; ~*day:* geneth-

birthmark *comb* nevi-, nevo-

bishop *base* episcop-

biting *comb* aceto-, keto-, oxal-, oxy-; *base* -acid-, -mord-

bitter *comb* picro-; *base* -acerb-, asper-, -mord-

bittern *base* botaur-, ixobrych

black *comb* atro-, melano-, piceo;

base -ebon-, fulig-, -nigr-. *Also see* "Colors" in Part III

black widow *base* latrodect-

blackbird *base* -icter-, merul-

bladder *comb* asco-, burs-, bursi-, burso-, ceco-, cyst-, -cyst , cysti-, cysto-, follic-, physa-, physali-, physo-, typhlo-, utri-, utric-, vesico-, vesiculi-, vesiculo-; *base* -sacc-, -thylac-

blame *base* culp-, reprehen-, -vituper-

blanket *base* -lodic-

blend *pre* co-; *comb* conjugato-, -ergasia, gameto-, gamo-, hapto-, junct-; *base* aps-, apt-, -greg-, -soc-; *suf* -ate, -ize

blight *comb* fungi-, -mycete, myceto-, -mycin, myco-, uredo-

blind *comb* caeco-, ceco-, typhlo-; *base* -lusc-

blink *base* -conniv-, -nict-

blister *comb* phlyc-, vesica-, vesico-, vesiculo-; *base* pustul-

blood *comb* haema-, haemo-, hema-, hemato-, hemo-, sangui-, sanguineo-, sanguino-; *base* cruent-, cruor-; ~*clot:* thrombo-; ~*condition or disease:* -aemia, cythemia, -emia; ~*fluid:* lympho-; ~*vessels:* hemangio-, vasculo-, vaso-

blooming *comb* thalero-; *base* flor-, vig-

blow *wind: base* anemo-, flat-, vent-; *punch: comb* plessi-; *base* cop-, -crot-, -cuss-, -plang-, puls-, -tus-, vapul-, -verber-

blue *comb* cyano-, glauco-; *base* adular-, aerug-, -azur-, -caes-, -cerul-, -lazul-, -livid-, -pavon-. *Also see* "Colors" in Part III

blueberry *base* vaccin-

bluebird *base* sial-², -turd-

blunder *base* culp-, delinq-, laps-, pecc-, sphal-

blunt *comb* obtusi-; *base* hebet-
boar *base* suid-
boasting *base* kompo-, thras-
boat (-shaped) *comb* navi-, scapho-,
scapulo-; *base* -cymb-
bobolink *base* -icter-
body *comb* physico-, physi-,
physio-, somato-, -some[1]; *base*
-corp-; *dead~: comb* necro-; *base*
-cadav-; *~defect:base* -hamart-;
~odor: brom-, ozostom-; *~organ
part: suf* -ite
bog *base* telmat; *peat~: base* turbar-
boil (up) *base* aestu-, -coct-, ferv-
bold *base* audac-, feroc-
bolt *base* gomph-, pessul-, -ser-
bond *comb* desmo-, ligamenti-, lig-
amento-, syndesmo-; *base* -caten-,
-vinc-; *double~: suf* -ylene
bone *comb* ossi-, osseo-, osteo-;
forearm~: ulno-; *~joining hipbones:* sacro-; *~membrane:* pe-
riosteo-; *frontal~:* fronto-; *bony
process: comb* stylo-
book *comb* biblio-; *base* -libr-;
~size: suf -mo; *~worm:* tinea-
border *base* fimbr-, -marg-,
propinq-, prox-, termin-. *See*
near
born *comb* -genic, -natal, -para,
-tocia, -toky; *base* geneth-, -nasc-,
partur-; *~in: suf* -an
boron *comb* boro-
both *comb* ambi-, ambo-; *~sides:*
amphi-, ampho-, bi-
bother *base* vex-
bottle *base* ampull-, lagen-;
leather~: utrei-, utri-
bottom *pre* sub-; *comb* basi-, fund-;
base -radic-
boundary *comb* orismo-; *base* fin-,
termin-
bowl *comb* crater-, cylico-, kylixo-
box *comb* pyx-; *~tree: base* bux-
boy *base* puer-

bragging *base* kompo-, thras-
brain *comb* cephal-, cerebri-, cere-
bro-, encephalo-
brambles *comb* bato-[2]
bran *base* furfur-, pityr-
branch *comb* clado-, rami-
brass *comb* chalco-; *base* -aenio-
brave *base* audac-, feroc-
brazen *base* contum-, impud-, pro-
cac-
bread *base* arto-, pan-[2]
breakfast *base* -jent-
break(ing) *comb* -clasia, -clasis,
-clastic, -rhegma, -(r)rhexis; *base*
agmat-, -fract-, -frag-, -frang-,
-rupt-
breast *comb* mammi-, mammo-,
mastia-, -masto, mazo-[2], stetho-;
base pect-; *~bone:* sterno-. *See*
nipple
breath *comb* -hale, -pnea, pneo-,
pneumato-, pneumo-, pneu-
mono-, pneusio-, pulmo-, spiro-[1];
base afflat-; *bad~:* -halit-, ozos-
tom-
breed *base* thremm-
brick *base* -later-, plinthi-
bridge *base* gephyr-, pont-
brief *comb* brachio-, brachisto-,
brachy-, brevi-, chamae-, hekisto-,
micro-, mini-, parvi-, parvo-,
steno-, tapino-; *base* -cort-, -curt-,
exig-; *suf* cle, -cula, -cule, -een, -
el, -ella, -en, -et, -ette, -idion,
-idium, -ie, -illa, -illo, -isk, -kin,
-le, -let, -ling, -ock, -ola, -ole,
-rel, -ula, -ule, -ulum, -ulus, -y
bright *comb* helio-; *base* -clar-,
-fulg-, -gano-, -luc-, -lumin-,
nitid-
brine *base* muri-
bring *base* -duc-, -fer-, -port- . *See*
carry
bring forth *comb* maieusi-, -parous;
base partur-

brisk *comb* ocy-, tacho-, tachy-; *base* alacr-, celer-, festin-, veloc-
bristle *comb* chaeti-, chaeto-, seti-
broad *comb* eury-, lati-, platy-
bromine *comb* bromo-
broom *comb* scop-, scopi-
brothel *base* lupan-
brother *comb* frater-, fratri-; *base* -adelph-
brown *comb* fusco-, phaeo-; *base* aen-, brun-, castan-, -fulv-, -gland-, lur-, mustel-, -spad-, -testac-. *Also see* "Colors" *in Part* III
bruise *base* -tus-
brush *base* muscar-
bubble *comb* pego-, physali-; *base* bullat-
buckthorn *base* -rhamn-
bud *base* gemm-[1]
buffalo *base* bubal-
buffoon *comb* balatro-
bug *comb* cimic-, core-[2], entomo-, insecti-, insecto-
build *base* -fabr-, -fac-, -fec-, -fic-, -struct-
bulb(ous) *comb* bulbo-; *base* cep-[2]
bulge *comb* -cele, -edema, ganglio-, phlogo-, phym-, -phyma, physa-, physo-, strum(i)-; *base* aug-, cresc-, physc-, strum-, -tum-, -turg-; *suf* -itis
bull *comb* tauri-, tauro-

bullfinch *base* pyrrhul-
bull-headed *base* contum-, obstin-, pervic-, proterv-
bully *base* -procac-
bundle *comb* fasciculato-, fascio-; *base* phacell-, -sarcin-
bunting *base* emberiz-, pyrrhul-
burden(ed) *comb* hypegia-, hypengy-, -ridden; *base* -oner-, paralip-
burdensome *pre* dys-; *comb* -bar, bary-, mogi-; *base* ardu-, stren-
burning *comb* causto-, igni- pyro-; *base* ard-[1], ars-, cauter-, celo-[2], combust-, crem-, phlog-, -ust-
bursting *base* -rrhexis-, -rupt-. *See* **breaking**
bury *base* -hum-
burying place *comb* kil(l)-. *See* **tomb**
business *base* -negot-
butcher *base* lania-
butter *comb* butyro-
butterfly *base* lepidopter-, papil-
buttocks *comb* -pygia, pygo-; *base* nati-, podic-
buzzard *comb* buteo-; *base* cathart-
buy *comb* onio-; *base* -empt-, -merc-, nundin-
by *pre* ad-, by-, epi-, peri-; *comb* juxta-; *base* -prox-; *~means of:* *pre* syn-

C

cabbage *base* brassic-
calcium *comb* calc-, calci-
calf *base* **animal:** vitul-; **leg:** sura-
call *base* appell-, -claim, -clam-, -dict-, -nom-, -voc-; *~upon: base* -prec-
calm *base* placid-, sedat-, tranquil-
camel *comb* cameli-

camp *base* castr-
cancel *base* oblit-
cancer *base* carcin(o)-
cap *base* -pile-
capable of being *suf* -able, -ibility, -ible, -ibly, -ile
capacious *base* ocho-[2]
capsule *comb* capsuli-, capsulo-

carbohydrate *suf* -ose[1]
carbon *comb* carbo-
carbon dioxide *comb* -capnia,
  capno-
carbuncle *comb* anthraco-
card *comb* carto-, charto-
cardinal *bird:* *base* pyrrhul-
careful *base* attent-, caut-, diligen-
caries *comb* cario-
carp *base* cyprin-
carry(ing) *comb* -fer, -ferous, -ger-
  ous, -parous, -pher, -phore,
  -phorous; *base* -port-, -vect-
cartilage *comb* chondr-, chondrio-,
  chondro-, xiphi-; ***eyelid~:*** tarso-
carve *comb* -glyph, glypto-
case *comb* angio-, chlamyd-, coleo-,
  meningo-, -theca, theci-, theco-
cash *comb* -penny ; *base* chremat-,
  -numm-, -pecun-, quaest-
cashew *base* anacard-
cassowary *base* casuar-
castor oil *base* ricinol-
cat *comb* aeluro-, ailuro-, gato-;
  base -fel-, gale-[3]
catch *comb* -tain; *base* -cap(t)-,
  -cathex-, -ger-, -hapt-, -prehend,
  prehens-, rap-, rep-, -ten-
caterpillar *base* bruch-, -camp-[2],
  eruc-
catfish *base* silur-
catkin *base* ament-[2], -juli-
cauliflower *base* brassic-
cause, causing *pre* be-, em-, en-[2],
  meta-, trans-; *comb* aetio-, -blast,
  -blastic, blasto-, -craft, ergo-,
  etio-, -facient, -fic, -fication, -gen,
  -genesis, -genic, -genous, -geny,
  -parous, -plasia, -plasis, plasmo-,
  -plast, -plastic, plasto-, -plasty,
  -poiesis, -poietic, -trope, -tropic,
  -tropism, tropo-, -tropous, -tropy,
  -urgy; *base* -fabr-, -fec-, -mut-,
  -vert-; *suf* -ate, -en, -fy, -ize, -otic
caused by *suf* -atory, -ic, -ing

caustic *comb* cauter-; ***acrimonious***
  base acerb-, mord-
cave *comb* speleo-, troglo-; *base*
  spelunc-
cavity *comb* alveolo-, antro-, atrio-,
  -coele, coelo-, parieto-, sino-,
  sinu-, syringo-, ventriculo-,
  vesiculo-, vestibulo-; *base* lacun-.
  See **hollow**
cease *comb* stasi-, -stasis, -stat; *base*
  fin-, termin-
cecum *comb* ceco-, typhlo-
cedar *base* cedr-
celebration *comb* -fest, -mas; *suf* -ia
celestial activity *comb* astro-
cell *comb* alveolo-, celli-, celluli-,
  cellulo-, -cyte, -cythemia, cyto-,
  -gonium, kyto-, -plasm, plasmo-
cellulose *comb* cello-
celom *comb* celo-[1]
Celt *comb* Celto-
cement *comb* glea-
cemetery *base* coemet, coimet-
center *comb* centr-, centri-, -cen-
  tric, centro-
centipede *base* chilopod-, scolopen-
  dri-
cereal *base* frument-
cervical *comb* cervico-
chaff *base* palea-
chain *base* caten-, vinc-
chair *base* cathedr-, sedil-
chalk *base* cimol-, -cret-, gypso-;
  [geology] *comb* cretaceo-
chamber *comb* alveolo-, atrio-,
  antro-, -coele, coelo-, parieto-,
  sino-, sinu-, sinuso-, syringo-,
  ventriculo-, vesiculo-, vestibulo-.
  See **hollow**
chamois *base* rupicap-
chance *comb* clero-, faust-, tycho-
change *pre* be-, em-, en-, meta-,
  trans-; *comb* aetio-, -blast, -blas-
  tic, blasto-, -craft, ergo-, etio-,
  -facient, -fic, -fication, -gen,

-genesis, -genic, -genous, -geny,
-parous, -plasia, -plasis, plasmo-,
-plast, -plastic, plasto-, -plasty,
-poiesis, -poietic, -trope, -tropic,
-tropism, tropo-, -tropous, -tropy,
-urgy; *base* camb-, -fabr-, -fec-,
-mut-, -vari-, -vert-; *suf* -ate, en,
-fy, -ize, -otic

channel *comb* aulo-, follic-, meato-,
poro-, salpingo-, siphono-,
soleno-, syringo-, tubi-, tubo-,
tubulo-, vasi-; *base* strig-

character *comb* etho-, -hood, quali-;
suf -ity

characteristic of *suf* -an^3, -ar, -ary,
-ate^2, -ean, -en, -esque, -ian, -ic,
-ical, -il, -ile, -ine, -ish, -istic,
-like, -ly, -ous, -ular, -ulent,
-ulose, -y. *See* **belonging to**

characterized by *suf* -acean,
-aceous, -acious, -aire, -al, -ate,
-ed^2, -eous, -ey, -ful, -gerous, -ial,
-ine, -ious, -itious, -oid, -orious,
-ory, -ose, -osity, -ous, -some,
-ular, -ulent, -ulose, -ulous, -
wise, -y^1

chariot *base* harmat-

chasm *base* vorag-

chastisement *comb* mastigo-,
rhabdo-; *base* castig-, peno-,
poine-, -pun-

chatter *base* garrul-. *See* **talk**

cheat *base* apat-, dolero-, ludif-

checked *comb* brady-; *base* -cunct-,
imped-, -mora-, -tard-. *See* **inhibit**

cheek *comb* bucco-, -genia, genio-,
geny-, mel(o)-^{2}, -paria, zygo-
matico-, zygomato-

cheerful *comb* chero-; *base* beati-,
felic-, jubil-, macar-

cheese *comb* tyro-; *suf* case-

chemicals *comb* chemo-

cherry *base* -ceras-

chest *comb* sterno-, stetho-,

thoracico-, thoraco-; *base*
pector-

chestnut *base* aescul-, -castan-

chew *base* manduc-, -mastic-, trog-

chickadee *base* par-^{2}

chicken *base* gallin-, pull-. *See* **cock**

chicory *base* cichor-

chief *comb* arch-^{1}, archi-, proto-;
base -prim-, -princip-

child *comb* paedo-^{2}, pedi-, pedo-^{2},
proli-, tecno-; *base* -fil-^{2}, -puer-,
tek-

childbirth *comb* lochio-, maieusi-,
-para, -parous, -tocia, toco-,
toko-, -toky; *base* -partur-

chimpanzee *base* sim-

chin *comb* -genia, genio-, geny-,
mento-

Chinese *comb* Chino-, Sino-

chisel *comb* scalpri-

chlorine *comb* chloro-, perchloro-

choice *base* -opt-^{1}, -vol-

choke *base* -pnig-

chore *comb* arti-, -craft, -ergasia,
ergasio-, -ergics, ergo-, -ergy,
organo-, -urgy; *base* -labor-,
lucubr-, oper-^{1}, -opus-, pono-^{2}

chromatin *comb* chromato-

chromium *comb* -chrome

chromosones: of a specified multiple of ___ *comb* -ploid

church *comb* ecclesiastico-, kil(l)-

chyle *base* chyl-

cilia *comb* cilii-, cilio-

circle *comb* ano-, annul-, crico-,
cyclo-, disco-, globi-, globo-,
glom-, gyro-, orbito-, -sphere,
sphero-, stilli-, zon-, zoni-;
base -anu-, -cing-, -cinct-,
-circin-, -circul-, -coron-,
-glomer-, -numm-, -orb-, -rot-,
-troch-

citizen (of) *base* -civ-; *suf* -an,
-ian, -ite

citric *base* citro-

city *comb* -burg(h), -polis, -ton, -ville; *base* -civ-, -urb-

civet *base* viverr-

clamor *base* crepit-, frem-, ligyr-, strep(i)-, strid-, stridul-. *See* **sound**

clan *base* -phrat-

clarion *base* -litu-

class names *suf* -ia

clatter *base* -strepit-

clavicle *comb* cleido-, clido-

claw *comb* -chela, cheli-, helo-, onycho-, -onychia; *base* -ungui-, ungul-

clay *comb* argillaceo-, argillo-, limo-[1], pelo-

cleanse *comb* balneo-; *base* ablut-, cathar-, -lav-, -mund-[2], -purg-

clear *comb* lampro-, luc-, luci-; *base* -clar-

cleaver *base* -dolabr-

cleft *comb* dicho-, -fid[2], fissi-, schisto-, schizo-, sulcato-, -tomy; *base* fatisc-, -par-, rim-. *See* **groove**

clever *base* ingen-

cliff *base* scopul-

climb *base* -ascend-, ascens-, -scal-, -scand-, -scans-

cloak *base* chlamyd-

clockwise *comb* dextr(o)-

clod *base* gleb-

close by *pre* a-, ac-, ad-, af-, ag-, al-, an-, ap-, ar-, as-, at-, by-, cis-, epi-, para-, peri-; *comb* juxta-, citra-, pene-, proximo-

closed, closure *comb* -atresia, atreto-, claustro-, cleido-, -cleisis, cleisto-, stego-; *base* -clithr-, -clud-, -clus-

clot *comb* thrombo-; *base* grum-

clothing *base* habil-, hesto-, -vest-

cloud *comb* fracto-, nephelo-, nepho-, nimbo-; *base* homichlo-, -nebul-, -nubi-; *rounded~:* mammato-

club *base* clavi-, rhopal-

clumps *comb* cespitoso-; *base* -glob-. *See* **tufts**

cluster *base* corymbi-, glom-, racem-

clutch *comb* -tain; *base* -cap(t)-, -cathex-, -ger-, -hapt-, -prehend, prehens-, rap-, rep-, -ten-

coal *comb* anthraco-; *base* -carb-

coast *shore: base* littor-, maritim-

cobweb *base* arachn-

coccus *comb* -coccal

coccyx *comb* coccy-, coccygo-

cock *base* alector-, alectry-

cockroach *base* blatt-[1]

coercion *comb* dyna-, dynamo-, mega-, megalo-, -megaly, -sthenia, stheno-; *base* -forc-, -fort-, -poten-, robor-

coil *comb* cirri-, cochlio-, gyro-, helico-, spiro-[2], strepto-; *base* stromb-. *See* **curl**

coin *base* numisma-, -numm-

coincide *base* concinn-, congru-, unanim-

coition *comb* -lagnia; *base* -coit-

cold *comb* cheima-, crymo-, cryo-, frigo-, gelo-, kryo-, pago-, psychro-, rhigo-; *base* alg-, glac-

collar *base* coll-[1]

collarbone *base* clavi-[1]

collection of *suf* -ad, -age, -ery, -hood, -ship

collodion *comb* collodio-

colon *comb* coli-[1], colo-

color *comb* chromato-, -chrome, chromo-; *base* -pigm-, -tinct-, -ting-; *colored: comb* -chroous; *two-colored: comb* dichro-. *Also see* "Colors" *in Part III*

colorless *comb* leuco-, leuko-

column *base* stylo-[2]; *small~:* columelli-

comb *base* cteno-; *~teeth:* pecti-
nato-
combat *comb* macho-, -machy,
pugn-; *base* -bell-, pugil-
combine *pre* co-; *comb* conjugato-,
-ergasia, gameto-, gamo-, hapto-²,
junct-; *base* aps-, apt-, -greg-,
-soc-; *suf* -ate, -ize
combustible *comb* ard-, ars-
come *base* -ven(t)-
comestibles *comb* bromato-,
-brotic, manduc-, opso-, -phage,
phago-, -phagous, -phagy, -sitia,
sitio-, sito-, -troph, -trophic,
tropho-, -trophy, -vora, -vore,
-vorous; *base* -alim-, -cib-, escul-,
-gust-, -nutr-; *partially di-
gested~:* chymo-
command *base* -imper-, juss-,
-mand-
commence *base* inaug-, incip-, init-
commercial names *suf* -co, -ine
common *comb* caeno-¹, ceno-²,
coeno-, pan-¹; *base* -commun-,
-vulg-; *~people: comb* demo-;
base -pleb-, -popul-
commotion *base* -agit-, -tumult-,
-turb-
community *base* synœc-
compact *dense: comb* dasy-, pycno-,
pykno-; *base* -crass-, -press-,
-spiss-; *small: comb* brachio-,
brachisto-, brachy-, brevi-,
chamae-, hekisto-, micro-, mini-,
nano-, parvi-, parvo-, -steno-;
base cort-, curt-; *suf* -cle, -cula,
-cule, -culum, -culus, -een, -el,
-ella, -en, -et, -ette, -idion,
-idium, -ie, -illa, -illo, -isk, -kin,
-le, -let, -ling, -ock, -ola, -ole,
-rel, -ula, -ule, -ulum, -ulus, -y
comparable *pre* para-, quasi-; *comb*
homeo-, omœo, homoio-, ho-
molo-, iso-, -phane, -phanic; *base*
simil-; *suf* -acean, -aceous, -al,

-an, -ar, -ary, -ean, -en, -eous,
-esque, -ful, -ic, -il, -ile, -ine,
-ing, -ish, -itious, -ize, -like, -ode,
-oid, -ose, -osity, -some, -tious,
-ular, -y
compel *See* **urge**
competence *base* quali-
competitive event *comb* -athlon,
-athon, -off²
complain *base* -quer-, -querul-
complement of *pre* co-
complementary *comb* counter-
complete(ly) *pre* be-, cata-, cath-,
de-, kata-, ob-, per-; *comb* holo-,
omni-, pan-, panto-, stone-, toti-
compound names *comb* tetrazo-;
suf -ide, -ole¹
comprehension *comb* -gnomy,
-gnosia, -gnosis, -gnostic, gnoto-,
ideo-, -noia, -nomy, -phrenic,
phrenico-, phreno-, psycho-,
-sophy; *base* -cogit-, -cogn-, epis-
tem-, ment(a)-, -noe-, -put-,
ratio-, -sci-
computer *comb* cyber-
concave *comb* concavo-
concealed *pre* sub-; *comb* calypto-,
crypto-; *base* occult-
concept *comb* -gnomy, -gnosia,
-gnosis, -gnostic, gnoto-, ideo-,
-noia, -nomy, phreno-, psycho-,
-sophy; *base* -cogit-, -cogn-, epis-
tem-, -noe-, -put-, ratio-, -sci-
concise *comb* brachio-, brachisto-,
brachy-, brevi-, chamae-, hekisto-,
micro-, mini-, parvi-, parvo-,
steno-, tapino-; *base* -cort-, -curt-,
exig-; *suf* cle, -cula, -cule,
-culum, -culus, -een, -el, -ella,
-en, -et, -ette, -idion, -idium, -ie,
-illa, -illo, -isk, -kin, -le, -let,
-ling, -ock, ola, -ole, -rel, -ula,
-ule, ulum, -ulus, -y
conclude *base* -fin-, termin-
condensed *comb* brachio-,

brachisto-, brachy-, brevi-,
chamae-, hekisto-, micro-, mini-,
parvi-, parvo, steno-, tapino-;
base -cort-, -curt-, exig-; *suf* -cle,
-cula, -cule-, culum, -culus, -een,
-el, -ella, -en, -et, -ette, -idion,
-idium, -ie, -illa, -illo, -isk, -le,
-let, -ling, -ock, -ola, -ole, -rel,
-ula, -ule, -ulum, -ulus, -y

condition *suf* -able, -acity, -acy,
-age, -ance, -ancy, -ant, -asis,
-asm, -ate, -atile, -ation, -cy,
-dom, -eity, -ence, -ency, -ent,
-ery, -esis, -ful, -hood, -iasis,
-ice[1], -ility, -ion, -ise, -ism, -ity,
-ling[3], -ma, -ment, -ness, -or[3],
-osis, -otic, -red, -ship, -sion, -sis,
-th, -tion, -tude, -ture, -ty[1], -ure,
-y[2]

conduct ***behavior:*** *comb* etho-; *base*
hexi-; ***lead:*** *comb* -arch, -duce,
duc(t)-, magist-; *base* hegemon-,
-reg-

cone *comb* coni-[2], conico-, cono-,
conoido-; ***pine~:*** strobil-

confer *base* -don-

configuration *comb* topo-

confine *comb* sphingo-, -strain,
-strict, syndesmo-; *base* -liga-,
-merinth-, -string-, -vinc-

conflict *comb* macho-, -machy; *base*
-bell-, -pugil-, -pugn-

confusion *comb* atax-, ataxi-,
-ataxia, ataxio-, ataxo-; *base*
misc-, -turb-

connected (with) *base* hirmo-, nex-;
suf -ar[2], -arious, -ary, -id[1], -wise;
~twins: *comb* -pagia, -pagus

conquer *base* vict-, -vinc-

consecrated *comb* hagio-, hiero-;
base -sacr-, -sanct-

consequence *comb* ergo-, -ergic,
-ergy; *suf* -age, -asm, -ata, -ation,
-ency, -ism, -ma, -ment, -mony,
-sion, -ure

consistent *comb* even-

constitution *comb* -ousia, -ousian;
base quid-

constrained *comb* -bound

constriction *comb* lepto-, stegno-,
steno-; *base* -stal-, -strict-. *See*
tightening

construction *comb* -craft, ergo-,
-fic, -urgy; *base* -fabr-, -fac-, -fic-.
See **make**

contagious *base* -tapin-

container *comb* angio-, asco-, bursi-,
burso-, ceco-, chlamyd-, chrysali-,
cisto-, coleo-, -cyst, cysti-, cysto-,
follic-, meningo-, pericardiaco-,
pericardio-, peritoneo-, phasco-,
physa-, physali-, physo-, -theca,
theci-, theco-, typhlo-, utri-,
utric, vesico-; *base* -sacc-, -thylac-

containing *comb* -filled, pleni-,
pleo-, pluri-; *base* -pler-, -plet-;
suf -acious, -ate, -ic, -ful, -lent,
-ose[2], -osity, -ous, -ulent, -y

contempt *base* fastid-

contentment *comb* chero-; *base*
beati-, felic-, jubil-, macar-

contest *comb* -athlon, -athon,
macho-, -machy, -off; *base* agon-

continent *base* -epeiro-

continual *base* assid-, contin-,
incess-, perpet-

contorted *comb* contorto-, gyro-,
helico-, pleco-, plecto-, spiro-,
strepho-, strepsi-, strepto-; *base*
-strob-, -stromb-, -stroph-, -tors-,
-tort-

contraction *comb* -chorea , choreo-,
-clonic, -clonus, -esmus, -ismus,
spasmo-; *base* -stal-, vellic-

contrary *pre* anti-, cata-, contra-,
contre-, cross-, dis-, hetero-, ob-,
un-, with-; *comb* counter-, enan-
tio-, oppositi-

control *base* magist-, maha-; ***loss***
of~: *comb* -crasia

controversy *base* eris-

converge *comb* -ergasia, gameto-, gamo-, hapto-, junct-; *base* -aps-, -apt-, -greg-, -soc-; *suf* -ate, -ize

conversation *comb* -claim, logo-, -logue, -lalia, -lexia, lexico-, -lexis, -lexy, -logy, -phone, hono-, -phony, verbi-, verbo-, voc-, voci-, -voke; *base* -clam-, -dict-, -loc(u)-, -loqu-, -orat-, rhet-

convex *comb* convexo-, gibboso-

cook *base* -coct-, mageir-, magir-

coot *base* fulic-

copious *base* ampl-, copi-, largi-

copper *comb* chalco-, cupreo-, cupri-, cupro-, cuproso-; *base* auricalc-. *Also see* "Colors" *in Part* III

copy *base* -mim-

coracoid bone *comb* coraco-

coral *comb* coralli-

cord *comb* -chorda, chord-, cordo-, funi-, tendo-; *base* cord-, resti-

core *comb* caryo-, karyo-, nucleo-

cork *comb* phello-; *base* suber-

cormorant *base* phalacrocorac-

corn *base* frument-, grani-; *ear of~:* spici-

cornea *comb* corneo-, kerato-

corpse *comb* necro-; *base* -cadav-

corpulent *base* obes-, pingu-

correct(ion) *comb* ortho-; *base* castig-, emend-

corruption *comb* lysi-, -lysis, lyso-, -lyte, -lytic, -lyze, phthino-, phthisio-, -phthisis, phthysio-, -phthysis, putri-, pyo-, pytho-, sapro-, septi-, septo-, septico-; *base* phthor-, vitia-

cortex *comb* cortico-, pallio-

cost of *suf* -age

costly *base* dapat-

cotton *base* xilin-

cough *base* -tuss-

count *base* calcul-, -comput-, -num-

counterclockwise *comb* laevo-, levo-

counterfeit *comb* pseudo-

countless *comb* myrio-; *base* innum-

country *base* -rur-, -rustic-; *of a~:* *suf* -ese, -ian; *~names: comb* -land; *suf* -ia

coupled *comb* conjugato-

courtesan *comb* cypriano-, hetaero-, porno-; *base* -meretric-, scort-; **brothel:** lupan-

courtesy *base* -comit-

cousin *base* -sobrin-

covenant *base* fedi-

cover(ed) with *pre* be-; *comb* calypto-, stegano-, stego-

covering *comb* lamelli-, lepido-, squamo-, tecti-, tegu-, -theca, theco-, theci-, veli-; *base* involver-, lorica-, oper-[2], -scut-, strag-. *See* **skin**

covert *pre* sub-; *comb* crypto-; *base* clandest-, furt-

covetousness *base* avar-, cup(id)-, pleonec-, pleonex-

cow *base* bou-, bov-, bu-, -vacc-

cowardly *base* pav-, timid-, trep-

cowl *base* cuculli-

crab *base* cancr-; **hermit~:** pagur-; **sea~:** gammar-

crack *comb* dicho-, -fid, fissi-, schisto-, schizo-, sulcato-, -tomy; *base* fatisc-, -par-, rim-

craft *base* techn-. *See* **make**

crane *comb* alector-, grallator-, grui-

crater *base* crateri-

craving *comb* eroto-, -lagnia, -mania, -orexia; *base* -appet-, conat-, -cup-, -libid-, -opt-, vell-; *suf* -urient

crazy *comb* lysso-, -mania; *base* ament-, dement-

creak *base* -crep-, -crepit-, strid-, stridul-

creased *base* -rug-

create/creation *pre* be-, em-, en-, meta-, trans-; *comb* aetio-, -blast , -blastic, blasto-, -craft, ergo-, etio-, -facient, -fic, -fication, -gen, -genesis, -genic, -genous, -geny, -parous, -plasia, -plasis, plasmo-, -plast, plastic, plasto-, -plasty, -poiesis, -poietic, -trope, -tropic, -tropism, tropo-, -tropous, -tropy, -urgy; *base* -fabr-, -fec-, -mut-, -vert-; *suf* -ate, -en, -fy, -ize, -otic

creep *base* -rept-

crescent *base* crescenti-, lunul-, menisc-

crest *comb* lopho-; *base* crist-

cricket *base* gryll-, locust-

crime *pre* dys-, mis-; *comb* caco-, enisso-, enosio-, kak-, kako-, mal-, male-, ponero-; *base* culp-, delict-, facin-, flagit-, hamart-, iniq-, nefar-, pecca-, perdit-, -prav-, sceler-, scelest-, turp-

crisp *comb* ulo-[3]

critical *comb* enisso-; *base* critico-

crocodile *base* crocodil-, -gavial-

crooked *comb* ancylo-, ankylo-, -campsis, campto-, campylo-, -clinal, -clinate, -cline, -clinic, clino-, -clinous, -clisis, curvi-, cyrto-, -flect , flex-, flexuoso-, lechrio-, loxo-, recurvo-, repando-, scolio-, -tort, -verge; *base* -clit-, -cliv-, sinu-

cross *comb* cruci-, stauro-

crosswise *comb* transverso-

crow *comb* coraci-, coraco-; *base* corvin-

crowd *comb* ochlo-

crown *base* corolli-, -coron-

cruel *base* agrio-

crushing *comb* stip-[2], tribo-, -tripsy

cry *tears: comb* dacryo-, fleb-, flet-, lachrim(o)-, lachrym(o)-, -plor-; *call out: comb* -claim; *base* -clam-, -plor-

crystal *comb* crystallo-

cube *comb* cubi-, cubo-; *base* tesser-

cuckoo *base* cucul-

cucumber *base* cucumi-

cudgel *base* fustig-

culpability *base* culp-, delinq-, laps-, -pecca-, sphal-

cultivation *comb* -ponic

culture *comb* ethno-

cumulus *comb* cumulo-

cunning *base* daedal-

cup (-shaped) *comb* calath-, calyc-, cotyle-, cotyli-, cotylo-, cupuli-, cyathi-, cyatho-, scyphi-, scypho-; *base* crin-, pocul-

curing *comb* -iatrics, -iatr(o)-, -iatry, medico-; *base* cur-, san-

curl, curly *comb* cirrhi-, cirrho-, cirri-, cirro-, ulo-[3]; *base* cincinn-, -crisp-. See **coil**

current *electrical: comb* rheo-; *water: comb* fluvio-; *base* -potam-, rheum-, -rip-; *contemporary: See* **new**

curse *base* anathem-

curved *comb* ancylo-, ankylo-, -campsis, campto-, campylo-, -clinal, -clinate, -cline, -clinic, clino-, -clinous, -clisis, curvi-, cyrto-, -flect, flex-, flexuoso-, lechrio-, loxo-, recurvo-, repando-, scolio-, -tort, -verge; *base* -clit-, -cliv-, sinu-

cushion *base* pulvin-, tylo-

custom *base* mor-[1], nomo-, -suet-

customer *base* empt-

cut *comb* -cide, cis-[2], -cise, -ectomy, inciso-, -sect, temno-, -tmesis, -tome, tomo-, -tomous, -tomy; *base* sec-

cutting *surgical: comb* -ectomy, -tome, -tomy

cuttlefish *base* -teuth-, sepi(a)-
cyanogen *comb* cyano-
cycle *comb* cyclo-; *base* circul-, orb-

cylinder *comb* cylindro-
cypress *base* cupress-
cyst *base* sacc-

D

dagger *base* sica-
damaging *comb* noci-, pesti-; *base* -nox-
damp *comb* hydro-, hygro-, udo-; *base* humect-, ulig-
dance *comb* choreo-; *base* orchest-, -salta-, tripud-
dandruff *base* furfur-, porrig-
danger *base* pericul-
Danish *comb* Dano-
dark(ness) *comb* ambly-, melan(o)-, nycto-, scoto-; *base* -achlu-, amaur-, fusc-, lyg-, obscur-, tenebr-
dart *base* tel-
dative *comb* dativo-
daughter *comb* fili-
daughter-in-law *base* -nur(us)-
dawn *base* -auror-, eos(o)-, luc-
day *base* diurn-, ephem-, hemer-, hodiern-, journ-, quotid-
daylight *base* -pheng-
deaf *base* coph-, -surd-
death *comb* mort(i)-, necro-, sapro-, thanato-; *base* exanim-, nerter-, obit-; *deadly:* phthart-
debility *comb* astheno-, -atrophia, lepto-, -plegia, -plegy; *base* -debil-, dimin-, enerv-, flacc-, labe-
decaying *comb* cario-, lysi-, -lysis, lyso-, -lyte, phthino-, phthisio-, -phthisis, putre-, putri-, pytho-, sapro-, septi-, septico-, septo-; *base* marcesc-, phthor-, tabe-; *suf* -ase
deceptive *base* apat-, dolero-, ludif-
decide *base* crit-[1]

decks *comb* -decker
decline *comb* -atrophia; *base* dimin-
decomposed *comb* septi-[2], septo-[1]
decomposing enzyme *suf* -ase
decrease *base* decresc-, dimin-
decree *base* -imper-, juss-, -mand-
deep *comb* batho-, bathy-; *base* profund-
deer *base* cervi-, elaph-
defeat *base* vict-, -vinc-
defecation *comb* -chezia, copro-, fim-, fimi-, kopro-, scato-, spatilo-, sterco-; *base* -fec(u)-
defect, bodily *comb* pero-; *base* -hamart-, -mutil-
defending *pre* pro-; *base* patroc-
defense *comb* -phylactic, phylacto-, -phylax, -phylaxis
deficiency *comb* isch-, oligo-, -penia
definition *comb* orismo-; *base* dior-
deformed *comb* pero-; *base* -mutil-
degree *suf* -ency
dehydrogenated *comb* dehydro-
deity *comb* theo-; *base* dei-
delayed *comb* brady-; *base* -cunct-, imped-, -mora-, -tard-. *See* late
delete *base* oblit-
deleterious *comb* noci-, pesti-; *base* -nox-, pericul-
delicate *comb* habro-, lepto-, subtil-, tenu-
delight *comb* chero-; *base* beati-, elat-, felic-, gaud-, jubil-, macar-
dementia *comb* lysso-, -mania; *base* ament-, dement-

demon *comb* daemono-, demono-; *base* diabol-, necyo-, satan-

demonstrating *comb* -deictic; *base* -monstr-

dense *comb* dasy-, pycno-, pykno-, -spiss-; *base* -crass-; ~*tufts:* cespitoso-

dentate *comb* dentato-

deny *base* -neg-

deoxygenated *comb* deoxy-

depart *base* relinq-

deposit of soft materials *comb* athero-

depraved *pre* dys-, mis-; *comb* caco-, enisso-, enosio-, kak-, kako-, mal-, male-, ponero-; *base* culp-, facin-, flagit-, hamart-, iniq-, nefar-, pecca-, perdit-, -prav-, sceler-, scelest-, turp-

deprive of *pre* ab-, apo-, be-, de-, des-¹, di-, dia-, dif-, dis-, e-, ec-, ef-, ex-, for-, off-, se-, with-; *comb* ectro-; *base* -spol-

depth *comb* batho-, bathy-; *base* -byss-

deputy *comb* vice-

derivative of *pre* meta-, para-

descended from *comb* -gone, -gonium, gono-, -gony, proli-; *suf* -ing

description *comb* -graphy

desert *comb* eremo-

deserving of *comb* -worthy

desire *comb* eroto-, -lagnia, -mania, -orexia; *base* -appet-, conat-, -cup-, -libid-, -opt-, vell-; *suf* -urient

destination *comb* teleo-, telo-, ultim(o)-; *base* -fin-, -termin-

destitute *comb* ptocho-, vidu-; *base*- mendic-, -paup-, -pov-

destroying *comb* lysi-, lyso-, -lysis, -lytic, -lyze, -phage, phago-, -phagous, -phagy; *base* -ate-⁴, perd-, phthart-, -vast-

determine *comb* -gnomy, -gnosia, -gnosis, -gnostic, gnoto-

detestation *comb* miso-, -phobe, -phobia, -phobic; *base* -invid-, -ira(sc)-, odi-

detrimental *comb* noci-, pesti-; *base* -nox-, pericul-

development *comb* -blast, -blastic, blasto-, -geny, -plasia, -plasis, -plast , -plastic, plasto-, -plasty, -trope, -tropism, tropo-, -tropous, -tropy; *base* -mut-, -vari-, -vert-; *late~:* serot-

device for measuring *comb* -meter

devil *comb* demono-, necyo-, satan-; *base* -diabol-

devoid *comb* ceno-, keno-; *base* -erem-, (ex)haur-, inan-, -vac(u)-

devotion to, excessive *comb* -latry; *suf* -ism

devour *comb* bromato-, -brotic, manduc-, -phage, phago-, -phagous, -phagy, -sitia, sitio-, sito-, -troph, -trophic, tropho-, -trophy, -vora, -vore, -vorous; *base* -alim-, -cib-, comest-, -ed-, escul-, glutt-, -gust-

dew *comb* droso-, -ror-

diaphragm *comb* -phrenic, phrenico-, phreno-

dice *base* alea-, astragal-, clero-, cubo-

die *See* **death**

different *comb* hetero-

difficult *pre* dys-; *comb* -bar, bary-, mogi-; *base* ardu-, stren-

dig *comb* orycto-; *base* fod-, -foss-

digest *comb* peps-, pept-, pepto-; ***partially~:*** *comb* chymo-

digestive fluid *comb* chyli-, chylo-, chymo-

digitalis *comb* digito-

dignity *base* celsi-

dilation *comb* -ectasia, -ectasis

dill *base* aneth-

dimension *comb* -footer, -sized; ~*of a sheet: suf* -mo. *Also see* "Dimension" in Part III

diminution *suf* -aster²

diminutive ending *suf* -cle, -cula, -cule, -culum, -culus, -een, -el, -ella, -en, -et, -ette, -idion, -idium, -ie, -illa, -illo, -isk, kin, -le, -let, -ling², -ock, -ola, -ole², -rel, -ula, -ule, -ulum, -ulus, -y³

dimness *comb* ambly-, melan(o)-, nycto-, scoto-; *base* -achlu-, amaur-, fusc-, lyg-, obscur-, opac-, tenebr-

dinner *comb* deipno-, prand-

dip *comb* -merge, -merse

directing *comb* -agogic, -agogue; *base* -vers-, -vert-

direction *comb*— ward, -ways, -wise; *suf* -ern, -ling³; ~*east:* euro-, -orient-; ~*north:* -borea-, septen-; ~*south:* -austr-, noto-; ~*west:* hesper-, occid-, -zephyr-. *Also see* "Direction" in Part III

dirt *comb* blenno-, -chezia, copro-, edaph-, fim(i)-, kopro-, miso-², myso-, -myxia, myxo-, paedo-¹, pedo-³, scato-, spatilo-, spurc-, stegno-, sterco-; *base* -fecu-, gleb-, hum-, macul-, molys-, rhypar-, rhypo-, rypo-, sord-

disastrous *base* funest-

discharge *flow: comb* rheo-, rheum-, -(r)rhage, -(r)rhagia, -(r)rhea, -(r)rhoea, -(r)rhoeica; *base* -flu(v)-, -fus-; *release: base* -miss-, -mit-, -pomp-

discipline *comb* mastigo-, rhabdo-; *base* castig-, peno-, poine-, -pun-

discontinue *comb* stasi-, -stasis, -stat; *base* fin-, termin-

discourse *comb* -claim, logo-, -logue, -lalia, -lexia, lexico-, -lexis, -lexy, -logy, -phone, hono-,

-phony, verbi-, verbo-, voc-, voci-, -voke; *base* -clam-, -dict-, -loc(u)-, -loqu-, -orat-, rhet-; *defective~: comb* -lalia, lalo-, -phasia, -phasic, -phasis, -phasy, -phemia, -phemy; *base* psell-

discover *base* heur-

disease *pre* dys-, mal-; *comb* loemo-, loimo-, noso-, -path, -pathic, patho-,-pathy; *base* aegr-, -morb-, -pecca-; ~*names: comb* -aemia, -emia; *suf* -asis, -ia, -itis, -oma, -osis; *skin~:* licheno-; ~*treatment: comb* -iatrics, iatro-, -iatry. *See* **disorder**

disfigured *comb* pero-; *base* -mutil-

disgorge *comb* -emesis, -emetic, emeto-

disgrace *base* sord-, turp-

disgust *base* fastid-

dish *comb* lecano-; *base* -leco-, scutel-

disk-shaped *comb* disco-; *base* -numm-

disorder *comb* atax-, ataxi-, -ataxia, ataxio-, ataxo-, -thymia, -phrenia, -phrenic; *base* -turb-; *of personality~: comb* -tonia

display *comb* -orama, phaeno-, pheno-; *base* -monstr-

dispute *base* velit-

dissimilar *comb* aniso-, anomalo-, anomo-, perisso-, poikilo-

dissolve *comb* lyo-, lysi-, -lysis, lyso-, -lyte, -lytic, -lyze; *base* -liqu-, -solu-, -solv-

distant *comb* disto-, tele-

distension *comb* -cele, -edema, ganglio-, phlogo-, phym-, -phyma, physa-, physo-, strum(i)-; *base* aug-, cresc-, physc-, strum-, -tum-, -turg-; *suf* -itis

distinct *separate: pre* dia-, dis-, for-, se-; *comb* -crit, dialy-, ideo-, proprio-, self-. *See* **divided;** *clear:*

comb lampro-, luc-, luci-; *base* -clar-

distress *base* aerumn-, vex-

divalent sulfur *comb* sulfo-

divergent *comb* divergenti-, divergi-, vari-

divided *pre* sub-; *comb* dicho-, -fid, fissi-, schisto-, schizo-, tomo-, -tomous, -tomy; ~*crosswise:* decuss-

dividing wall *comb* sept(o)-²

divination *comb* -mancy, -mantic; *base* augur-, hariol-, vatic-. *Also see* "Divination" in Part III

dizziness *comb* dino-²; *base* vertig-

do *pre* em-, en-; *comb* -craft, ergo-, -facient, -fic, -fication, -gen, -genesis, -genic, -genous, -geny, ideo-, -plast, -plastic, plasto-, -plasty, poiesis, -poietic,-urgy; *base* -fabr-, -fac-, -fec-¹; *suf* -ate, -en, -fy, -ize

docile *base* moriger-

doctor *comb* iatro-; *base* -med-

doctrine *suf* -ism, -logy

dodo *base* did-

doer *suf* -an, -ant, -ard, -arian, -art, -ary, -ast, -ator, -ee, eer, -en, -ent, -er, -ette, -ier, -ist, -le, -man, -nik, -o, -or, -person, -people, -ster, -woman

dog *comb* cyno-, kyno; *base* -can-¹

dogma *comb* dogmato-

doleful *comb* lype-; *base* dolor-, fleb-, flet-, luct-, trist-

doll *comb* paedo-²

dolphin *base* delphin-

domain of *suf* -dom²

donkey *base* as-, ono-

door *comb* osti-, porto-; *base* valv-

dormouse *base* glir-, myox-

dorsum *comb* dorsi-, dorso-, nota-, noto-, opistho-; *base* -terg-

dose *comb* poso-

dotted *comb* punctato-; *base* -stigm-

double *pre* bi-, bin-, bis-, di-², dy-, twi-; *comb* ambi-, ambo-, amphi-, ampho-, deutero-, deuto-, dicho-, diphy-, diplo-, disso-, double-, dui-, duo-, duplicato-, duplici-, dyo-, gemin-, zygo-. *Also see* "Numbers" in Part III

doubtful *base* ambig-, ancip-, apor-, dub-, vagu-

dove *base* columb-

down (from) *pre* a-, ab-, abs-, cata-, cath-, de-, kata-

downcast *comb* lype-; *base* dolor-, fleb-, flet-, luct-, -trist-

dozen *comb* dodeca-, duodec-, duodecim-, duoden-

dragon *base* draco-, draconi-

dragonfly *base* libell(ul)-

draw *art: comb* -gram, graph(o)-, -pict-; ***pull:*** *base* -duct-, -tract-; ~*forth:* *base* -haur-, -haust-

dread *comb* -phobe, -phobia, -phobic, phobo-; *base* pavid-, tim(or)-, trem-, trep-. *Also see* "Fear" in Part III

dream *comb* oneiro-

dregs *base* fec-²

drink *comb* pino-, poto-; *base* -bib-, pocul-; ~*made from __ : suf* -ade

dripping *base* driri-

drive *base* -pel-, -pul-

driving away, out *comb* -fuge

drooping *comb* -ptosia, -ptosis; *base* -flacc-. *See* **bent**

drop ***liquid:*** *comb* gutti-, stilli-; *base* stact-, stagm-; ***fall:*** *comb* -ptosia, -ptosis; *base* -cad-, -cas-, -cid-

dropping *base* stalac-, stalag-

drugs *comb* pharmaco-; *base* medic-

drum *comb* tympano-

drunk *base* inebr-, methys-, temul-

dry *comb* carpho-, xero-; *base* arid-, celo-[2], cherso-, -sicc-

dry out *base* marces-, marcid-

duck *base* anat-, fuligul-

dull *base* hebet-, obtus-, -tard-; *~vision: comb* ambly-

dung *comb* -chezia, copro-, fimi-, kopro-, scato-, spatilo-, sterc(o)-; *base* -fec(u)-, -merd-; *~hill:* sterquil-

during *pre* con-, in-, inter-, per-

dusk *base* -crepus-, lyg-

dusky *comb* fusc-, fusco-, -phaein, phaeo-, phein-, pheo-

dust *comb* coni-[1], -conia, conio-, konio-; *base* amath-, pulver-; *dusty place:* conist-

duty *comb* hypegia-, hypengy-; *base* paralip-

dwarf *comb* chamae-, nan(n)o-,

dwelling *comb* ekist-; *base* -aed-, -cali-, -dom-, -edi-; *suf* -age

E

each *comb* katheno-

eager *base* avid-, cupid-

eagle *base* aet-, aquil-

ear *comb* auri-[1], auriculo-, oto-. *See* **sound**

early *pre* ante-, pre-; *comb* prim-, primi-, primo-, proto-; *~period: pre* eo-; *comb* paleo-, protero-

earth *comb* agro-, -gaea, geo-, hum-; *base* secul-, tellur-, -terr-

earthquake *comb* seismo-, tromo-

earwig *base* forficul-

east *base* euro-, -orient-

easy *base* -facil-

eating *comb* bromato-, -brotic, manduc-, -phage, phago-, -phagous, -phagy, -sitia, sitio-, sito-, -troph, -trophic, tropho-, -trophy, -vora, -vore, -vorous; *base* -alim-, -cib-, comest-, -ed-[1], escul-, glutt-, -gust-

eccentric *comb* aetheo-, anom(o)-, anomalo-. *See* **irregular**

educate *comb* -pedia; *base* -didact-, doc-, -paed-

eel *base* anguill-, -cyclostom-, -muraen-

effect *comb* -ergy

efficient *base* efficac-, habil-, quali-

effort *base* conat-, peir-

egg *comb* oo-, ovario-, ovi-[1], ovo-; *~yolk:* lecith-, lecitho-, vitell-; *~shaped:* ovato-

Egyptian *comb* Egypto-

eight *comb* octa-, octo-, ogdo-; *~hundred:* octocent-. *Also see* "Numbers" in Part III

eighteen *comb* duodeviginti-, octakaideca-

eighth *base* octan-

eighty *base* octogen-, octoges-

eland *base* taurotrag-

elation *base* jubil-

elbow *base* -ancon-

elderly *comb* gerasco-, gero-, geronto-, grand-, presby-, presbyter-; *base* -antiqu-, -sen-, -vet-; *~woman:* grao-

electric(al) *comb* electro-, galvano-; *~induction: comb* inducto-

elementary *base* prim-, -rud-; *~particle: comb* stoichio-; *suf* -on

elephant *base* elephant-, pachyderm-

elevation *comb* acro-, alti-, alto-, bato-, hypsi-, hypso-; *base* procer-

eleven *comb* endeca-, hendeca-, undeca-, undecim-. *Also see* "Numbers" in Part III

elk *base* cerv-

elm *base* ulm-

emaciated *base* tab-. *See* **wasting away**

emanation *comb* atmo-, -capnia, capno-, vapo-, vapori-; *base* nebul-

embarrassment *base* pud-, verecund-

embezzle *base* pecul-

emboss *base* toreut-

embryo(nic) *comb* -blast, -blastic, blasto-, -blasty; *base* embry-

emendation *comb* ortho-; *base* castig-, emend-

emerald *base* smaragd-

eminent *comb* over-

emotions *comb* thymo-; ***disordered~:*** -thymia

empty *comb* ceno-³, keno-; *base* -erem-, (ex)haur-, inan-, -vac(u)-

emu- *base* rat-

emulation *base* zelo-

enamel *comb* amelo-

encounter *base* congress-, congru-

encourage *base* -hort-

end *comb* teleo-, telo-, ultim-, ultimo-; *base* -fin-, -termin-; ***endless:*** apeiro-

enduring *base* diuturn-, dur(o)-, perenn-, perm-, stabil-

enema *base* clysm-; clyst-

enemy *base* advers-, hostil-, inimic-

energy *comb* dyna(mo)-

engage in *suf* -ize

English *comb* Anglo-

engrave *comb* -glyph, glypto-

enigmatic *comb* enigmatico-

enlarged *pre* ad-, extra-, hyper-, super-; *comb* auxano-, auxo-, multi-, myria-, myrio-, out-, over-, -plasia, pleni-, pleo-, pleio-, pleon-, plethys-, plio-, pluri-, pol-

laki-, poly-; *base* ampl-, -aug-, -cresc-, dilat-, -fold-, pler-, -plet-

enormous *comb* bronto-, dino-, giganto-, mega-, megalo-, -megaly

enter *comb* intro-; *base* ingress-

enthusiasm *base* ard-, alacr-, -ferv-, zelo-

entice *base* lenocin-

entire(ly) *pre* be-, cata-, de-, kata-, ob-, per-; *comb* holo-, omni-, pan-, panto-, stone-, toti-

entrance *comb* porto-

entreaty *base* litan-, -preca-

enveloped *pre* be-; *comb* calypto-, stegano-, stego-

environment *comb* -cole, -colent, -colous, eco-, oeco-, oiko-; *base* -aed-, -dom-, -edi-

envy *base* -invid-

enzymes *comb* zym-, zymo-; *suf* -ase

epidemic *base* luet-, morb-, pestil-

epoch *comb* -cene

equal(ly) *pre* co-; *comb* equi-, homalo-, homo-, homolo-, iso-, pari-, tauto-

equivalent *pre* para-, quasi-; *comb* homeo-, omœo-, homoio-, homolo-, iso-, -phane, -phanic; *base* simil-; *suf* -acean, -aceous, -al, -an, -ar, -ary, -ean, -en, -eous, -esque, -ful, -ic, -il, -ile, -ine, -ing, -ish, -itious, -ize, -like, -ode, -oid, -ose, -osity, -some, -tious, -ular, -y

erase *base* oblit-

erect *comb* ithy-, ortho-, recti-; *base* ard-³

ermine *base* mustel-

error *base* culp-, delinq-, laps-, pecc-, sphal-

eruption *comb* -anthema

erythrocyte *comb* erythro-

essence *base* -ousia, -ousian, quid-

eternal *comb* ever-; *base* etern-, perpet-, semper-

ethers *suf* -ole

ethical *comb* ethico-

ethmoid bone *comb* ethmo-

European *comb* Euro-, Europaeo-, Europeo-

eustachian tube *comb* salpingo-

even *level: comb* homalo-, homolo-, plani-, plano-, plate-, platy-; *number:* artio-. *See* equal

evening *comb* -noct(i)-, nyct(o)-; *base* crepus-, -vesper-

event *comb* -athlon, -athon, -machy, -off. *See* festival

everlasting *base* assid-, contin-, incess-, perpet-

every *comb* katheno-, omni-, pan-, pant(o)-

evil *pre* dys-, mis-; *comb* caco-, iniq-, kak(o)-, mal(e)-, ponero-; *base* -prav-, sceler-, turp-

evolution *comb* -genesis. *See* creation

examination *comb* -opsy, -scope, -scopic, scopo-, -scopy; *base* -(in)quir-, -(in)quis-, -scrut-

example of *comb* -type; *suf* -ism

excessive *pre* hyper-, super-, ultra-; *comb* over-, poly-; *~craving: comb* -lagnia, -mania; *~devotion: comb* -latry; *suf* -ism; *~drinking and eating: base* crapul-; *~flow: comb* -(r)rhagia, -(r)rhage, -(r)rhagy

exchange *base* -allac-, -allag-, -allaxis-, camb-

excision *comb* -(ec)tomy

excite *comb* agito-; *base* -cit-

exclaim *base* clam-, vocif-

exclude *pre* ab-, apo-, be-, de-, des-, di-, dia-, dif-, dis-, e-, ec-, ef-, ex-, for-, off-, se-, with-; *comb* ectro-; *base* -spol-

excrement *comb* -chezia, copro-,

fimi-, kopro-, scato-, spatilo-, sterco-; *base* -fec(u)-, -merd-

exertion *comb* -ergasia, ergasio-, -ergic, ergo-, -ergy, -orial, -pragia, -praxia, -praxis; *suf* -esce, -escence, -escent, -esis; *quality of~: comb* -pragia

exhaustion *comb* pono-; *base* -fatig-, -kopo-, -lass-

exhibit *comb* phaeno-, pheno-; *base* -monstr-

existence *comb* onto-; *base* -esse-

exit *base* egress-, relinq-

expansion *comb* -ectasia, -ectasis; *base* -dilat-

experienced *base* -vet-

experiment *base* peir-

extended *comb* dolicho-, -footer, longi-, macro-, maxi-; *base* procer-; *~words:* sesquipedal-

extent *comb* quant(i)-; *suf* -age, -ful, -ling[3]

external *comb* ect(o)-, exo-, extra-

extinct mammal form *comb* -there, therio-, thero-

extol *base* laud-

extra *pre* hyper-, super-. *See* increased

extremity *comb* acro-, aorto-, -mele, -melia[1], melo-[3]

exultation *comb* chero-; *base* beati-, felic-, jubil-, macar-

eye *comb* eid(o)-, oculi-, oculo-, op-, ophthalmo-, -opia, opsi-, -opsia, -opsis, opso-[2], -opsy, optico-, opto-, -scope, -scopic, -scopy; *base* blep-, ommat-, -spec-, -spic-, -vid-, -vis-; *cornea of~: comb* corneo-, kerato-; *corner of~:* canth(o)-; *~covering:* sclero-; *iris of~:* irido-; *~lash:* cili-; *~lid:* blepharo-, tarso-; *one-eyed:* lusc-; *pupil of~:* core(o)-,

-coria, coro-, -koria, pupillo-;
~retina: retino-
eyebrows *base* ophry-; *space be-*tween~:* glabello-
eyelet *comb* ocelli-

F

fabricate/fabrication *pre* be-; *comb* -craft, ergo-, -facient, fic-, -fication, -plastic, -plast, plasto-, -plasty, -poiesis, -poietic, -urgy; *base* aedi-, edi-, -fabr-, -fac-, -fec-; *suf* -ate, -fy, -ize

face *comb* facio-, prosop(o)-, -visaged

faceted *comb* -hedral, -hedron

fact of being *suf* -cy, -ency

faded *base* -marc-

fail(ure) *pre* dis-; *base* atychi-, kak-orrhaph-

fainting *base* asthen-

faith *comb* -ousia; *base* -cred-, -fid-[1], -pist-; *suf* -ism

fake *see* **false**

falcon *base* accipit-, falconi-, raptor-

fall *base* -autumn-

falling *comb* -ptosia, -ptosis; *base* -cad-, -cas-, -cid-

fallopian tube *comb* salpingo-

false *comb* mytho-, pseudo-; *base* fict-, kibdelo-, -mendac-, notho-

fame/famous *base* celebr-, laud-, -lustr-

family *base* cogn-, famil-, stirp-

family names [zoology] *suf* -idae

famine *comb* limo-[2]

fan *base* rhipi-; *~like:* flabelli-, rhipido-

far *comb* disto-, tele-

farewell *base* vale-

farming *base* agricol-, agricult-, arat-

fascia *comb* fascio-

fast *comb* ocy-, tacho-, tachy; *base* alacr-, -celer-, veloc-

fasten *base* -hapto-[2], pegm-. *See* **bind**

fasting *comb* limo-[2]

fat *comb* adip(o)-, lipo-[1], pimel(o)-, pio-, stearo-, steato-; *base* -aliph-, lipar-, -obes-, -pingu-, sebo-; *~degeneration:* comb* -demia

father *comb* pater-, patri-

father-in-law *base* socer-

fatigue *comb* pono-; *base* -fatig-, -kopo-, lass-

fault *base* culp-, delinq-, laps-, -pecca-, sphal-

fear *comb* -phobe, -phobia, -phobic, phobo-; *base* pavid-, tim(or)-, -trem-, -trep-. *Also see* "Fear" in Part III

feast day *suf* -fest, -ia, -mas

feather(like) *comb* penni-, pennati-, pinnati-, pinnato-, pinni-, plum(i)-, pteno-, pter, ptero-, pterono-, -pterous, pterygo-, -pteryl, ptilo-. *See* **wing**

feces *comb* -chezia, copro-, fim(i)-, kopro-, scato-, spatilo-, sterco-; *base* -fec(u)-, -merd-

feeble *comb* astheno-, -atrophia, lepto-, -plegia, -plegy; *base* -debil-, dimin-, enerv-, flacc-, labe-

feeding on *comb* bromato-, -brotic, manduc-, -phage, phago-, -phagous, -phagy, -sitia, sitio-, sito-, -troph, -trophic, tropho-, -trophy, -vora, -vore, -vorous; *base* -alim-, -bosc-, -cib-, -gust-feel *comb* -aphia, -apsia, hapt(o)-, -path, -pathic, patho-, -pathy, sensi-, senso-, sensori-, thigmo-; *base* -palp-, -sens-, -sent-, -tact-, -tang-

feet long *comb* -foot(er)

feign *comb* pseudo-; *base* -simula-

felicity *comb* chero-; *base* beati-, felic-, jubil-, macar-

female *comb* gyn(e)-, gyneco-, gyneo-, gyno-, -gynous, -gyny, -para, she-, thely-, -wife; *base* femin- muliebr-, mulier-; *suf* -a⁴, -en, enne, -ess, -ette, -ice², -ine, -stress, -trice, -trix; *elderly~:* grao-

ferment *social: base* -agit-, -tumult-, -turb-

fermentation *comb* zym(o)-

fern *comb* pterido-; *base* filic-

ferret *base* mustel-, viverr-

ferric iron *comb* ferri-

fervor *base* ard-, alacr-, -ferv-, zelo-

festival (names) *comb—* athon, -fest, -mas; *base* -heort-; *suf* -ia

fetus *comb* brepho-, cyo-, embryo-, kyo-; *~membrane: comb* allanto-, amnio-

fever *comb* febri-, pyreto-, -pyrexia

few *comb* oligo-; *base* pauc(i)-

fiber *base* erio-, fibri-, ino-

fibril-shaped *comb* fibrilloso-

fibrin *comb* fibrino-

fibrous matter *comb* fibro-, fibroso-, funi-, strom-; *~growth:* ino-; *~tissue:* fascio-

fibula *base* peroneo-

fictitious *comb* pseudo-

fiddle *base* pandur-

field *comb* agri-, agro-; *base* agrest-, camp-¹

fifteen *base* pentakaideca-, quindec-. *Also see* "Numbers" *in Part III*

fifty *base* pentaconta-, pentacosta-, quinquagen-, quinquages-

fig *base* -fici-, -syc-

fight *comb* macho-, -machy, pugn-; *base* -bell-, pugil-

figure *comb* icono-, -form; *base* schem-; *~with (x) angles:* -gon; *~with (x) surfaces:* -hedral, -hedron

filament *comb* fili-, filio-, filamento-, filo-, mito-, nemato-; *base* stema-

filled with *comb* -filled, plen(i)-; *base* -pler-, -plet-; *suf* -acious, -ate, -ic, -id², -ful, -ose, -osity, -ous, -ulent, -y

filter *base* col-²

filth *comb* blenno-, -chezia, copro-, fim(i)-, kopro-, miso-, myso-, -myxia, myxo-, paedo-, pedo-, scato-, spatilo-, spurc-, stegno-, sterco-; *base* -fec-², molys-, rhypar-, rupo-, rhypo-, rypo-, sord-; *filthy talk:* borbor-

fin *comb* pinni-, pterygo-

final stage *comb* eschato-, teleo-, telo-, ultim(o)-; *base* -fin-, -termin-

finch *base* fringill-

find *base* heur-

fine *comb* habro-, lepto-, subtil-, tenu-

finger *comb* -dactyl, dactylo-, -dactylous, -dactyly, digiti-; *~like: comb* digitato-; *~ring: comb* dactylio-

fingernail *comb* -onychia, onycho-

Finnish *comb* Finno-

fir *base* abiet-

fire *comb* igni-, pyr(o)-; *base* ard-, ars-, flagr-, flamm-, incend-, phlog-

firefly *base* lampyr-

firm *comb* duro-, sclero-

first *comb* arch-, fore-, pre-, primi-, primo-, pro-, proso-, protero-, proto-; *base* -princip-

fish(like) *comb* icthyo-, pisci-; *base* halieut-; *bony~:* scopeli

fishing *base* riv-
fissure *comb* fissuri-, rim-
fist *base* pug-, pygm-
fit *seizure: comb* -agra, -lepsia, -lepsis, -lepsy, -leptic; *capable: comb* -worthy; *suf* -able, -ibility, -ible, -ile
five *comb* cinque-, penta-, quin-, quinque-, quint(i)-; *~hundred:* quincent-. *Also see* "Numbers" *in* Part III
fixation *comb* -lagnia, -philia; *surgical~:* -pexy
fixed *comb* stasi-, -stasis, -stat, stato-; *base* stabil-
flag *comb* vexillo-
flamingo *base* phoenicopter-
flammable *comb* ard-, ars-
flank *comb* laparo-
flash *comb* sela-; *base* -fulg-, stilpno-
flask *base* lagen-, ampul-
flat *comb* plain-, plani-, plano-[1], plat-[1], platy-; *~plain:* pedion-
flattery *base* adul-, bland-
flatulence *comb* physa-
flavin *comb* -flavin, flavo-
flaw *base* culp-, delinq-, laps-, pecc-, sphal-
flax *comb* byssi-, linar-
flea *base* psyll-[2], puli-
flee *base* avers-, drapeto-, fug-, -phygo-
flesh *comb* carni-, carnoso-, creo-, kreo-, -sarc, sarco-. *See* skin
flexible *base* agil-, facil-, ingen-
flight *comb* avi; *base* -fug-. *See* flying
fling *comb* -bole, -bolic, bolo-, -boly; *base* ballist-, -jact-, -jacula-, -ject-
flipper *comb* pinni-, pterygo-
flock *base* -greg-
flood *base* -antlo-, diluv-, inund-; *~tide:* plemyr-

floor (soilbed) *base* edaph-
flora *comb* botano-, herbi-, -phyte, phyto-; *base* veget-; *suf* -aceae, -ad, -ales, -eae, -ia
flour *comb* aleuro-; *base* farin-
flower *comb* antho-, -anthous, flori-, -florous; *~garland: base* corolli-
flow(ing) *comb* rheo-, rheum-, -(r)rhage, -(r)rhagia, -(r)rhea, -(r)rhoea, -(r)rhoeica; *base* -flu(v)-, -fus-
fluid *comb* -plasm, plasmo-; *base* -liqu-, -ner-
fluorescence *comb* fluo(ro)-
fluorine *comb* fluo-, fluor(o)-
flute *comb* aulo-
fly *insect: base* cyclorraph-, musc-[1], myia-
flying *comb* aero-, avia-, avio-, aviono-. *See* wing
foam *base* aphro-, -spum-
focused on *comb* -centered, -centric
foe *base* advers-, hostil-, inimic-
fog *comb* fracto-, nephelo-, nepho-; *base* brum-[2], calig-, homichlo-, nebul-, -nub-
fold *comb* -plex, plicato-, plici-, -ptych
follow(ing) *pre* epi-, meta-, post-; *comb* after-, hind-, postero-; *base* -secut-, -sequ-; *suf* -an
folly *see* foolish
food *comb* bromato-, -brotic, manduc-, opso-, -phage, phago-, -phagous, -phagy, -sitia, sitio-, sito-, -troph, -trophic, tropho-, -trophy, -vora, -vore, -vorous; *base* -alim-, -cib-, escul-, -gust-, -nutr-; *partially digested~:* chymo-. *Also see* "Food" *in* Part III.
foolish *base* fatu-, inan-, moro-, stult-
foot *comb* ped-[1], pedati-, -pede, pedi-, pedo-[1], -poda, -pode,

-podium, -pod, podo-, -podous, -pus *base* -plant-; *~sole:* -pelm-, plant-

footprint *comb* ichno-, stibo-

for *pre* pro-

forbid *base* prohib-

force *comb* dyna-, dynamo-, mega-, megalo-, -megaly, -sthenia, stheno-; *base* -forc-, -fort-, -poten-, robor-

forceps *base* labido-

forearm *comb* ulno-

forehead *comb* metopo-

foreign(er) *comb* perisso-, xeno-; *base* -ali-

foremost *comb* arch-, archi-, proto-; *base* -prim-, -princip-

forest *comb* dendri-, dendro-, -dendron, hylaeo-, saltu-, silvi-, xylo-; *base* arbor-, nemo(r), -sylv-

forever *comb* ever-; *base* etern-, perpet-, semper-

forget *base* leth-

forked *base* -furc-

form, a *comb* eid(o)-, -form, -morph, -morphic, -morphism, morpho-, -morphous; *base* -figur-, -schem-

form, to *pre* be-; *comb* aetio-, etio-; *base* -fabr-, fac-, fec-, fic-

formation *pre* em-, en-, meta-, trans-; *comb* -blast, -blastic, blasto-, -craft, ergo-, etio-, -facient, -fic, -fication, -gen, -genesis, -genic, -genous, -geny, -parous, -plasia, -plasis, plasmo-, -plast, -plastic, plasto-, -plasty, -poiesis, -poietic, -trope, -tropic, -tropism, tropo-, -tropous, -tropy, -urgy; *base* -fec-, -mut-, -vert-; *suf* -ate, -en, -fy, -ize, -otic

fornicate *base* copul-, scort-, stupr-

fortification *base* castella-

fortune *luck: comb* tycho-; *base*

faust-; *wealth: comb* pluto-; *base* opul-

forty *base* quadragen-, quadrages-

forward *pre* fore-, pre-, pro-[1]; *comb* antero-, proso-

fossil *base* oryct-; *suf* -ite

foul *dirt: comb* blenno-, -chezia, copro-, edaph-, fim(i)-, kopro-, miso-, myso-, -myxia, myxo-, paedo-, pedo-, scato-, spatilo-, spurc-, stegno-, sterco-; *base* -fecu-, gleb-, hum-, macul-, molys-, rhypar-, rhypo-, rypo-, sord-; *evil: pre* dys-, mis-; *comb* caco-, iniq-, kak(o)-, mal(e)-, ponero-, -prav-, turp-

foundation *comb* base-, basi-, baso-

fountain *base* cren-[2], pego-

four(th) *comb* quadr-, quadrato-, quadri-, quadru-, quart-, quarter-, quarti-, quat-, quater-, tetarto-, tetra-, tessera-; *~cycles:* tetra-, cyclo-; *~hundred:* quadricent-; *~times:* tetrakis-. *Also see* "Numbers" in Part III

fourteen *base* quattuordec-, tessaradeca-, tetradeca-, tetrakaideca-

fowl *base* gallin-

fox *base* alopec-, vulpi-

foxglove *comb* digito-

fraction *base* -par-[1], parti-; *~of a meter: comb* -meter

fracture *comb* -clasia, -clasis, -clastic, rhegma-, -(r)raghia, -(r)rhexis; *base* agmat-, -fract-, frag-, -frang-, -rupt-; *bone~:* catagm-

fragile *see* **frail**

fragment *comb* clasmato-, -fid; *base* frust-, -par-

frail *comb* lepto-; *base* -asthen-, coupho-, -debil-, koupho-

framework *base* pegm-

fraudulent *base* apat-, dolero-, ludif-

freckle *base* lentig-
free *comb* eleuthero-; *base* -liber-, vac(u)-
freeing *comb* lyo-, lysi-, -lysis, lyso-, -lyte, -lytic, -lyze; *base* -liqu-, -solu-, -solv-
freezing *comb* cheima-, crymo-, cryo-, frigo-, gelo-, kryo-, pago-, psychro-, rhigo-; *base* alg-, glac-
French *comb* Franco-, Gallo-
frenzied *base* frenet-
frequent *comb* pluri-, pollaki-, poly-; *base* crebr-; *suf* -le. See **repeatedly**
fresh *comb* thalero-; *base* -nov-
friction *comb* tribo-, -tripsy; *base* trit-
friendship *comb* socio-; *base* -am-, amic-¹, comit-
fright *see* **fear**
frigid *see* **freezing**
fringe *comb* crosso-; *base* -fimbr-, lacin-, thysan-; *small~:* fimbrilli-; *~with hairs:* fimbriato-
frog *comb* batracho-, bufo-, phryno-, rani-; *base* polyped-
from *pre* a-², ab-, abs-, apo-, e-, ex-, with-
front *pre* ante-, pre-, pro-; *comb* antero-, fore-, proso-
frontal bone *comb* fronto-
frost *base* cryo-, gel-¹, kryo-, pachno-, pago-, pruin-, rhigo-

froth *base* -spum-
fructose *comb* fructi-, fructo-
fruit *comb* -carp, -carpic, carpo-¹, -carpous, pomi-, pomo-; *base* -frug-¹; *~sugar:* fructi-, fructo-
fruitfly *base* drosophyl-, trypet-
fugitive *base* drapeto-
full of *comb* -filled, pleni-, pleo-, plero-, pluri-; *base* -pler-, -plet-; *suf* -acious, -ate, -ic, -ful, -ilent, -ose², -osity, -ous, -ulent, -y
fun *comb* chero-
function *suf* -ate³, -ise
functionally disordered *pre* para-
funeral rites *base* epicid-, thren-
fungus *comb* fungi-, morilli-, -mycete, mycet(o)-, -mycin, myco-, uredo-; *base* bolet-
funnel *comb* choano-, infundibuli-
fur *base* dora-
furious *base* chol-, -invid-, -ira-, -margy
furnish with *pre* be-; *suf* -ate
furrow *comb* holco-, stria-, striato-, strio-, sulcato-; *base* -scrobic-, strig-
fusion *pre* co-; *comb* conjugato-, -ergasia, gameto-, gamo-, hapto-, junct-; *base* aps-, apt-, -greg-, -soc-; *suf* -ate, -ize
futile *base* futil-, inutil-, mataeo-

G

gable *base* fastig-
gain *base* lucr-, quaest-
gall *bile:* *comb* bili-, chol(e)-, gall-; *tumorous plant tissue:* cecid-
galvanic *comb* galvano-
gambling *base* alea-
gamete *comb* gameto-

ganglion *comb* ganglio-
gangrene *base* sphacel-
gap *base* -apert-, -cav-, fenest-, foram-, œgo-, oigo-, osti-, patul-, pylo-, rim, valv-
garb *base* habil-, hesto-, -vest-
garden *comb* horti-

garlic *base* alli-, scoro-

gas *comb* aeri-, aero-, gaso-, pneumo-; ***stomach~:*** physa-, physo-

gash *comb* -cide, cis-, -cise, -ectomy, inciso-, -sect, temno-, -tmesis, -tome, tomo-, -tomous, -tomy; *base* sec-

gastric *comb* chyli-, chylo-, chyma-

gate *comb* porto-; *base* osti-, -pyl-

gathered together *comb* cumulo-; *base* acerv-, -sor-

gelatin *comb* gelatino-

generate *comb* aetio-, etio-, -gen, geno-, -genesis, -genic, -genous, -geny, -gone, -gonium, gono-, -gony, -phyletic. *See* cause

genital(s) *comb* genito-; *base* -aede-; ***female~:*** colpo-; ***male~:*** phallo-

gentle *base* -len-, mansue-, miti-, moll-

geological epoch *comb* -cene

geometric figure *comb* -gon, -hedral, -hedron

gerbil *base* cricet-

German *comb* Germano-, Teutano-, Teuto-

germinal *comb* -blast, blasto-, -blasty, -carp, -carpic, carpo-, -carpous, sperma-, -spermal, spermatio-, spermato-, spermi-, -spermic, spermo-, -spermous, sporo-; *base* semin-

germs *comb* bacilli-, bacillo-, -bacter, bacteri-, bacterio-

get *base* -cap-, -cep-, -cip-, -dyte-

ghost *base* phantas-, phasm-, spectr-

gibbon *base* hylobat-

gift *base* don-, dor-, mun-

gigantic *comb* bronto-, dino-, giganto-, mega-, megalo-, -megaly, super-. *See* large

gills *comb* -branchia, branchio-

ginger *base* zingiber-

giraffe *base* artiodactyl-

girdle *comb* zoni-, zono-; *base* -cing-, zoster-. *See* band

give *base* -don-; ***~birth:*** *base* -partur-; ***~way:*** *base* -ced-, -cess-

glacier *comb* glacio-

gland *comb* adeni-, adeno-, balani-, balano-; ***swollen~:*** strum(i)-

glass(y) *comb* crystallo-, hyalo-, vitreo-, vitri-, vitro-. *See* mirror

gleam *comb* sela-; *base* -fulg-, gano-, lustr-, rutil-, stilpno-

glittering *base* stilpno-

globe *comb* ano-, annul-, crico-, cyclo-, disco-, globi-, globo-, glom-, gyro-, orbito-, -sphere, sphero-, stilli-, zon-, zoni-; *base* -anu-, -cing-, -cinct-, -circin-, -circul-, -coron-, -glomer-, -numm-, -orb-, -rot-, -troch-

gloomy *base* fusc-, obscur-, tenebr-

glowworm *base* lampyr-

glue (like) *comb* colleto-, -glea, -glia, glio-, glutin-, kollo-; *base* coll-²

glum *comb* lype-; *base* dolor-, fleb-, flet, luct-, -trist-

glutted *comb* -filled, pleni-, pleo-, plero-, pluri-; *base* -pler-, -plet-; *suf* -acious, -ate, -ic, -ful, -ilent, -ose, -osity, -ous, -ulent, -y

glycerin, glycerol, glycogen *comb* glico-, gluco-

gnash *base* brux-, frend-, mol-

gnat *base* culici-

gnaw *base* -trog-. *See* chew

gnu *base* connochaet-

go *comb* -grade, -motive, -plania , plano-; *base* -bat-, -ced-, -cess-, -cur(s)-, -grad-, -gress-, -mob-, -vad-, -vas-; ***~away:*** out-; ***~into:*** -dyte-; ***~forward:*** pro-; ***~toward:*** -bound, -petal

goal *comb* teleo-, telo-, ultim(o)-; *base* -fin-, -termin-

goat *comb* capri-, egagro-, trago-; *base* hircin-

goblet *base* pocul-

God *comb* theo-; *base* dei-

goiter *base* strum(i)-

gold(en) *comb* auri-[2], auro-, chrys(o)-. *Also see* "Colors" in Part III

goldfish *base* cyprin-

gonad *comb* gonado-

good *pre* bene-, eu-; *base* agath-, bon-, prob-

goodbye *base* vale-

goods *base* empor-, -merc-

goose *base* anser-, cheno-

gorgeous *comb* calli-, callo-; *base* kal-, pulchr-

gorilla *base* -pong-

gourd *base* cucurbit-

government *comb* -archy, -cracy, -crat(ic); *base* gubern-

grab *base* rap-, rep-. *See* grasp

graceful *comb* habro-

grafting *base* surcul-

grain *comb* grani-; *base* farr-, farrag-, -frument-

gram *comb* -gram

grandfather *base* av(us)-

grandmother *base* av(ia)-

granite *comb* graniti-; **like, of~:** grano-

granular *comb* coni-, -conia, conio-, granulo-

grape (like) *comb* acini-, botry-, staphylo-, vini-, vino-, viti-; *base* racem-, -rhag-, -uvi-, -uvu-

grasp *comb* -tain; *base* -cap(t)-, -cathex-, -ger-, -hapt-, -prehend, prehens-, -ten-

grass *base* agrost-, gramin-

grasshopper *base* acrid-, gryll-, locust-

grave *comb* -taph, tapho-; *base* sepul-

gravel *base* glare-

gray *comb* glauco-, -phaein, phaeo-, pheo-, polio-; *base* caesi-, -can-[2], -gris-, -tephr-. *Also see* "Colors" in Part III

grazing *base* pascu-

grease *base* lipar-, sebo-, unct-, ungu-

great *size: comb* macro-, magni-, maxi-, plethys-; *base* -ampl-, -maj-; *suf* -fold. *See* gigantic

greater *pre* super-; *comb* meizo-, out-

greed *base* avar-, avid-, cup(id)-, edac-, gulos-, pleonec-, pleonex-

Greek *comb* Graeco-, Greco-; *base* Hellen-

green *comb* chloro-, glauco-, olivaceo-; *base* -beryl-, caes-, oliv-, porrac-, pras-, smaragd-, thall-, thallas-, verd-, -vir-, virid-. *Also see* "Colors" in Part III

gridiron *base* graticul-

grief *comb* lype-; *base* dolor-, fleb-, flet-, luct-, trist-

grind *base* -brux-, frend-, mol-

grit *comb* ammo-, aren-, arenaceo-, glare-, psammo-, sabul-

groin *comb* bubo-, inguino-

groove *comb* bothr-, -glyph, glypto-, stria-, striato-, strio-, sulcato-; *base* canalic-, sulc-. *See* cleft

grope *base* pselaph-

ground *base* edaph-, geo-, -hum-, -terr-

group (of) *suf* -age, -ery, -hood, -ship

group names [zoology] *suf* -ini

grouse *base* gallinac-, tetrao-

grove *suf* -etum

grow, growth *comb* auxano-, auxeto-, auxo-, -blast, -blastic, blasto-, -blasty, -colous, -crease, -culture, -nastic, -nasty, onco-, -physis, -plasia, -plasis, -plast, -plastic, plasto-, plethys-, verruci-;

base -aug, -cresc-; *suf* -oma, -ome; ~*in:* -cole, -colent, -colous; ~*together:* symphyo-
guess *base* -stoch-
guide *base* gubern-
guilt *base* -culp-
gull *base* gavi-, lar-

gullet *comb* esophago-, œsophago-
gulp *base* glutt-
gum-yielding *comb* gutti-
gums *comb* gingivo-, oulo-, ulo-[2]
gyrating *comb* gyro-
gyroscope *comb* gyro-

H

habit *base* -hexi-
habitat *comb* -cole, -colent, -colous, eco-, oiko-; *base* -aed-, -dom-, -edi-
hailstone *base* grandin-, chalax-
hair/hairlike *comb* capilli-, chaet(o)-, cilii-, cilio-, -coma, comi-, como-, crin(i)-, dasy-, fimbr-, fimbrilli-, pili-, pilo-, piloso-, -trich, -tricha, tricho-, villoso-; *base* hirsut-, hispid-, lanug-, -thrix-, vill-
half *pre* demi-, hemi-, semi-; *comb* dicho-, mezzo-; *base* dimid-
halibut *base* hippogloss-
halogen *comb* halo-; *suf* -ine
halt *comb* stasi-, -stasis, -stat, stato-; *base* fin-, termin-
hammer *comb* malleo-; *base* mall-, sphyr-
hampered *comb* brady-; *base* -cunct-, imped-, -mora-, -tard-
hand *comb* cheiro-, chiro-, hand-, mani-, manu-
handle *base* ansa-, manubr-
hang *comb* cremo-; *base* -pend-, -pens-
happening every __ *suf* -ly
happiness *comb* chero-[1]; *base* beati-, felic-, jubil-, macar-
harbor *base* limen-
hard *comb* duro-, sclero-; ~*palate:*

comb uranisco-, urano-; ~*shell:* *base* lorica-. *See* **difficult**
hare *base* cunic-, lago-, lepor-
harlot *comb* cypriano-, hetaero-, porno-; *base* meretric-, scort-
harmful *comb* noci-, pesti-; *base* -nox-, pericul-
harmony *pre* co-; *base* concinn-, congru-, -eiren-, -iren-, -pac-, -pax, unanim-
harsh *comb* caco-; *base* acerb-, asper-
haste *base* alacr-, celer-, festin-, subit-; *comb* ocy-, tacho-, tachy-
hatchet *base* dolabr-, pelec-, securi-
hate(d) *comb* miso-, -phobe, -phobia, -phobic; *base* -invid-, -ira(sc)-, odi-
haul(ing) *comb* -fer, -ferous, -gerous, -parous, -pher, -phore, -phorous; *base* -port-, -vect-
having *comb* -echia; *suf* -acean, -aceous, -al, -ate[2], -ed[2], -ful, -gerous, -ial, -ine, -ious, -itious, -ory, -ous, -some, -ulent, -ulous, -wise, -y; *base* -ten-; ~*parts:comb* -fold
hawk *base* accipit-, buteo-, falco-, hieraco-
hawthorn *base* -crataeg-
hazard *base* pericul-
head *comb* capit-, cephal-, -cephalic, cephalo-, -cephalous,

-cephaly, cranio-, kephalo-; *having a ___ head:* -headed; *type of~:* -pated

headstrong *base* contum-, obstin-, pervic-, proterv-

healing *comb* -iatrics, -iatr(o)-, -iatry, medico-; *base* cur-, san-

health *base* salub-, san-. *See* **sickness**

heap(ing) *comb* cumulo-; *base* acerv-, -sor-

hearing *comb* acou-, acoust-, audi(o)-, auri-, echo-, -ecoia, oto-, -phone, phono-, -phony, -phthong, soni-, sono-, sonoro-

heart *comb* cardi-, -cardia, cardio-, -cardium, cordato-, cordi-, pericardiaco-, pericardio-; *~attack: base* angin-; *~cavity: comb* atrio-; *~shaped: comb* cordato-

heartbreak *comb* lype-; *base* dolor-, fleb-, flet-, luct-, trist-

heat *comb* cal(e)-, calo-, calor(i)-, pyr(o)-, -therm, thermo-, -thermy; *base* aest-, caum-, ferv-

heave *comb* -bole, -bolic, bolo-, -boly; *base* -ballist-, -jact-, -jacula-, -ject-

heavens *comb* ourano-, urano-; *base* cael-, cel-

heavy *comb* -bar, bari-, baro-, grav(i)-; *base* -obes-, -pond-

Hebrew *comb* Hebraico-

hedgehog *base* echin-, erinac-

heel-bone *comb* calcaneo-, ptern-

height *comb* acro-, alti-, alto-, bato-[1], hypsi-, hypso-; *base* procer-

hell *base* acheron-, avern-, infern-, -styg-

helmet *base* cassidi-, -gale-

help *base* -(ad)jut-, -(ad)juv-, -auxil-

helpful *comb* chreo-, chresto-; *base* -util-

hemispheric *comb* hemispherico-

hen *base* gallin-

heptillion *comb* yotta-; *~th:* yocto-

herd *base* -greg-

heredity *comb* heredo-

heresy *base* heresio-

hermit *base* eremit-; *~crab:* pagur-

hernia *comb* -cele, celo-[1], hernio-

heron *base* arde-, grallator-

herring *comb* harengi-; *base* clupe-, halec-

hesitate *base* cunct-

hexillion *comb* zetta-; *~th:* zepto-

hiccup *base* singult-

hidden *pre* sub-; *comb* calypto-, crypto-; *base* occult-; *hiding place:* latib-. *See* **covered**

hide *animal: comb* pelli-; *conceal:* *See* **hidden**

high(er) *pre* meta-, super-; *comb* acro-, alti-, alto-, hypsi-, hypso-

higher valence *pre* per-; *suf* -ic

highest *comb* acro-

highway *comb* hodo-, -ode, odo-; *base* -iter-, -via-

hill *base* coll-[3]

hinge *base* gingly-

hip *comb* cotyle-, cotyli-, cotylo-, coxo-, ischi(o)-

hiss *base* -sibil-

historical *comb* historico-

hit *comb* plessi-; *base* cop-, -crot-, -cuss-, -plang-, puls-, -tus-, vapul-, -verber-

hoard *comb* cumulo-; *base* acerv-, -sor-

hoax *base* ludif-

hog *base* hyos-

hold *comb* -tain; *base* -cap(t)-, -cathex-, -ger-[1], -hapt-, -prehend, prehens-, -ten-; *~back:* prohib-

holder *comb* angio-, asco-, bursi-, burso-, ceco-, chlamyd-, chrysali-, cisto-, coleo-, -cyst, cysti-, cysto-, follic-, meningo-, pericardiaco-, pericardio-, peritoneo-, phasco-, physa-, physali-, physo-, -theca, theci-, theco-, typhlo-, utri-, utric, vesico-; *base* -sacc-, -thylac-

hole *base* cav-, foramin-, lacun-, troglo-. *See* **opening**

holler *base* clam-, vocif-

hollow *comb* cava-, -cave, cavi-, cavo-, -coele, coelo-, cotyle-, cotyli-, cotylo-, koilo. *See* **cavity**

holly *base* ilic-

holy *comb* hagio-, hiero-, sanct(i)-; *base* -sacr-

home (of) *comb* eco-, ekist-, nosto-, oeco-, oiko-; *base* aed-, -dom-, edi-; *suf* -age

honest *base* prob-

honey *comb* mell(i)-

honeycomb *comb* favoso-; *base* fav-

honor *base* timo-

honorable *pre* bene-, eu-; *base* agath-, bon-, prob-

hood *base* calyptri-, cuculli-

hook *base* hamat-, -unci-

hookworm *base* ancylostom-

hope *base* -sper-

hormone names *comb* -kinin

horn, hornlike *comb* cerat(o)-, -corn, corneo-, corni-, cornu-, kerat(o)-

hornbill *base* bucerot-, bucorac-

hornblower *comb* keraulo-

hornet *comb* vespi-; *base* -sphec-

horse *comb* equ(i)-, hippo-, -hippus; *base* caball-, caval-

horsefly *base* taban-

horseshoe *base* hippocrepi-

horsetail *base* equiset-

hospital *base* nosocom-

host *base* -hosp-, -xen-

hostile *pre* anti-; *base* inimic-

hot *comb* cal(e)-, calo-, calor(i)-, pyr(o)-, thermo-, -thermy; *base* aestu-, caum-, ferv-

hour *comb* horo-

house *comb* eco-, ekist-, oeco-, oiko-; *base* aed-, -dom-[1], edi-; *suf* -age

how many *base* quot-

howl *base* ulul-[1]

hub *comb* centr-, centri-, -centric, centro-

huge *comb* bronto-, dino-, giganto-, mega-, megalo-, -megaly

hull *ship:* *base* naut-; **husk:** *base* follic-, -lemma[2], putamin-

human *comb* anthrop(o)-, humano-. *See* **people**

humid *comb* hydro-, hygro-, udo-; *base* humect-, madefac-, -rig-

hummingbird *base* trochil-

humorous *comb* comico-

hump *comb* cypho-, gibboso-, hybo-, lordo-, scoli-; *base* -kyph-

hundred *comb* cent(i)-, hecato-, hecto-, hekto-; *~twenty:* hecaton-icosa-

hunger *base* esur-; *~for:* *comb* eroto-, -lagnia, -mania, -orexia; *base* -appet-, conat-, -cup-, -libid-, -opt-, vell-; *suf* -urient

hunt *base* venat-

hurl *comb* -bole, -bolic, bolo-, -boly; *base* ballist-, -jact-, -jacula-, -ject-

hurricane *base* lilaps-

hurry *base* accel-, celer-, festin-

hurt *comb* noci-; *base* -nox-, vuln-. *See* **pain**

husband *base* conjug-, marit-

hushed *comb* hesy-; *base* -plac-, quiesc-, -tacit-

husk *comb* follic-, -lemma[2], putamin-

hut *base* -cali-

hydraulic *comb* hydraulico-

hydrides *suf* -ine

hydrocarbon *suf* -ene; *~radical:* *suf* -ylene; *~paraffin series:* *suf* -ane; *~plus nitrogen:* *comb* diazo-

hydrogen *comb* -hydric
hydroxyl *radicals: comb* -hydric;
   ~group: comb hydroxy-
hygiene *base* salub-, san-
hyoid bone *comb* hyo-

hypnotism *comb* hypno-; *base*
   mesmer-
hyrax- *comb* chero-[2], hyraci-,
   hyraco-
hysteria *comb* hyster(o)-

I

ice *comb* glacio-, pago-; *base* gel-[1]
icicle *base* stiri-
icon *comb* icono-
idea *comb* -gnomy, -gnosia, -gnosis,
   -gnostic, gnoto-, ideo-, -noia,
   -nomy, phreno-, psycho-, -sophy
   base -cogit-, -cogn-, epistem-,
   -noe-, -put-, ratio-, -sci-
identical *pre* co-; *comb* equi-,
   homo-, iso-, pari-, tauto-
idiot *base* fatu-, inan-, moro-, stult-
idle *base* oti-, pigrit-
idol *comb* idolo-
ignorant *base* hebet-, obtus-, -tard-
ileac plus, ileum *comb* ileo-, ilio-
ill(ness) *pre* dys-, mal-; *comb* noso-,
   -path, -pathic, patho-, -pathy;
   base aegr-, -morb-, -pecca-, vale-
   tud-; *~names: comb* -aemia,
   -emia; *suf* -asis, -ia, -itis, -oma,
   -osis; *~treatment: comb* -iatrics,
   iatro-, -iatry. See disorder
illumination *comb* actino-, luci-,
   phengo-, phos-, photo-; *base* clar-,
   -luc-, -lum-
illusory *comb* pseudo-; *base* -phan-
   tas-, phasm-
image *comb* icono-; *base* agalma-
imbibe *comb* pino-, poto-; *base*
   -bib-, pocul-
imitate *base* emul-, -mim-
immature *comb* paedo-[2], pedo-;
   base juven-. See undeveloped
immense *comb* bronto-, dino-, gi-
   ganto-, mega-, megalo-, -megaly

immobility *comb* -plegia, -plegy
immorality *pre* dys-, mis-; *comb*
   caco-, enisso-, enosio-, kak-,
   kako-, mal-, male-, ponero-; *base*
   culp-, facin-, flagit-, hamart-,
   iniq-, nefar-, pecca-, perdit-,
   -prav-, sceler-, scelest-, turp-
immortal *comb* ever-; *base* etern-,
   perpet-, semper-
immovable *comb* stasi-, -stasis,
   -stat, stato-; *base* stabil-
immune *comb* immuno-
impaired *base* vitia-
impartial *comb* equi-
impede *comb* isch-, koly-, -penia,
   rhopo-, -strain, -strict; *base*
   angust-, -string-; *suf* -en
imperfection *base* culp-, delinq-,
   laps-, -pecca-, sphal-
imperfectly *pre* demi-, hemi-, semi-;
   comb -atelia, atelo-
imperforate *comb* -atresia, atreto-
impervious to *comb* -proof, -tight
impetus *base* horm-
important *base* grav-
imposter *base* phenac-, phenak-
impoverished *comb* ptocho-, vidu-;
   base -mendic-, -paup-, penur-,
   -pov-
improved *comb* melior-, out-
impulse *base* ate-[4]
in *pre* eis-, em-, en-[1], il -, im-, in-,
   ir-; *comb* endo-, ento-, entre-,
   eso-, inter(o)-, intra-, intro-; *~a*
   specified way: suf -ly, -ways,

-wise; ~*back: pre* meta-; *comb*
post-, postero-; ~*common: comb*
caeno-, ceno-; ~*front of: pre* ante-,
fore-, ob-, prae-, pre-, pro-;
~*some order: suf* -ly; ~*the direc-*
tion of: suf -ad, -ly, -ward, -ways,
-wise; ~*the manner of: suf* -like,
-ways; ~*the style of: suf* -ese,
-esque
inaccuracy *base* culp-, delict-, laps-,
pecc-, sphal-
inadequacy *comb* isch-, oligo-,
-penia
inaudible *comb* hesy-; *base* -plac-,
quiesc-, -tacit-
inborn *comb* innato-
incapable of being *suf* -less. See
not
incense *comb* -thymia[2]; *base* kniss-,
liban-, thur-
incessant *base* assid-, contin-,
incess-, perpet-
incipient *base* incip-, -init-; *suf*
-esce, -escence, -escent.
incised *comb* eroso-. See **groove**
inciting *comb* -agogic, -agogue
incline *comb* -clinal, -clinate,
-cline, -clinic, clino-, -clinous,
-clisis, lechrio-, loxo-, plagio-;
base -cliv-
incomplete *pre* demi-, hemi-, semi-;
comb -atelia, atelo-; *suf* -esce,
-escence, -escent
incorrect *base* dys-, mis-
increased *pre* ad-, extra-, hyper-,
super-; *comb* auxano-, auxo-,
multi-, myria-, myrio-, out-,
over-, -plasia, pleni-, pleo-, pleio-,
pleon-, plethys-, plio-, pluri-, pol-
laki-, poly-; *base* -aug-, -cresc-,
-fold-, -pler-, -plet-. See **grow**
indefinite *base* ambig, dub-, ancip-
index *comb* sema-, -seme, semeio-,
semio-
India *comb* Indo-[2]

indicate *comb* phaeno-, pheno-;
base -monstr-
indigence *comb* -penia, ptocho-,
vidu-; *base* -mendic-, -paup-,
penur-, -pov-
indigo *comb* indi-, indo-[1]
indirect *comb* loxo-, plagio-; *base*
ambag-
indisposed *pre* dys-, mal-; *comb*
noso-, path, -pathic, patho-,
-pathy; *base* aegr-, cachex-,
-morb-, -pecca-, valetud-
individual *suf* -aholic, -aire, -an,
-ant, -ard, -arian, -art, -ary, -ast,
-ate, -ator, -ee, -eer, -en, -ent,
-er, -ette, -eur, -fer, -ician, -ier,
-ior, -ist, -le, -ling, -man, -nik,
-o, -or, -person, -people, -ster,
-woman, -yer
indolent *base* pigr-
inebriated *base* inebr-, methys-,
temul-
inert gas *suf* -on
ineffectual *base* futil-, inutil-,
mataeo-
inexpensive *base* vili-
infection *comb* lysi-, lyso-, -lysis,
-lyte, -lytic, -lyze, phthisio-,
-phthisis, phthysio-, -phthysis,
putre-, putri-, pyo-, pytho-,
sapro-, septi-, septico-, septo-,
toxi-, toxico-, toxo-; *base* phthor-,
vitia-
inferiority *pre* hypo-, sub-, under-;
comb hystero-[2]; *base* hesson-; *suf*
-aster[2]
infinity *base* apeiro-. See **forever**
infirm *pre* dys-, mal-; *comb* noso-,
path, -pathic, patho-, -pathy; *base*
aegr-, cachex-, -morb-, -pecca-,
valetud-
inflammation *comb* erysi-,
phlog(o)-; *suf* -itis. See **swelling**
inflorescence *comb* thyrsi-, thyrso-
infuse *comb* -enchyma[2]; *suf* -ate

ingest *comb* bromato-, -brotic, manduc-, -phage, phago-, -phagous, -phagy, -sitia, sitio-, sito-, -troph, -trophic, tropho-, -trophy, -vora, -vore, -vorous; *base* -alim-, -cib-, comest-, -ed-, escul-, glutt-, -gust-

inguinal *comb* inguino-

inhabit(ant) *comb* -cole, -colent, -colous; *suf* -an, -ite

inhale *comb* -hale, -pnea, pneo-, pneumato-, pneumo-, pneumono-, pneusio-, pulmo-, spiro-; *base* afflat-

inhere *base* -sid-, situ-

inhibit *comb* isch-, koly-, -penia, -strain, -strict; *base* -string-; *suf* -en. See **checked**

iniquity *pre* dys-, mis-; *comb* caco-, iniq-, kak(o)-, mal(e)-, ponero-; *base* -prav-, sceler-, turp-

initial *comb* arch-, fore-, pre-, primi-, primo-, pro-, proso-, protero-, proto-; *base* -princip-

initiate *base* inaug-, incip-, init-

injection *base* trypan-

injudicious *base* fatu-, inan-, moro-, stult-

injurious *comb* noci-, pesti-; *base* -nox-, pericul-

injury *comb* noci-, traumato-; *base* -nox-

ink *base* atrament-

innkeeper *base* caupon-

inquiry *base* erot-, -quir-, -rog-

insanity *comb* lysso-, -mania; *base* ament-[1], dement-

insatiable *base* avid-, edac-, gulos-

inscribe *comb* -gram, -graph, -grapher, -graphic, grapho-, -graphy, grapto-, -logue; *base* -scrib-, -script-, typo-

insect *comb* cimic-, core-[2], entomo-, insecti-, insecto-. See **mite**

insert *base* calar-, calat-, pon-, pos-

inside *pre* eis-, em-, en-[1], il -, im-, in-[1], ir-; *comb* endo-, ento-, entre-, eso-, inter(o)-, interno-, intra-, intro-; *from~:* entostho-

insolent *base* contum-, impud-, procac-

inspection *comb* -opsy, -scope, -scopic, scopo-, -scopy; *base* -(in)quir-, -(in)quis-, -scrut-

instance of *suf* -ism

instantly *base* subit-

instep *comb* tarso-

instruct *comb* -pedia; *base* -didact-, doc-, -paed-

instrument (of) *suf* -ment[1], -ure; *medical~:* -tome; *scientific~:* -stat

insufficient *pre* demi-, hemi-, semi-; *comb* -atelia, atelo-

insult *base* contum-

intact *pre* be-, cata-, de-, kata-, ob-, per-; *comb* holo-, omni-, pan-, panto-, stone-, toti-; *base* integr-

intellect *comb* -gnomy, -gnosia, -gnosis, -gnostic, -gnoto, ideo-, -noia, -nomy, phren(o)-, psycho-, -sophy, thymo-, -witted; *base* -cogit-, -cogn-, ment(a)-, -noe-, -put-, -ratio-, -sci-

intelligent *base* sapien-

intensifier *pre* em-, en-, in-, za-

intercourse *comb* -lagnia; *base* -coit-, copul-

interfunctioning *comb* -ergasia, ergasio-

intermix *pre* co-; *comb* conjugato-, -ergasia, gameto-, gamo-, hapto-, junct-; *base* aps-, apt-, -greg-, -soc-; *suf* -ate, -ize

interpretation *base* -hermen-

interrogate *base* -pet-, -quir-, -quis-, -rog-

intestinal pouch *comb* caeco-, ceco-, typhlo-

intestines *comb* entero-, ileo-, ilio-,

intestino-, jejuno-; *base* viscer-;
~*worm:* ascari-

intimidated *base* -pavid-, -tim-,
trepid-. *See* **fear**

intoxicated *base* -inebr-, -meth-,
temul-

intractable *base* contum-, obstin-,
pervic-, proterv-

invent *base* -heur-

inverse *pre* anti-, contra-, contre-,
dis-, hetero-, ob-, un-; *comb*
back-, counter-, enantio-,
oppositi-

invisible *pre* sub-; *comb* calypto-,
crypto-; *base* occult-

involuntary movement *comb*
-chorea-, choreo-, -clonic,
-clonus, spasmo-; *base* -stal-; *suf*
-esmus, -ismus

iodine *comb* iodo-

ion *comb* iono-

irate *base* chol-, -invid-, -ira-,
-margy

iris *comb* irido-

Irish *comb* Hiberno-

iron *comb* ferri-, ferro-, sidero-[1]

irregular *comb* allo-, anomalo-,
anomo-, poecilo-, poikilo-;
~*shape:* *comb* amorpho-

irridium *comb* iridico-, iridio-

irrigation *comb* -clysis

irritate *base* erethis-

ischium *comb* ischi(o)-

island *base* insul-

isomer *comb* pseudo-

isthmus *base* isthm-

Italy *comb* Italo-

itch *comb* acari-, scabi-; *base* -prur-,
psor-

ivory *base* ebur-

ivy *base* ciss-, -heder-

J

jackass *base* as-[2], asin-

jackdaw *base* gracul-

jagged *comb* serrato-; *base* cren-[1],
lacin-

jail *base* -carcer-

jam *comb* emboli-, embolo-; *base*
-byon-, -farct-

jaundice *comb* icter(o)-

jaw *comb* genia-, genio-, geny-[1],
gnatho-, -gnathous, mandibulo,
maxillo-; ~*bone:* *base* -siagon-

jay *base* garrul-

jealous *base* -emul-

jeer *comb* catagelo-, katagelo-

jeopardy *base* pericul-

jejunum *comb* jejuno-

jellyfish *base* discophor-

jerk *comb* -chorea, choreo-,
-clonic, -clonus, -esmus, -ismus,

spasmo-, -tonic; *base* -stal-,
-vellic-

jest *base* joco(s)-, jocu(l)-

jewel *base* -gemm-[2]

Jewish *comb* Judaico-, Judaeo-,
Judeo-

jilt *base* relinq-, repud-

jingling *base* tinn-

job *comb* arti-, -craft, -ergasia,
ergasio-, -ergic, ergo-, -ergy,
organo-, -urgy; *base* -opus-,
pono-; *suf* -arian

join *comb* -ergasia, gameto-, gamo-,
hapto-, junct-; *base* -aps-, -apt-[1],
-greg-, -soc-; *suf* -ate, -ize; ~*together:* *pre* co-; *comb* conjugato-

joint *body*~: *comb* arthr(o)-,
articul-; ~*socket:* gleno-; *jointed:*
base -enarthra-

joke *base* joco(s)-, jocu(l)-
journey *comb* hodo-, -ode, odo-, via-; *base* -itin-, peregrin-
joy *comb* chero-; *base* beati-, elat-, felic-, gaud-, jubil-, macar-
judging *comb* -gnomy, -gnosia, -gnosis, -gnostic; *base* -crit-[1], -judic-, krit-, -soph-
jug *base* urcei-
juice *comb* opo-; *base* -suc-

jump *base* -salta-
junction *pre* co-; *comb* conjugato-, -ergasia, gameto-, gamo-, hapto-, junct-; *base* aps-, apt-, -greg-, -soc-; *suf* -ate, -ize
jurisdiction *suf* -dom, -ric
justice *comb* dike-
juvenile *comb* paedo-, pedi-, pedo-, proli-, tecno-; *base* -fil-, -puer-, tek-

K

kangaroo *base* macropod-
keel *base* -carin-
keen *base* -acer(b)-
keep *comb* -serve, -tain; *base* custod-, -ten-; *~away:* *comb* alex-, alexi-, alexo-
keg *comb* dolio-
kernel *comb* caryo-, karyo-; *base* -nucl-
kestrel *base* falco-
ketone *comb* keto-; *suf* -one
key *comb* clavi-[1], cleido-, clido-
kick *base* -calcitr-
kidney *comb* nephro-, pyelo-, reni-, reno-
kidney-bean *base* phaseol-
killing *comb* -cidal, -cide, -cidious, -cidism; *base* -dacn-, trucid-
kind *category:* *comb* -type; *suf* -atic; *gentle:* *base* -len-, mansue-, miti-, moll-
kindle *comb* causto-, igni- pyro-; *base* ard-[2], ars-, cauter-, celo-, combust-, crem-, phlog-, -ust-
kinetic *comb* cine-, -drome, dromo-, -dromous, excito-, kine-, -kinesi(a), -kinesis, -kinetic, kineso-, kineto-, kino-, -motive, -pragia, -praxia, -praxis, tremo-; *base* -stal-

kinfolk *base* cogn-, famil-, stirp-
king *base* basil-, reg(n)-
kingfisher *base* halcyon-
kinked *comb* cirri-, cochlio-, gyro-, helico-, spiro-, strepto-; *base* stromb-. *See* **curl**
kiss *base* basiat-, oscul-; *tongue~:* cataglott-
kitchen *base* culin-
kite *bird:* *base* milv-
knack *base* -apt-, -habil-, -poten-, -qual-; *suf* -bility, -ful, -ship
knavish *pre* dys-, mis-; *comb* caco-, kak-, kako-, mal-, male-, ponero-; *base* facin-, flagit-, iniq-, nefar-, perdit-, -prav-, sceler-, scelest-, turp-
knead *base* subig-
knee *base* gen(u)-
knife *comb* cultell-, cultri-, sica-
knit together *base* -hapto-, pegm-
knob *comb* clavato-; *base* condyl-, umbo-
knock *base* -puls-
knot *base* -nod-, -tylo-
knowledge *comb* -gnomy, -gnosia, -gnosis, -gnostic, gnoto-, ideo-,

-noia, -nomy, -phrenic, phrenico-, phreno-, psycho-, scio-², -sophy; *base* -cogit-, -cogn-, epistem-,

ment(a)-, -noe-, -put-, ratio-, -sci-
kudu *base* tragelaph-

L

---

labia minora *comb* nympho-
labor *childbirth:* *comb* lochio-, -para, -parous, -tocia, toco-, toko-, -toky; *work:* *comb* -craft, ergic, -ergy, ergo-, -urgy; *base* ardu-, oper-¹, pono-
laborious *pre* dys-; *comb* -bar, bary-, mogi-; *base* ard³-, stren-
laceration *comb* sparasso-; *base* -sparax-
lacking *pre* a-, an-¹, dis-, ex-, il-, im-, in-, un-; *comb* lipo-²; *base* penur-, -priv-; *suf* -less; *~a part:* *comb* ectro-; *~an opening:* *comb* -atresia, atreto-
lactic *comb* lacto-
ladder *base* scala-; *~rung:* climac-
lady *comb* gyn(e)-, gyneco-, gyneo-, gyno-, -gynous, -gyny, -para, thely-, -wife; *base* -femin-, muliebr-, mulier-; *suf* -en, -enne, -ess, -ette, -ice, -ine, -stress, -trice, -trix
lake *comb* limno-; *base* lacus-
lamb *base* -agn-
lame *base* claud-, debil-
lamentation *base* thren-
lamp *base* lampad-, lucern-, lychn-
lamprey *base* cyclostom-
land *comb* agri-, agro-, choro-, geo-; *base* tellur-, -terr-
language *comb* -glossia, gloss(o)-, -glot, glotto-, lingui-, linguo-; *suf* -ese. See **word**
larch *base* larix-
large(r) *pre* super-; *comb* -fold,

macro-, magni-, maxi-, plethys-; *base* -ampl-, grandi-, -maj-. *See* **gigantic**
larva *comb* larvi-
larynx *comb* guttur-, laryngo-
lassitude *comb* pono-; *base* -fatig-, -kopo-, lass-
last *base* eschato-, -fin-, termin-, -ultim-
lasting *base* diuturn-, dur(o)-, perenn-, perm-, stabil-
late *comb* opsi-¹, serot-. *See* **tardy**
later *pre* meta-, post-; *comb* hystero-²
latest *comb* neo-
latex *comb* latici-
lattice *base* cancell-, clathr-, cratic-
laugh *comb* gel-²; *base* cachinn-, -ris-
laurel *base* daphn-
law *comb* juris-, nomo-, thesmo-; *base* jud-, jur-, leg-², regul-
lawless *comb* anomo-
lawsuit *base* litig-
laxative *base* chalast-
layer(ed) *comb* -decker, lamelli-, lamini-, lamino-, -plex, strati-, strato-
lazy *base* oti-, pigrit-
lead *conduct:* *comb* -arch, -duce, duc(t)-, magist-; *base* hegemon-, -reg-; *metal:* *comb* molybdo-, plumbo-
leading *comb* -agogic, -agogue
leaf *comb* foli(i)-, -folious, petalo-, -phyll, phyllo-, -phyllous; *base*

bract-, clad-, frondi-; ~*buds: base*
gemm-[1]; ~*like: comb* foliato-
lean *comb* angusti-, dolicho-, lepto-,
mano-, stegno-, steno-, tenu-;
base areo-, gracil-, isthm-, maci-,
stal-, strict-
leap *base* salta-
learn *base* disc-, -math, soph-
leather *base* alut-, cori-, pelli-,
utri-[1]; ~*bottle:* utrei-, utric-
leave *base* relinq-
leech *base* bdell-, discophor-,
hirud-, sanguisug-
leek *base* porr-, praso-
left *comb* laeo-, laevo-, levo-,
sinistro-; ~*handed:* scaev-
leg *base* -cnem-, -crur-, -scel-; *condition of~: comb* -scelia
legend *comb* mytho-, stori-; *base*
fabul-, -narr-,
length *base* meco-. See **long**
leniency *base* clem-[2]
lens *comb* phaco-, phako-, -phakia
leopard *base* pard-
less *pre* demi-, hypo-, mis-, sub-,
subter-; *comb* meio-, mini-, mio-,
oligo-; *base* dimin-, hesson-,
-pauc-
lettuce *base* lactuc-
level *comb* homalo-, homolo-,
plain-, plani-, plano-[1], platy-; *base*
plat-
lever *base* -mochl-
liability *comb* hypegia-, hypengy-;
base paralip-
lice *comb* pedicul-, phthiro-
lick *base* lamb-, ligur(r)-, ling-[4]
licorice *base* glycyr-
lid *base* oper-[2]
lie *untruth: base* mendac-; *recline:
base* -cub-, -cumb-
life *comb* bio-, -biosis, vita-, vivi-,
zoo-, -zoic, -zooid; *base* -anim-
ligament *comb* desmo-, ligamenti-,
ligamento-, syndesmo-

light *not dark: comb* actino-, luci-,
phengo-, phos-, photo-; *base* clar-,
-luc-, -lum-; *not heavy: base*
levi(t)-
lighthouse *base* fan-, phar-
lightning *comb* astra-; *base* astraph-,
fulgur-, fulmin-
like *pre* para-, quasi-; *comb* homeo-,
omœo, homoio-, homolo-, iso-,
-phane, -phanic; *base* simil-; *suf*
-acean, -aceous, -al[3], -an, -ar,
-ary, -ean, -en, -eous, -esque, -ful,
-ic, -il, -ile, -ine, -ing, -ish,
-itious, -ize, -like, -ode[2], -oid,
-ose[2], -osity, -some[2], -tious, -ular,
-y
likeness *comb* icono-, -opsis, -vult-
liking *comb* -phile, -philia, -philiac,
-philic, -philism, philo-, -philous
lily *base* lili-, -lirio-
limb *comb* -mele, -melia[1], melo-[3]
lime *CaO: comb* calcareo-; *base*
calc-; *fruit:* tilia-
limit *comb* isch-, koly-, -penia,
-strain, -strict ; *base* -fin-, -string-,
termin-; *suf* -en; *limited to: comb*
-specific, specio-
linden *base* tilia- (tiliaceous)
line *comb* lineo-, -stichia, sticho-,
-stichous; *wavy~: comb* gyroso-
link *pre* co-; *comb* conjugato-,
-ergasia, gameto-, gamo-, hapto-,
junct-; *base* aps-, apt-, -greg-,
-soc-; *suf* -ate, -ize
lion *base* leo(n)-
lips *comb* cheilo-, chilo-, labio-;
base labi-
liquid *base* flu-, -ner-. See **water**
little *comb* brachisto-, brachy-,
brevi-, chamae-, micro-, mini-,
nano-, parvi-, parvo-, pauci-,
steno-; *base* -curt-, exig-; *suf* -cle,
-cula, -cule, -culum-, -culus,
-een, -el, -ella, -en, -et, -ette, -
idion, -idium, -ie, -illa, -illo, -isk,

-kin, -le, -let, -ling, -ock, -ola,
-ole, -rel, -ula, -ule, -ulum, -ulus,
-y

liver *comb* hepatico-, hepato-; *base*
jecor-

living *comb* bio-, vivi-, -zoic,
-zooid; *base* -anim-, -vit-;
~*among:* comb -colous; ~*in: suf*
-an

lizard *comb* -saur, sauro-, -saurus;
base lacert-, stellio-

load *base* oner-

loaded *comb* -filled, pleni-, pleo-,
plero-, pluri-; *base* -pler-, -plet-;
suf -acious, -ate, -ic, -ful, -ilent,
-ose, -osity, -ous, -ulent, -y

lobe *comb* lobulato-; *ear: comb*
auriculo-

lobster *base* astac-, -gammar-,
homar-

location *comb* -land, loc(o)-, situ-,
-stead, topo-, -topy; *suf* -age,
-arium, -ary, -ensis, -ery, -orium,
-ory. *Also see* "Location" in Part
III

lock *comb* clido-; *base* cleid-

locust *base* locust-

loins *comb* laparo-, lumbo-,
osphy(o)-

long *comb* dolicho-, -footer, longi-,
macro-, maxi-; *base* procer-;
~*words:* sesquipedal-

look *comb* eid(o)-, oculo-, ommat-,
-opia, opsi-, -opsia, -opsis, opso-,
-opsy, ophthalmo-, optico-, opto-,
-scope, -scopic, scopo-, -scopy,
visuo-; *base* -blep-, -scrut-, -spec-,
-spic-, -vid-

loosen *comb* lyo-, lysi-, -lysis, lyso-,
-lyte, -lytic, -lyze; *base* -liqu-,
-solu-, -solv-

loss of control *comb* -crasia, -crasy

loss of knowledge *comb* -agnosia

lot *comb* clero-

loudness *base* crepit-, frem-, ligyr-,
strep(i)-, strid-, stridul-. *See*
sound

louse *base* pedicul-, phthir-, phthyr-

love *comb* -phile, -philia, -philiac,
-philic, -philism, philo-, -philous;
base -agap-, -am-, charit-

loveplay *comb* paizo-, paraphil-

low(er) *pre* hypo-, infero-, infra-,
sub-, subter-, under-; *comb*
chamae-, infero-, tapino-; *base*
hystat-

luck *base* faust-, tych-

ludicrous *base* fatu-, inan-, moro-,
stult-

lumbar *comb* lumbo-

lump *base* gleb-, glom-

lunch *base* prand-

lung(s) *comb* -pnea, pneo-, pneu-
mato-, pneumo-, pneumono-,
pulmo-, pulmoni-, pulmono-,
spiro-

lust *comb* eroto-, -lagnia, -mania;
base appet-, -cup-, -libid-, tentig-

luster *comb* sela-; *base* -fulg-, gano-,
lustr-, pheng-, rutil-, stilpno-

lye *base* lixiv-

lying down *base* -cub-, -cumb-,
supin-

lymph(atic) *comb* lymphato-, lym-
pho-; ~*nodes: comb* lymphadeno-;
~*vessels: comb* lymphangio-

lynx *base* lync-

lyre *base* lyri-

lyric *comb* lyrico-

M

macaw *base* psittac-
machine(s) *comb* mechano-
mackerel *base* scombr-
mad *comb* -margy; *base* frenet-,
-fur-, -ira-
made of *suf* -en, -ic
madness *comb* lysso-, -mania; *base*
ament-, dement-
magic *base* mago-
magnetic force *comb* magneto-
magnify *base* ampl-, aug-. *See* increased
magpie *base* corv-, garull-
maim(ed) *comb* pero-; *base* -mutil-
main *comb* arch(i)-[1], proto-; *base*
-prim-, -princip-; ~**land**: *comb*
epeiro-
make, making *pre* em-, en-; *comb*
-craft, ergo-, -facient, -fer, -fic,
-fication, -gen, -genesis, -genic,
-genous, -geny, -gerous, ideo-,
-parous, -phor, -phorous, -plast,
-plastic, plasto-, -plasty, poiesis,
-poietic, -urgy; *base* -fabr-, -fac-,
-fec-[1]; *suf* -ate, -atory, -en, -ic,
-ing, -fy, -ize, -otic
Malay *comb* Malayo-
male *comb* andr(o)-, -androus,
-andry, arrheno-, masculo-; *base*
viril-
malevolent *pre* dys-, mis-; *comb*
caco-, iniq-, kak(o)-, mal(e)-,
ponero-; *base* -prav-, sceler-,
turp-
malformed *comb* pero-; *base*
-mutil-
malfunction *pre* dys-
malnutrition *comb* -atrophia,
-atrophic
manage *base* ger-[1]
manatee *base* trichec-
mane *base* jubat-

manganese *comb* mangani-,
mangano-
mangle *comb* sparasso-; *base* lacer-,
lania-, sparax-. *See* maim
manifest *comb* luci-, phanero-,
pheno-; *base* -clar-
mankind *comb* anthropo-
manner *comb* -wise
mantle *comb* pallio-
manufactured product *suf* -ite
many *comb* multi-, myria-, myrio-,
pluri-, poly-, sychno-; ~*colored*:
comb poecilo-; ~*times*: *comb* pol-
laki-. *See* increased
map *comb* carto-, charto-
maple *base* acer-[2]
marble *base* -marm-
marine *comb* halo-, mari-, thalasso-,
thalatto-; *base* naut-, nav-, pelag-
mark *base* stigm-
marlin *base* istiophor-
marmoset *comb* callithri-
marmot *base* sciur-
marriage *comb* gameto-, gamo-,
-gamous, -gamy; *base* conjug-,
marit-, -nub-, -nupt-
marrow *comb* -myelia, myelo-
Mars *comb* areo-[1]
marsh *comb* helo-[2], palud-, palus-,
ulig-
marten *base* mustel-
martin *base* hirund-
masculine *comb* andro, -androus,
-andry, arrheno-, masculo-; *base*
viril-
master *comb* magist-, maha-; *base*
heri-
mastoid *comb* mastoido-
matching *pre* para-, quasi-; *comb*
homeo-, omœo, homoio-,
homolo-, iso-, -phane, -phanic;
base simil-; *suf* -acean, -aceous,

-al, -an, -ar, -ary, -ean, -en,
-eous, -esque, -ful, -ic, -il, -ile,
-ine, -ing, -ish, -itious, -ize, -like,
-ode, -oid, -ose, -osity, -some,
-tious, -ular, -y
material for *suf* -ing
matter *comb* hylo-
maxilla *comb* maxillo-
maxim *base* gnom-
maximum *pre* hyper-
meadow *base* prat-; *~lark:*
icter-
meager *comb* oligo-, -penia,
ptocho-, vidu-; *base* -mendic-,
-paup-, penur-, -pov-
meal *comb* deipno-; *base* cen-,
coen-, prand-. *See* **food.** *Also see*
"Food" in Part III
means *suf* -cle, -ment[1]
measure *comb* -meal, -meter,
-metric(s), metro-, -metry
meat *comb* -burger, carni-, carnoso-,
creo-, kreo-, -sarc, sarco-; *~market:* macell-
mechanical *comb* mechanico-; *base*
banaus-
medical *comb* medico-; *base* -san-;
~treatment: comb -iatrics, iatro-,
-iatry
medicine *base* pharma(co)-
mediocre *pre* hypo-, sub-, under-;
comb hystero-; *base* hesson-; *suf*
-aster
meditate *base* melet-
medium *comb* mesati-, metrio-. *See*
middle
meeting *base* congress-, congru-
melt *comb* lyo-, lysi-, -lysis, lyso-,
-lyte, -lytic, -lyze; *base* -liqu-,
-solu-, -solv-
membrane *comb* chorio-, choroid-,
hymeno-, membrano-; *eyeball~:*
sclero-; *fetal~:* allant(o)-, amnio-;
~partition: comb mediastino-;
mucous~: comb muci-, muco-,

mucoso-; *~sheath: comb*
meningo-
memory *comb* -mnesia, -mnesis;
base -mem-, -mnem-
meninges *comb* meningo-
menstrual *comb* emmen-, -menia,
men(o)-
mental *comb* -gnomy, -gnosis,
-gnostic, -gnoto, ideo-, -noia,
-nomy, phren(o)-, psycho-,
-sophy, thymo-; *base* -cogit-,
-cogn-, -noe-, -put-, -ratio-, -sci-;
~disorder: comb -mania, -phrenia, -phrenic, phrenico-, phreno-,
-thymia[1]
merchandise *base* empor-, empt-
mercy *base* clem-[2], mansue-
mere *comb* psilo-
mesentery *comb* meso-
metacarpus *comb* metacarpo-
metal *comb* metalli-, metallo-;
~plate: base -elasmo-
metatarsus *comb* metatarso-
meteor names *suf* -id[1]
meteorological front *comb* fronto-
method *comb* -craft; *suf* -ade, -age,
-al, -ance, -ancy, -asis, -asm,
-ation, -cy, -ence, -ency, -ery,
-esis, -iasis, -ice, -ics, -ing, -ion,
-ism, -ment, -osis, -otic, -sion,
-sis, -th, -tion, -tious, -ture, -ure,
-y, -ysis
methyl *comb* metho-
middle *comb* centri-, -centric,
centro-, medi(o)-, mesati-, mesio-,
meso-, mezzo-, mid-
mighty *comb* dino-. *See* **powerful**
mild *base* -len-, mansue-, miti-[1],
moll-
milk(y) *comb* galact(o)-, lacti-,
lacto-
mill *base* molend-
million *comb* mega-
millionth *comb* micro-
millipede *base* arthropod-, diplopod

mind *comb* -gnomy, -gnosis, -gnostic, -gnoto, ideo-, -noia, -nomy, phren(o)-, psycho-, -sophy, thymo-, -witted; *base* -cogit-, -cogn-, ment-², -noe-, noo-, -put-, -ratio-, -sci-; *~disorder: comb* -mania, -phrenia, -phrenic, -thymia

mine *base* bothro-

mineral *suf* -ite, -lite

mink *base* mustel-

minnow *base* cyprin-

minor *insignificant: base* -nuga-. See **small**. *child: comb* paedo-, pedi-, pedo-, proli-, tecno-; *base* -fil-, -puer-, tek-

mint *base* menth-

miracle *comb* thaumato-

mirror *comb* catoptro-, eisoptro-, enoptro-, spectro-

misery *base* aerumn-

missile *base* ballist-

missing *pre* a-, an-, des-¹, dis-, ex-, il-, im-, in-, ir-, un-; *comb* lipo-; *base* paralip-, -priv-; *suf* -less; *~a part: comb* ectro-; *~an opening: comb* -atresia, atreto-

mist *comb* fracto-, nepho-, nephelo-; *base* calig-, -nebul-, -nub-

mistake *base* culp-, delict-, laps-, pecc-, sphal-

mistletoe *comb* ixo-

mite *comb* acari-, acarin-, acaro-, miti-². See **termite**

miter *base* mitri-

mixed, mixture *comb* mixo-, -crasia; *base* farrag-, -misc-, -phyr-, -temp-

mob *comb* ochlo-

mobility *comb* cine-, -drome, dromo-, -dromous, excito-, kine-, -kinesi(a), -kinesis, -kinetic, kineso-, kineto-, kino-, -motive, -pragia, -praxia, -praxis, tremo-; *base* -stal-

mockery *base* deris-

mockingbird *base* -mim-

moderate *base* metrio-. See **medium**

modern *comb* neo-. See **new**

modesty *base* -pud-, verecund-

modification *comb* allo-, anomalo-, anomo-, poikilo-; *base* -mut-. See **change**

moisture *comb* hydro-, hygro-; *base* humect-, mad-, ulig-

molded *comb* -plast, -plastic, plasto-, -plasty

mole *blemish: base* nev(o)-; *animal: base* talp-

mole rat *base* zemni-

mollusks *comb* malaco-; *base* mollusc-

money *comb* -penny ; *base* chremat-, -numm-, -pecun-, quaest-

mongoose *base* viverr-

monkey *base* cebo-, pithec-

monster *comb* terato-; *base* pelor-

month *base* mens-

monthly *base* emmen-

mood *comb* thymo-

moon *comb* luni-, lunu-, seleno-

moose *base* cervi-

moral *pre* bene-, eu-; *base* agath-, bon-, prob-

moray *base* muraen-

morbid condition *comb* -iasis; *suf* -oma

more *pre* ad-, extra-, super-; *comb* auxano-, auxeto-, auxo-, multi-, myria-, myrio-, out-, over-, -plasia, pleni-, pleo-, pleio-, pleon-, plethys-, plio-, pluri-, pollaki-, poly-; *base* -aug-, -cresc-, -fold-, -pler-, -plet-. See **addition**

morning *base* -matut-

mortal *base* thneto-, thripto-

mortgage *base* -pign-

mosquito *comb* anophel-, culici-; *base* aed-

moss *comb* bryo-; *base* musc-[2],
sphagn-, splachn-
most *comb* pleisto-
moth *base* arct-, phalaen-, tinea-
mother *comb* mater-, matri-, metr-,
-para
mother-in-law *base* socrus-,
penther-
motion *comb* cine-, -drome,
dromo-, -dromous, excito-, kine-,
-kinesi(a), -kinesis, -kinetic,
kineso-, kineto-, kino-, -motive,
-pragia, -praxia, -praxis, tremo-;
base -stal-
motor *comb* moto-
mountain *comb* oreo-, oro-[2]; *base*
-mont-; *~ash:* sorb-[2]
mourning *comb* lype-; *base* dolor-,
-fleb-, -flet-, -luct-, trist-
mouse *base* mur-[1], myo-[2]
mouth *comb* -mouthed, or-[1], oro-,
stomato-, -stome, -stomous; *roof
of~: comb* palato-, uranisco-,
urano-; *~wash:* collut-
move *comb* -grade, -motive,
-plania, plano-[2]; *base* -bat-, -ced-,
-cess-, -cur(s), -grad-, -gress-,
-mob-, -mot-, mov-, -vad-, -vas-;
~away: comb allelo-, out-; *~for-
ward: comb* pro-; *~toward: comb*
-petal
movies *base* cine-
muck *comb* blenno-, -chezia, copro-,
lim-, muci-, muco-, myco-, myso-,
-myxia, myxo-, p(a)edo-, scato-,
stegno-, sterco-; *base* -fecu-, -fim-,
molys-, rhypar-
mucus *comb* blenno-, muci-, muco-,
mucoso-, -myxia, myxo-
mud *comb* pelo-; *base* -lim-, lut-
mulberry *base* -mor-[2], -mur-[3]
mulish *base* contum-, obstin-,
pervic-, proterv-

mullet *base* mugil-
multiform *comb* polymorpho-
multitude *comb* ochlo-
mummy *base* mummi-
murder *comb* -cidal, -cide, -cidious,
-cidism; *base* dacn-, trucid-
murky *comb* ambly-, melano-,
nycto-, scoto-; *base* achlu-,
amaur-, fusc-, lyg-, obscur-, opac-,
tenebr-
murmur *base* frem-, mussit-,
susurr-
muscle *comb* musculo-, myo-[1],
-tonic; *~tension:* -tonia
mushroom *comb* agar-, fungi-,
myco-. *See* fungus
music *comb* melo-[1], musico-, -tonic
musk *base* -mosch-
muskrat *base* cricet-
mussel *base* mytil-
mustard *base* sinap-
musty *base* mucid-
mutable *pre* be-, em-, en-, meta-,
trans-; *comb* aetio-, -blast, -blas-
tic, blasto-, -craft, ergo-, etio-,
-facient, -fic, -fication, -gen,
-genesis, -genic, -genous, -geny,
-parous, -plasia, -plasis, plasmo-,
-plast, -plastic, plasto-, -plasty,
-poiesis, -poietic, -trope, -tropic,
-tropism, tropo-, -tropous, -tropy,
-urgy; *base* camb-, -fabr-, -fec-,
-mut-, -vari-, -vert-; *suf* -ate, en,
-fy, -ize, -otic
mutter *see* murmur
mutual *pre* co-, enter-, inter-, syl-,
sym-, syn-, sys-; *comb* allelo-,
hama-, symphyo-, synchro-; *base*
-allac-, -allag-, -allaxis-, -mutu-
myrtle *base* myrti-
mystical *comb* mystico-
myth *comb* mytho-

N

nail *comb* helo-[1], onych-,-onychia, onycho-, scolo-; *base* clav-, ungui-

naked *comb* gymno-, nudi- psilo-

name *comb* nomato-, -nomia, onomato-, -onym; *base* appell-, -nom-, -nym-

names of *~acids: suf* -onic; *~alcohols: suf* -itol; *~animals: suf* -id, -ida, -idae, -iformes, -zooic; *~bacteria: suf* -ella; *~classes: suf* -acea, -aceae, -ia, -oidea; *~companies: suf* -co, -ine; *~compounds: suf* -ide, -idine; *~country: comb* -land; *suf* -ia; *~directions: suf* -ern; *~diseases: comb* -aemia, -emia; *suf* -asis, -ia, -itis, -osis; *~electronic devices: comb* -tron; *~enzymes: suf* -ase; *~families: suf* -idae; *~festivals: comb* -fest, -mas; *suf* -ia; *~genera: suf* -aria, -odus, -soma; *~groups: comb* -zoa, -zoon; *suf* -aria, -id, -ini; *~hormones: suf* -kinin; *~meteors: suf* -id; *~minerals: suf* -lite; *~neutral substances: suf* -in ; *~numerals, collective: suf* -ad; *~orders: suf* -acea, *~plants: suf* -ad, -ales, -ia; *~radicals: suf* -yl; *~super-families: suf* -oidea; *taxonomic~: suf* -ota, -ote

narcotics *comb* leth-, mecon-, narco-

narrow *comb* angusti-, areo-, dolicho-, isthm-, lepto-, stegno-, steno-; *base* -phim-, -stal-, -strict-, -tenu-

nasal *comb* nasi-, naso-, rhino-

nationality *suf* -an, -ean, -ian, -ish, -ite, -n

nature *comb* -ousia, -ousian; *base* quid-

natural *comb* innato-, physico-, physi-, physio-

navel *comb* omphalo-, umbilici-

near *pre* a-, ac-, ad-, af-, ag-, al-, an-, ap-, ar-, as-, at-, by-, cis-[1], epi-, para-, peri-; *comb* juxta-, citra-, pene-, plesio-, proximo-; *base* propinq-. *See* **adjacent**

nebulous *base* ambig, dub-, ancip-

neck *comb* atlo-, cervico-, coll-[1], jug-, trachelo-; *base* -auchen-

necklace *base* monil-

needle *comb* aci-, acicul-; *base* acer-[1], -aichm-, -belon-

negatives *pre* a-, ab-, an-, anti-, apo-, cata-, de-, dis-, dys-, ex-, il-, im-, in-, ir-, mal-, mis-, ne-, non-[1], ob-, un-; *comb* anti-, -atresia, atreto-, contra-, counter-, ectro-, lipo-, mal-, neutro-, nihil-, no-, nulli-, with-; *base* -priv-; *suf* -less

neglect *base* paralip-

neighbor *base* geiton(o)-

neoplasm *suf* -oma

nephew *base* nepo-

nerve *comb* ganglio-, nervi-, nervo-, neuro-

nest *base* -cali-, nid(i)-

net/network *comb* dictyo-, -plex, reti-, reticulato-, reticulo-

nettle *comb* cnido-; *base* -urtic-

neutral(izing) *pre* anti-; *comb* neutro-

neutral substances *suf* -in

new *comb* caeno-[2], caino-, cainoto-, -cene, ceno-[1], cenoto-, kaino-, kainoto-, neo-, thalero-; *base* -nov-[1]

NH *comb* *~acid radicals:* -imido; *~nonacid radicals:* imino-

nicknames *suf* -y[3]

night *comb* nocti-, nycta-, nycti-,

nycto-; *base* -crepus-, -vesper-;
all~: *comb* -pannychy
nightingale *base* philomel-
nightmare *base* malneiro-
nimbleness *comb* ocy-, tacho-,
　tachy-; *base* alacr-, celer-, festin-,
　veloc-
nine *comb* ennea-, nona-; *base*
　-nov-[2]; **~hundred:** enneacent-.
　Also see "Numbers" *in Part III*
nineteen *base* enneakaideca-, unde-
　viginti-
ninety *base* enneaconta-, nonagen-,
　nonages-
ninth *base* non-[2]
nip *base* vellic-
nipple *comb* mamilli-, papilli-,
　papillo-, papilloso-, thelo-, umbo-.
　See **breast**
niter *comb* nitro-
nitrogen *comb* azo-, nitro-, nitroso-;
　~plus hydrocarbon: diazo-
NO radical *comb* nitro(so)-
nod *base* nut(a)-
noise *base* crepit-, frem-, ligyr-,
　strep(i)-, strid-, stridul-. *See*
　sound
noiseless *comb* hesy-; *base* -plac-,
　quiesc-, -tacit-
nonacid radical *comb* -amine,
　amino-
none *comb* nulli-. *See* **negatives**
nonsense *base* fatu-, inan-, moro-,
　stult-
noon *base* merid-
normal *comb* normo-
Norman *comb* Normano-
north *base* borea-, septen-
northern lights *comb* aurora-
nose *comb* nasi-, naso-, rhino-,
　rhyncho-, -rrhyncha. *See* **beak**.
　~bleed: epistax-; **~blowing:**
　emunct-; **snub~:** simo-; **sneer:**
　mycter-
nostrils *base* nari-

not *pre* a-[3], ab-, an-[1], apo-, cata-,
　de-, dis-, ex-, il-, im-, in-, ir-,
　mis-, ne-, non-[1], ob-, un-; *comb*
　anti-, contra-, counter-, mal-,
　neutro-, no-, nulli-, with-; *suf*
　-less
not having *pre* a-, an-, des-, dis-,
　ex-, il-, im-, in-, ir-, un-; *comb*
　-atresia, atreto-, ectro-, lipo-; *base*
　-priv-; *suf* -less
notch *comb* crenato-, crenulato-.
　See **jagged**
nothing *base* nihili-
notion *comb* -gnomy, -gnosia,
　-gnosis, -gnostic, gnoto-, ideo-,
　-noia, -nomy, phreno-, psycho-,
　-sophy *base* -cogit-, -cogn-, epis-
　tem-, -noe-, -put-, ratio-, -sci-
nourishment *comb* bromato-,
　-brotic, manduc-, opso-, -phage,
　-phago, -phagous, -phagy, -sitia,
　sitio-, sito-, -trophia, -trophic,
　tropho-, -trophy, -vora, -vore,
　-vorous; *base* -alim-, -cib-, -gust-,
　-nutr-, thrept-
noxious *comb* noci-, pesti-; *base*
　-nox-, pericul-
nucleus *comb* caryo-, karyo-,
　nucleo-
number *base* -numer-; **even~:** *comb*
　artio-; **uneven~:** *comb* impari-,
　perisso-; **a number of:** *suf* -age,
　-some[3]. *Also see* "Numbers" *in*
　Part III
numbness *comb* narco-; *base* torp-
numerals *base* arithm-; **cardinal~:**
　suf -teen; **collective~:** *suf* -ad;
　ordinal~: *suf* -eth, -th. *Also see*
　"Numbers" *in Part III*
numerous *comb* multi-, myria-,
　myrio-, pluri-, poly-, sychno-
nurse *comb* threptero-
nut, nut-shaped *comb* caryo-,
　karyo-, nuci-, nucleo-
nuthatch *base* sitt-

nutmeg *base* myrist-
nutrition *comb* bromato-, -brotic,
  manduc-, opso-, -phage, -phago,
  -phagous, -phagy, -sitia, sitio-,
sito-, -trophia, -trophic, tropho-,
-trophy, -vora, -vore, -vorous;
base -alim-, -cib-, -gust-, -nutr-,
thrept-

O

oak *base* querc(i)-; *evergreen~:*
  cerr-
oar *comb* -reme, remi-
oats *base* aven(i)-
obedient *base* moriger-
obese *comb* adip(o)-, lipo-,
  pimel(o)-, pio-, stearo-, steato-;
  base -aliph-, lipar-, -obes-,
  -pingu-, sebo-
object of an action *suf* -ate
objective *comb* teleo-, telo-,
  ultim(o)-; *base* -fin-, -termin-
oblige *base* -mand-
oblique *comb* loxo-, plagio-; *base*
  ambag-
oblong *comb* oblongo-
obscenity *base* aischro-, borbor-,
  copro-, fescinn-
obscure *comb* enigmato-; *base*
  ambig, dub-, ancip-
observe *comb* eid(o)-, oculo-,
  ommat-, -opia, opsi-, -opsia,
  -opsis, opso-, -opsy, ophthalmo-,
  optico-, opto-, -scope, -scopic,
  scopo-, -scopy, visuo-; *base* -blep-,
  -scrut-, -spec-, -spic-, -vid-
obsessed with *comb* -aholic,
  -lagnia, -philia, -ridden
obstinate *base* contum-, obstin-,
  pervic-, proterv-
obstructed *comb* brady-; *base*
  -cunct-, imped-, -mora-, -tard-
obstruction *comb* emboli-, embolo-;
  base -byon-, -farct-
obtain *base* -cap-, -cep-, -cip-,
  -dyte-

obtuse *comb* obtusi-
obvious *comb* lampro, luc-, luci-;
  base -clar-
ocean *comb* halo-, mari-, thalasso-,
  thalatto-; *base* aequor-, naut-,
  nav-, pelag-
occipital *comb* occipito-
occupation *comb* arti-, -craft,
  -ergasia, ergasio-, -ergic, ergo-,
  -ergy, organo-, -urgy; *base* -opus-,
  pono-; *suf* -arian
odd-numbered *comb* impari-
odor *comb* brom(o)-, -odic, odori-,
  odoro-, -olent, olfacto-, -osmia,
  osmo-[1], osphresio-, ozo-, ozono-;
  base fet-, nidor-. *See also* "The
  Senses" in Part III
of *suf* -acean, -aceous, -ac[2], -ad[2], -al,
  -an, -ar, -arious, -ary, -atic,
  -ative, -atory, -eae, -ean, -eous,
  -ery, -etic, -ial, -ian, -ic, -id, -il,
  -ile, -ina, -inae, -ine, -ing, -ious,
  -istic, -ite, -itic, -itious, -itive,
  -ive, -oidea, -ory, -otic, -tious,
  -tive, -ular
off *pre* ab-, apo-, de-, ex-, for-
offering *base* -don-, -thy-
office *suf* -acy, -ate[3], -cy, -dom,
  -ship
offspring *comb* proli-
often *comb* pluri-, pollaki-, poly-;
  base crebr-; *suf* -le
oil *comb* elaeo-, elaio-, eleo-, olea-,
  -oleic, oleo-
ointment *comb* myro-; *base* -unct-,
  ungu-

old *comb* archaeo-, archeo-, eo-,
gerasco-, gero-, geronto-, grand-,
paleo-, presbyo-; *base* -antiq-,
-sen-, -vet-; *~age:* ger-[2];*~woman:*
grao-

omission *pre* a-, an-, dis-, ex-, il-,
im-, in-, ir-, un-; *comb* lipo-; *base*
-priv-; *suf* -less; *~of an opening:*
comb -atresia, atreto-;*~of a part:*
comb ectro-

on *pre* ana-, epi-, ob-, sur-; *~both
sides: comb* amph(i)-; *~the left
side: comb* laeo-, laevo-, levo-,
sinistro-; *~the other side: pre*
trans-; *~the outside: pre* epi-;
~the right side: comb dexio-, dex-
tro-; *~the side: pre* by-; *comb* lat-
eri-, latero-; *~this side of: pre* cis-;
comb citra-; *~top: pre* super-

one *comb* eka-, haplo-, heno-,
mono-, uni-; *~and one-half:*
comb sesqui-; *~billion: comb* giga-;
~billionth: comb nan(n)o-; *~by
one:* katheno-; *~fifth:* quint-;
~fourth: comb tetarto-; *~half:*
comb demi-, dicho-, dimid-,
hemi-, mezzo-, semi-; *~heptil-
lion: comb* yotta; *~heptillionth:*
comb yocto-;*~hexillion: comb*
zetta-; *~hexillionth: comb* zepto-;
~hundred: comb centi-, hecato-,
hecto-, hekto-; *~hundredth: comb*
centi-; *~million: comb* mega-;
~millionth: comb micro; *~quad-
rillion: comb* femto-; *~quad-
rillionth: comb* peta-;*~quintil-
lion: comb* atto-; *~quintillionth:*
comb exa-; *~thousand: comb*
chili-, kilo-; *~thousandth: comb*
milli-; *~trillion: comb* pico-;
~trillionth: comb tera-. *See also*
"Numbers" in Part III

one who __ *suf* -aholic, -aire, -an,
-ant, -ar[2], -ard[2], -arian, -art, -ary,
-ast, -ate, -ator, -ee, -eer, -en,

-ent, -er, -ette, -eur, -fer, -ician,
-ier, -ior, -ist, -le, -man, -nik, -o,
-or, -person, -people, -ster,
-woman, -yer; *~is well versed in
__:* -logist

one-eyed *base* lusc-

one's own *comb* heauto-, idio-, pro-
prio-, self-, sui-

onion *base* cep-[2], cromny-

ooze *base* ulig-

opaque *comb* glauco-

open space *comb* agora-, ceno-,
keno-

opening *base* -apert-, -cav-, fenest-,
foram-, œgo-, oigo-, osti-, patul-,
pylo-, rim, valv-; *lack of~: comb* -
atresia, atreto-; *surgical~:* -stomy

operation *comb* -ectomy

opinion *base* gnom-

opium *base* -mecon-

opossum *base* didelph-

opposite *pre* anti-, contra-, contre-,
dis-, hetero-, ob-, un-; *comb* back-,
counter-, enantio-, oppositi-

option *base* -opt-, -vol-

opulence *comb* chryso-, pluto-; *base*
chrem-, -opul-, pecun-

oracle *comb* chresmo-

orange *fruit: base* -hesperid-; *color:*
base auranti-. *Also see* "Colors" in
Part III

orangutan *base* -pong-

orb *comb* ano-, annul-, crico-,
cyclo-, disco-, globi-, globo-,
glom-, gyro-, orbito-, -sphere,
sphero-, stilli-, zon-, zoni-; *base*
-anu-, -cing-, -cinct-, -circin-,
-circul-, -coron-, -glomer-,
-numm-, -orb-, -rot-, -troch-

orbit *comb* orbito-

orchid *comb* orchido-[1]

order *placement: comb* -tactous,
taxi-, -taxia,-taxis, taxo-, -taxy;
base -pon-, -pos-; *command: base*
imper-, -jus-, -mand-

ordinary people *comb* demo-; *base* -pleb-, -popul-

organ *comb* organo-; *suf* -ite; ***having female~:*** *comb* -gynous; ***having male~:*** *comb* -androus

organic *comb* organo-

origin *comb* aetio-, -blast, blasto-, -blasty, -carp, -carpic, carpo-, -carpous, etio-, -gen, -genic, -genesis, -genous, -geny, -gone, -gonium, gono-, -gony, -phyletic, sperma-, spermal, spermatio-, spermato-, spermi-, -spermic, spermo-, -spermous, sporo-; *base* -init-; *suf* -esce, -escence, -escent

original *comb* archaeo-, primi-, primo-, proto-

originate *base* inaug-, incip-, init-

oriole *base* -icter-

osmium *comb* osmio-

osmosis *comb* osmo-[2]

osprey *base* ossifrag-

ostrich *base* -rat-, struthi-

other *comb* allo-, alter-, hetero-; *base* -ali-[2]

otter *base* -lutr-

out of *pre* e-, ec-, ef-, ex-. *See* **outside**

outcome *comb* ergo-, -ergic, -ergy; *suf* -age, -asm, -ata, -ation, -ency, -ism, -ma, -ment, -mony, -sion, -ure

outgrowth *comb* cele-, -edema, ganglio-, -phym(a); *base* -tum-

outside *pre* epi-, exo-, extra-, extro-, para-, preter-; *comb* ecto-, extero-, foris-, out-. *See* **out of**

outskirts *base* limin-, marg-

ovary *comb* gyn(o)-, -gynous, -gyny, oario-, oophoro-, ovario-

over ***above:*** *pre* ano-, meta-, ob-, preter-, super-, supra-, sur-, sursum-; *comb* over-; ***again:*** *pre* ana-, re-; *base* -palin-; ***excessive:*** *pre* hyper-, super-, ultra-; *comb* over-, poly-

overflow *base* antlo-, diluv-, inund-

oversight *base* culp-, delict-, laps-, pecc-, sphal-

overt *comb* lampro-, luc-, luci-, -phane, phanero-, -phanic, -phany, pheno-; *base* -clar-, -schem-, -spec-, -spic-

overthrow *base* vict-, -vinc-

overweight *base* obes-, pingu-

ovum *comb* oo-, ovario-, ovi-[1], ovo-

owl *base* strigi-, tyto-, ulul-[2]

ox *comb* bou-, bov-, bu-

oxygen *comb* oxa-, oxy-[2]; ***deprived of~:*** *comb* deoxy-

oyster *comb* ostrei-, ostreo-; *base* -ostrac-

ozone *comb* ozono-

P

pack together *base* stip-[2]

pad *comb* tylo-

page size *suf* -mo

pain *comb* alge-, algesi-, -algia, algo-, -algy, -dynia, noci-, -odynia, odyno-, pono-[1]; *base* dolor-, -nox-; ***sudden~:*** *comb* -agra. *See* **suffering**

paint *base* -pict-, pigm-

pairs *pre* bi- *comb* conjugato-, didymo-, diplo-, zyga-, zygo-

palate *comb* palato-, uranisco-, urano-, velar-

paleontological *comb* paleo-

palliative *base* anet-, -len-, miti-[1]

pallium *comb* pallio-

palm *hand: comb* palmati-,
  palmato-; *tree: base* palmac-
pan *comb* lecano-
pancreas *comb* pancreato-, pancreo-
pander *comb* leno- (lenocinant)
panic *comb* -phobe, -phobia,
  -phobic, phobo-; *base* pavid-,
  tim(or)-, -trem-, -trep-. *Also see*
  "Fear" in Part III
paper *comb* carto-, charto-, papyro-
papillary *comb* papilli-, papillo-,
  papilloso-
papule *comb* papulo-
papyrus *comb* papyro-
parachute (using) *comb* para-
parade *comb* -cade
paraffin series: hydrocarbon *suf*
  -ane
parakeet *base* psittac-
paralysis *comb* -plegia, -plegy
paramount *comb* arch-, archi-,
  proto-; *base* -prim-, -princip-
parasite *base* colaco-, parasit-,
  pothiri-, trypano-, vermin-
parasol *base* umbell(i)-, umbrell(i)-
parched *comb* carpho-, xero-; *base*
  arid-, celo-, cherso-, -sicc-
parchment *base* pergamen-
parent form *comb* proto-
parietal *comb* parieto-
parrot *base* psittac-
parsley *base* petrosel-
part(s) *comb* -fold, -meran,
  -mer(e), mer(o)-[1], -merous, par-,
  parti-
participant *suf* -ade; ~*in govt: comb*
  -crat
particular *comb* -specific
partition *comb* parieto-, -phragma,
  phragmo-, septo-; *base* -mur-
partly *comb* demi-, hemi-, semi-;
  ~*serious:* serio-
partridge *base* gallinac-, -perdic-,
  -perdri-
parturient *comb* -para

pass *base* -bat-
passage *comb* isthm-, meato-, over-,
  poro-, soleno-; *base* -bat-
past *comb* preter-
paste *base* glutin-. *See* glue
pastoral care *base* poimen-
patch *comb* emboli-, embolo-,
  -plakia
path *comb* -ode[1], odo-; *base* -itin-,
  -via-
pathetic *base* fleb-, trist-
pawn *base* pign-
pay *base* -pend-, -pens-
pea *comb* pisi-
peace *base* -eiren-, -iren-, -pac-,
  -pax-
peach *base* persic-
peacock *base* pavon-
peak *comb* coryph-
peanut *base* arach-
pear *comb* apio-, piri-, piro-, pyri-
pearl *base* margarit-
peat bog *base* turbar-
pebble *comb* pesso-, psepho-; *base*
  calcul-. *See* stone
peculiar *comb* aetheo-, anom(o)-,
  anomalo-. *See* irregular
peculiarity of *suf* -ism
peel *comb* -lemma[2]
pejorative *suf* -aster, -erel
pelican *base* onocrot-, pelecan-
pelvis *comb* pelvi-, perineo-,
  pyelo-
pen *base* styl-
penguin *base* sphenisc-
peninsula *base* chersones-
penis *comb* peo-, phall(o)-; *base*
  med-, mentul-
pennant *base* vexill-
penniless *comb* -penia, ptocho-,
  vidu-; *base* -mendic-, -paup-,
  penur-, -pov-
people *comb* dem(o)-, ethno-; *base*
  anthrop-, -pleb-, -popul-, -vulg-
pepper *base* piper-

perception *comb* -esthesia, -esthe-
sio, percepto-
perch *fish:* base perc- *sit:* base -sess-
percussion *comb* pless(i)-; *base*
-crot-, -cuss-, -puls-, -tus-, vapul-,
verber-
perforation *comb* -tresia. *See* tear
perfume *comb* myro-, -thymia[2]
pericardial *comb* pericardiaco-,
pericardio-
peril *base* pericul-
perineum *comb* perineo-
period *time: comb* back-, chrono-,
eo-, horo-, paleo, protero-, yester-;
menstrual: comb emmen-,
-menia, meno-
periosteum *comb* periosteo-
perishable *base* caduc-, fragil-
peritoneum *comb* meso-, perito-
neo-
permanent *base* diuturn-, dur(o)-,
perenn-, perm-, stabil-
pernicious *comb* noci-, pesti-; *base*
-nox-, pericul-
perpetual *base* assid-, contin-, in-
cess-, perpet-
person *suf* -aholic, -aire, -an, -ant,
-ard, -arian, -art, -ary, -ast, -ate,
-ator, -ee, -eer, -en, -ent, -er,
-ette, -eur, -fer, -ician, -ier, -ior,
-ist, -le, -ling[1], -man, -nik, -o,
-or[2], -person, -people, -ster,
-woman, -yer
personal *comb* idio-, proprio-, self-
perspiration *comb* sudori-; *base*
-hidr-, -suda-
persuade *base* -duc-
pertaining to *suf* -ac[2], -acean,
-aceous, -ad, -al, -an, -ar[2], -ari-
ous, -ary, -atic, -ative, -atory,
-eae, -ean, -eous, -ery, -etic, -ial,
-ian, -ic, -id, -il, -ile, -ina, -inae,
-ine, -ing, -ious, -istic, -ite, -itic,
-itious, -itive, -ive, -oidea, -ory,
-otic, -tious, -tive, -ular

pest *comb* pesti-, vermin-
pestilence *comb* loemo-, loimo-. *See*
disease
petal *comb* petuli-, -sepalous
petroleum *comb* petro-
petty *base* pusill-, rhopo-
pharynx *comb* pharyngo-
pheasant *base* alector-, gallinac-,
phasian-
phenanthrene *comb* phenanthro-
phenol *base* carbol-; *suf* -ol
phenyl *comb* pheno-
philosophical *comb* philosophico-
phonetic *comb* phonetico-
phosphorous *comb* phospho-,
phosphoro-
phrase *comb* phraseo-
phylum *comb* phylo-
physical *comb* physi-, physico-,
physio-; *~love:* eroto-
piece *comb* clasmato-, -fid; *base*
frag-, frust-, -par-
pig *base* porcin-, sui-
pig-headed *base* contum-, obstin-,
pervic-, proterv-
pigeon *base* columb-, palumb-,
perister-, pullastr-
pile *base* -acerv-, conger-, -cumul-
pillar *comb* column-, stylo-[2]; *~like:*
paxill-; *small~:* columelli-
pillow *base* pulvin-
pimp *base* leno-
pimple *comb* pustulo-
pin *base* acu-, belon-
pinch *base* -rrhexo-
pine *base* -peuce-, pin-; *~cone:*
strobil-
pineapple *base* bromel- (bromeliaceous)
pipe *comb* aulo-, follic-, salpingo-,
siphoni-, siphono-, solen(o)-, sy-
ringo-, tubi-, tubo-, tubuli-, vasi-;
base calam-, fistul-, -syr-
pistil *comb* gyn(o)-, -gynous, -gyny
pit *base* -taph(o)-, taphro-

pitcher *comb* urcei-, urceo-
pitted *base* bothr-, fov-, scrobic-
place, a *comb* -land, loco-, situ-, -stead, topo-,-topy, ubi-; *suf* -ensis; ~*of:* *suf* -age; ~*for:* *suf* -arium, -ary, -cle, -ery, -orium, ory. *Also see* "Location" *in Part* III
place, to *comb* -thesis, -thetic; *base* -pon-, -pos-; *suf* -en
placenta *base* mazo-[1], placenti-
plait *comb* pleco, plecto-
plane *surface:* *comb* explanato-, plani-, plano-[1]
plant growth: unequal *comb* -nastic, -nasty
plants *comb* botano-, herbi-, -phyte, phyto-, vegeti-, vegeto-; *suf* -ad, -aceae, -ales, -eae, -ia
plastic surgery *comb* -plasty
plate *comb* lamelli-, lamini-, lamino-, placo-; *base* -tect-; **metal~:** *comb* elasmo-
platinum *comb* platini-, platino-
platypus *base* monotrem-, pro-tother-
play *comb* -lude
please *base* delect-, -plac-, volupt-
pleasure *base* -hedon-, volupt-
pleura *comb* pleuro-
plover *base* charadr-, pluvial-
pluck *base* -tillo-, -vellic-
plug *comb* emboli-, embolo-; *base* -byon-, -farct-
plunge *comb* -merge, -merse
plural *suf* -a, -acea, -aceae, -ae, -des[2], -eae, -en[2], -es, -i, -ia, -ata, -ota, -s; **collective~:** *suf* -ana
pod *base* kelyph-, siliqu-
poems *comb* rhapso-; *base* -metr-, muso-; *suf* -ad
pointed *comb* acantho-, aceto-, acetyl-, acid-, acro-, acu-, acuti-, cusp-, mucro-, oxy-[1], spiculi-, spiculo-, stylo-[1]; *base* -acerb-, aci-,

-aichm-, -aichur-, -belon-, fastig-, muric-, -punct-, -piq-, -pung-, stigm-
points, having *comb* punctato-
poison *comb* tox(i), toxico-, -toxin, toxo-[1], veneno-
polar *comb* polari-
polecat *base* mustel-
police officer *base* alyt-
polished *base* levig-, xest-
political *comb* politico-
pollen *comb* palyn-, pollini-
pollute *base* -turp-
polymer of *pre* meta-
pomegranate *base* balaust-
pond, pool *comb* limno-; *base* lacus-, stagn-
poor *deficient:* *comb* -isch-, oligo-, -penia; *penniless:* *comb* ptocho-, vidu-; *base* -mendic-, -paup-, penur-, -pov-; *quality:* *comb* caco-, kako-
poppy *comb* opio-, papaver-; *base* -mecon-
porcelain *base* poticho-
porcupine *base* hystric-
pore *comb* pori-, poro, poroso-
pork *base* porcin-
porphyritic rock *comb* -phyre
porpoise *base* delphin-, phoecaen-
portal *comb* porto-
portion *base* par-[1]
position *office:* *suf* -acy, -ate, -cy, -dom, -ship
possessing *comb* -echia; *suf* -acean, -aceous, -al, -ate, -ed, -ful, -gerous, -ial, -ine, -ious, -itious, -ory, -ous, -some, -ulent, -ulous, -wise, -y; *base* -ten-; ~*parts:* *comb* -fold
possibility *suf* -atile
postage stamp *base* philatel-, timbro-
posterior *comb* postero-
potassium *comb* kal(i)-
potency *comb* dyna-, dynamo-,

mega-, megalo-, -megaly, -sthe-
nia, stheno-; *base* -forc-, -fort-,
-poten-, robor-; *~to do or be: suf*
-bility

pouch *comb* angio-, asco-, burs(o)-,
-ceco, chlamyd-, chrysali-, coleo-,
-cyst, cysti-, cysto-, follic-,
meningo-, pericardiaco-, pericar-
dio-, peritoneo-, physa-, physali-,
physo-, theca-, theco-, typhlo-,
utric-, vesico-; *base* marsup-,
-sacc-, scrot-, -thylac-

poultry *base* gallin-

pound *comb* -cuss-, plessi-, rhabdo-;
base -cop-, -crot-, fustig-, plang-,
puls-, quass-, vapul-, -verber-

pour *base* -chys-, -chyt-, -flu-, -fus-

poverty *comb* -penia, ptocho-,
vidu-; *base* -mendic-, -paup-,
penur-, -pov-

power(ful) *comb* -crat, crato-,
dyna-, dynamo-, mega-, megalo-,
-megaly, stheno-; *base* -forc-,
-fort-, imper-, -poten-; *~to do or
be: suf* -bility

practice of *comb* -craft; *suf* -ade,
-age, -al, -ance, -ancy, -asis, -asm,
-ation, -cy, -ence, -ency, -ery,
-esis, -iasis, -ice, -ics, -ing, -ion,
-ism, -ment, -osis, -otic, -sion,
-sis, -th, -tion, -tious, -ture, -ure,
-y, -ysis

practitioner *suf* -ician, -ist

praise *base* encom-, -laud-

pray *base* litan-, orat-, -prec-, -rog-

preaching *base* kery-

precipice *base* -cremno-

predilection for *comb* philo-

pregnancy *comb* -cyesis, toco-; *base*
gestat-, -gravid-, -maieusi-

prehistoric *comb* eo-, paleo-, proto-

preparation *pre* pre-

present *base* -don-

preserver *suf* -sote

press together *base* stip-[2]

pressure *comb* bar(o)-, -piesis,
piezo-, -tonia, -tonic, tono-; *base*
thlips-

pretend *comb* pseudo-; *base* fict-,
-simul-

preventing *pre* anti-; *base* imped-,
prohib-

previous *pre* pre-; *comb* back-,
yester-

prickly *comb* echinato-, echino-,
echinulato-, echinuli-; *base*
-urtic-

priest *base* presbyter-, sacerdot-

primary *comb* archi-, proto-; *base*
-prim-, -princip-

primate *comb* -pithecus

primitive *comb* archi-, paleo-,
prisc-, proto-

principal *comb* arch(i)-[1], prim-,
proto-

principle of *suf* -ism

print *comb* -type

prior to *pre* pre-; *comb* back-,
yester-

proceed *comb* -grade, -motive, -pla-
nia , plano-; *base* -bat-, -ced-,
-cess-, -cur(s)-, -grad-, -gress-,
-mob-, -vad-, -vas-; *~away:* out-;
~into: -dyte-; *~forward:* pro-;
~toward: -bound, -petal

process of *comb* -craft; *suf* -ade,
-age, -al, -ance, -ancy, -asis, -asm,
-ation, -cy, -ence, -ency, -ery,
-esis, -iasis, -ice, -ics, -ing, -ion,
-ism, -ment[1], -osis, -otic, -sion,
-sis, -th, -tion, -tious, -ture, -ure,
-y, -ysis

procession *comb* -cade

proclamation *base* kery-

procure *base* -cap-, -cep-, -cip-,
-dyte-

produce/producing *comb* -facient,
-ferous, -fic, -fication, -gen, -gen-
esis, -genic, -genous, -geny, -ger-
ous, ideo-, -parous, -phor,

-phorous, -plast, -plastic, plasto-,
-plasty, poiesis, -poietic, -urgy; *suf*
-ate, -atory, -ic, -fer, -ing, -otic
product of *comb* -geny[2], -gony; *suf*
-ade, -ery, -ment[1]
proficiency *base* -apt-, -habil-,
-poten-, -qual-; *suf* -bility, -ful,
-ship
profit *base* lucri-, quaest-
profusion *base* ampl-, copi-, larg-
projectile *base* -ballist-
promoting *base* -gog-
propagate *base* thremm-
propel *comb* -bole, -bolic, bolo-,
-boly; *base* ballist-, -jact-, -jacula-,
-ject-
proper *comb* cyrio-, kyrio-, ortho-
properties *suf* -ics
prophetic *comb* fati-, vati-
propitiatory *base* hilasm-, ilast-
proposition *comb* -lemma[1]
prosperity *comb* chryso-, pluto-;
base chrem-, -opul-, pecun-
prostate *comb* prostato-
prostitute *comb* cypriano-, hetaero-,
porno-; *base* -meretric-, scort-;
brothel: lupan-
protected against *comb* -proof
protecting from *comb* para-[1]
protection *comb* -phylactic, phy-
lacto-, -phylax, -phylaxis
protein *comb* proteo-
protein hydrolysis *suf* -ose
protest *base* -quer-, -querul-
protoplasm *comb* -plasmo-, -plast
protuberance *comb* condyl(o)-,
gibboso-, hybo-, papillo-,
ramoso-, thelo-, umbo-
proverb *base* parem-, paroem-
provide *pre* be-; *base* -don-; *suf* -ate
provided with *comb* -echia; *suf*
-able, -ate, -ed[2], -ious, -ous,
proving *comb* -deictic
proximity *pre* a-, ac-, ad-, af-, ag-,
al-, an-, ap-, ar-, as-, at-, by-, cis-,

epi-, para-, peri-; *comb* juxta-,
citra-, pene-, proximo-
proxy *comb* allelo-, allo-, alter-,
hetero-; *base* -ali-
psychosis *comb* lysso-, -mania; *base*
ament-, dement-
ptarmigan *base* tetraon-
pubescent *base* hebe-
pubic *comb* pubio-, pubo-
public *comb* demo-; *base* -pleb-,
-vulg-
puke *comb* -emesis, -emetic, emeto-
pull *base* -tillo-, -tract-, vell-
pulley *comb* trochi-, trocho-
pulmonary *comb* pulmo-
pulse *comb* sphygmo-; *base* -crot-
pumpkin *base* pepo-
puncture *comb* -centesis; *base*
stigm-
punishment *comb* mastigo-,
rhabdo-; *base* castig-, peno-,
poine-, -pun-[1]
pupil *eye:* *comb* core-[1], coreo-,
-coria, coro-, -koria, pupillo-;
student: *base* -discip-
puppet *base* pupa
purchase *comb* onio-; *base* -empt-,
-merc-, nundin-
purify *base* cathar-. *See* **cleanse**
purple *comb* purpureo-; *base* ama-
ranth-, blatt-[2], indi-, indo-,
phenic-, porphyr-, -pun-[2]. *Also
see* "Colors" in Part III
purpose *comb* teleo-, telo-
purse *comb* burs(o)-, marsup-,
phasco-
purslain *base* portulac-
pursue *base* secut-, sequ-
pus *comb* purulo-, pyo-. *See* **infection**
push *comb* -trude; *base* -pel-, -pul-,
trus-
put *base* -pon-, -pos-; *suf* -en;
~in the form of: *suf* -ate; *~to-
gether:* *comb* -thesis, -thetic; *base*

cond-, -fabr-, -fac-, -fec-, -fic-,
-struct-
putrefying *comb* cario-, lysi-, lyso-,
-lysis, -lyte, -lytic, phthino-,
phthisio-, -phthisis, putre-, putri-,

pytho-, sapro-, septi-, septico-,
septo-; *base* marcesc-, phthor-,
tabe-; *suf* -ase
pylorus *comb* pyloro-
pyrites *comb* pyrito-

Q

quadrillion(th) *comb* femto-, peta-
quaff *comb* pino-, poto-; *base* -bib-,
pocul-
quail *base* coturn-, gallinac-
quake *base* -pav-, -trem-
qualified *comb* -potent; *suf* -able,
-ible, -ile; *in an ~way:* -bly
quality of *suf* -able, -acity, -acy,
-age, -ance, -ancy, -ant, -asis,
-asm, -ate, -atile, -ation, -cy,
-dom, -eity, -ence, -ency, -ent,
-ery, -esis, -ful, -hood, -iasis,
-ice[1], -ility, -ion, -ise, -ism, -ity,
-ling, -ma, -ment, -ness, -or[3],
-osis, -otic, -red, -ship, -sion, -th,
-tion, -tude, -ture, -ty[1], -ure, -y[2]
qualm *comb* -phobe, -phobia,
-phobic, phobo-; *base* pavid-,
tim(or)-, -trem-, -trep-. *Also see*
"Fear" in Part III
quantity *base* -quant-; *suf* -age,
-ful
quarrel *comb* -machy; *base* litig-,
pugil-, -pugn-, -rix-
quarter *base* quadr-
quash *comb* lysi-, lyso-, -lysis,
-lytic, -lyze, -phage, phago-, -
phagous, -phagy; *base* -ate-[4],
perd-, phthart-, -vast-

quaver *comb* tremo-; *base* pav-,
trep-
queen *base* regin-
quell *comb* stasi-, -stasis, -stat,
stato-; *base* fin-, termin-
quest *comb* -petal, -quire, -quiry;
base indag-, -rog-, -scrut-
question *base* erot-, -quir-, -rog-
quickness *comb* ocy-, tacho-,
tachy-; *base* alacr-, celer-, festin-,
veloc-
quicksand *base* syrt-
quiet *comb* hesy-; *base* -plac-,
quiesc-, -tacit-
quinine *base* cinchon-
quintillion(th) *comb* atto-, exa-
quirky *comb* aetheo-, anom(o)-,
anomalo-. *See* **irregular**
quisling *base* prodit-
quit *base* relinq-
quite *pre* be-, cata-, cath-, de-,
kata-, ob-, per-; *comb* holo-,
omni-, pan-, panto-, stone-, toti-
quivering *comb* -chorea, choreo-,
-clonic, -clonus, -esmus, -ismus,
spasmo-; *base* -stal-, -vellic-

R

rabbit *base* cunic-, lago-, lepor-
rabies *base* lyss-
raccoon *base* arctoid-, procyon-
race *group:* *comb* -ethno, geno-, phylo-
race course *comb* -drome, dromo-, dromous
radiant *comb* helio-; *base* fulg-, nitid-; *~energy:* *comb* bolo-², radio-, spectro-
radicals *suf* -yl, -ylene; *two~:* *comb* bi-
radicle *comb* radiculo-, rostell-
radioactive *comb* radio-
radish *base* raphan-
rag *base* pann-
railroad *base* siderodromo-
rain *comb* hyeto-, pluvio-; *base* imbri-, nimb-, ombr-
rainbow *base* irid-
raise *cultivate:* *base* -ponic; *lift:* levat-
ram *comb* crio-, krio-; *base* -ariet-
rank *comb* -rater; *suf* -cy, -dom², -ship
rap *comb* plessi-; *base* cop-, -crot-, -cuss-, -plang-, puls-, -tus-, vapul-, -verber-
rape *base* rap-, rep-, stupr-
rapid *comb* ocy-, tacho-, tachy-; *base* alacr-, celer-, festin-, veloc-
rare *comb* mano-, spano-; *base* -areo-²
rash *comb* -anthema
rat *base* mur-
ratio, inverse *pre* sub-
rattlesnake *base* crotal-
raven *comb* coraci-, coraco-; *base* corvin-
ravenous *base* avid-, edac-, gulos-
raw *base* omo-²

ray *comb* radio-, radiato-; *base* bolo-², -rad-
razor *base* xyr-
reading *comb* -legia; *base* lect-, -leg-¹
real *base* ver-
realm *suf* -dom, -ric
rear *comb* hind-. *See* **behind**
reasoning *comb* -gnomy, -gnosia, -gnosis, -gnostic, -gnoto, ideo-, -noia, -nomy, -phrenic, phrenico-, phreno-, psycho-, -sophy, thymo-, -witted; *base* -cogit-, -cogn-, ment(a)-, -noe-, -put-, -ratio-, -sci-
rebuke *base* increp-
receiver *comb* -ceptor; *base* -cap-, -cip-; *suf* -ee
recent *comb* -cene, ceno-¹, neo-, nov-
receptacle *comb* angio-, asco-, bursi-, burso-, ceco-, chlamyd-, chrysali-, cisto-, coleo-, -cyst, cysti-, cysto-, follic-, meningo-, pericardiaco-, pericardio-, perito-neo-, phasco-, physa-, physali-, physo-, -theca, theci-, theco-, ty-phlo-, utri-, utric, vesico-; *base* -sacc-, -thylac-
reciprocal *pre* co-, inter-, syl-, sym-, syn-, sys; *comb* allelo-, hama-, symphyo, synchro-; *base* -allac-, -allag-, -allaxis-, -mutu-
recline *base* -cub-, -cumb-
recognition *comb* -gnosis, -gnostic
reconstructive surgery *comb* -plasty
rectification *comb* ortho-; *base* cas-tig-, emend-
rectum *comb* procto-, recto-
red *comb* carmino-, erysi-, erythro-, phoeni-, pyhrro-, rhodo-, roseo-,

testaceo-; *base* coccin-, coquel-,
cruent-, -ereuth-, ferrug-, fuc-,
grenat-, -later-, minia-, murex-,
nacar-, -rub-, -rud-, -ruf-, -rut-.
Also see "Colors" *in Part III*
redundant *comb* perisso-
reed *comb* aulo-, follic-, salpingo-,
siphoni-, siphono-, solen(o)-,
syringo-, tubi-, tubo-, tubuli-,
vasi-; *base* arundi-, calam-, fistul-,
-syr-
refuse to *pre* dis-
region *comb* choro-
regular *comb* cyrio-, kyrio-,
homalo-, homolo-, ortho-
regulate *base* -temp-
regurgitate *comb* -emesis, -emetic,
emeto-
reject *base* relinq-
relate *base* narr-
relating to *suf* -acean, -aceous, -ad[2],
-al, -an, -ar, -arious, -ary, -atic,
-ative, -atory, -eae, -ean, -eous,
-ery, -etic, -ial, -ian, -ic, -id, -il,
-ile, -ina, -inae, -ine, -ing, -ious,
-istic, -ite, -itic, -itious, -itive,
-ive, -oidea, -orious, -ory, -otic,
-tious, -tive, -ular
relatives *base* cogn-, famil-, stirp-
release *base* -miss-, -mit-, -pomp-
relieving *comb* lyo-, lysi-, -lysis,
lyso-, -lyte, -lytic, -lyze; *base*
-liqu-, -solu-, -solv-
relics *comb* lipsano-, reliq-
religion *comb* religio-, theo-
remember *comb* -mnesia, -mnesis;
base -mem-, -mnem-
remote *comb* disto-, tele-
remove *pre* ab-, abs-, apo-, be-, de-,
des-, di-, dia-, dif-, dis-, e-, ec-,
ef-, ex-, for-, off-, se, with-; *comb*
ectro-
repair *comb* ortho-; *base* castig-,
emend-
repeatedly *comb* batto-, pollaki-;

base epana-, -iter-, palin-; *suf* -er.
See **frequent**
replacement *comb* allelo-, allo-,
alter-, hetero-; *base* -ali-
replete *comb* -filled, pleni-, pleo-,
plero-, pluri-; *base* -pler-, -plet-;
suf -acious, -ate, -ic, -ful, -ilent,
-ose, -osity, -ous, -ulent, -y
reply *base* apocris-. *See* **say**
repress *comb* stasi-, -stasis, -stat,
stato-; *base* fin-, termin-
reproach *comb* enisso-, enosi-
reproduce *comb* aetio-, -blast,
blasto-, -blasty, -carp, -carpic,
carpo-, -carpous, etio-, -gen,
-genic, -genesis, -genous, -geny,
-gone, -gonium, gono-, -gony,
-phyletic, sperma-, -spermal,
spermato-, spermi-, -spermic,
spermo-, sporo-; *base* -init-; *suf*
-esce, -escence, -escent
reptile *comb* echidno-, -glypha,
herpeto-, -ophidia, ophidio-,
ophio-, -saur, sauro-, -saurus;
base angui-, batrach-, colubr-,
reptil-, -serp-, viper-
repulsion *base* fastid-
request *base* -pet-, -quir-, -quis-,
-rog-
require *base* exig-
rescued *comb* eleuthero-; *base*
-liber-, vac(u)-
resembling *pre* para-, quasi-; *comb*
homeo-, homoio-, homolo-, iso-,
-opsis, -phane, -phanic, -phany,
pheno-; *base* simil-; *suf* -acean,
-aceous, -al, -an, -ar, -ary, -ean,
-en, -eous, -esque, -ful, -ic, -il,
-ile-, -ine, -ing, -ish, -istic, -isti-
cal, -itious, -ize, -like, -ode, -oid,
-oidal, -ose, -osity, -some, -tious,
-ular, -y
resentment *base* -invid-
reservoir *base* lacco-
resin *comb* resino-

resistant to *comb* -proof, -tight;
  ~disease: comb immuno-
resourceful *base* agil-, facil-, ingen-
respiration *comb* -pnea, pneo-,
  pneumato-, pneumo-, pneu-
  mono-, pneusio-, pulmo-, respi-
  rato-, spiro-[1]; *base* -hal-
responsibility *comb* hypegia-,
  hypengy-; *base* paralip-
responsive to *comb* -trope, -tropic,
  -tropism, tropo-, -tropous,
  -tropy
rest *base* oti-
restless *comb* agito- *base* -turb-
restrained *comb* brady-; *base*
  -cunct-, imped-, -mora-, -tard-
restriction *comb* isch-, koly-,
  -penia, rhopo-, -strain, -strict;
  base angust-, -string-; *suf* -en. *See*
  tie
result (of) *comb* ergo-, -ergic,
  -ergy; *suf* -age, -asm, -ata, -ation,
  -ency, -ism, -ma, -ment[1], -mony,
  -sion, -ure
retaliation *comb* counter-
retention *comb* -echia, -tain; *base*
  -cathex-, -ten-
reticular *comb* reticulo-
retina *comb* retino-
return *pre* re-; *comb* nosto-
reveal *comb* phaeno-, pheno-; *base*
  -monstr-
reversal *comb* allo-; *base* -vers-,
  -vert-
reverse *pre* anti-, de-
revile *base* vituper-
revulsion *comb* miso-, -phobe,
  -phobia, -phobic; *base* -invid-,
  -ira(sc)-, odi-
rhinoceros *base* ceratorh-
rhombus *comb* rhombo-
rib *comb* costi-, costo-
ribbon *comb* taeni-, taenio-, -tene,
  teni-; *base* lemnisc-
rice *base* oryzi-, rizi-

riches *comb* chryso-, pluto-; *base*
  chrem-, -opul-, pecun-
ridge *comb* crebri-, lopho-; *base*
  -carin-
ridicule *comb* catagelo-, katagelo-
ridiculous *base* fatu-, inan-, moro-,
  stult-
right *comb* recti-; *~angle: comb*
  ortho-; *~side: comb* dexio-, dex-
  tro-; *correct: comb* ortho-; *base*
  emend-
righteous *pre* bene-, eu-; *base*
  agath-, bon-, prob-
rigid *comb* ancylo-, ankylo-, tetano-
rind *comb* -lemma[2]
ring *comb* annul-, ano-[2], crico-,
  cyclo-, disco-, globo-, gyro-,
  -sphere, sphero-, stilli-; *base*
  -anu-, -cinct-, -cing-, -circin-,
  -circul-, -coron-, -glomer-,
  -numm-, -orb-, -rot-, -troch-,
  -zon-; *finger~:* dactylio-;
  ~shaped: ano-[2]
ringing *base* tinn-, tintinn-
ringlet *comb* cirr(h)i-, cirr(h)o-
ripe *base* -matur-
rise *base* -cresc-, -surg-
risky *base* pericul-
rivaling *pre* anti-
river *comb* fluvio-, potamo-; *base*
  amn-, flum-, -rip-
roach *base* blatt-
road *comb* hodo, -ode, odo-; *base*
  -iter-, -via-
roadrunner *base* cucul-
roar *base* -frem-
robber *comb* clepto-, klepto-, lesto-;
  base -furt-, harpax-, latro-, pred-
robin *base* -turd-
robust *comb* -proof, dur(o)-; *base*
  -forc-, -fort-
rock *comb* -lithic, litho-, pesso-,
  petri-, petro-, sax(i)-; *base* -lapid-,
  -rupes-, rupic-; *suf* -ite
rod (shaped) *comb* bacilli-, bacillo-,

bacul-, fusi-, fuso-, rhabdo-, vergi-; *base* coryn-, ferul-, -rad-, virgul-

Roman *comb* Romano-

romantic *comb* romantico-

roof *comb* stego-, tecti-, tegu-; *~of mouth: comb* palato-, uranisco-

rooster *comb* alector-, alectry-

root *comb* radiculo-, rhizo-, -rrhiza; *base* -radic-, -stirp-

rope *comb* funi-, resti-, schoeno-

rose *comb* rhodo-, roseo-

rotary *comb* cyclo-, roti-, troch-, trochalo-, trochi-, trocho-

rotten *comb* lysi-, lyso-, -lysis, -lyte, phthysio-, -phthysis, putre-, putri-, pytho-, sapro-, septi-, septo-; *base* -putr-

rough *comb* asper-. trachy-; *base* -rud-, salebr-

round *comb* ano-, annul-, convexo-, crico-, cyclo-, disco-, gibboso-, globi-, globo-, glom-, gyro-, orbito-, rotundi-, rotundo-, -sphere, sphero-, stilli-, tereti-, tereto-, trochi-, trocho-, zon-, zoni-; *base* -anu-, -cing-, -cinct-, -circin-, -circul-, -coron-, -glomer-, -numm-, -orb-, -rot-, strongyl-; ***partly~: comb*** orbiculato-

route *comb* -ode, odo-; *base* -itin-, -via-

routine *comb* -craft; *suf* -ade, -age,

-al, -ance, -ancy, -asis, -asm, -ation, -cy, -ence, -ency, -ery, -esis, -iasis, -ice, -ics, -ing, -ion, -ism, -ment, -osis, -otic, -sion, -sis, -th, -tion, -tious, -ture, -ure, -y, -ysis

rows *comb* -stichia, sticho-, -stichous

rubbing *comb* tribo-, -tripsy; *base* trit-

rude *base* contum-, impud-, procac-

rue *base* rut-

rug *base* lodic-

ruination *comb* lysi-, lyso-, -lysis, -lytic, -lyze, -phage, phago-, -phagous, -phagy; *base* -ate-[4], perd-, phthart-, -vast-

ruler *comb* -arch[2], gubern-; *base* -reg-

ruling *comb* -archy, -ocracy; *base* -regn-

rump *comb* podic-, pygia, pygo-; *base* nati-

run *comb* -drom(e), dromo-, -dromous; *base* curr-, -cur(s)-

rune *comb* runo-

rupture *comb* -clasia, -clasis, clastic, frag-, -rhegma, -(r)rhexis; *base* -fract-, -frang-, -rupt-

rush *hurry: base* curr-, impet-, -vad-, -vas-; ***plant:*** -junc-

Russia(n) *comb* Russo-

rust *base* rubig-

S

sable *base* zibel-

sac *comb* angio-, asco-, bursi-, burso-, ceco-, chlamyd-, chrysali, coleo-, -cyst, cysti-, cysto-, follic-, meningo-, pericardiaco-, pericar-

dio-, peritoneo-, physa-, physali-, physo-, -theca, theco-, typhlo-, utri-[2], utric-, vesico-; *base* marsup-, -sacc-, -thylac-

saccharin *comb* saccharo-

sacrifice *base* -thy-
sacred *comb* hagio-, hiero-; *base* -sacr-, -sanct-
sacrum *comb* sacro-
saddle *base* ephipp-
sadness *comb* lype-; *base* dolor-, fleb-, flet-, luct-, -trist-
safe from *comb* -proof, -tight
saffron *base* -croce-
sail *base* navig-
sailfish *base* istiophor-
saint *comb* hagio-
salad *base* acetar-
saliva *comb* ptyal(o)-, sial¹-
salmon *comb* salmoni-
salt *comb* alo-, halo-, sali-, salino-; *base* sals-; *suf* -ate, -ite
salvation *base* soter-
same *pre* co-; *comb* equi-, homo-, iso-, pari-, tauto-; *~time: comb* hama-; *base* -simul-
sand *comb* ammo-, arenacio-, psammo-; *base* aren-, sabul-, saburr-
sand grouse *base* pterocl-
sandpiper *base* charadr-, -tring-
sandwich *comb* -burger
sarcastic *base* acerb-, mord-
sated *comb* -filled, pleni-, pleo-, plero-, pluri-; *base* -pler-, -plet-; *suf* -acious, -ate, -ic, -ful, -ilent, -ose, -osity, -ous, -ulent, -y
saucer *base* acetabul-
sausage(-shaped) *base* allant(o)-, botul-
savage *base* agrio-
save *base* salv-, serrato-
saw *tool: comb* pri-, prion-, runcin-, serrato-, serri-
sawdust *base* scobi-
say *comb* -claim, logo-, -logue, -lalia, -lexia, lexico-, -lexis, -lexy, -logy, -phone, phono-, -phony, rhet-, verbi-, verbo-, voc-, voci-, -voke; *base* -clam-, -dict-,

-loc(u)-, -loqu-, narr-, -orat-, -phat-, -phem-
scabbard *comb* coleo-
scale *base* -libra-
scales *comb* lamelli-, lepido-, squamato-, squamo-, squamoso-, squaroso-; *base* -pholid-, -scut-
scalloped *comb* cren-, crenato-, crenulato-
scandal *comb* -gate
scapula *comb* scapulo-
scar *comb* ulo-¹; *base* -cica-
scarce *comb* mano-, spano-; *base* -areo-
scared *base* -pavid-, -tim-, trepid-. *See* fear
scatter *comb* -sperse; *base* -spor-
scenery *comb* -scape
scent *comb* brom(o)-, odori-, odoro-, olfacto-,-osmia, osmo-, osphresio-, ozo-, ozono-
school *base* schol-
science *comb* -graphy, -logic, -logical, -logy, techno-, -techny; *suf* -ics
scimitar *comb* acinaci-
scintillation *comb* sela-; *base* -fulg-, stilpno-
scissors *base* forfic-, -psalid-
sclera *comb* sclero-
scold *base* increp-
scope of *suf* -ure
scorn *base* deris-
scorpion *base* pedipalp-
Scottish *comb* Scoto-
scourge *comb* cnido-, mastigo-; *base* flagell-, -piq-, -urtic-
scrap *comb* clasmato-, -fid; *base* frag-, frust-, -par-
scratch *comb* amycho-, scab-, titillo-
scrotum *comb* didym(o)-, orchido-, orchio-, oscheo-; *base* -scrot-
scrub *comb* balneo-; *base* ablut-, cathar-, -lav-, -mund-, -purg-

sculpt *comb* glyph-, glypt-
scurvy *base* -scorb-
Scythian *comb* Scytho-
sea *comb* enalio-, halo-, mare-,
  mari-, thalasso-, thalatto-; *base*
  aequor-, naut-, nav-, pelag-;
  ~shore: paral-, thino-
sea horse *base* hippocamp-
sea urchin *base* echin-
seagull *base* -lar-
seal *animal: comb* phoc(o)-; *stamp:*
  base -sigil-, sphrag-
search(ing) *comb* -petal, -quire,
  -quiry; *base* indag-, -rog-, -scrut-.
  See **turn towards**
seasons *comb* horo-; *fall: base* -au-
  tumn-; *spring: base* -vern-; *sum-*
  mer: base -aestiv-; *winter: base*
  -hibern-, -hiem-
seat *base* cathedr-, sedil-
seaweed *comb* phyceae-, -phyceous,
  phyco-; *base* -fuc-
sebum *comb* sebo-
second/secondary *pre* bi-, para-²,
  super-; *comb* deuter(o)-, deuto-.
  See **two**
second-rate *pre* hypo-, sub-, under-;
  comb hystero-; *base* hesson-; *suf* -
  aster
secret *pre* subter-; *comb* calypto-,
  crypto-; *base* arcan-, occult-
secretion *comb* crino-, -crine; *wax-*
  like~: comb cerumini-
sect *suf* -arian
secure *comb* -proof, -tight
see *comb* eid(o)-, oculo-, ommat-,
  -opia, opsi-, -opsia, -opsis, opso-,
  -opsy, ophthalmo-, optico-, opto-,
  -scope, -scopic, scopo-, -scopy,
  visuo-; *base* -blep-, -scrut-, -spec-,
  -spic-, -vid-. *Also see* "The Senses"
  in Part III
seeds *comb* -carp, -carpic, carpo-,
  -carpous, -sperm, -spermal, sper-
  matio-, spermato-, spermi-,

-spermic, spermo-, -spermous,
  -spore, spori-, sporo-, -sporous;
  base semin-
seek(ing) *comb* -petal, -quire,
  -quiry; *base* -rog-, -scrut-. *See*
  turn towards
seemingly *pre* quasi-
segment *comb* clasmato-, dicho-,
  -fid², fissi-, schisto-, schizo-,
  -tomy; *base* -par-
seize *comb* -tain; *base* -cap(t)-,
  -cathex-, -ger-, -hapt-, plag-,
  -prehend, prehens-, rap-, rep-,
  -ten-
seizure *comb* -agra, -lepsia, -lepsis,
  -lepsy, -leptic
selection *base* -opt-, -vol-
self *comb* auto-, ego-, idio-, ipse-,
  proprio-, self-, tauto-; *base* -ille-;
  ~indulgence: apolaust-
selfishness *base* avar-, avid-,
  cup(id)-, edac-, gulos-, pleonec-,
  pleonex-
self-moving *comb* auto-
sell *base* empor-, -merc-, vend-
send *base* -miss-, -mit-¹, -pomp-
sensation *comb* -esthesia, esthesio-,
  hapto¹-, sensi-, senso-, sensori-.
  Also see "The Senses" in Part III
senseless *base* -stup-
sensory *comb* sensori-
sepals *comb* sepalous
separate *pre* apo-, dia-, dis-, for-,
  se-; *comb* chori-, choristo-, crit-²,
  dicho-, dialy-
sequel *following: pre* epi-, meta-,
  post-; *comb* after-, hind-, pos-
  tero-; *base* -secut-, -sequ-; *suf*
  -an; *outcome: comb* ergo-, -ergic,
  -ergy; *suf* -age, -asm, -ata, -ation,
  -ency, -ism, -ma, -ment, -mony,
  -sion, -ure
Serbia *comb* Serbo-
serenity *base* -eiren-, -iren-, -pac-,
  -pax-

series *base* -hirmo-
serious *base* grav-
sermon *base* -homil-, kery-
serous fluid *base* ichor-
serrated *comb* serrato-; *base* cren-[1], lacin-. *See* **notched**
serum *comb* oro-, orrho-, sero-
serviceable *comb* chreo-, chresto-; *base* -util-
set *comb* -thesis, -thetic; *base* -pon-, -pos-; *suf* -en; ~*apart:* *base* sacr-
seta *comb* chaet(o)-
settlement *comb* ekist-; *base* -dom-; *suf* -age
seven *comb* hebdo-, hepta-, septem-, sept(i)-[1]; ~*hundred:* septinginti-. *Also see* "Numbers" in Part III
seventeen *base* heptakaideca, septendecim-
seventh *base* septim-
seventy *base* septuagen-, septuages-, septuagint-
sever *comb* -cide, cis-, -cise, -ectomy, inciso-, -sect, temno-, -tmesis, -tome, tomo-, -tomous, -tomy; *base* sec-
several *comb* multi-, pluri-, pollaki-, poly-
sew *base* -sutil-
sewer *base* cloac-
sex organs *comb* genito-; *base* -aede-; *female~:* colpo-; *male~:* phallo-
sexual *comb* aphrodisio-, eroto-, gameto-, gamo-, -gamous, -gamy, geno-, gonado-, -gone, -gonium, gono-, -gony, nympho-; *base* -coit-, -cyprid-, -vener-[1]; ~*intercourse:* subagit-; ~*uncertainty:* gynandro-
shabby *base* sord-, turp-
shadow *comb* scia-, scio-[1], skia-; *base* -opac-, -umbr-
shaft *comb* calam-, cauli-, caulo-, cormo-, culm-, ferul-, paxill-,

scapi-, thyrsi-, thyrso-; *base* festuc-, stip-
shaggy *base* -hispid-, vill-
shaking *base* agit-, -cuss-, lab-, pav-, quass-, tremo-, trep-, vibro-
shallow *base* lev-, parv-
shame *base* pud-, verecund-
shape, a *comb* eid(o)-, -form, -morph, -morphic, -morphism, morpho-, -morphous; *base* -figur-, -schem-
shaped like *comb* -form, -oid, -oidal. *Also see* "Shapes" in Part III
shapeless *comb* amorpho-
shark *base* carcharin-, gale-[2], selach-, sphyrn-, squal-
sharp *comb* acantho-, aceto-, acetyl-, acid-, acro-, acu-, acuti-, cusp-, echino-, mord-, oxal-, oxy-[1], spiculi-, spiculo-, stylo-[1]; *base* acer-[1], -acerb-, -aichm-, -aichur-, asper-, -belon-, muric-, -punct-, -piq-, pung-, xyr-
shatter *comb* -clasia, -clasis, -clastic, -rhegma, -(r)rhexis; *base* agmat-, -fract-, -frag-, -frang-, -rupt-
shave *base* tonsor
shears *base* forfic-, psalid-
sheath *comb* angio-, chlamyd-, coleo-, meningo-, -theca, theci-, theco-, vagini-, vagino-. *See* **container**
shed *comb* lyo-, lysi-, -lysis, lyso-, -lyte, -lytic, -lyze; *base* -liqu-, -solu-, -solv-
sheep *base* ovi-[2], verv-. *See* **lamb**
sheet *bed~:* lodic-; *layer:* lamin-; *winding~:* sindon-
shell *comb* conchi-, kelyph-, lorica-, -ostraca, ostraco-, testaceo-
shield *comb* aspido-, peltati-, peltato-, pelti-, pelto- *base* clype-, scut-

shift *base* camb-, -fabr-, -fec-, -mut-, -vari-, -vert-. *See* **change**

shiny *base* fulg-, gano-, lustr-, pheng-, rutil-, sela-, stilpno-

ship *base* nau-, naut-, nav-

shoe *base* -calce-, -crep-

shoot *base* **weapon:** -ballist-, -jacul-; **plant:** surcul-

shopkeeper *base* capel-

shore *base* littor-

shortage *comb* isch-, oligo-, -penia

shorter *comb* brachisto-, brachy-, brevi-, chamae-, hekisto-, micro-, mini-, parvi-, parvo-, steno-, tapino-; *base* -curt-, exig-; *suf* -cle, -cula, -cule, -een, -el, -ella, -en, -et, -ette, -idion, -idium, -ie, -illa, -illo, -isk, kin, -le, -let, -ling, -ock, -ola, -ole, -rel, -ula, -ule, -ulum, -ulus, -y

shoulder *comb* acromio-, humero-, omo-[1]; **~blade:** *comb* scapuli-, scapulo-; *base* spatul-

shout *base* clam-, vocif-

show *comb* phaeno-, pheno-; *base* -monstr-

showers *comb* hyeto-, pluvio-; *base* imbri-, ombr-

shrew *base* soric-, tupai-

shrimp *base* macrur-

shrine *comb* aedi-

shrink *base* dimin-

shrivel *base* marces-, marcid-

shroud *base* sindon-

shrub *base* thamn- (thamnium); **shrublike:** *comb* fruticuloso-

shun *base* phygo-

shut *comb* -atresia, atreto-, claustro-, cleido-, -cleisis, cleisto-, stego-; *base* clithr-, -clud-, -clus-

shyness *base* tim-, verecund-

Sicilian *comb* Siculo-

sickle(-shaped) *comb* drepani-, falci-

sickness *pre* dys-, mal-; *comb* noso-, path, -pathic, patho-, -pathy; *base* aegr-, cachex-, -morb-, -pecca-, valetud-

side *pre* by-; **on or near~:** *comb* lateri-, latero-, pleuro-

sieve *comb* coli-[2], coscino-, cribri-, ethmo-

sift *base* -cern-

sight *comb* eid(o)-, oculo-, ommat-, -opia, opsi-[2], -opsia, -opsis, opso-, -opsy, ophthalmo-, optico-, opto-, -scope, -scopic, scopo-, -scopy, visuo-; *base* -blep-, -scrut-, -spec-, -spic-, -vid-, vis-

sign(al) *comb* sema-, -seme, semeio-, semio-

silent *comb* hesy-; *base* -tacit-

silica/silicon *comb* siliceo-, silici-, silico-

silk *comb* metax-, seri-, sericeo-, serico-

silkworm *base* -bombyc-

silly *base* fatu-, inan-, moro-, stult-

Silurian *comb* Siluro-

silver(y) *comb* argenti-, argento-, argyro-, glauco-, plat-[2]. *Also see* "Colors" *in Part III*

similar *pre* para-, quasi-; *comb* -esque, homeo-, homoeo-, homoio-, homolo-, iso-, -phane, -phanic; *base* simil-; *suf* -acean, -aceous, -al, -an, -ar, -ary, -ean, -en, -eous, -esque, -ful, -ic, -il, -ile-, -ine, -ing, -ish, -itious, -ize, -like, -ode, -oid, -ose, -osity, -some, -tious, -ular, -y

simple *base* facil-. *See* **single**

sin *comb* enisso-, enosio-; *base* -culp-, hamart-, -pecca-

sincere *base* prob-, ver-

sinew *comb* chord-, -chorda, cord-

single *comb* eka-, haplo-, heno-, mono-, uni-

sink **decline:** *comb* -atrophia; *base*

dimin-; *decrease:* base decresc-,
dimin-
sinuous *comb* -enchyma[1]
siphylis *comb* syphilo-
sister *base* -soror-
sit *base* -cathis-, -kathis-, -sed-,
-sess-; *~in:* -sid-
situated *comb* out-
six *comb* hexa-, seni-, sexi-, sexti-,
sise-; *~hundred:* hexacosi-, sex-
cent-; *~times:* hexakis-. *Also see*
"Numbers" in Part III
sixteen *base* hexadeca-, hexa-
kaideca, sedecim-
sixth *base* sext-
sixty *base* hexaconta-, sexagen-,
sexages-
size *comb* -footer, -sized; *~of a
sheet: suf* -mo. *Also see* "Dimension" in Part III
skeleton *comb* skeleto-
skill *comb* -craft, -ship, techno-
skin *comb* chorio-, cut(i)-, -derm,
-derma, dermato-, -dermatous,
-dermis, dermo-, dora-; *base* -
pell-; *~disease:* licheno-; *~eleva-
tion: comb* papulo-; *~itch: comb*
acar-, scabi(o)-; *base* -prur-,
-psor-. *See* **flesh**
skirmish *base* velit-. *See* **battle**
skull *comb* -cephalic, cephalo-,
-cephalous, -cephaly, cranio-,
occipito-, orbito-
skunk *base* mephit-, mustel-
sky *base* coeli-
skylark *base* alaud-
slab *base* -pinac-, -pinak-
slag *base* scoria-
slander *base* calumn-
slanting *comb* -clinal, -clinate,
-cline, -clinic, clino-, -clisis,
lechrio-, loxo-, plagio-; *base*
-cliv-. *See* **bent**
slaughter *base* trucid-
Slav *comb* Slavo-

slave *comb* dulo-; *base* -serv-
sleep *comb* hypno-, somni-; *base*
carot-, -dorm-, -sopor-
sleeplessness *base* agrypn-
slender *comb* lepto-, steno-, -tenu-;
base -areo-, gracil-
slide *base* laps-
slightly *pre* sub-; *suf* -aster[2]
slime *comb* blenno-, -chezia, copro-,
lim-, muci-, muco-, myco-, myso-,
-myxia, myxo-, p(a)edo-, scato-,
stegno-, sterco-; *base* -fecu-, -fim-,
molys-, rhypar-
slippery *base* -lubric-
slope *comb* -clinal, -clinate, -cline,
-clinic, clino-, -clisis, klino-,
lechrio-, loxo-, plagio-; *base* -clit-,
-cliv-
sloth *animal:* base xenarthr-; *indo-
lence: base* pigr-, segn-
slow *comb* brady-; *base* -cunct-,
lent-, -pigr-, -tard-
slug *base* limac-
sly *base* daedal-
small(er) *comb* brachisto-, brachy-,
hekisto-, micro-, mini-, nano-,
parvi-, parvo-, steno-; *base* -curt-,
exig-; *suf* -cle, -cula, -cule,
-culum, -culus, -een, -el, -ella,
-en, -et, -ette, -idion, -idium, -ie,
-illa, -illo, -isk, kin, -le, -let,
-ling, -ock, -ola, -ole, -rel, -ula,
-ule, -ulum, -ulus, -y
smart *base* sapien-
smell *comb* brom(o)-, -odic, odori-,
odoro-, -olent, olfacto-, -osmia,
osmo-[1], osphresio-, ozo-, ozono-;
base fet-, nidor-. *See also* "The
Senses" in Part III
smelt *base* -ather-
smile *base* ris-
smoke *comb* -capnia, capno-; *base*
-fum-
smooth *comb* even-, leio-, lisso-;
base -glabr-, -levig-, -lubr-, psilo-

smother *base* -pnig(er)-
smut *base* aischro-
snail *base* cochlea-, gastropod-, limac-
snake *comb* -glypha, herpeto-, echidno-, -ophidia, ophio-; *base* angui-, colubr-, reptil-, serpen-, viper-; ~*charmer:* psyll-
snapper *base* lutjan-
snatch *base* -rap-, -rep-
sneer *base* mycter-
sneeze *base* ptarm-, sternut-
snipe *base* charadr-, scolopac-
snore *base* rhonch-, stertor-
snout *comb* rhyncho-, -rrhyncha; *base* proboscbase-, rostell-, -rostr-. *See* **beak**
snow *base* -chion-, -chium-, ning-, niv-
soak up *comb* -sorb[1]; *base* bib-
soap *base* sapon(i)-
sober *base* **abstinent:** nephal-; **serious:** grav-
social belief *suf* -arian
society *comb* anthropo-, socio-
socket *comb* alveolo-; *base* -gomph-
sodium *comb* -natremia, sodio-
soft *comb* -malacia, malaco-; *base* hapal-, -len-, malax-, -moll-; ~*deposit: comb* athero-; ~*palate:* velar-
soil *comb* agro-, paedo-[1], pedo-[3]; *base* edaph-, -hum-, -terr-
soldier *comb* -milit-
sole of the foot *base* pelm-, -plant-
solid *comb* stereo-
solitary *comb* auto-, eremo-, mono-, soli-, uni-. *See* **one**
somewhat *pre* demi-, hemi-, semi-; *comb* -atelia, atelo-; *suf* -esce, -escence, -escent, -y[1]
son *base* fili-
son-in-law *base* -gener-
song *comb* asmato-, lyrico-, melo-[1], musico-; ~*birds:* oscin-

soot *base* fulig-
soothing *base* anet-, -len-, miti-[1]
sorcery *base* -venefic-
sordid *base* sord-, turp-
soreness *comb* alge-, algesi-, -algia, algo-, -algy, -dynia, noci-, -odynia, odyno-, pono-; *base* dolor-, -nox-
sorrow *comb* lype-; *base* dolor-, -fleb-, -flet-, -luct-[1], trist-
soul *comb* pneumato-, thumo-, -thymia, thymo-; *base* -anim-, -spirit-
sound *comb* acou-, acoust-, audi(o)-, auri-, echo-, oto-, -ecoia, -phone, phono-, -phony, -phthong, soni-, sono-, sonoro-. *See* **noise**
soundness *base* salub-, san-
sour *base* acer-, acid-, amar-
source *comb* aetio-, -blast, blasto-, -blasty, -carp, -carpic, carpo-, -carpous, etio-, -gen, -genic, -genesis, -genous, -geny, -gone, -gonium, gono-, -gony, -phyletic, sperma-, -spermal, spermato-, spermi-, -spermic, spermo-, sporo-; *base* -init-; *suf* -esce, -escence, -escent
south *comb* austro-, noto-
sow *base* sativ-, sator-, sparg-
Spanish *comb* Hispano-, Ibero-
sparing *base* frug-[2]
spark *base* -scintill-, spinthar-
sparrow *base* passer-
sparse *comb* oligo-; *base* pauc(i)-
spasm *comb* -chorea, choreo-, -clonic, -clonus, -esmus, -ismus, spasmo-, -tonic; *base* -stal-, -vellic-
spatula *comb* spathi-, spatuli-
speak, speech *comb* -claim, logo-, -logue, -lalia, -lexia, lexico-, -lexis, -lexy, -logy, -phone, phono-, -phony, verbi-, verbo-,

voc-, voci-, -voke; *base* -clam-, -dict-, garrul-, -loc(u)-, -loqu-, -orat-, phat-, -phem-, rhet-; *defective~: comb* -lalia, lalo-, -phasia, -phasic, -phasis, -phasy, -phemia, -phemy; *base* psell-

spear *comb* hastato-, hasti-; *~head:* lonch-

specialist *suf* -ician, -ist, -ologist

speckled *base* -psar-. *See* **spotted**

specter *base* phantas-, phasm-, spectr-

spectroscope *comb* spectro-

speed *comb* tacho-, tachy-, veloci-; *base* -celer-, festin-

sphenoid bone *comb* spheno-

spherical *comb* ano-², annul-, crico-², cyclo-, disco-, globi-, globo-, glom-, gyro-, orbito-, sphaero-, -sphere, spherico-, sphero-, stilli-, zon-, zoni-; *base* anu-, -cing-, -cinct-, -circin-, -circul-, -coron-, -glomer-, -numm-, -orb-, -rot-, -troch-

spider *comb* arachn(o)-, araneo-; *base* arene-, phalang-; *black widow~: base* latrodect-

spike *comb* helo-¹, scolo-, spiculi-, spiculo-; *~of corn:* spici-; *succulent~: comb* spadici-

spill *base* -chys-, -chyt-, -flu-, -fus-

spin *comb* gyro-¹

spinal cord *comb* -myelia, myelo-

spindle *comb* fusi-, fuso-, fusu-

spine *comb* aculei-, rachi(o)-, rhach(i)-, -rrhachia, spini-, spino-, spinoso-, spinuloso-, spondylo-, vertebro-

spiny *comb* acantho-, aceto-, acetyl-, acid-, acro-, acu-, acuti-, cusp-, echinato-, echino-, echinulato-, echinuli-, oxal-, oxy-, spiculi-, spiculo-, stylo-; *base* -acerb-, -aichm-, -aichur-, -belon-, muric-, -punct-, -piq-, -punct-

spiral *comb* cirri-, cochlio-, gyro-, helico-, spiri-, spiro-², strepto-, stromb-

spirit *comb* pneumato-; *base* -anim-

spirits *base* phantas-, phasm-, spectr-

spitting *comb* -ptysis. *See* **saliva**

spleen *comb* lieno-, splenico-, spleno-

splendid *base* lustr-

split *comb* dicho-, -fid-, -fissi-, schisto-, schizo-, -tomy; *base* -par-, -crev-

spoil *comb* lysi-, lyso-, -lysis, -lytic, -lyze, -phage, phago-, -phagous, -phagy; *base* -ate-⁴, perd-, phthart-, -vast-, vitia-

spoke *a brace: base* -rad-; *talked: See* **speak**

sponge-like *comb* spongio-, spongo-

spontaneous *comb* ultro-

spoon *base* cochlea-

spore *comb* -spore, spori-, sporo-, -sporous

spot *comb* celido-

spotted *comb* ocelli-; *base* -macul-, psar-, -stict-, -variol-

spouse *base* conjug-, marit-, uxor-

spread *expand: comb* -ectasia, -ectasis; *base* -dilat-; *scatter: base* sparg-

spring *leap:* salta-; *season:* primaver-, -vern-; *water: base* cren-², pego-, scatur-

sprinkle *base* sparg-, -sperg-, -spers-

spurious *comb* kibdelo-, pseudo-; *base* -notho-

squama *comb* squamato-, squamo-, squamoso-, squaroso-

square *base* quadr-

squid *base* cephalopod-, teutho-

squinting *base* -strab-, -strabism-

squirrel *base* sciur-

stable *base* diuturn-, dur(o)-, perenn-, perm-, stabil-

stag *base* cerv-, elaph-

stage player *base* -histrion-

stagger *base* titub-

stain *base* -macul-, spil-, -tinct-, -ting-

stairs *base* -climac-

stalactite *comb* stalacti-

stalk *shaft:* *comb* calam-, cauli-, caulo-, cormo-, culm-, ferul-, paxill-, scapi-, thyrsi-, thyrso-; *base* festuc-, stip-¹; **hunt:** *base* -venat-

stamens *comb* -androus, stamini-

stamp *comb* -type, sigil-; *postage~:* *base* philatel-, timbro-

standard *comb* ortho-; *base* -regul-

standing still *comb* stasi-, -stasis, -stat, stato-

staphylococcus *comb* staphylo-

star *comb* aster-¹, astro-, -sidere, sidero-², stelli-

starch *comb* amyl(o)-

starfish *base* asteroid-, echinoderm-

starling *base* psar-², sturn-

start *base* inaug-, incip-, init-

starting to be *suf* -esce, -escence, -escent

state of *suf* -able, -acity, -acy, -age, -ance, -ancy, -ant, -asis, -asm, -ate, -atile, -ation, -cy, -dom, -ence, -ency, -ent, -ery, -esis, -ful, -hood, -iasis, -ice¹, -ility, -ion, -ism, -ity, -ling, -ma, -ment, -mony, -ness, -or, -osis, -otic, -red, -ship, -sion, -th, -tion, -tude, -ture, -ty, -ure, -y

stationary *comb* stasi-, -stasis, -stat, stato-; *base* stabil-

statue *base* agalma-

status *suf* -ship

stay *remain:* *base* contin-, dur-, perpet-; *delay:* *comb* brady-; *base* -cunct-, imped-, -mora-, -tard-

steady *base* perm-, stabil-

steal *comb* clepto-, klepto-, lesto-; *base* -furt-, harpax-, klope-, ladron-, latro-, -rept-

steam *comb* atmo-

steel *base* chalyb-

steep *base* ard-³, precip-

steering *comb* -agogic, -agogue; *base* -vers-, -vert-

stem *comb* cauli-, caulo-, cormo-, scapi-; *base* calam-, culmi-, sarment-

stench *comb* brom(o)-, odori-, odoro-, olfacto-, -osmia, osmo-, osphresio-, ozo-, ozono-; *base* fet-, -mephit-, putr-

step *comb* -basia, bato-, -grade; *base* -ambul-, -gress-

stepdaughter *base* privign-

stepfather *base* vitric-

stepmother *base* noverc-

stepson *base* privign-

sternum *comb* sterno-

stick *comb* scop(i)-; *base* carph-, ramul-, -sarment-, surcul-, virgul-

sticky *base* agglut-, ixo-, visc(o)-. *See* **glue**

stiff *comb* ancylo-, ankylo-, tetano-

still *base* eremo-, hesy-

stimulating *comb* excito-; *base* stig-

sting *comb* cnido-, mastigo-; *base* -piq-, -urtic-

stirrup *base* stap-

stitch *base* rhaps-, sutil-

stomach *comb* gastero-, -gastria, gastro-; *~opening:* *comb* pyloro-. *See* **belly**

stone *comb* -lith(o), pesso-, petri-, petro-, psepho-, sax(i)-; *base* -lapid-, -rup-; *suf* -lite; *~using stage:* *comb* -lithic

stooping *comb* kypho-, scolio

stop *comb* stasi-, -stasis, -stat; *base* fin-, termin-

stopper *comb* emboli-, embolo-

stork *base* ciconi-, grallator-, pellarg-

storm *base* orag-, procell-

story *comb* mytho-

straight *comb* ithy-, ortho-, recti-

strain *comb* -piesis, piezo-; *base* col-², colar-, colat-, -tens-

strange(r) *comb* perisso-, xeno-; *base* -ali-, peregrin-

strap *base* himant-, -ligul-, lora-

stratum *comb* strati-, strato-. *See* **layer**

straw *comb* carpho-, culmi-, festuc-, stramin-

strawberry *base* fragar-

stream *comb* fluvio-; *base* -potam-, rheum-, -rip-

strength *comb* dyna-, dynamo-, mega-, megalo-, -megaly, -sthenia, stheno-; *base* -forc-, -fort-, -poten-, robor-; *~to do or be: suf* -bility

strenuous *pre* dys-; *comb* -bar, bary-, mogi-; *base* ardu-, stren-

stretch *comb* -tend, teno-, tensio-, tono-

stricture *comb* isch-, koly-, -penia, rhopo-, -strain, -strict; *base* angust-, -string-; *suf* -en

strife *base* eris-

strike *comb* plessi-, -cuss-; *base* -cop-, -crot-, plang-, -puls-, -tus-, -vapul-, -verber-

string *base* linon-

stripped *comb* gymno-, nudi-, psilo-

stroke *comb* -plexia

strong *comb* -proof, dur(o)-; *base* -forc-, -fort-. *See* **strength**

struggle *comb* macho-, -machy; *base* agon-

stubborn *base* contum-, obstin-, pervic-, proterv-

studded *comb* clavato-

study *base* disc-, -math, soph-

stuff up *base* -byon-

stupid *base* hebet-, obtus-, -tard-

stupor *comb* carot-, narco-

sturgeon *base* acipenser-, sturi(m)-

stutter *base* balbut-, blesi-, -psell-

styloid *comb* stylo-

suberic acid *comb* subero-

subject to *suf* -ize

submissive *base* moriger-

subordinate *pre* sub-, under-

subsequent to *pre* cis-. *See* **following**

substance *comb* -ousia, -ousian

substitute *pre* pro-¹; *suf* -ette

succeed *base* -cap-, -cep-, -cip-

succinct *base* brev-. *See* **short**

suck *comb* -suge; *base* -haur-, -haust-, -myz-

sudden *base* subit-. *See* **quickness**

suffering *comb* -path, -pathic, patho-, -pathy. *See* **pain**

sugar *comb* gluco-, glycero-, glyco-, levul-, saccharo-, sucr-

suggestive of *pre* para-, quasi-; *comb* homeo-, homoio-, homolo-, iso-, -phane, -phanic; *base* simil-; *suf* -acean, -aceous, -al, -an, -ar, -ary, -ean, -en, -eous, -esque, -ful, -ic, -il, -ile, -ine, -ing, -ish, -itious, -ize, -like, -ode, -oid, -ose, -osity, -some, -tious, -ular, -y¹

suitable for *base* concinn-; *suf* -il, -ile, -like, -ly

sulfate *comb* sulfato-

sulfur *comb* sulfo-, sulfureo-, sulpho-, thia-, thio-

summit *base* coryph-

summon *base* appell-, -claim, -clam-, -dict-, -nom-, -voc-; *~upon: base* -prec-

sumptuous *base* dapat-

sun *comb* helio-, sol-; *~bathing:* apricat-; *~shade: comb* umbelli-, umbello-, umbraculi-

superior *pre* pre-, super-; *comb* over-

superlatives *suf* -est, -most

supplement *pre* a-, ac-, ad-, af-, ag-, al-, an-, ap-, ar-, as-, at-, co-, extra-, para-, super-, syn; *comb* inter-. *See* **more**

supporting *pre* pro-; *comb* -pher; *base* patroc-; *~part: comb* -podium, scapi-; *base* paxill-, sterigm-, -stip-[1]. *See* **carrying**

suppress *base* fin-, termin-

suppurative *comb* pyo-. *See* **putrefying**

supreme *comb* arch-, archi-, proto-; *base* -prim-, -princip-

surf *comb* cuma-

surfaces *comb* -hedral, -hedron, topo-, -topy

surfeit *base* ampl-, copi-, larg-

surgeon *base* chirur-, medic-

surgical operation *comb* -ectomy, -pexy, -stomy, tomo-, -tomous, -tomy

surly *base* acerb-, moros-

surpassing *pre* ex-, extra-, meta-, over-, para-, pre-, preter-, super-, supra-, sur-, ultra-

surplus *base* ampl-, copi-, larg-

surrounding *pre* be-, circum-, peri-; *comb* amphi-, ampho-; *base* -zon-, -cing-, -cinct-

suture *comb* -(r)rhaphy

swallow *bird: base* chelid-, hirund-, -sturn-; *ingest: comb* -phage, phago-, -phagous, -phagy; *base* -glut-

swamp *base* palud-, palus-

swan *base* cycn-, cygn-

sway *base* nuta-, -vacil-

sweat *comb* sudori-; *base* -hidr-, -suda-

sweet *comb* mell(i)-; *base* -dulc-, -hedy-, suav-

swelling *comb* -cele, -edema, ganglio-, phlogo-, phym-, -phyma, physa-, physo-, strum(i)-; *base* aug-, cresc-, physc-, strum-, -tum-, -turg-; *suf* -itis

swift *bird: base* cypsel-; *fast: comb* ocy-, tacho-, tachy-; *base* -celer-, veloc-

swim *comb* necto-; *base* -nata-

swine *base* porcin-, sui-

Swiss *base* Helvet-

sword(like) *comb* ensi-, gladi-, machaero-, xiphi-, xipho-

swordfish *base* xiphi-

symbol *comb* sema-, -seme, semeio-, semio-

symmetry *comb* pari-; *base* concinn-, congru-, symmetr-

synchronized *comb* synchro-

syphilis *comb* -luetic

Syrian *comb* Syro-

system *suf* -ics

T

tablet *base* pinac-, tabell-

tacit *comb* hesy-; *base* -tacit-

tail *comb* caudo-, -cerca, -cercal, cerco-, uro-[1]

tailor *base* sartor-

take *base* -cap(t)-, -cep[1]-, -empt-

take hold of *comb* -tain; *base* -capt-, -cathex-, -ger-, -hapt-, -prehend, prehens-, rap-, rep-, -ten-

taker *comb* -ceptor

tale *base* -fabul-, mytho-, -narr-, storitalented *base* ingen-

talk(ing) *comb* -claim, glosso-,
-lalia, lalo-, -lexia, lexico-, -lexis,
-lexy, logo-, -logue, -logy, -phone,
phono-, -phony, verbi-, verbo-,
voc-, voci-, -voke; *base* -clam-,
-dict-, garrul-, -loc(u)-, -loqu-,
-orat-, -phem-, rhet-; *filthy~:*
borbor-. *Also see* **speak/speech**

tallness *comb* acro-, alti-, alto-,
bato-, hypsi-, hypso-, longi-; *base*
procer-

tallow *comb* seb(o)-

talon *base* ungui-, ungul-

tame *base* cicur-, mansue-

tan *base* fulv-. *Also see* "Colors" in
Part III

tapered *base* fastig-

tapeworm *comb* taeni-, teni-

tapir *base* pachyderm-

tarantula *base* theraphos-

tardy *comb* brady-; *base* -cunct-,
-tard-. *See* **late**

tarsier *base* lemur-

tartar *comb* tartro-

tasseled *base* crosso-, -thysan-

taste *comb* -geusia; *base* -geum-,
-geumat-, -gust-, -sapor-. *Also see*
"The Senses" in Part III

tattoo *base* stigm-

taurine *comb* tauro-

tavern *base* caupon-

tawny *base* melin-, mustel-

tea *base* -thei-

teach *comb* -pedia; *base* -didact-,
doc-, -paed-

tear *rip:* *comb* sparasso-; *base* lacer-,
-lania-, sparax-; *cry:* *comb*
dacry(o)-, lachrim-, lachrym-,
lacrimo-; *base* fleb-, flet-, -plor-

tease *comb* tantalo-; *base* vex-

technical *comb* techno-

technique *comb* -craft; *suf* -ade,
-age, -al, -ance, -ancy, -asis, -asm,
-ation, -cy, -ence, -ency, -ery,

-esis, -iasis, -ice, -ics, -ing, -ion,
-ism, -ment, -osis, -otic, -sion,
-sis, -th, -tion, -tious, -ture, -ure,
-y, -ysis

teeth *see* **tooth**

television *comb* tele-, video-

tell *comb* -claim, logo-, -logue,
-lalia, -lexia, lexico-, -lexis, -lexy,
-logy, -phone, phono-, -phony,
rhet-, verbi-, verbo-, voc-, voci-,
-voke; *base* -clam-, -dict-,
-loc(u)-, -loqu-, narr-, -orat-,
-phat-, -phem-

temperament *comb* -natured

temple *head:* *comb* temporo-;
church: *comb* aedi-; *base* -nao-

temporal *base* -secul-

ten *comb* dec(a)-, decem-, deka-;
one tenth: *comb* deci-; *ten and __:*
suf -teen; *~thousand:* myria-;
x times ten: *suf* -ty^2. *Also see*
"Numbers" in Part III

ten thousand *comb* myria-, myrio-

tending to *pre* pro-; *comb* -phile,
-philia, -philiac, -trope, -tropic;
suf -able, -ative, -ish, -istic, -isti-
cal, -ive, -like, -some^2, -orial,
-ulous, -y^1

tendon *comb* tendo-, teno-,
tenonto-

tendril *comb* cirr(h)i-, cirr(h)o-,
pampin-

tennis *base* sphair-

tension *comb* tasi-, taso-, -tonia,
-tonic, tono-

tentacles *comb* actino-, tentaculi-;
base brach-, cornic-, flagell-

tentative *base* ambig-, ancip-, apor-,
dub-, vagu-

terminate *comb* stasi-, -stasis, -stat;
base fin-, termin-

termite *base* isoptero-, termit-

tern *base* stern-

terrified *base* -pavid-, -tim-, trepid-.
See **fear**

terrifying *comb* dino-[1]
territory *suf* -land
testicle *comb* didym(o)-, orchido-[2], orchio-, oscheo-; *base* -scrot-
testing *comb* -opsy, -scope, -scopic, scopo-, -scopy; *base* -(in)quir-, -(in)quis-, -scrut-
testy *base* acerb-, mord-
tetanus *comb* tetano-
thalamus *comb* thalamo-
thallium *comb* thallo-
thankful *base* grat-
the *pre* al-[2]
theater *comb* theatro-
theory *suf* -ism, -logy
thermoelectric *comb* thermo-
thick *comb* cespitoso-, dasy-, hadro-, pachy-, pycno-, pykno-, visc(o)-; *base* -crass-, -spiss-
thief *comb* clepto-, klepto-, lesto-; *base* -furt-, harpax-, ladron-, latr(o)
thigh *comb* mero-[2]
thin *comb* angusti-, dolicho-, lepto-, maci-, mano-, stegno-, steno-, tenu-; *base* -areo-[2], gracil-, -isthm-, stal-, -strict-
thing that is ___ *suf* -ance, -ee, -er, -tion, -tious
think *see* **thought**
third *base* -tert-, trient-, trito-
thirst *comb* dipso-; *base* siti-. *See* **dry**
thirteen *base* tredecim-, triskaideka-
thirty *base* triaconta-, triceni-, triges-, trigint-
thong *base* lor-. *See* **strap**
thorax *comb* thoracico-, thoraco-
thorny *comb* acantho-, echino-, rhamn-, spiculi-, spiculo-, spini-; *base* -muric-, -urtic-
thought *comb* -gnomy, -gnosia, -gnosis, -gnostic, gnoto-, ideo-, -noia, -nomy, phreno-, psycho-,
-sophy; *base* -cogit-, -cogn-, epistem-, -heur-, ment-[2], -noe-, -put-, ratio-, -sci-; *insane~:* *comb* lysso-, -mania; *base* ament-, dement-
thousand *comb* chili-, kilo-; *~th:* milli-
thread(like) *comb* filamento-, fili-, filio-, filo-, mit-[2], nemato-; *base* -nema-, stema-
threat *base* min-
three *comb* ter-, tri-, triakis-, triplo-, trito-; *base* -tern-, -tert-; *~dimensional:* *comb* stereo-; *~fourths:* triquadr-; *~hundred:* trecent-. *Also see* "Numbers" in Part III
threshing *base* trit-
threshold *base* -limin-, marg-, propinq-, prox-
thrift *base* frug-[2], pars-
throat *comb* gutturo-, laryngo-, pharyngo-, -throated, tracheo-; *base* fauc-, jug-
through *pre* cata-, cath-, dia-, per-, trans-
throughout *pre* ana-; *comb* -wide
throw *comb* -bole, -bolic, bolo-[1], -boly; *base* -ballist-, -jact-, -jacula-, -ject-
thrush *base* -musicap-, -turd-, cichlo-
thrust *base* -pel-, -pul-, -trude-, -trus-
thumb *base* pollic-
thunder *comb* bronte-, bronto-, cerauno-, kerauno-; *base* fulmin-, tonitr-
thymus *comb* thymo-
thyroid *comb* -thyrea, thyreo-; *~gland:* *comb* thyro-
tibia *comb* tibio-; *base* -cnem-
tick *base* acar-, ixod-
tickle *comb* titillo-
tide *base* aestu-, estu-
tie *comb* sphingo-, -strain, -strict,

syndesmo-; *base* -liga-, -merinth-, -string-, -vinc-. *See* **restriction**

tiger *base* tigr-

tightening *comb* isch-, koly-, -penia, -strain, -strict; *base* -string-; *suf* -en. *See* **constriction**

tile *base* imbricato-, tegul-

tillage *comb* -culture

tilting *comb* -clinal, -clinate, -cline, -clinic, clino-, -clisis, lechrio-, loxo-, plagio-; *base* -cliv-

time *comb* back-, chrono-, horo-, yester-; *base* -tempor-; *~period: pre* eo-; *comb* aev-, -cene, paleo-, protero-. *Also see* "Time" in Part III

timid *base* pav-, trep-, verecund-

tin *base* cassiter-, stann-

tiny *comb* brachisto-, brachy-, brevi-, chamae-, micro-, mini-, nano-, parvi-, parvo-, pauci-, steno-; *base* -curt-, exig-; *suf* -cle, -cule, -een, -el, -ella, -en, -et, -ette, -idion, -idium, -ie, -illa, -illo, -isk, -kin, -le, -let, -ling, -ock, -ola, -ole, -rel, -ula, ule, -ulum, -ulus, -y

tip *comb* -apical, apico-; *base* cacumen-

tired *comb* pono-; *base* -fatig-, kopo-, -lass-

tissue *comb* fascio-, histio-, histo-, -sarc, sarco-; *dead~:* necro-

titan *comb* titano-[1]

titanium *comb* titano-[2]

titmouse *base* par-[2]

to *pre* a-, ac-[1], ad-[1], af-, ag-, al-[1], an-[2], ap-, ar-[1], as-[1], at-, il-, im-, in-, ir-, ob-; *comb* -bound; *base* pros-; *suf* -ad, -ly, -ward, -ways, -wise; *~the other side: pre* trans-

toad *comb* batracho-, bufo-, phryno-

today *base* hodie-

toe *comb* dactyl(o)-, -dactylous, -dactyly, digiti-; *base* halluc-

together *pre* co-[1], inter-, syl-, sym-, syn-, sys-; *comb* allelo-, hama-, symphyo-, synchro-; *base* -mutu-, -simul-

toil *base* aerumn-. *See* **difficult** and **work**

tomb *comb* -taph, tapho-; *base* sepulc-

tomorrow *base* crastin-

tone *comb* tonia-, -phone, phono-, -phony; *base* son-

tongue *comb* -glossia, glosso-, -glot, lamino-, lingu(o)-; *base* -ligul-; *~kissing:* cataglott-

tonsil *comb* tonsillo-

tooth *comb* dentato-, denti-, dento-, dont-, -odont(o), -odus, -toothed; *canine~:* laniar-; *~disease: comb* cario-; *lacking~: base* edent-, coryph-; *wisdom~: base* cranter-

top *crest: comb* cory-, coryph-, stromboli-; *base* cacum-, culm-; *~shaped: comb* turbinato-

topical *comb* topo-, -topy

torch *base* lampad-, lychn-

tornado *base* -lilaps-

tortoise *base* -chelon-, emydo-, testud-. *See* **turtle**

totally *pre* be-, cata-, cath-, de-, kata-, ob-, per-; *comb* holo-, omni-, pan-, panto-, stone-, toti-

totter *base* -lab-

touch *comb* aphe-, -aphia, -apsia, hapto-[1], sensori-, thigmo-; *base* -palp-, -sent-, -tact-, -tang-. *Also see* "The Senses" in Part III

toughness *comb* dyna-, dynamo-, mega-, megalo-, -megaly, -sthenia, stheno-; *base* -forc-, -fort-, -poten-, robor-

tour *comb* hodo-, -ode, odo-, via-; *base* -itin-, peregrin-

toward *pre* a-, ac-[1], ad-[1], af-, ag-, al-[1], an-[2], ap-, ar-[1], as-[1], at-, il-, im-, in-, ir-, ob-; *comb* -bound, -petal; *base* pros-; *suf* -ad[3], -ly, -ward, -ways, -wise

tower *base* pyrgo-, turri-

town *comb* -burg(h), -ton, -ville; *base* urb-

toxic *comb* tox(i), toxico-, -toxin, toxo-, veneno-

trace *comb* ichno-; *base* indag-, vestig-

trachea *comb* tracheo-

track *comb* ichno-

trade *base* empor-, merc-, nundin-; *~names:* co-[2]

train *comb* siderodromo-

trait *suf* -able, -acity, -acy, -age, -ance, -ancy, -ant, -asis, -asm, -ate, -atile, -ation, -cy, -dom, -eity, -ence, -ency, -ent, -ery, -esis, -ful, -hood, -iasis, -ice, -ility, -ion, -ise, -ism, -ity, -ling, -ma, -ment, -ness, -or, -osis, -otic, -red, -ship, -sion, -th, -tion, -tude, -ture, -ty, -ure, -y

traitor *base* prodit-

tranquility *base* -eiren-, -iren-, -pac-, -pax-

transcending *pre* trans-

transfer *carry:* *comb* -fer, -ferous, -gerous, -parous, -pher, -phore, -phorous; *base* -port-, -vect-; *change:* *base* camb-, -fabr-, -fec-, -mut-, -vari-, -vert-; *suf* -ate, en, -fy, -ize, -otic

transgression *comb* enisso-, enosio-; *base* -culp-, hamart-, -pecca-

transitory *base* caduc-

transmission *comb* -cast

transparent *comb* diaphano-, hyalo-, -phane

transplant *base* chim-

transport *comb* -fer, -ferous, -gerous, -parous, -pher, -phore, -phorous; *base* -port-, -vect-

transverse *comb* cross-

trap *comb* -thera

trapezoid *comb* trapezi-

travel *comb* hodo-, dromo-, odo-; *base* -itiner-, -peregrin-, -via-. *See* **wander**

tray *base* hypocrater-

treat with *suf* -ate, -ize

treatment *comb* -iatrics, iatro-, -iatry; *base* -com-

tree(like) *comb* dendri-, dendro-, -dendron, silvi-, xylo-; *base* -arbor-. *See* **woods**

tremble *comb* tremo-; *base* pav-, trep-; *earth~:* tromo-

trepidation *comb* -phobe, -phobia, -phobic, phobo-; *base* pavid-, tim(or)-, -trem-, -trep-. *Also see* "Fear" in Part III

triangular *comb* delta-, triangulato-, trigono-

tribe *comb* phylo-

trifling *base* -nuga-

trillion *comb* tera-; *-th:* pico-

trilobytes *comb* -paria

trip *comb* hodo-, -ode, odo-; *base* -itiner-, -peregrin-, -via-

triple *comb* triplicato-, triplo-; *base* -ter(n)-

trouble *base* aerumn-. *See* **grief**

trout *base* -trocto-, trutt-

truffle *comb* hydno-

trumpet *base* buccin-

trunk *comb* cormo-. *See* **stem**

trust *base* -cred-. *See* **belief**

truth *base* aleth-, -ver-

try *base* conat-, peir-

tube *comb* aulo-, follic-, salpingo-, siphoni-, siphono-, soleno-, tubi-, tubo-, tubuli-, tubulo-, vasi-; *base* fistul-, -syr-; *~shaped: comb* syringo-

tuberculosis *comb* tuberculo-; *base* phthisi-, phthisio-, -phthisis
tufts *comb* cespitoso-; *base* carph-, crin-, crist-, flocc-
tumor *comb* -cele, onco-, phym-, -phyma, struma-; *suf* -oma
tumult *base* -agit-, -tumult-, -turb-
tunnel *base* cunicul-
turbine *comb* turbo-
turbot *base* psett-, scophthalm-
turkey *base* gallinac-, meleagr-
Turkey *comb* Turco-, Turko-
turn *comb* gyro-, helico-, roti-, strepho-, strepsi-, strepto-, stroph(i)-, trepo-, -verge, vortici-; *base* -vers-, -vert-, -volut-, -volv-; *~towards or away:* *comb* -trope, -tropic, -tropism, tropo-, -tropous, -tropy
turnabout *comb* allo-; *base* -vers-, -vert-
turnip *base* napi-
turpentine *base* terebinth-
turtle *comb* chelo(n)-; *base* -anaps-, chelys-, -testud-, -turtura-. *See* tortoise
twelve *comb* dodeca-, duodec-, duodecim-, duoden-
twenty *comb* eico-, icosa-, icosi-, viginti-; *base* vicesim-; *~four:* icositetra-

twice *pre* bi-, di-[1]; *~per time period:* *pre* semi-
twigs *comb* scop(i)-; *base* carph-, ramul-, -sarment-, surcul-, virgul-
twilight *base* -crepus-, -lyg-
twin(s) *comb* diplo-, zygo-; *base* -didym-, gemelli-, gemin-; *conjoined~:* *comb* -pagia, -pagus. *See* two
twisted *comb* contorto-, gyro-, helico-, pleco-, plecto-, spiro-, strepho-, strepsi-, strepto-; *base* -strob-, -stromb-, -stroph-, -tors-, -tort-
twitching *comb* -chorea, choreo-, -clonic, -clonus, -esmus, -ismus, spasmo-; *base* -stal-, -vellic-
two *pre* bi-, bin-, bis-, di-, du-; *comb* ambi-, ambo-, amphi-, ampho-, deutero-, deuto-, dicho-, diphy-, diplo-, disso-, double-, duo-, duplicato-, duplici-, dyo-, gemelli-, twi-, zygo-; *base* -didym-, gemin-; *~colored:* *comb* dichro-; *~hundred:* *base* ducen-; *~wings:* *comb* diptero-. *Also see* "Numbers" in Part III
tympanic *comb* myringo-
type *comb* -type, typo-
typhoid *comb* typho-

U

ulcer *comb* helco-
ulna *comb* cubito-, ulno-
umbilicus *comb* omphalo-
umbrella *comb* umbell(i)-, umbraculi-, umbrelli-
unaffected by *suf* -proof
unalterable *base* immut-

unceasing *base* assid-, contin-, incess-, perpet-
uncertain *base* ambig-, ancip-, apor-, dub-, vagu-
uncle *base* -avunc-, patru-
unclean *comb* blenno-, -chezia, copro-, fim(i)-, kopro-, myso-,

-myxia, myxo-, paedo-, pedo-,
scato-, spatilo-, spurc-, stegno-,
sterco-; *base* -fecu-, molys-,
rhypar-, rhypo-

unconscious *base* -stup-

under *pre* hypo-, infra-, sub-, subter-; *comb* infero-, under-; *base*
cunicul-; ~*world:* infern-

understanding *comb* -gnomy,
-gnosia, -gnosis, -gnostic; *base*
-crit-, -judic-, -soph-

undertaking *pre* entre-

undeveloped *comb* -atelia, atelo-.
See **immature**

undiscerning *base* hebet-, obtus-,
-tard-

undivided *base* integ-, tot-

undo *pre* de-

undulation *comb* flexuoso-; *base*
-sinu-. *See* **wave**

uneasy *base* agit-, mov-, trepid-,
turb-

unequal *comb* aniso-, inequi-,
impari-, perisso-

uneven *comb* anomalo-, anomo-,
perisso-, poikilo-, sinuato-, sinuoso-; *base* salebr-

unfinished *pre* demi-, hemi-, semi-;
base -atelia, atelo-; *suf* -esce,
-escence, -escent

unguent *base* -aliph-, unct-

unhappy *comb* lype-; *base* dolor-,
fleb-, flet, luct-, -trist-

unimportant *base* -nuga-

union *comb* -ergasia, gameto-,
gamo-, -gamous,-gamy; *base*
-greg-, -junct-, -soc-

unit *comb* -mer(e), mero-

unite *pre* co-; *comb* conjugato-,
-ergasia, gameto-, gamo-, hapto-,
junct-; *base* aps-, apt-, -greg-,
-soc-; *suf* -ate, -ize

universe *comb* -cosm, cosmo-

unlike *pre* anti-, contra-, contre-,
dis-, hetero-, ob-, un-; *comb*

back-, counter-, enantio-,
oppositi-

unlit *comb* ambly-, melan(o)-,
nycto-, scoto-; *base* -achlu-,
amaur-, fusc-, lyg-, obscur-,
tenebr-

unprofitable *base* mataeo-

unquenchable *base* avid-, edac-,
gulos-

unreasonable *base* alogo-

unsatisfactory *pre* hypo-, sub-,
under-; *comb* hystero-; *base*
hesson-; *suf* -aster

unsaturated acid *comb* -enoic

unspecified *base* ambig, dub-,
ancip-

untrustworthy *base* apat-, dolero-,
ludif-

unusual *comb* aetheo-, anom(o)-,
anomalo-. *See* **irregular**

unwell *pre* dys-, mal-; *comb* noso-,
-path, -pathic, patho-, -pathy;
base aegr-, -morb-, -pecca-,
valetud-

up *pre* ana-, ano-; *comb* super-,
supra-; ~*to: pre* epi-

upheaval *base* -agit-, -tumult-,
-turb-

upon *pre* ana-, epi-, ob-, super-,
sur-

upper side *comb* supero-

upright *comb* ortho-, prob-, recti-

uproar *base* crepit-, frem-, ligyr-,
strep(i)-, strid-, stridul-. *See*
sound

upward *pre* ano-[1], ex-

uranium *comb* uranoso-

urea *comb* ure(a)-

ureter *comb* uretero-, urethro-

urge *base* horm-, -hort-, -suade,
-suas-

uric acid *comb* uri-, urico-

urine/urinary tract *comb* ouro-,
ure(a)-, ureo-, uretero-, -uretic,
urini-, urino-, uro-[2], -ury; *base*

-mict-, -ming-; ***diseased condi-*
tion of~:** *comb* -uria
urn *comb* urcei-, urceo-
usage *base* mor-[1]
used for doing *comb* -chresis; *suf* -le
useful *comb* chreo-, chresto-; *base* -util-
useless *base* futil-, inutil-, mataeo-
usual *comb* normo-
utensil *base* skeuo-

uterus *comb* hyster(o)-[1], metra-, metro-, utero-
utter *comb* -claim, logo-, -logue, -lalia, -lexia, lexico-, -lexis, -lexy, -logy, -phone, phono-, -phony, rhet-, verbi-, verbo-, voc-, voci-, -voke; *base* -clam-, -dict-, -loc(u)-, -loqu-, narr-, -orat-, -phat-, -phem-
uvula *comb* staphylo-, uvulo-

V

vacant *comb* ceno-, keno-; *base* -erem-, (ex)haur-, inan-, -vac(u)-
vaccine *comb* vaccino-
vagina *comb* colp(o)-, elytr(o)-, kolpo-, vagini-, vagino-. *See* **vulva**
vague *base* ambig, dub-, ancip-
vagus nerve *comb* vago-
vain *comb* mataeo-
valence *comb* -valent; ***lower~:*** *suf* -ous
validating *comb* -deictic
values *comb* axio-[2]
valve *comb* valvi-, valvulo-
vampire *base* vespertil-
vanishing *base* marc-
vanquish *base* vict-, -vinc-
vapor *comb* atmo-, -capnia, capno-, vapo-, vapori-; *base* halit-, -nebul-
variation *comb* allo-, anomalo-, anomo-, poikilo-; *base* -mut-. *See* **change**
vas deferens *comb* vaso-
vase *comb* urcei-
vast *comb* bronto-, dino-, giganto-, mega-, megalo-, -megaly
vault *base* fornic-
veal *base* vitul-
vegetable *comb* vegeti-, vegeto-; *base* lachan-, oler-, olit-

vegetation *comb* botano-, herbi-, -phyte, phyto-; *base* veget-; *suf* -aceae, -ad, -ales, -eae, -ia
vehicle *comb* amaxo-, -mobile; *base* -ocho-[1]
veiled *pre* sub-; *comb* calypto-, crypto-; *base* occult-
vein *comb* cirso-, phlebo-, vene-, veni-, veno-, venoso-, -venous; ***enlarged~:*** *comb* varici-, varico-
velvet *base* velut-
ventral *comb* abdomino-, celio-, laparo-, ventro-
ventricle *comb* ventriculo-
veracity *base* aleth-, -ver-
verdegris *base* aerug-
verge *base* marg-, propinq-, prox-
vermin *base* pesti-, vermin-
versatile *base* agil-, facil-, ingen-
verse *comb* rhapso-, -stichia, sticho-, -stichous
vertebra *comb* spondylo-, vertebro-; ***top~:*** *comb* atlanto-, atlo-
vertigo *base* illyngo-
verve *base* ard-, alacr-, -ferv-, zelo-
very *pre* per-; *comb* stone-
vesicle *comb* vesiculi-, vesiculo-
vessel *comb* angio-, vasculo-, vasi-, vaso-; ***serving~:*** *base* skeuo-
vestibule *comb* vestibulo-

viands *comb* bromato-, -brotic, manduc-, opso-, -phage, phago-, -phagous, -phagy, -sitia, sitio-, sito-, -troph, -trophic, tropho-, -trophy, -vora, -vore, -vorous; *base* -alim-, -cib-, escul-, -gust-, -nutr-; ***partially digested~:*** chymo-

vibration *comb* pallo-, tremo-, vibro-

vice *comb* enisso-, enosio-; *base* -culp-, hamart-, -pecca-

vicious *base* flagit-, iniq-, perdit-, -prav-, turp-

victory *base* nic-

view, a *comb* -scape

view, to *comb* eid(o)-, oculo-, ommat-, -opia, opsi-, -opsia, -opsis, opso-, -opsy, ophthalmo-, optico-, opto-, -scope, -scopic, scopo-, -scopy, visuo-; *base* -blep-, -scrut-, -spec-,-spic-, -vid-

village *comb* -burg(h), -ton ,-ville

villainous *pre* dys-, mis-; *comb* caco-, enisso-, enosio-, kak-, kako-, mal-, male-, ponero-; *base* culp-, facin-, flagit-, hamart-, iniq-, nefar-, pecca-, perdit-, -prav-, sceler-, scelest-, turp-

vine *comb* clem-[1], viti-; *base* -ampel-, pampin-

vinegar *comb* acet(o)-, acetyl-, acid-, keto-; *See* **sharp**

violate *base* temerat-

violet *comb* indo-[1]; *base* ianth-, -viol-. *Also see* "Colors" in Part III

viper *comb* echidno-

virgin *comb* partheno-

virtuous *pre* bene-, eu-; *base* agath-, bon-, prob-

virus *comb* ***genus:*** -virus; ***family:*** -viridae; ***subfamily:*** -virinae

viscera *comb* splanchno-, viscero-

visible *comb* lampro-, luc-, luci-, -phane, phanero-, -phanic, -phany, pheno-; *base* -clar-, -schem-, -spec-, -spic-

vision *comb* eid(o)-, oculo-, ommat-, -opia, opsi-, -opsia, -opsis, opso-, -opsy, ophthalmo-, optico-, opto-, -scope, -scopic, scopo-, -scopy, visuo-; *base* -blep-, -scrut-, -spec-, -spic-, -vid-

vitality *comb* bio-, -biosis, vita-, vivi-, zoo-, -zoic, -zooid; *base* -anim-

vitiated *comb* lysi-, lyso-, -lysis, -lyte, phthysio-, -phthysis, putre-, putri-, pytho-, sapro-, septi-[2], septico-, septo-[1]; *base* -marces-, -putr-, tabe-; *suf* -ase

vitriol *comb* vitriolico-

vocabulary *comb* glosso-, -glot, -lexia, lexico-, -lexis, -lexy, logo-, -logue, -logy, verbo-; *base* -lingu-, -locu-, -loqu-, rhema-

voice *comb* -claim, logo-, -logue, -lalia, -lexia, lexico-, -lexis, -lexy, -logy, -phone, phono-, -phony, -phthong, rhet-, verbi-, verbo-, voc-, voci-, -voke; *base* -clam-, -dict-, -loc(u)-, -loqu-, -orat-, -phat-, -phem-

void *comb* ceno-, keno-; *base* -erem-, (ex)haur-, inan-, -vac(u)-

voltaic *comb* volta-

voluminous *base* ampl-, copi-, magn-

voluntary *comb* ultro-. *See* **free**

vomit *comb* -emesis, -emetic, emeto-

voracious *base* avid-, edac-, gulos-

vortex *comb* vortici-

vote *base* suffrag-

voyage *base* -curs-, itiner-, -navig-, peregrin-, via-

vulgar ***obscene:*** *base* aischro-, borbor-, copro-, fescinn-; ***ordinary:*** *comb* demo-; *base* -pleb-, -popul-

vulture *base* -vultur-

vulva *comb* episio-, vulvi-, vulvo-. *See* **vagina**

W

wading bird *base* grallator-
wagon *base* plaustr- (plaustrary)
wail *base* plang-, -plor-, -ulul-[1]
wait *comb* brady-; *base* -cunct-,
  imped-, -mora-, -tard-
walk *comb* -basia, bato-, -grade;
  base -ambul-, -gress-
wall *comb* parieto-, -phragma,
  septo-; *base* herco-, -mur-[2],
  teicho-, ticho-, vall-
walnut *base* juglan-
walrus *base* oben-
wand *comb* rhabdo-
wander *comb* -plania, plano-[2]; *base*
  err-, -peregrin-, -vag(r)-. *See*
  travel
wanting *pre* hypo-, sub-, under-;
  comb hystero-; *base* hesson-; *suf*
  -aster
wanton *base* meretric-, scort-
war *base* arm-, -bell-, milit-,
  polem-
warbler *base* vermivor-
ward off *base* alexi-, alexo-
warmth *comb* cal(e)-, calo-,
  calor(i)-, pyro-, -therm, thermo-,
  thermy; *base* aest-, caum-, ferv-
warn *base* -mon-
wart *base* verruci-
wash *comb* balneo-; *base* ablut-,
  cathar-, -lav-, -mund-[2], -purg-
wasp *comb* vespi-; *base* sphec-,
  sphek-
wasting away *comb* phthino-,
  phthisio-, -phthisis; *base* tab-
watchman *base* excub-, custod-,
  vigil-
water *comb* aqua-, aque-, aqui-,
  hydro-, hyeto-, hygro-; *base* -rip-
waterless *comb* carpho-, xero-; *base*
  arid-, celo-, cherso-, -sicc-
wave *comb* cuma-, cyma-, cymato-,

cymo-, -enchyma, flexuoso-, gy-
  roso-, kymo-, sinuato-, sinuoso-;
  base -fluct-, -unda-, -undul-
wax *comb* cero-, cerumini-
way *comb* hodo-, -ode[1], odo-, via-;
  base -itin-
weakness *physical: comb* astheno-,
  -atrophia, lepto-, -plegia, -plegy;
  base -debil-, dimin-, enerv-, flacc-,
  labe-; *spiritual: base* culp-,
  delinq-, laps-, -pecca-, sphal-
wealth *comb* chryso-, pluto-; *base*
  chrem-, -opul-, pecun-
weapon *comb* hoplo-
weary *comb* pono-; *base* -fatig-,
  kopo-, lass-
weasel *base* arctoid-, gale-[1], -mustel-
weave *base* tex-
web *comb* hypho-
wed *comb* gameto, gamo-, -gamous,
  -gamy; *base* conjug-, marit-,
  -nub-, -nupt-
wedge-shaped *comb* spheno-; *base*
  cuneo-
weed *base* runc-
week *base* -hebdom-
weep *base* dacryo-, fleb-, flet-,
  lachrim-, lachrym-, plor-
weevil *base* curculion-
weight *comb* -bar, baro-, bary-,
  gravi-; *base* obes-, -pond-
well *condition: pre* bene-, eu-; *base*
  -san-,-salub-; *water: comb*
  phreato-, putea-
west *base* hesper-, -occid, zephyr-.
  See direction
wet *comb* hydro-, hygro-, udo-;
  base humect-, madefac-, -rig-. *See*
  water
whale *base* -balaen-, cet(o)-
wheat *base* silig-, tritic-
wheedle *base* leno-

wheel *comb* cyclo-, roti-, trochalo-, trochi-, trocho-, -wheeler. *See* **circle**

where *base* -ubi-. *See* **location**

whip(like) *comb* flagello-, mastigo-; *base* lora-

whirl *comb* dino-², vortici-

whirlpool *base* vorag-

whisper *base* psithur-, susurr-

whistle *base* sibil-

white *comb* leuco-, leuko-; *base* -alb-, alut-, -cand-, ceruss-, ebur-, -lac-, -niv-. *Also see* "Colors" in Part III

whole *pre* be-, cata-, de-, kata-, ob-, per-; *comb* holo-, omni-, pan-, panto-, stone-, toti-; *base* integr-

whore *comb* cypriano-, hetaero-, porno-; *base* -meretric-, scort-; **brothel:** lupan-

wicked(ness) *pre* dys-, mis-; *comb* caco-, enisso-, enosio-, kak-, kako-, mal-, male-, ponero-; *base* culp-, facin-, flagit-, hamart-, iniq-, nefar-, pecca-, perdit-, -prav-, sceler-, scelest-, turp-

wicker *base* vimin-

wide *comb* eury-, lati-, platy-; *base* ampl-

widow *base* -vidu-

wife *comb* uxori-; *base* conjug-, marit-

wild *base* agrio-

wild animal *comb* -there, therio-, thero-; *base* -fer-

will *comb* -bulia, ultro-; *base* -vol-

willow *base* itea-, salic-

win *base* vict-, -vinc-

wind *comb* anemo-; *base* -flat-, -vent-; **north~:** *base* -borea-; **south~:** *comb* austro-; **west~:** *comb* zephyro-; *base* favon-

winding *comb* flexuoso-; *base* -sinu-

window *base* -fenestr-

windpipe *comb* bronch(i)-, bronchio-, broncho-, laryngo-, tracheo-

wine *comb* oeno-, oino-, vini-, vino-, viti-

wing *comb* ala-, ali-¹, pteno-, -pter, pterido-, pterigo-, ptero-, -pterous, pterygo-, pteryl-, ptib-, ptilo-; **having two~:** *comb* diptero-; **~case:** elytri-

wink *base* conniv-, nict-

winter *base* brum-¹, cheima-, hibern-, hiema-

wipe out *comb* lysi-, lyso-, -lysis, -lytic, -lyze, -phage, phago-, -phagous, -phagy; *base* -ate-⁴, perd-, phthart-, -vast-

wisdom *base* -jud-, sapient-, -soph-

wish *base* desid-, -opt-¹, -vell-, -vol-

witchcraft *base* -venefic-

with *pre* co-, inter-, para-, syl-, sym-, syn-, sys-; *comb* allelo-, hama-, symphyo-, synchro-; *base* -mutu-

withdraw **leave:** *base* relinq-; **remove:** *pre* ab-, abs-, apo-, be-, de-, des-, di-, dia-, dif-, dis-, e-, ec-, ef-, ex-, for-, off-, se, with-; *comb* ectro-

wither *base* marces-, marcid-

within *pre* eis-, em-, en-¹, il-, im-, in-¹, ir-; *comb* endo-, ento-, eso-, intero-, intra-, intro-; **from~:** *comb* entostho-

without **missing:** *pre* a-, an-, dis-, ex-, in-; *comb* lipo-; *base* priv-; *suf* -less; **outside:** *pre* epi, exo-, extra-, para-, preter; *comb* ecto-, extero-, out-

woe *comb* lype-; *base* dolor-, fleb-, flet-, luct-, trist-

wolf *comb* lyco-; *base* -lup-

wolverine *base* -mustel-

woman *comb* gyn(e)-, gyneco-, gyneo-, gyno-, -gynous, -gyny,

-para[3], thely-, -wife; *base* -femin-,
muliebr-; *suf* -en, -enne, -ess,
-ette, -ice, -ine, -stress, -trice,
-trix; *old~:* grao-
womb *comb* hyster(o)-[1], metra-,
metro-, utero-
wombat *base* phascolom-
wonder *comb* thaumato-; *base*
-mir-
wood *comb* erio-, hyle-, hylo-,
ligni-, ligno-, xylo-, -xylous, ylo-
woodcock *base* -charadr-, gallinag-,
scolopac-
woodlouse *base* -onisc-
woodpecker *base* -pici-
woods *base* nemo(r)-, saltu-, silv-.
See **forest**
wool *comb* lani-; *base* -flocc-, -lana-,
mallo-, -ulo-[3]; *wooly: comb* dasy-
words *comb* -glossia, glosso-, -glot,
-lexia, -lexis, lexico-, -lexy,
lingu(o)-, logo-, -logue, -logy,
phraseo-, -phrastic, verbi-, verbo-;
base -lex-, -locu-, -loqu-, rhema-,
vocab-; *suf* -ese; *long~: base*
sesquipedal-; *~unit: suf* -eme
work *comb* arti-, -craft, -ergasia,
ergasio-, -ergics, ergo-, -ergy,
organo-, -urgy; *base* -labor-,
lucubr-, oper-[1], -opus-, pono-[2]
workable *comb* chreo-, chresto-;

base -util-
world *comb* -cosm, cosmo-, -gaea;
base mund-[1], secul-, -tellur-,
-terr-
worm *comb* ascari-, filari-,
helminth(o)-, nemato-, scoleci-,
scoleco-, taeni-, vermi-; *base*
lumbric-, oxyur-, tered-, tinea-
worry *base* vex-
worse *pre* sub-; *base* degen-, pejor-
worship *comb* -latry; *base* cult-,
vener-[2], -venerat-; *one who~:*
comb -later
worthlessness *base* futil-, inutil-,
mataeo-, -nuga-, -vili-; *suf* -aster[2]
worthy of being *suf* -able, axio-;
base -dign-
wound *comb* helco-, traumato-;
base sauciat-, -vuln-
wrapping *base* involver-
wren *base* troglodyt-
wrestling *base* luct-[2]
wrinkle *comb* corrugato-, rhyti-;
base -crisp-, -rug-
wrist *comb* carpo-[2]
write *comb* -gram, -graph, -gra-
pher, -graphic, grapho-, -graphy,
grapto-, -logue; *base* -scrib-,
-script-, typo-
wrong *pre* dys-, mis-. *See* **wicked**

X

X-rays *comb* radio-, roentgeno-
X-shaped *base* decuss-

xiphoid process *comb* xiphi-,
xipho-

Y

yam *base* dioscorea-
yarn *base* fabul-, mytho-, narr-, stori-

yawl *base* nav-, scaph-
yawn *base* oscit-

year *base* -ann-, -enn-; *period of two~:* bienn-; *period of three~:* trienn-; *period of four~:* quadrenn-; *period of five~:* quinquenn-; *period of six~:* sexenn-; *period of seven~:* septenn-; *period of eight~:* octenn-; *period of nine~:* novenn-; *period of ten~:* decenn-. See "Numbers" in Part III

yearly *base* annivers-

yearn for *comb* eroto-, -lagnia, -mania, -orexia; *base* -appet-, conat-, -cup-, -libid-, -opt-, vell-; *suf* -urient

yeast *base* ferment-, prozym-, zym(o)-

yell *base* -clam-, vocif-

yellow *comb* chrys(o)-, flavido-, flavo-, -icter-, lurido-, luteo-, ochreo-, ochro-, xantho-; *base* aen-, croce-, -fulv-, gambog-, gilv-, -helv-, jaun-, lur-, lut-, -melin-, safran-, vitell-. *Also see* "Colors" in Part III

yesterday *base* hestern-, prid-

yew *base* tax-

yield *base* ced-, -cess

yoke *comb* jug-, zyga-, zygo-; *base* zeug-, zeux-

yolk *comb* lecith(o)-, vitelli-, vitello-

young *base* jun-, -juven-, nov-. *See* **child**

yttrium *comb* yttro-

Z

zany *base* fatu-, inan-, moro-, stult-

zeal *base* ard-, alacr-, -ferv-, zelo-

zebra *base* -zebr-

zenith *comb* -apical, apico-

zero *comb* nihil-, nulli-. *See also* "Negatives" in Part III

zest *comb* agito-; *base* alacr-, ard-, avid-, cupid-, ferv-, hedon-, volupt-, zelo-

zinc *comb* zinco-

zirconium *comb* zirconio-

zygoma *comb* zygomatico-, zygomato-

PART III
Categories

ANIMALS

aardvark edent- (edentate)
adder colub- (colubrine)
agouti dasyproct- (dasyproctidae)
albatross diomed- (diomedeidae);
  procellar- (procellariid)
alligator eusuch- (eusuchian)
anchovy engraul- (engraulid)
angel fish pterophyll- (pterophyllous)
ant formic- (formicine); myrmec-
  (myrmecine); myrmeco- (myme-
  cology); myrmic- (mymicine)
anteater myrmecophag- (myrmecophagine)
antelope alcelaph- (alcelaphine);
  bubal- (bubaline)
ape pithec- (pithecoid); -pithecus
  (Australopithecus); sim- (simian)
armadillo dasypod- (dasypodid);
  tolypeut- (tolypeutine)
ass as- (assinine); ono (onolatry)
auk alcid- (alcidine)
badger melin- (meline); mustel-
  (mustelid)
barracuda percesoc- (percesocine);
  sphyraen- (sphyraenoid)
bat desmodont- (desmodontid);
  megacheiropter- (megacheiropteran); microcheiropter- (microcheiropteran); noctilion- (noctilionid); pterop- (pteropine);
  vespertil- (vespertilian)
bear arcto- (cynarctomachy); urs-
  (ursine)
beaver castor- (castoreum)
bee api- (apiarian); bomb-
  (bombid); melisso- (melissean)
beetle coleopter- (coleopteral);
  scarab- (scaraboid)
bird avi- (avian); orneo- (orneoscopic); orni- (ornithology); or-
  nitho- (ornithological); volucr-

(volucrine); *flycatching~:* musci-
cap- (muscicapine); *hanging nest
building~:* pendulin- (penduline);
perching~: passer- (passerine);
singing~: oscin- (oscine);*wad-
ing~:* grall- (gralline)
bittern botaur- (botaurus); ixo-
  brych- (ixobrychus)
black widow spider latrodect- (latrodectus)
blackbird icter- (icterine); merul-
  (meruline)
bluebird sial- (Sialia); turd- (turdine)
boar suid- (suidian)
bobolink icter- (icterine)
buffalo bubal- (bubaline)
bug cimic- (cimicoid); entomo-
  (entomology); insecti- (insecticide); insecto- (insectology)
bull taur- (tauriform)
bullfinch pyrrhul- (pyrrhuline)
bunting emberiz- (emberizine);
  pyrrhul- (pyrrhuloxine)
butterfly lepidopter- (lepidopter-
  ous); papil- (papilionaceous)
buzzard buteo- (buteonine);
  cathart- (cathartine)
calf vitul- (vituline)
camel camel- (cameline)
cardinal pyrrhul- (pyrrhuloxine)
carp cyprin- (cyprinoid)
cassowary casuar- (casuarina)
cat aeluro- (aelurophile); ailuro-
  (ailurophobe); feli- (feline); gale-
  (galeanthropy); gato- (gatophobia)
caterpillar bruch- (bruchus);
  -camp- (campodean); eruc- (eruciform)
catfish silur- (silurid)
centipede chilopod- (chilopodal);
  scolopendr- (scolopendriform)

chamois rupicap- (rupicaprine)
chickadee par- (parine)
chicken gallin- (gallinaceous); pull- (pullet)
chimpanzee sim- (simid)
civet viverr- (viverrine)
cock alector- (alectoromancy); alectry- (alectryomachy)
cockroach blatt- (blatta)
coot fulic- (Fulicinae)
cormorant phalacrocorac- (phalacrocoracine)
cow bou- (boustrophedon); bov- (bovine); bu- (bulimia); vacc- (vaccine)
crab cancri- (cancrine); gammar- (gammarolite)
crane alector- (alectorine); grallator- (grallatorial); grui- (gruiform)
cricket gryll- (gryllid); locust- (locustarian)
crocodile crocodil- (crocodilian); gavial- (gavialoid)
crow coraci- (coraciform); coraco- (coracoid); corvin- (corvine)
cuckoo cucul- (cuculine)
cuttlefish sepi- (sepiacean); -teuth- (teuthologist)
deer cervi- (cervine); elaph- (elaphine)
dodo did- (didine)
dog cani- (canine); cyn- (cynanthropy); kyn- (kynanthropy)
dolphin delphin- (delphine)
donkey ono- (onocentaur)
dormouse glir- (gliriform); myox- (myoxine)
dove columb- (columbine)
dragonfly libellul- (libellulid)
duck anat- (anatine); fuligul- (fuliguline)
eagle aet- (aetites); aquil- (aquiline)
earwig forficul- (forficulid)
eel anguill- (anguilliform); cy-

clostom- (cyclostome); muraen- (muraenoid)
eland taurotrag- (Taurotragus oryx)
elephant elephant- (elephantine); pachyderm- (pachydermic)
elk cerv- (cervine)
emu rat- (ratite)
ermine mustel- (musteline)
falcon accipit- (accipitrine); falcon- (falconry); raptor- (raptorial)
ferret mustel (musteline); viverr- (viverrine)
finch fringill- (fringilline)
firefly lampyr- (lampyrid)
fish icthyo- (icthyoid); pisci- (piscine); *bony~:* scopeli- (scopeliform)
flamingo phoenicopter- (phoenicopteroid)
flea puli- (pulicine)
fly cyclorrhaph- (cyclorrhaphous); musc- (muscid); myia- (myiasis)
fox alopec- (alopecoid); vulp- (vulpine)
frog batracho- (batrachoid); bufo- (bufotenine); phryno- (phrynoderma); polyped- (polypedatid); rani- (ranine)
fruitfly drosophil- (Drosophilidae); trypet- (Trypetidae)
gerbil cricet- (cricetine)
gibbon hylobat- (hylobatine)
giraffe artiodactyl- (artiodactylous)
gnat culici- (culiciform)
gnu connochaet- (Connochaetes)
goat caprin- (caprine); egagro- (egagropile); hircin- (hircine); trago- (tragopan)
goldfish cyprin- (cyprinid)
goose anser- (anserine); cheno- (Chenopod)
gorilla pong- (pongid)
grasshopper acrid- (acridid); gryll- (gryllotalpa); locust- (locustid)

grouse gallinac- (gallinaceous); tetrao- (tetraonid)

gull gavi- (Gaviae); lar- (larine)

halibut hippogloss- (hippoglossoid)

hare cunic- (cuniculous); lago- (lagotic); lepor- (leporine)

hawk accipit- (accipitrine); buteo- (buteonine); falco- (falconine); hieraco- (hieracosophic)

hedgehog echin- (echinate); erinac- (erinaceous)

heron arde- (ardeid); grallator- (grallatorial)

herring clupeo- (clupeoid); halec- (halecomorphous); harengi- (harengiform)

hog hyos- (hyoscyamine)

hookworm ancylostom- (Ancylostoma)

hornbill bucerot- (Bucerotinae); bucorac- (Bucoracinae)

hornet -sphec- (sphecoid); vespi- (vespine)

horse caball- (caballine); caval- (cavalry); equ- (equine); hippo- (hippology); -hippus (eohippus)

horsefly taban- (tabanid)

hummingbird trochil- (trochiline)

hyrax chero- (cherogril)

jackass asin- (asinine)

jackdaw gracul- (graculine)

jay garrul- (garruline)

jellyfish discophor- (discophoran)

kangaroo macropod- (macropodine)

kestrel falco- (falconine)

kingfisher halcyon- (halcyonine)

kite milv- (milvine)

kudu tragelaph- (Tragelaphus)

lamb agn- (agnification)

leech bdell- (bdellatomy); discophor- (discophorous); hirud- (hirudine); sanguisug- (sanguisugous)

leopard pard- (pardine)

lion leo- (leonine)

lizard lacert- (lacertilian); saur- (saurian); sauro- (sauropod); -saurus (icthyosaurus); stellio- (stellion)

lobster astac- (astacian); gammar- (gammarolite); homar- (homarine)

locust locust- (locustarian)

louse pedicul- (pediculous); phthir- (phthiriasis); phthyr- (phthyriasis)

lynx lync- (lyncean)

macaw psittac- (psittacine)

mackerel scombr- (scombroid)

magpie corv- (corvoid); garrul- (garruline)

manatee trichec- (Trichechus)

marlin istiophor- (istiophorid)

marmoset callithric- (callithricid)

marmot sciur- (sciurid)

marten mustel- (musteline)

martin hirund- (hirundine)

meadowlark icter- (icterine)

millipede arthropod- (arthropodal); diplopod- (diplopodal)

mink mustel- (musteline)

minnow cyprin- (cyprinid)

mite acar- (acaroid); miti- (miticide)

mockingbird mim- (mimine)

mole talp- (talpine)

mole-rat zemn- (zemnine)

mollusk malaco- (malacological); mollusc- (molluscous)

mongoose viverr- (viverrine)

monkey cebo- (cebocephalic); pithec- (pithecoid)

moose cerv- (cervine)

mosquito aed- (aedine); anophel- (anopheline); culici- (culicid)

moth arct- (arctian); phalaen- (phalaenoid); tinea- (tineid)

mouse mur- (murine); myo- (myomancy)

mullet mugil- (mugiloid)
muskrat cricet- (cricetid)
mussel mytil- (mytiloid)
nightingale philomel-
(philomelian)
nuthatch sitt- (Sitta)
opossum didelph- (didelphine)
orangutan pong- (pongoid)
oriole icter- (icterine)
osprey ossifrag- (ossifrage)
ostrich rat- (ratite); struthi-
(struthious)
otter lutr- (lutrine)
owl strigi- (strigine); tyto- (Tytonidae); ulul- (ululant)
ox bou- (boustrophedon); bov-
(bovine); bu- (bulimia)
oyster ostrac- (ostracine); ostrei-
(ostreiform); ostreo- (ostreophage)
parakeet psittac- (psittacine)
parrot psittac- (psittacine)
partridge gallinac- (gallinaceous);
-perdic- (perdicine); perdri- (perdricide)
peacock pavon- (pavonine)
pelican onocrot- (onocrotal); pele-
can- (pelecanid)
penguin sphenisc- (spheniscan)
perch perc- (perciform)
pheasant alector- (alectorine); gal-
linac- (gallinaceous); phasian-
(phasianine)
pig porcin- (porcine); sui- (suilline)
pigeon columb- (columbaceous);
palumb- (palumbine); perister-
(peristeronic); pullastr- (pullastrine)
platypus monotrem-
(monotremal); protother- (Prototheria)
plover charadr- (charadrine); plu-
vial- (pluvialine)
polecat mustel- (musteline)
porcupine hystric- (hystricine)

porpoise delphin- (delphine);
phoecaen- (Phoecaenoides)
poultry gallin- (gallinaceous)
ptarmigan tetraon- (tetraonid)
quail coturn- (coturnine); gallinac-
(gallinaceous)
rabbit cunic- (cuniculous); lago-
(lagotic); lepor- (leporine)
raccoon arctoid- (arctoidean); pro-
cyon- (procyonine)
ram ariet- (arietine); crio- (criocephalous); krio- (krioboly)
rat mur- (murine)
rattlesnake crotal- (crotaline)
raven coraci- (coraciiform); coraco-
(coracomorphic); corvin-
(corvine)
reptile batrach- (batrachian); her-
peto- (herpetology); -ophidia
(Thanatophidia); ophio- (ophiolatry); reptil- (reptilian); saur-
(saurian); -saurus (icthyosaurus);
serp- (serpentine)
rhinoceros ceratorh- (ceratorhine)
roach blatt- (blattid)
roadrunner cucul- (cuculid)
robin turd- (turdine)
sable zibel- (zibeline)
sailfish istiophor- (istiophorid)
salmon salmoni- (salmoniform)
sandgrouse pterocl- (pteroclid)
sandpiper charadr- (charadrine);
tring- (tringoid)
scorpion pedipalp- (pedipalpous)
sea horse hippocamp- (hippocampine)
sea urchin echin- (echinoid)
seagull lar- (laroid)
seal phoc- (phocine)
shark carchar- (carcharinid); gale-
(galeod); selach- (selachoid) *ham-
merhead~:* sphyrn- (Sphyrna);
squal- (squaloid)
sheep ovi- (ovine); verv- (vervecine)

shrew soric- (soricine); tupai- (tupaiid)
shrimp macrur- (macruran)
silkworm bombyc- (bombycine)
skunk mephit- (mephitine); mustel- (mustelid)
skylark alaud- (alaudine)
sloth xenarth- (xenarthral)
slug limac- (limacine)
smelt ather- (atherine)
snail cochlea- (cochleiform); gastropod- (gastropodal); limac- (limacine)
snake angui- (anguiform); colubr- (colubrine); echidno- (echidnotoxin); -glypha (episthoglypha); herpeto- (herpetology); ophid- (ophidian); ophio- (ophiolatry); reptil- (reptilian); serpen- (serpentine); viper- (viperine)
snapper lutjan- (lutjanid)
snipe charadr- (charadrine); scolopac- (scolopaceous)
sparrow passer- (passerine)
spider arachn- (arachnoid); arene- (areneiform); phalang- (phalangium)
squid cephalopod- (cephalopodal); teutho- (teuthologist)
squirrel sciur- (sciurine)
stag cerv- (cervine); elaph (elaphine)
starfish asteroid- (asteroidean); echinoderm- (echinodermatous)
starling psar- (psarolite); sturn- (sturnoid)
stoat mustel- (musteline)
stork cicon- (ciconine); grallator- (grallatorial); pelarg- (pelargic)
sturgeon acipenser- (acipenserine); sturion- (sturionic)
swallow chelid- (chelidonian); -hirund- (hirundine); sturn- (sturnoid)
swan cycn- (cycnean); cygn- (cygnine)

swift cypsel- (cypseline)
swine porc- (porcine); su- (suoid)
swordfish xiphi- (xiphioid)
tapeworm taeni- (taenioid); teni- (teniacide)
tapir pachyderm- (pachydermoid)
tarantula theraphos- (theraphosid)
tarsier lemur- (lemuroid)
termite isoptero- (isopterous); termit- (termitarium)
tern stern- (sternine)
thrush cathar- (Catharus); cichlo- (cichlomorphous); muscicap- (muscicapine); turd- (turdiform)
tick acar- (acarine); ixod- (ixodid)
tiger tigr- (tigrine)
titmouse par- (parine)
toad batrach- (batrachian); bufo- (bufonite); phryno- (phrynoderma)
tortoise chelon- (chelonian); emydo- (emydosaurian); testud- (testudineous)
trout trocto- (troctolite); trutt- (truttaceous)
turbot psett- (psettaceous); scophthalm- (Scophthalmus)
turkey gallinac- (gallinaceous); meleagr- (meleagrine)
turtle anaps- (anapsid); chelon- (chelonian); -chelys (Lepidochelys); testud- (testudinal); turtura- (turturring)
vulture vultur- (vulturine)
walrus oben- (obenid)
warbler vermivor- (Vermivora)
wasp sphec- (sphecid); vesp- (vespine)
weasel arctoid- (arctoidean); gale- (phascogale); mustel- (musteline)
weevil curculion- (curculionid)
whale balaen- (balaenoid); cet- (cetaceous)
wolf lup- (lupine); lyc- (lycanthropy)

wolverine mustel- (musteline)
wombat phascolom- (phascolo-mian)
woodcock charadr- (charadrine); gallinag- (gallinaginous); scolopac- (scolopacine)
woodlouse isopod- (isopodous); onisc- (onisciform)
woodpecker pic- (picine)
worm ascari- (ascariasis); filari-
(filariform); helminth-(helminthoid); lumbric (lumbri-ciform); oxyur- (oxyurifuge); scolec- (scolecoid); scoleci-(scoleciform); scoleco (scoleco-brotic); taeni- (taeniiphobia); tered- (teredines); tinea- (tineid); vermi- (vermiform)
wren troglodyt- (troglodytine)
zebra zebr- (zebrine)

THE BODY

abdomen abdomino- (ab-dominocentesis); alv- (alvine); celio- (celiomyositis); celo- (celo-scope); laparo- (laparotomy); ven-tri- (ventricumbent); ventro-(ventrodorsal); *abdominal sac:* peritoneo- (peritoneoclysis); *dis-tended~:* ventricoso- (ventricoso-globose)
adrenal gland adreno- (adreno-toxin)
amniotic sac amnio- (amniocente-sis)
ankle bone astragalo- (astragalon-avicular); tali- (taligrade); talo-(talocalcaneal)
antibodies -valent (multivalent)
anus ano- (anorectal)
arm acromio- (acromioclavicular); brachio- (brachiocephalic)
armpit axill- (periaxillary)
artery arterio- (arteriosclerosis); -venous (intravenous)
atlas *vertebra:* atlanto- (atlantoax-ial); atlo- (atloid)
atrophy tabe- (tabescent)
auricle atrio- (atrioventricular)
backbone rachi- (rachicentesis); ra-chio- (rachiometer); rhach- (rha-chitis); -rrhachia (glycorrhachia)
bile bili- (biligenic); chole- (chole-
cyst); cholo- (chololith); gall-(gallbladder)
birthmark nevi- (nevoid); nevo-(nevosity)
blister phlyc- (phlyctenous); pus-tul- (pustule); vesica- (vesica-tory); vesico- (vesicoprostatic); vesiculo- (vesiculo-pustular)
blood cruent- (incruent); cruor-(cruorin); haema- (haema-chrome); haemo- (haemogastric); hema- (hemachrome); hemato-(hematogenic); hemo- (hemo-philia); sangui- (sanguicolous); sanguineo- (sanguineous); san-guino- (sanguino-purulent); *~clot:* thrombo- (thrombo-phlebitis); *~condition or disease:* -aemia (hyperaemia); -cythemia (leucocythemia); -emia (leu-kemia); *~fluid:* lympho- (lym-phocyte); *~vessels:* hemangio-(hemangiosarcoma); vasculo-(vasculitis); vaso- (vasoconstric-tor)
body corp- (corporeal); physico-(physicochemical); physi- (physi-atrics); physio- (physiotherapy); somato- (somatology); -some (chromosome); *dead~:* cadav-(cadaver); necro- (necrosis);

~*defect:* hamart- (hamartoma);
~*odor:* brom- (bromidrosis);
~*organ part:* -ite (somite)
bone ossi- (ossification); osseo-
(osseomucin); osteo- (osteoplasty); *forearm~:* ulno- (ulnoradial); *frontal~:* fronto- (fronto-
parietal); ~*joining hipbones:*
sacro- (sacroiliac); ~*membrane:*
periosteo- (periosteophyte); *bony
process:* stylo- (stylohyoid)
brain cephal- (cephalitis); cerebri-
(cerebritis); cerebro- (cerebrospinal); encephalo- (encephalocele)
breast mammi- (mammiferous);
mammo- (mammogram); -mastia
(macromastia); masto- (mastodynia); mazo- (mazoplazia); stetho-
(stethoscope); ~*bone:* pect- (pectoral); sterno- (sternoclavicular)
breath afflat- (afflatus); -hale (exhale); halit- (halitosis); ozostom-
(ozostomia); -pnea (apnea);
pneo- (pneograph); pneumato-
(pneumatometer); pneumo-
(pneumobacillus); pneumono-
(pneumonophorous); pneusio
(pneusiobiognosis); pulmo- (pulmnonary); spiro- (spirograph)
buttocks nati- (natiform); -pygia
(steatopygia); pygo- (pygopod)
cartilage chondr- (chondrify);
chondrio- (chondriosome); chon-
dro- (chondroblast); xiphi- (xipi-
oid); *eyelid~:* tarso- (tarsoplasty)
cecum ceco- (cecostomy); typhlo-
(typhlostomy)
cell alveolo- alveolopalatal); celli-
(celliferous); celluli- (celullifer-
ous); cellulo- (cellulo-fibrous);
-cyte (lymphocyte); -cythemia
(leukocythemia); cyto- (cytology); -gonium (sporogonium);

kyto- (kytometry); -plasm (neoplasm); plasmo- (plasmolysis)
cellulose cello- (cellophane)
celom celo- (celomate)
cervical cervico- (cervicodorsal)
cheek bucco- (buccolabial); -genia
(microgenia); genio- (genioplasty); geny- (genyplasty); melo-
(meloplasty); zygomatico- (zygomatico-auricular); zygomato- (zy-
gomato-temporal)
chest pector- (pectoral); sterno-
(sternocostal); stetho- (stethomet-
ric); thoracico- (thoracico- abdominal); thoraco- (thoracotomy)
chin -genia (microgenia); genio-
(genioplasty); geny- (genyplasty);
mento- (mentoplasty)
chromosomes -ploid (diploid)
chyle chyl- (chylaqueous)
clavicle cleido- (cleidomastoid);
clido- (clidomastoid)
clot grum- (grumous); thrombo-
(thrombo-phlebitis)
coccyx coccy- (coccyalgia); coc-
cygo- (coccygodynia)
collarbone clavi- (clavicle)
colon coli- (coliform); colo-
(coloenteritis)
cornea corneo- (corneoiritis); ker-
ato- (keratotomy)
corpse cadav- (cadaverous); necro-
(necrophilia)
cyst- sacc- (sacculation)
dandruff porrig- (porriginous)
defecation -chezia (hematochezia);
copro- (coprolagnia); fecu- (feculent); fim- (fimetic); fimi- (fimicolous); kopro- (koprophilia);
merd- (immerd); scato- (scatology); spatilo- (spatilomancy);
sterco- (stercoraceous)
diaphragm -phrenic (gastrophrenic); phrenico- (phrenicotomy); phreno- (phrenogastric)

ear auri- (auricular); auriculo- (auriculo-temporal); ot- (otitis); oto- (otopyosis)

elbow ancon- (anconitis)

embryo- -blast (mesoblast); -blastic (osteoblastic); blasto- (blastoderm); -blasty; embry- (embryonic)

ethmoid bone ethmo- (ethmoturbinal)

eustachian tube salpingo- (salpingitis)

eye eido- (eidoptometry); oculi- (oculiform); oculo- (oculomotor); op- (opalgia); ophthalmo- (ophthalmoscope); -opia (diplopia); opsi- (opsiometer); -opsis (coreopsis); ommat- (ommatophore); opsi- (opsiometer); opso- (opsoclonus); -opsy (achromatopsy); optico- (optico-papillary); opto- (optometry); -scope (telescope); -scopic (microscopic); -scopy (bioscopy); spec- (inspect); spic- (conspicuous); vid- (video); vis- (visual); ~*brow:* ophry- (ophryosis); *cornea:* corneo- (corneoiritis); kerato- (keratotomy); *corner of~:* cantho- (canthoplasty); ~*covering:* sclero- (sclerotomy); *iris of~:* irido- (iridomotor); ~*lash:* cili- (ciliary); ~*lid:* blephar- (blepharotomy); *retina:* retino- (retinoschisis). *See* **pupil**

face facio- (facioplegia); prosopo- (prosopagnosia); -visaged (round-visaged)

fallopian tube salpingo- (salpingotomy)

fibula peroneo- (peroneo-calcaneal)

finger -dactyl (dactyliology); dactylo- (dactylology); -dactylous (tridactylous); -dactyly (brachydactyly); digiti- (digitigrade)

fingernail -onychia (leukonychia); onycho- (onychphagy)

foot ped- (pedal); pedi- (pedicure); pedo- (pedopathy); pod- (podalgia); ~*sole:* pelm- (antiopelmus); plant- (plantigrade)

forearm ulno- (ulnoradial)

forehead metopo- (metoposcopy)

freckle lentig- (lentigo)

frontal bone fronto- (fronto-parietal)

gall bili- (biligenic); chole- (cholecyst); gall- (gallbladder)

gastric chyli- (chyliferous); chylo- (chylocyst); chymo- (chymopoiesis)

genitals aede- (aedeagus); genito- (genitourinary); *female~:* colpo- (colpospasm); *male~:* phallo- (phallocampsis)

gland adeni- (adeniform); adeno- (adenomere); balani- (balanitis); balano- (balanorrhagia)

goiter strumi- (strumiferous)

gonad gonado- (gonadopathy)

groin bubo- (bubonocele); inguino- (inguinoscrotal)

gullet esophago- (esophagus); oesophago- (oesophagalgia)

gums gingivo- (gingivoglossitis); oulo- (oulorrhagy); ulo- (uloglossitis)

hair capilli- (capilliform); crini- (criniferous); pili- (piliform); pilo- (piloerection); piloso- (piloso-fimbriate); hirsut- (hirsute); lanug- (lanugo); thrix- (streptothrix)

hand cheiro- (macrocheiria); chiro- (chiromancy); mani- (manipulate); manu- (manual)

head capit- (decapitate); cephal- (cephalitis); -cephalic (dolichocephalic); cephalo- (cephalocentesis); -cephalous (brachycephaloius); -cephaly (dolichocephaly); cranio- (craniotomy); kephalo- (kephalotomy)

heart cardi- (cardiagra); -cardia (tachycardia); cardio- (cardiology); -cardium (myocardium); cordato- (cordato-ovate); cordi- (cordiform); pericardiaco- (pericardiaco-phrenic); pericardio- (pericardiostomy)

heel bone calcaneo- (calcaneofibular)

hernia -cele (perineocele); celo- (celotomy); hernio- (herniotomy)

hip cotyle- (cotyledonary); cotyli- (cotyliform); cotylo- (cotylosacral); coxo- (coxodynia); ischio- (ischiocapsular)

hyoid bone hyo- (hyoidal)

intestinal pouch caeci- (caeciform); ceco- (cecostomy); typhlo- (typhlostomy)

intestines entero- (enteropathy); ileo- (ileostomy); ilio- (iliosacral); intestino- (intestino-vesical); jejuno- (jejunocolostomy); viscer- (visceroptosis)

iris irido- (iridomotor)

jaw -genia (microgenia); genio- (genioplasty); geny- (genyplasty); gnatho- (gnathodynamics); -gnathous (prognathous); mandibulo- (mandibulo-maxillary); maxillo- (maxillo-palatine)

jejunum jejuno- (jejunoplasty)

joint arthro- (arthrodynia); articul- (multiarticular); ~*socket:* gleno- (gleno-humeral)

kidney nephro-; pyelo-; reni-; reno-

knee genu- (genuflect)

labia minora nympho- (nymphoncus)

larynx guttur- (gutturo-labial); laryngo- (laryngoscope)

leg cnem- (gastrocnemius); crur- (crural); scel- (isosceles)

limb -mele (phocomele); -melia (macromelia); melo- (melorheostosis)

lips cheilo- (cheiloplasty); chilo- (chiloplasty); labio- (labiodental)

liver hepatico- (hepaticostomy); hepato- (hepatogastric); jecor- (jecorary)

loins laparo- (laparotomy); lumbo- (lumbodorsal); osphyo- (osphyocele)

lumbar lumbo- (lumbosacral)

lungs -pnea (apnea); pneo- (pneograph); pneumato- pneumatometer); pneumo- pneumobacillus); pneumono- (pneumonophorous); pneusio (pneusiobiognosis); pulmo- (pulmnonary); pulmoni- (pulmonigrade); pulmono- (pulmonobranchous); spiro- (spirometer)

lymph lymphato- (lymphatolysis); lympho- (lymphocyte)

marrow -myelia (micromyelia); myelo- (myelogenic)

mastoid mastoido- (mastoidohumeral)

membrane chorio- (choriocele); choroid- (choroideremia); hymeno- (hymenogeny); membrano- (membranocartilaginous); *eyeball~:* sclero- (sclerotomy); *fetal~:* allanto- (allanto-chorion); amnio (amniocentesis)-; *mucous~:* muci- (muciparous); muco- (mucoprotein); mucoso- (mucoso-granular); *~sheath:* meningo- (meningocele)

mole nevo- (nevoid)

mouth -mouthed (open-mouthed); oro- (orolingual); stomato- (stomatalgia); -stome (cyclostome); -stomous (megastomous);

roof of~: palato- (palatonasal);
uranisco- (uraniscoplasty); urano-
(uranoschisis)

mucus blenno- (blennostasis);
muci- (muciparous); muco- (mucoprotein); mucoso- (mucoso-
granular); -myxia (hypomyxia);
myxo- (myxomycete)

muscle musculo- (muscu-
lophrenic); myo- (myocardium);
-tonic (myatonic); -tonia (isotonia)

navel omphalo- (omphalitis); um-
bilici- (umbiliciform)

neck atlo- (atloid); auchen- (maerauchenia); cervico- (cervicodorsal); coll- (decollate); jug- (jugu-
late); trachelo- (trachelodynia)

nipple mamilli- (mamilliform); pa-
pilli- (papilliform); papillo-
(papillomatosis); papilloso- (pa-
pilloso-asperate); thelo- (perithelium); umbo- (umbonulate)

nose nasi- (nasion); naso- (nasolabial); rhino- (rhinology)

nostrils nari- (narial)

occipital occipito- (occipito-axial)

ovary oario- (oariopathy);
oophoro- (oophoritis); ovario-
(ovariocentesis)

ovum oo- (oogamous); ovario-
(ovariocele); ovi- (oviduct); ovo-
(ovolecithin)

palate palato- (palatonasal);
uranisco- (uraniscoplasty); urano-
(uranoschisis); velar- (labiovelar)

palm palmati- (palmatifid);
palmato- (pelmatopeltate)

pancreas pancreato- (pancreatotomy); pancreo- (pancreopathy)

pelvis pelvi- (pelvimeter); perineo-
(perineocele); pyelo- (pyelocysti-
tis)

penis med- (medorthophobia);
mentul- (mentulate); peo-
(peotomy); phall- (phallic)

pericardial pericardiaco- (pericardiaco-phrenic); pericardio- (pericardiostomy)

perineum perineo- (perineocele)

periosteum periosteo- (periosteophyte)

peritoneum meso- (mesogastrium);
peritoneo- (peritoneoclysis)

perspiration hidr- (anhidrosis);
suda- (sudatory); sudori- (sudorific)

pharynx pharyngo- (pharyngology)

pimple pustulo- (pustulocrusta-
ceous)

placenta mazo- (mazolysis); pla-
centi- (placentiform)

pleura pleuro- (pleurotomy)

prostate prostato- (prostatectomy)

pubic area pubio- (pubiotomy);
pubo- (pubofemoral)

pulse crot- (catacrotic); sphygmo-
(sphygmograph)

pupil core- (corelysis); coreo-
(coreoplasty); -coria (isocoria);
coro- (coroplastic); -koria (leuko-
coria); pupillo- (pupillometer)

pus purulo- (purulo-gangrenous);
pyo- (pyogenic)

pylorus pyloro- (pylorodiosis)

rash -anthema (enanthema)

rectum procto- (proctology); recto-
(rectoscope)

retina retino- (retinoschisis)

rib costi- (costiform); costo- (costotome)

saliva ptyal- (ptyalogogue); sialo-
(sialorrhea)

scapula scapulo- (scapuloclavicular)

scar cica- (cicatrix); ulo- (ulodermatitis)

scrotum didymo- (didymalgia); or-
chido- (orchidotomy); orchio-
(orchiocele); oscheo- (oscheitis);
scrot- (scotocele)

shoulder acromio- (acromioclavicular); humero- (humero-cubital); omo- (omodynia); scapuli- (scapulimancy); scapulo- (scapuloclavicular); spatul- (spatulamancy)

sinew chord- (chorditis); chorda- (chordamesoderm); cord- (corotomy)

skeleton skeleto- (skeleto-trophic)

skin chorio- (choriocele); cuti- (cutisector); derm- (dermabrasion); -derm (endoderm); -derma (scleroderma); dermato- (dermatology); -dermatous (xerodermatous); -dermis (epidermis) ; dermo- (dermoneural); dora- (doramania); pell- (pellagra)

skull -cephalic (dolichcephalic); cephalo- (cephalometry); -cephalous (brachycephalous); -cephaly dolichocephaly); cranio- (craniofacial); occipito- (occipito-axial); orbito- (orbitonasal)

socket alveolo- (alveolopalatal); gomph- (gomphosis)

sphenoid bone spheno- (sphenocipital)

spinal cord -myelia (micromyelia); myelo- (myelogenic)

spine rachi- (rachicentesis); rhachi- (rhachitis); -rrhachia (glycorrhachia); spini- (spini-acute); spino- (spinobulbar); spinoso- (spinoso-dentate); spinuloso- (spinuloso-serrate); spondylo- (spondylitis); vertebro- (vertebroiliac)

spleen lieno- (lieno-gastric); splenico- (splenico-phrenic); spleno- (splenocele)

sternum sterno- (sternoclavicular)

stomach -gastria (microgastria); gastro- (gastroenteritis)

sweat hidr- (anhidrosis); suda- (sudaminal); sudori- (sudoriparous)

temple temporo- (temporomandibular)

tendon tendo- (tendolysis); teno- (tenotomy); tenonto- (tenontodynia)

testicle didymo- (didymalgia); orchido- (orchidotomy); orchio- (orchiocele); oscheo- (oscheitis); scrot- (scotocele)

thalamus thalamo- (thalamocortical)

thigh mero- (merocele)

thorax thoracico- (thoracicoabdominal); thoraco- (thoracoplasty)

throat fauc- (faucal); gutturo- (gutturo-labial); jugo- (jugo-maxillary); laryngo- (laryngoscope); pharyngo- (pharyngology); tracheo- (tracheotomy)

thumb pollic- (pollicate)

thymus thymo- (thymokinetic)

thyroid -thyrea (hypothyrea); thyreo- (thyreotomy); thyro- (thyromegaly)

tibia cnem- (cnemis); tibio- (tibiotarsal)

toe -dactyl (dactyliology); dactylo- (dactylology); -dactylous (tridactylous); -dactyly (brachydactyly); digiti- (digitigrade); halluc- (hallucar)

tongue -glossia (macroglossia); glosso- (glossoplegia); -glot (polyglot); lamino- (lamino-alveolar); ligul- (liguliform); linguo- (linguopalatal)

tonsil tonsillo- (tonsillotomy)

tooth cranter- (syncranterian); dentato- (dentato-serrate); denti- (dentifrice); dento- (dentosurgical); dont- (periodontal); laniar- (laniariform); odont- (macrodont); -toothed (gap-toothed)

trachea tracheo- (tracheobronchitis)
tumor -cele (cystocele); -oma (sarcoma); onco- (oncologist); phym- (phymatosis); -phyma (osteophyma); struma- (strumectomy)
ulcer helco- (helcoplasty)
ulna cubito- (cubito-carpal); ulno- (ulnoradial)
umbilicus omphalo- (omphalitis)
ureter uretero- (ureterostomy); urethro- (urethroscopy)
urine mict- (micturient); ming- (bradymingent); ouro- (ouromancy); urea- (ureapoiesis); ureo- (ureometer); uretero- (ureterostomy); -uretic (diuretic); urini- (uriniparous); urino- (urinometer); uro- (urolith); -ury (strangury)
uterus hystero- (hysterodynia); metra- (metratonia); metro- (metrorrhagia); utero- (uterovaginal)
uvula staphylo- (staphylorrhaphy); uvulo- (uvulectomy)
vagina colpo- (colpocele); elytro- (elytroplasty); kolpo- (kolposcope); vagini- (vaginismus); vagino- (vaginomycosis)
vagus nerve vago- (vagotropic)
vein cirso- (cirsotomy); phlebo- (phlebotomy); varici- (variciform); varico- (varicocele); vene- (venesection); veni- (venipuncture); veno- (venostomy); venoso- (venoso-reticulated); -venous (intravenous)
ventral abdomino- (abdominoscrotal); celio- (celiopathy); laparo- (laparoscope); ventro- (ventrotomy)
ventricle ventriculo- (ventriculoatrial)
vertebra atlanto- (atlantoaxial); atlo- (atloaxoid); spondylo- (spondylopyosis); vertebro- (vertebrocostal)
vesicle vesiculi- (vesiculigerous); vesiculo- (vesiculo-pustular)
vomit -emesis (hematemesis); -emetic (antiemetic); emeto- (emetophobia)
vulva episio- (episiotomy); vulvi- (vulviform); vulvo- (vulvovaginal)
wart verruci- (verruciform)
windpipe bronchi- (bronchiectasis); bronchio- (bronchiogenic); broncho- (bronchoscope); laryngo- (laryngostenosis); tracheo- (tracheomalacia)
womb hystero- (hysteropexy); metra- (metralgia); metro- (metrophlebitis); utero- (uterolith)
wrist carpo- (carpoptosis)
xiphoid process xiphi- (xiphisternum); xipho- (xiphoiditis)
yawn oscit- (oscitation)
zygoma zygomatico- (zygomaticoauricular); zygomato- (zygomatotemporal)

COLORS

Black

blue-black nigr- (nigrosine)
deep-black melan(o)- (melanous)
ebony-black ebon- (ebonize)
inky-black atro- (atroceruleous)
reddish-black piceo- (piceo-ferruginous)
sooty-black fulig- (fuliginated)

Blue

black-blue livid- (lividity)
dark-blue cyan(o)- (cyanean)
gray-blue caes- (caesious)
green-blue aerug- (aeruginous);
 glauco- (glaucous)
milky-blue adular- (adularescent)
peacock blue pavon- (pavonine)
sea-blue cumat- (cumatic)
sky-blue azur- (azureous); -cerul-
 (cerulean); lazul- (lazuline)

Brown

acorn-brown gland- (glandaceous)
chestnut-brown castan- (castaneous); -spad- (spadiceous)
dark-brown brun- (brunneous);
 fusco- (fuscous)
dusky-brown phaeo- (phaeophyll)
reddish-brown testac- (testaceous)
yellow-brown fulv- (fulvous);
 gland- (glandaceous); lur- (lurid);
 mustel- (musteline)

Copper

brassy-yellow copper chalco-
 (chalcography)
gold-copper auricalc- (auricalceous)
red-brown copper cupr- (cupre-
 ous); cupreo- (cupreo-violaceous); cuproso- (cuproso-ferric)

Gold

copper-gold auricalc- (auricalceous)
yellow-gold aur- (aurulent);
 chryso- (chrysography)

Gray

ash-gray tephr- (tephroite)
blue-gray caesi- (caesious)
dusky-gray phaeo- (phaeophyll);

-phaein (haemophaein); pheo-
 (pheochrome)
pale-gray polio- (poliomyelitis)
pearl-gray gris- (griseous)
silvery-gray glauco- (glaucodot)
white-gray can- (canescent)

Green

blue-green caes- (caesious); glauco-
 (glaucous)
dusky-green oliv- (olivaceous); oli-
 vaceo- (olivaceo-cinereous)
emerald-green smaragd- (smaragdine)
fresh-green thall- (thallium); -
 virid- (viridescence)
grass-green verd- (verdurous)
leek-green porrac- (porraceous);
 pras- (prasine)
light-green/blue beryl- (berylline)
sea-green thalass- (thalassine)
slightly-green vir- (virescence)
yellow-green chloro- (chlorophyl-
 lose)

Orange

fruit-orange auranti- (aurantiaceous)

Purple

bright-purple blatt- (blattean)
dark-purple porphyr- (porphyrin)
metallic purple indi- (indirubin);
 indo- (indophane)
red-purple amaranth- (amaranthine); phenic- (phenicine); -pun-
 (puniceous)
standard-purple purpureo- (pur-
 purescent)

Red

blood-red cruent- (cruentous)
brick-red later- (lateritious);
 testaceo- (testaceo-fuscous)

bright-red -rub- (rubicund)
brownish-red -ruf- (rufescent)
cinnabar-red minia- (miniaceous)
copper-red pyhrro- (pyrrhotite)
crimson-red carmino- (carmino-
   philous)
dark-red -rut- (rutilant)
deep-red grenat- (grenatite)
healthy-red -rud- (ruddy)
inflamed-red erysi- (erysipelatous)
orange-red nacar- (nacarine);
   pyrrho- (pyrrho-arsenite)
poppy-red coquel- (coquelicot)
purple-red erythro- (erythrean);
   murex- (murexide); phoeni-
   (phoeniceous)
rose-red rhodo- (rhodophyllose);
   roseo (roseo-cobaltic)
rouge-red fuc- (fucate)
rusty-red ferrug- (ferruginous)
scarlet-red coccin- (coccineous)
vermillion-red minia- (miniaceous)

Silver

blue-silver glauco- (glaucescent)
white-silver argyro- (argyranthe-
   mous)
white-silver argent(i)- (argenteous)

Tan

light-brown fulv- (fulvous)

Violet

metallic-violet indi- (indirubin);
   indo- (indophane)
purple-blue ianth- (ianthine); io-
   (iopterous); -viol- (violaceous)

White

intense-white cand- (candescent)
ivory-white ebur- (eburnine)
lead-white ceruss- (cerussal)
leathery-white alut- (alutaceous)
milk-white lac- (lacteous)
pale-white leuco- (leucous)
snow-white niv- (niveous)
standard-white alb- (albicant)
yellowish-white ochroleuc-
   (ochroleucous)

Yellow

bright-yellow gambog- (gambogian)
brown-yellow fulv- (fulvous); lur-
   (lurid); ochreo- (ochreous)
canary-yellow melin- (meline)
gold-yellow chryso- (chrysocrous)
greenish-yellow icter- (icterus);
   jaun- (jaundice)
honey-yellow helv- (helvine)
lemon-yellow citr- (citreous)
light-yellow xantho- (xanthous)
metallic-yellow aen- (aeneous)
orange-yellow safran- (safranin)
pale-yellow flav- (flavescent);
   flavido- (flavido-cinerascent);
   gilv- (gilvous); helv- (helvenac);
   lurido- (lurido-cinerascent);
   ochro- (ochrocarpous)
red-yellow luteo- (luteous)
saffron-yellow croce- (croceous)
yolk-yellow lut- (lutein); vitell-
   (vitelline)

DIMENSIONS

deep batho- (bathometer); bathy
(bathysphere)

gigantic bronto- (brontosaurus);
dino- (Dinotherium); giganto-
(gigantology); mega- (megalith);
megalo- (megalopolis); -megaly
(hepatomegaly); super- (super-
nova)

high acro- (acrophobia); alti-
(altimetry); alto- (altostratus);
hypsi- (hypsicephalic); hypso-
(hypsodont); super- (superstructure)

large ampl- (amplification); -fold
(hundredfold); grand- (grandi-
flora); macro- (macrocosm);
magni- (magnifying); maj-
(majority); maxi- (maximum);
plethys- (plethysmometry); super-
(supertanker)

long dolicho- (dolichocephalic);
-footer (ten-footer); longi- (longi-
caudate); macro- (macropterous);
maxi- (maxicoat); procer- (pro-
cercoid)

low chamae- (chamaerops); hypo-
(hypocaust); infero- (inferolateral); infra- (infrapatellar); sub-
(subway); subter- (subteraque-
ous); under- (underground)

narrow/thin angusti- (angustifoliate); areo- (areolation); dolicho-
(dolichocephalic); gracil-
(gracile); isthm- (isthmian);
lepto- (leptorrhine); phim- (phimosis); -stal- (staltic); stegno-
(stegnotic); steno- (stenosis);
-strict- (stricture); tenu- (tenu-
ity)

short brachisto- (brachistocephaly);
brachy- (brachypterous); brevi-
(abbreviation); chamae- (chamaerops); curt- (curtate); exig-[2]
(exiguous); mini- (minidrama)

small -cle (particle); -cule (molecule); -culum (curriculum);
-culuc (fasciculus); -een (colleen);
-el (satchel); -ella (umbrella); -en
(kitten); -et (rivulet); -ette (kitchenette); hekisto- (hekistotherm);
-idion (enchiridion); -idium
(peridium); -ie (laddie); -illa
(cedilla); -illo (cigarillo); -isk
(asterisk); -kin (lambkin); -le
(icicle); -let (ringlet); -ling (duckling); micro- (microcassette);
mini- (minibus); nano- (nanosecond); -ock (hillock); -ola (variola); -ole (variole); parvi- (parvi-
potent); parvo- (parvoline); -rel
(wastrel); -ula (fibula); -ule (ampule); -ulum (speculum); -ulus
(homunculus); -y (Billy)

thick cespitoso- (cespitoso-arbores-
cent); -crass- (crassitude); dasy-
(dasymeter); hadro- (hadrosaur);
pachy- (pachyderm); pycno- (pycnometer); pykn(o)- (pyknic);
spiss- (spissatus); visco- (viscos-
ity)

wide ampl- (amplitude); eury-
(eurygnathous); lati- (latisternal);
platy- (platypellic)

DIRECTIONS

away from, apart a-² (avert); ab-² (abduct); abs-² (abstruse); apo- (apogeotropism); be- (bereave); de- (deplane); des- (descant); di-² (divest); dia- (diagnose); dif- (differ); dis-¹ (dismiss); e- (emigrate); ec- (ecdemic); ectro- (ectrotic); ef- (efferent); ex- (expatriate); for- (forgo); off-¹ (offload); se- (separate); with- (withdraw)

backward retro- (retroversion); opiso- (opisometer)

down a-² (abate); ab-² (abdicate); abs-² (abscond); cata- (catacomb); cath- (cathepsin); de- (decumbent); kata- (katabatic)

east euro- (euroboreal); orient- (orienteering)

forward antero- (antero-frontal); fore- (foredeck); pre- (preaxial); pro-¹ (projection); proso- (prosogaster)

into eis- (eisegesis); em-¹ (emigrate); en-¹ (entomb); il- (illuminate); im- (immerse); in- (instill); ir- (irradiate)

left laeo- (laeotropic); laevo- (laevogyrate); levo- (levorotatory); sinistro- (sinistrocular)

north borea- (boreal); septen- (septentrion)

out of e- (eject); ec- (eccentric); ef- (effluence); ex- (expulsion)

right dexio- (dexiotropic); dextro- (dextrorotatory)

south austr- (Austronesia); noto- (notothere)

toward a-¹ (ascribe); ac- (acclaim); ad- (advance); -ad (dorsad); af- (affirm); ag- (aggrade); al- (allege); an- (announce); ap- (approve); ar- (arrive); as- (assent); at- (attrition); -bound (eastbound); il- (illuminate); im- (impel); in- (inboard); ir- (irrigate); -ly (northerly); ob- (object); -ward (outward)

up ana- (anabatic); ano- (anoopsia); ex- (extol); super- (superscript); sur- (surmount);

west hesper- (hesperian); occid- (occident); zephyr- (zephyrean)

DIVINATION

To extract the root which shows the method being used, simply drop the
*-**mancy**, which signifies telling the future.*

air *blowing or moving:* aeromancy; *visions in the sky:* chaomancy

angels angelomancy

animals *behavior:* zoomancy; *movement:* theriomancy

appearance or form of a person schematomancy

arrows with incised marks or words belomancy

ashes cineromancy, spodomancy; *~of a sacrifice:* tephromancy

ass head, boiled cephalonamancy

ax (balanced on a bar) axinomancy

barley meal alphitomancy

basin of water lecanomancy

Bible verses (randomly selected) bibliomancy

birds ornithomancy; ornomancy

blood hematomancy; *~dripping in patterns:* dririmancy

bones osteomancy, osteomanty; *~marked as dice:* astragalomancy

bowl of water cylicomancy, kylixomancy

brass vessels (sound of) chalcomancy

breastbone sternomancy

bubbles rising in a fountain pegomancy

cake dough (sprinkled on sacrificial victim) crithomancy

candles (blowing them out) pneumancy

cards cartomancy, chartomancy

cat (jumping and landing) ailuromancy, felidomancy

cheese (patterns of coagulation) tyromancy

cloud formations chaomancy

coals (burning) anthracomancy

contour of the land topomancy

counting mathemancy

crystal gazing crystallomancy; spheromancy

cup scyphomancy

dead people (communication with) egromancy, necromancy, necyomancy, psychomancy, sciamancy, sciomancy, thanatomancy

devil or demons demonomancy, necyomancy

dice (or beans with points or marks on them) astragalomancy, cleromancy, cubomancy

digging things up oryctomancy

dirt (thrown on ground to produce patterns) geomancy

dots or points (drawn at random, originally on the ground) geomancy

dreams oneiromancy, sompnary

dust amathomancy

eggs oomancy, ovomancy

embryonic sac amniomancy

entrails of a human anthropomancy, splanchnomancy

evil spirits demonomancy, necyomancy

false divination pseudomancy

feces (examination of) scatomancy, spatilomancy, stercomancy

feet (soles of) paedomancy, pedomancy

figs or fig leaves botanomancy, sycomancy

fingernails onychomancy

fire empyromancy, pyromancy

fish (examining heads or entrails) icthyomancy

flour aleuromancy

flowers anthomancy

foolish divination moromantie

footsteps ichnomancy

forehead wrinkles metopomancy

fountain pegomancy

glass vessels (figures appearing in) gastromancy

gods (speaking through oracles) theomancy

handwriting chartomancy, graptomancy

hatchet axinomancy

head cephalomancy

heavens ouranomancy, uranomancy

horses (neighing) hippomancy

human features and form collimancy, frontimancy, metopomancy, physiognomancy, schematomancy

icons iconomancy

idols idolomancy

incense burning knissomancy, libanomancy

key cleidomancy, clidomancy
kidneys nephromancy
lamp or torch flame lampadomancy, lychnomancy
largest object nearby macro-
mancy
laughter gelomancy
laurel tree or leaves daphnomancy
lead, molten (motions and figures
in) molybdomancy
leaves phyllomancy; *tea~:* folio-
mancy, theimancy
letters (of a person's name) nomancy, onomancy, onomato-
mancy, onomomancy
lines *on the forehead:* frontimancy,
metopomancy; *on the ground:*
geomancy; *on the neck:* collimancy; *on the palms:* cheiromancy, chiromancy; *on the soles:*
paedomancy, pedomancy
lip reading labiomancy
logarithms logarithmomancy
lots cleromancy
Lucifer necyomancy
magic magastromancy
meteors meteoromancy
mice movements myomancy
mirrors catoptromancy, enoptromancy
molten lead (dropped on water)
molybdomancy
moon selenomancy
names (including number of letters
in) nomancy, onomancy, ono-
matomancy
neck wrinkles collimancy
numbers arithmancy, arithmo-
mancy
nursing baby (choice of breast)
mazomancy
objects offered in sacrifice hieromancy
onions cromniomancy, cromnyo-
mancy

oracle's rapturous statements
chresmomancy, theomancy
palm reading cheiromancy, chiromancy
paper (written on) chartomancy
pearls margaritomancy
pebbles pessomancy, psephomancy
plants botanomancy, floromancy
playing cards cartomancy
pointed objects aichmomancy
posture ichnomancy
random lines or passages of books
stichomancy
rings dactyliomancy, dactylomancy
rod rabdomancy, rhabdomancy
rooster (choosing grains of corn)
alectoromancy, alectryomancy
sacred objects, sacrificial offerings
hieromancy
sage botanomancy
salt alomancy, halomancy
secret means cryptomancy
serpents ophiomancy
sheep (shoulder blade) spatulamancy
shells conchomancy
shield aspidomancy
shoulder blades (charred or
cracked) armomancy, omo-
platoscopy, scapulimancy; *~of
sheep:* spatulamancy
sieve (suspended on shears) coscinomancy
sleep meconomancy
smallest object nearby micromancy
smoke (ascent and motion) capnomancy
snakes ophiomancy
soles of feet (lines on) paedomancy,
pedomancy
soul (emotional and ethical disposi-
tions) psychomancy, thumomancy
spinning (in a marked circle until
dropping) gyromancy

spots maculomancy
spring of water pegomancy
stars astromancy, sideromancy, uranomancy
sticks or wands rhabdomancy, xylomancy
stomach rumblings gastromancy
stones (or stone charms) lithomancy
stranger (studying the first one to appear) xenomancy
straws (burning) sideromancy
sword machaeromancy
teeth odontomancy
things seen over one's shoulder retromancy
thunder brontomancy, ceraunomancy
tide (motion and appearance) hydromancy
time chronomancy
tongue hyomancy
torch flame lampadomancy, lychnomancy
tree bark (writing on) stigonomancy
twitching limbs spasmatomancy, spasmodomancy

umbilical cord (number of knots in) omphalomancy
urine ouromancy, urimancy, urinomancy, uromancy
verses or poems rhapsodomancy
walking ambulomancy
wand rhabdomancy
water hydromancy, ydromancy; *~in a basin or shallow bowl:* cylicomancy, kylixomancy, lecanomancy; *~fountain or spring:* pegomancy
wax (melted and dropped in water) ceromancy
weather aeromancy, meteoromancy
weights zygomancy
wheel tracks trochomancy
wild animals theriomancy
wind (observation of) aeromancy, austromancy
wine (its color, sound, etc. when poured) oenomancy, oinomancy
wood (pieces of) xylomancy
words logomancy
writing *on bark of a tree:* stigonomancy; *on paper:* chartomancy

THE ENVIRONMENT

NOTE: For mammals, birds, insects, and fish, see "Animals" in this section.

air aer- (aerate); aeri- (aeriferous); aero- (aerobic); anemo- (anemometer); atmo- (atmosphere); flat- (flatulent); physo- (physometra)
ash tree fraxin- (fraxinella); melia- (meliaceous)
atmosphere -bar (isobar); baro- (barometric)

beach littor- (littoral); thino- (thinolite)
beech faga- (fagaceous)
birch betul- (betulaceous)
blooming flor- (floriferous); thalero- (thalerophagous); vig- (vigorous)
bog telmat- (telmatology); turbar- (turbarian)

box-tree bux- (buxiferous)
branch clado- (cladophyll); rami-
  (ramify)
buckthorn rhamn- (rhamneous)
bud gemm-¹ (gemmate)
bug cimic- (cimicoid); entomo-
  (entomology); insecti- (insecticide); insecto- (insectology). *Also
  see* "Animals" in Part III
carbon dioxide -capnia (acapnia);
  capno- (capnomancy)
cedar cedr- (cedrine)
celestial activity astro- (astronomy)
chasm vorag- (voraginous)
clay argillaceo- (arenaceo-argillaceous); argillo- (argillo-calcareous); limo- (limo-cretaceous);
  pelo- (pelophilous)
cloud fracto- (fracto-stratus);
  homichlo- (homichlophobia);
  mammato- (mammato-cumulus);
  nebul- (nebulous); nephelo-
  (nephelometer); nepho- (nephology); nubi- (nubiferous)
coal anthraco- (anthracomancy);
  carb- (carbonize)
coast littor- (littoral); maritim-
  (maritime)
cold alg- (algid); cheima- (cheimaphilic); crymo- (crymophilic);
  cryo- (cryogenics); frigo- (frigorific); gel- (regelation); kryo-
  (kryometer); pago- (pagophagia);
  psychro (psychrometer); rhigo-
  (rhigosis)
continent epeiro- (epeirogenic)
cone, pine strobil- (strobiliform)
copper auricalc- (auricalceous);
  chalco- (chalcocite); cupreo-
  (cupreo-violaceous); cupri-
  (cupriferous); cupro- (cupromagnesite); cuproso- (cuproso-ferric)
coral coralli- (corallidomous)
country *rural:* rur- (ruralize); rus-
  tic- (rusticity); *nation:* -ese

(Japanese); -ia (India); -ian (Syrian); -land (Ireland)
crater crateri- (crateriform)
cypress cupress- (cupressineous)
darkness achlu- (achluophobia);
  amaur- (amaurosis); ambly- (amblyopia); crepus- (crepuscular);
  fusc- (fuscous); lyg- (lygaeid);
  melan- (melatonin); nyct- (nyctitropic); obscur- (obscurity);
  tenebr- (tenebrous)
dawn auror- (auroral); eo- (eosophobia)
day diurn- (diurnal); ephem-
  (ephemeris); hemer- (monohemerous); hodiern- (hodiernal);
  journ- (journal); quotid- (quotidian)
decomposing enzyme -ase (amylase)
desert eremo- (eremophyte)
dry arid- (aridity); carpho-
  (carphology); celo- (celosia); sicc-
  (desiccate); xero- (xerophyte)
dust amath- (amathophobia); coni-
  (coniosis); -conia (fibroconia);
  conio- (coniofibrosis); conist-
  (conistery); konio- (koniosis);
  pulver- (pulverize)
earth agro- (agronomy); -gaea (Paleogaea); geo- (geocentric); hum-
  (inhumation); secul- (secular);
  tellur- (intratelluric); terr- (ter-
  restrial); *~quake:* seismo- (seis-
  mograph); tromo-(tromometry)
elm ulm- (ulmaceous)
environment eco- (ecology); oeco-
  (oecology); oiko- (oikofugic)
evening crepus- (crepuscule); nocti-
  (noctilucent); nycto- (nyctophobia); vesper- (vespertine)
fall autumn- (autumnal)
fern filic- (filiciform); pterido-
  (pteridology)
fir abiet- (abietic)

flax byssi- (byssinosis)
flood antlo- (antlophobia); diluv-
(diluvial); inund- (inundation)
flora -phyte (microphyte); phyto-
(phytogenesis)
flower antho- (anthomania); -an-
thous (monanthous); flori-
(floriferous); -florous (multiflorous)
fog calig- (caliginous); homichlo-
(homichlophobia); nebul- (nebulous); nephelo- (nephelological);
nepho- (nephology); nubi- (nubiform)
forest arbor- (arboreal); dendri-
(dendritic); dendro- (dendrophilous); -dendron (rhododendron);
hylaeo- (hylaeosaurus); nemor-
(nemoricole); saltu- (saltuary);
silvi- (silviculture); sylv- (sylvan);
xylo- (xylophage)
fountain cren- (crenic); pego-
(pegomancy)
foxglove digito- (digitalis)
frost cryo- (cryophyte); gel-
(gelid); kryo- (kryometer);
pachno- (pacnolite); pago- (pagophagia); pruin- (pruinose); rhigo-
(rhigolene)
fungus fungi- (fungicide); -mycete
(schizomycete); myceto- (mycetoma); -mycin (streptomycin);
myco- (mycology); uredo- (ure-
dospore)
garden horti- (horticultural)
glacier glacio- (glaciologist)
granite graniti- (granitiform)
grass gramin- (graminivorous)
hawthorn crataeg- (crataegin)
holly ilic- (ilicic)
hot aestu- (exaestuating); cale-
(caleficient); calo- (caloreceptor);
caum-; (caumesthesia) calori-
(calorimetry); ferv- (effervesce);
pyro- (pyromania); thermo-

(thermonuclear); -thermy
(diathermy)
hurricane lilaps- (lilapsophobia)
ice gel- (gelation); glacio- (glacio-
logical); pago- (pagophagia); icicle: stiri- (stiriated)
island insul- (insular)
isthmus isthm- (isthmian)
ivy heder- (hederated)
lake lacus- (lacustrine); limno-
(limnologist)
land agri- (agrichemical); agro-
(agrology); choro- (chorography);
geo- (geothermal); tellur- (telluric); terr- (subterranean)
larch larix- (larixinic)
laurel daphn- (daphmomancy)
leaf bract- (bracteate); clad-
(cladanthous); foliato- (foliation);
-folious (multifolious); frondi-
(frondescence); petalo- (petalody);
-phyll (sporophyll); phyllo- (phyl-
lomania); -phyllous (diphyllous)
lettuce lactuc- (lactucarium)
lightning astra- (astraphobia); ful-
gur- (fulgurant); fulmin- (fulmination)
lily lili- (liliform); lirio- (liriodoen-
dron)
linden tilia- (tiliaceous)
maple acer- (aceric)
marble marm- (marmoreal)
marsh helo- (helobius); palud-
(paludicolous); palus- (palustrine); ulig- (uliginous)
meadow prat- (pratal)
meteorological front fronto- (frontogenesis)
mineral -ite (anthracite); -lite
(chrysolite)
mist calig- (caliginous); homichlo-
(homichlophobia); nebul- (nebulous); nephelo- (nephelological);
nepho- (nephology); nubi- (nubiform)

mistletoe ixo- (ixolite)

moisture humect- (humectant); hydro- (hydrobiology); hygro- (hygrophyte); ulig- (uliginose)

moon luni- (lunisolar); lunu- (lunulate); seleno- (selenodesy)

moss bryo- (bryophytic), musc- (emuscation); sphagn- (sphagnous); splachn- (splachnoid)

mountain mont- (ultramontane); oro- (orogeny); ~ash: sorb- (sorbose)

mud lim- (limivorous); pelo- (peloid)

mulberry mor- (moriform); mur- (muriform)

mushroom myco- (mycotoxin)

myrtle myrti- (myrtiform)

nettle cnido- (cnidophore); urtic- (urticaceous)

night -crepus- (crepuscule); nocti- (noctiluca); nycta- (nyctalopia); nycti- (nyctitropism); nycto- (nyctophobia); vesper- (vespertilionine); all~: -pannychy (psychpannychy)

oak querc- (quercitron)

ocean enalio- (enaliosaur); halo- (halosaurian); mari- (mariculture); naut- (nautical); nav- (navigation); pelag- (archipelago); thalasso- (thalassocracy); thalatto- (thalattology)

orchid orchido- (orchidology)

oxygen oxa- (oxazine); oxy- (oxyacid)

ozone ozono- (ozonosphere)

peat bog turbar- (turbary)

pebble calcul- (calculous); pesso- (pessomancy); psepho- (psephology)

peninsula cherson- (chersonese)

petal petuli- (petuliform); -sepalous (trisepalous)

pine -peuce (peucedaneous); pin- (pinaceous); ~cone: strobil- (strobiliform)

plants -aceae (Rosaceae); -ad (cycad); -ales (Liliales); botano- (botanomancy); -eae (Gramineae); herbi- (herbicidal); -ia (zinnia); -phyte (macrophyte); phyto- (phytography); vegeti- (vegetivorous); vegeto- (vegetoalkaline)

pollen pollini- (pollinosis)

pond lacus (lacuscular); limno- (limnophilous); stagn- (stagnal)

poppy mecon- (meconidine); opio- (opiomania); papaver- (papaverous)

precipice cremno- (cremnophobia)

purslain portulac- (portulaceous)

pyrites pyrito- (pyritohedron)

quicksand syrt- (syrtic)

radiant emissions aurora- (aurora australis)

rain hyeto- (hyetograph); imbri- (imbriferous); ombro- (ombrometer); pluvio- (pluviograph)

reservoir lacco- (laccolite)

river amn- (amnicolist); flum- (fluminal); fluvio- (fluvio-terrestrial); potamo- (potamologist); rip- (riparian)

rock -ite (anthracite); lapid- (lapidary); -lithic (neolithic); litho- (lithotomy); pesso- (pessomancy); petri- (petrification); petro- (petroglyph); rupes- (rupestrine); rupic- (rupicolous); saxi- (saxifrage)

rose rhodo- (rhodochrosite); roseo- (roseola)

rue rut- (rutaceous)

sand ammo- (ammocete); aren- (arenicolous); arenacio- (arenacio-argillaceous); psammo- (psammophilous); sabul- (sabulosity); saburr- (saburration)

sea enalio- (enaliosaur); halo- (halosaurian); mari- (mariculture); naut- (nautical); nav- (navigation); pelag- (archipelago); thalasso- (thalassocracy); thalatto- (thalattology); ~*shore:* thino- (thinolite)

seasons horo- (horology); *fall:* autumn- (autumnal); *spring:* vern- (vernal); *summer:* aestiv- (aestival); *winter:* hibern- (hibernal); hiem- (hiemal)

seaweed fuc- (fucivorous); phyceae- (Rhodophyceae); -phyceous (Rhodophyceous); phyco- (phycology)

shell conchi- (conchiferous); lorica- (illoricated); -ostraca (Leptostraca); ostraco- (ostracoderm); testaceo- (testaceology)

shore littor- (littoral)

shrub fruticuloso- (fruticuloso-ramose)

sky coeli- (coelicolist)

snow chion- (chionodoxa); -chium (hedychium); ning- (ninguid); niv- (niveous)

soil agro- (agronomy); edaph- (edaphic); hum- (exhumation); paedo- (paedogenic); pedo- (pedology); terr- (terrarium)

spring of water cren-^{2} (crenic); pego- (pegomancy)

star aster- (asteraceous); astro- (astonomy); -sidere (hagiosidere); sidero- (siderostat); stelli- (stelliferous)

stone -ite (anthracite); lapid- (lapidary); -lithic (neolithic); litho- (lithotomy); pesso- (pessomancy); petri- (petrification); petro- (petroglyph); rupes- (rupestrine); rupic- (rupicolous); saxi- (saxifrage)

straw carpho- (carphology); culmi- (culmicolous); festuc- (festucine); stramin- (stramineous)

stream fluvio- (fluviomarine); potam- (potamoplankton); rip- (riparian)

sun helio- (heliotropic); sol- (solarium)

swamp palud- (paludism); palus- (palustrine)

tendril cirri- (cirrigerous); cirro- (cirro-pinnate); pampin- (pampiniform)

thunder bronte- (bronteon); bronto- (brontology); cerauno- (ceraunoscope); fulmin- (fulminic); kerauno- (keraunograph); tonitr- (tonitrual)

tornado lilaps- (lilapsophobia)

tree arbor- (arboreal); dendri- (dendritic); dendro- (dendrophilous); -dendron (rhododendron); silvi- (silviculture); xylo- (xylophage)

twigs ramul- (ramulose); sarment- (sarmentaceous); scopi- (scopiform); surcul- (surculose); virgul- (virgulation)

twilight crepus- (crepuscular); lyg- (lygaeid)

universe -cosm (macrocosm); cosmo- (cosmology)

vegetation -aceae (Rosaceae); -ad (cycad); -ales (Liliales); botano- (botanomancy); -eae (Gramineae); herbi- (herbicidal); -ia (zinnia); -phyte (macrophyte); phyto- (phytography); vegeti- (vegetivorous); vegeto- (vegeto-alkaline)

vine ampel- (ampelopsis); pampin- (pampiniform); viti- (viticulture)

water aqua- (aquatic); aque- (aqueduct); aqui- (aquiclude); hydro- (hydrophilous); hyeto- (hyetology); hygro- (hygrometry); rip- (riparian)

weed runc- (runcation)
well phreato- (phreatic); putea-
(puteal)
whirlpool vorag- (voraginous)
willow itea- (iteatic); salic- (salicaceous)
wind anemo- (anemometer); vent-
(ventilation); **north~:** -borea (boreal); **south~:** austro- (austromancy); **west~:** zephyro- (zephyranth); favon- (favonian)
wood erio- (eriometer); hyle-
(hylephobia); hylo- (hylopha-

gous); ligni- (lignivorous); ligno-
(lignoceric); xylo- (xylophage);
-xylous (epixylous); ylo- (ylo-
mancy)
woods nemor- (nemoricole); saltu-
(saltuary); silv- (silvics); sylv-
(sylvan)
world -cosm (macrocosm); cosmo-
(cosmography); -gaea (Paleogaea); mund- (mundane); secul-
(secular); tellur- (telluric); terr-
(terrain)
yew tax- (taxaceous)

FEAR OR DISLIKE OF...

To extract the word part, simply drop "phobia" from each word.

abuse, sexual contreltophobia
accidents dystichiphobia
acid soils acidophobia
acorns balanophobia
aging gerascophobia
air aerophobia, anemophobia,
pneumatophobia
airplanes aeronautophobia, aerophobia, aviatophobia, avionophobia, aviophobia
airsickness aeronausiphobia
alkaline soils basiphobia, basophobia
alligators eusuchophobia
amnesia amensiophobia, amnesi-
phobia
ancestors patroiophobia
anger cholerophobia
angina anginophobia
animals zoophobia; **wild~:** agrizoophobia, theriophobia
ants myrmecophobia
arts and crafts technophobia

ashes of cremation spodophobia
asymmetry asymmetriphobia
atomic explosions atomosophobia
bacteria bacteriophobia, microbio-
phobia
baldness peladophobia, phalacrophobia
banners/bumper stickers vexillo-
phobia
base or low pursuits tapinophobia
bats desmodontophobia, pteropo-
phobia
beaches thinophobia
beards pogonophobia
bears arctophobia
beds clinophobia
bees apiophobia, apiphobia,
melissophobia
beggars/street people ptocho-
phobia
being afraid phobophobia
being alone autophobia, monophobia, eremophobia

being beaten rhabdophobia, vapulophobia
being beautiful callophobia
being bound merinthophobia
being buried alive taphephobia, taphophobia
being burned caustophobia
being clean balneophobia
being contagious tapinophobia
being dirty automysophobia
being pinched rrhexophobia
being ridiculed catagelophobia
being scolded enissophobia
being scratched amychophobia
being shot ballistophobia
being stared at ophthalmophobia, scopophobia, scoptophobia
bicycles cyclophobia
birds ornithophobia
Blacks negrophobia
blindness scotomaphobia, typhlophobia
blood haemaphobia, hemaphobia, hematophobia, hemophobia
blushing ereuthophobia, erythrophobia, erytophobia
boasting kompophobia
boats scaphophobia
body odor autodysosmophobia, bromidrosiphobia
bogs telmatophobia
books bibliophobia
boozing dipsophobia
breasts, developing mastophobia
bridges gephyrophobia
brothers adelphophobia
buffoons balatrophobia
bulls taurophobia
buttocks pygophobia
buzzards buteophobia
cancer carcinophobia, carcinomatophobia
cars ochophobia; *riding in~:* amaxophobia
cattle boustrophobia

cats aelurophobia, ailurophobia, elurophobia, felinophobia, galeophobia, gatophobia
caves speleophobia
Celts Celtophobia
cemeteries coimetrophobia
changes tropophobia, metathesiophobia
chatter, meaningless garrulophobia
chemicals chemophobia
chickens alektorophobia
childbirth lochiophobia, maieusiophobia, parturiphobia, tocophobia
children pediophobia, pedophobia
China/the Chinese Sinophobia
chins geniophobia
choking pnigerophobia, pnigophobia
cholera cholerophobia
churches ecclesiaphobia
clergy hierophobia
clocks/watches chronometrophobia
closed spaces claustrophobia, cleisiophobia, cleithrophobia, clithrophobia
clothes vestiphobia, vestiophobia
clouds nephophobia
cockroaches blattophobia
coitus coitophobia
cold cheimaphobia, cheimatophobia, frigophobia, psychrophobia, psychropophobia
colors chromatophobia, chromophobia; *black:* melanophobia; *blue:* caerulophobia; *brown:* fuscophobia; *copper:* chalcophobia; *gold:* aureophobia; *gray:* phaeophobia; *green:* verdophobia; *orange:* aurantiphobia; *purple:* porphyrophobia; *red:* erythrophobia; *silver:* argentophobia; *tan:* fulvophobia; *violet:* indophobia; *white:* leukophobia; *yellow:* xanthophobia

comets cometophobia
commitment zygophobia
computers cyberphobia, computer-
phobia
constipation coprostasophobia
cooking mageiricophobia
corpse necrophobia
crevices chasmophobia
criticism enissophobia
critics criticophobia
cross or crucifix staurophobia
crossing a bridge gephyrophobia
crossing busy streets agylophobia,
agyrophobia, dromophobia
crowds demophobia, enochlo-
phobia, ochlophobia
crystals crystallophobia
cyclones anemophobia
dampness hygrophobia
dancing choreophobia, choropho-
bia, orchestrophobia
darkness achluophobia, lygopho-
bia, nyctophobia, scotophobia
dawn eosophobia
daylight phengophobia
death necrophobia, thanatophobia
decaying matter pythophobia, septophobia
defecation, painful defecalgesio-
phobia
deformity dysmorphophobia
demons and devils daemono-
phobia, demonophobia, necyo-
phobia
dental work dentophobia, odontophobia
dependence soteriophobia
depth bathophobia
design or ultimate ends teleophobia
diabetes diabetophobia
dinner parties deipnophobia
dirt misophobia, molysmophobia,
mysophobia, rhypophobia
disease loimophobia, nosophobia,

pathophobia; *specific~:* monopathophobia
disorder ataxiophobia, ataxophobia
dizziness dinophobia, vertigopho-
bia
doctors iatrophobia
dogs cynophobia, kynophobia
dolls paedophobia, pediophobia,
pedophobia,
double vision diplopiaphobia,
diplophobia
drafts aerophobia, anemophobia
dreams oneirophobia
drink alcoholophobia, dipso-
manophobia, methyphobia, poto-
phobia
drugs pharmacophobia
dryness xerophobia
duration chronophobia
dust amathophobia, koniophobia;
dusty surfaces: conistrophobia
dwarfs nanophobia
earthquakes seismophobia
eating phagophobia
eels anguillophobia
electricity electrophobia
emotions thymophobia
empty rooms cenophobia, kenophobia
England/the English Anglophobia
erection *maintaining:* ithyphallophobia; *loss of:* medomalaco-
phobia
everything panophobia, panphobia,
pantaphobia, pantophobia
excrement coprophobia, koprophobia, scatophobia
exhaustion kopophobia
experimenting peirophobia
eyes ommatophobia, ommetapho-
bia; *~opening:* optophobia
fabrics textophobia
faces prosopophobia
failure atychiphobia, kakorraphia-

phobia, kakorraphiophobia, kakorrhaphiophobia
fainting asthenophobia
falling basophobia
falling downstairs climacophobia
falling in love philophobia
fat lipophobia, obesiophobia
father-in-law soceraphobia
Fathers of the early church paterophobia
fatigue kopophobia, ponophobia
fear phobophobia
feathers pteronophobia
feces coprophobia, koprophobia, scatophobia
fever febriphobia, pyrexeophobia, pyrexiophobia
fighting machophobia
filth rhypophobia, rypophobia, rupophobia
fire arsonophobia, pyrophobia
fish ichthyophobia
flashes selaphobia
flatulence physaphobia
flood antlophobia
flowers anthophobia
flute aulophobia
flying aeronautophobia, aerophobia, aviatophobia, avionophobia, aviophobia
fog homichlophobia, nebulaphobia, nephophobia
food cibophobia, sitiophobia, sitophobia,
foreigners xenophobia
foreplay malaxophobia, paizophobia, sarmassophobia
forests hylephobia, hylophobia, xylophobia, ylophobia
fountains pegophobia
France/the French Francophobia, Gallophobia
freedom eleutherophobia
French kissing cataglottophobia
friendship sociophobia

frogs batrachophobia
frost cryophobia, pagophobia, rhigophobia
fun cherophobia
funeral rites epicidiophobia, threnatophobia
fur doraphobia
gambling aleaphobia
garlic alliumphobia, scorophobia
gay people homophobia
genitals: genitophobia; *female~:* colpophobia, eurotophobia, kolpophobia; *male~:* phallophobia
Germany/the Germans Germanophobia, Teutophobia, Teutonophobia
germs bacillophobia, bacteriophobia, spermophobia
ghosts phantasmophobia, phasmophobia, spectrophobia
glass crystallophobia, hyalophobia, hyelophobia, vitreophobia
God deiphobia, theophobia
going to bed clinophobia
gold aurophobia
good news euphobia
graves taphophobia
gravity barophobia
Greece/the Greeks Grecophobia, Hellenophobia
growing old gerascophobia, gerontophobia
hair chaetophobia, trichophobia; *curly~:* ulophobia; *~disease:* trichopathophobia; *excessive~:* hypertrichophobia
Halloween Samhainophobia
happiness cherophobia
heart attack or disease anginophobia, cardiophobia
heat thermophobia
heaven ouranophobia, uranophobia
heights: *looking down:* acrophobia, altophobia, batophobia, hypsi-

phobia, hypsophobia; *looking up:* anablephobia, anablepophobia
hell Avernophobia, Hadephobia, stygiophobia
heredity patroiophobia
heresy heresiophobia
holy things hagiophobia, hierophobia
home and environment domatophobia, ecophobia, oecophobia, oikophobia; *returning~:* nostophobia
homosexuals homophobia
hornets vespiphobia
horses equinophobia, hippophobia
hospitals nosocomephobia
human beings anthropophobia
hurricanes lilapsophobia
hydrophobia hydrophobophobia
hypnotism hypnophobia, mesmerophobia
ice cryophobia, gelophobia
ideas gnotophobia, ideophobia
illness nosophobia, pathophobia; *specific~:* monopathophobia; *wasting~:* tabophobia
immobility of a joint ankylophobia
imperfection atelophobia
inability to stand basiphobia, basophobia
infection molysmophobia, mysophobia, septophobia
infinity apeirophobia
injections trypanophobia
injury traumatophobia
insanity dementophobia, lyssophobia, maniaphobia
insects acarophobia, entomophobia, insectophobia, isopterophobia; *stinging~:* cnidophobia
Ireland/the Irish Celtophobia, Hibernophobia
irrational destruction atephobia
isolation eremophobia
Italy/Italians Italophobia

itching acarophobia, scabiophobia
Japan/the Japanese Japanophobia
jealousy zelophobia
Jews Judaeophobia, Judeophobia, Judophobia
jumping catapedaphobia
justice dikephobia
kidney disease albuminurophobia
killing dacnophobia
kissing philemaphobia, philematophobia; *tongue~:* cataglottophobia
kleptomania kleptophobia
knees genuphobia
knowledge epistemophobia, gnosiophobia
lacerations sparassophobia
ladders scalaphobia
lakes limnophobia
large objects megalophobia
laughter gelophobia
lawsuits litigaphobia
learning sophophobia
left side levophobia, sinistrophobia
leprosy lepraphobia, leprophobia
lice pediculophobia, phthiriophobia
light phengophobia, photophobia; *glaring~:* photoaugiaphobia, photoaugiophobia
lightning astraphobia, astrapophobia
liquids aquaphobia, hygrophobia
lizards stelliophobia
lobsters homariphobia
lockjaw tetanophobia
loneliness eremiphobia, eremophobia
long waits macrophobia
loud noise ligyrophobia
love philophobia
lying mythophobia
machines mechanophobia
many things polyphobia
marriage gametophobia, gamophobia, nuptophobia

materialism hylephobia
meat carnophobia, kreophobia
medicine pharmacophobia
meeting people anthropophobia
memories mnemophobia, nostophobia
men androphobia, arrhenophobia
meningitis meningitophobia
menstruation menophobia
metals metallophobia
meteors meteorophobia
mice muriphobia, murophobia,
   myosophobia
microbes bacilliphobia, microbio-
   phobia, microphobia
milk galactophobia
mind psychophobia
mirrors catoptrophobia, eisoptro-
   phobia, spectrophobia
missiles ballistophobia
mistletoe ixophobia
mites acarophobia
moisture hygrophobia
money chrematophobia
monotony homophobia
monstrosities teratophobia
moon selenophobia
mornings matutinophobia
mortality thriptophobia
mother-in-law pentheraphobia
moths phalaenophobia
motion kinesophobia, kinetophobia
motor vehicles motorphobia
mountains orophobia
mummies mummiphobia
mushrooms mycophobia
music melophobia, musicophobia
myths mythophobia
names nomatophobia, onomatophobia
narcotics lethophobia, meconopho-
   bia
narrowness anginaphobia, steno-
   phobia
navels omphalophobia

needles aichmophobia, belonophobia
neglect of duty paralipophobia
new things cainophobia, cainotophobia, cenotophobia, kainopho-
   bia, kainotophobia, neophobia
night noctiphobia, nyctophobia
nipples, being seen through clothing thelophobia
nocturnal emissions oneirogmo-
   phobia
noise acousticophobia, ligyrophobia, phonophobia
Northern lights auroraphobia
nosebleeds epistaxiophobia
nuclear weapons nucleomitophobia
nudity gymnophobia, nudiphobia,
   nudophobia
numbers arithmophobia, numero-
   phobia; *uneven~*: perissophobia
nurses threpterophobia
nutritional food threptophobia
oceans thalassophobia
odors olfactophobia, ophresiopho-
   bia, osmophobia, osphresiophobia; *foul~*: bromidrophobia, bromidrosiphobia
old people gerontophobia
one thing monophobia
oneself autophobia
open spaces agoraphobia, cenophobia, kenophobia; *high~*: aeroacro-
   phobia
opinions of others allodoxaphobia
opposite sex heterophobia
otters lutraphobia
owls strigiphobia
pain algiaphobia, algophobia,
   odynephobia, odynophobia,
   ponophobia; *from light sensitiv-
   ity:* photaugiaphobia, photaugio-
   phobia
pairs didymophobia
paper papyrophobia
parasites parasitophobia, pothirio-

phobia, trypanophobia, verminophobia
parents-in-law soceraphobia
peace eirenophobia
peanut butter arachibutyrophobia
pellagra pellagrophobia
penis: peophobia; *erect~:* ithyphallophobia, medorthophobia; *visible contour of~:* medectophobia
people anthropophobia, demophobia
perfume myrophobia
philosophy philosophobia
physical love erotophobia
places topophobia
planning for the future teleophobia
plants botanophobia
pleasure hedonophobia
poetry metrophobia, musophobia
pointed objects aichmophobia, aichurophobia
poison iophobia, toxicophobia, toxiphobia, toxophobia
politicians politicophobia
pollen palynophobia
popes papaphobia
poverty peniaphobia
precipices cremnophobia
pregnancy maieusiophobia, tocophobia
prickly objects echinophobia
progress prosophobia
propriety orthophobia
prostitutes cyprianophobia, cypridophobia, cypriphobia, cyprinophobia, scortophobia
public places agoraphobia
public speaking glossophobia
pumpkins, especially jack-o'-lanterns pepophobia
punishment mastigophobia, poinephobia, rhabdophobia
puppets pupaphobia
purposive effort hormephobia
pus pyophobia

quarrels rixophobia
quicksand syrtophobia
rabies hydrophobophobia, lyssophobia
railways siderodromophobia
rain hyetophobia, ombrophobia, pluviophobia
rape stupraphobia, virgivitiphobia
rattlesnakes crotalophobia
razors xyrophobia
rectal disease proctophobia, rectophobia
referring to oneself autophoby
relatives syngenesophobia
religion theophobia
religious ceremonies teletophobia
reproach enissophobia, enisiophobia
responsibility hypegiaphobia, hypengyophobia, paralipophobia
reptiles batrachophobia, herpetophobia
ridicule catagelophobia, katagelophobia
riding in a car amaxophobia
right side dextrophobia
rivers potamophobia
robbers harpaxophobia
room full of people koinoniphobia
ruin atephobia
Russia/the Russians Russophobia
rust iophobia, rubigophobia
sacred things hagiophobia, hierophobia
sadness lypephobia
saints hagiophobia
salt halophobia
sand psammophobia
Satan Satanophobia
sausage allantophobia
scabies scabiophobia
scarring ulophobia
school didaskaleinophobia, scholionophobia
scissors forficophobia

scotomas scotomaphobia
scratches amychophobia
sea pelagophobia, thalassophobia
secretions crinophobia
secrets calyptophobia
semen spermatophobia, spermophobia
sermons homilophobia, keryophobia
sexual intercourse coitophobia, cypridophobia, erotophobia, genophobia
sexual perversion paraphobia
shadows sciaphobia, sciophobia
sharks carcharinophobia, selachophobia
sharp objects aichmophobia, belonophobia
shellfish ostraconophobia
shock hormephobia
sinning enissophobia, enosiophobia, hamartophobia, peccatiphobia, peccatophobia
sisters sororophobia
sitting cathisophobia, kathisophobia, thaasophobia
skin dermatophobia
skin diseases dermatopathophobia, dermatosiophobia
skin of animals doraphobia
skunks mephitophobia
sleep hypnophobia, somniphobia
slime blennophobia, myxophobia
small objects microphobia, tapinophobia
smells olfactophobia, osmophobia, osphresiophobia
smoke capnophobia
smothering pnigerophobia, pnigophobia
snakes herpetophobia, ophiciophobia, ophidiophobia, ophiophobia
snoring rhonchophobia
snow chionophobia

society anthropophobia, sociophobia
solitude autophobia, eremiophobia, eremophobia, ermitophobia, isolophobia, monophobia
sorcery veneficophobia
sound acousticophobia ~of certain words: onomatophobia
sourness acerbophobia, acerophobia
spasms choreophobia
speaking aloud phonophobia
speech defect laliophobia, lalophobia
speed tachophobia
spiders arachnephobia, arachnophobia
spiny creatures echinophobia
spirits demonophobia, phantasmaphobia, pneumatiphobia, spectrophobia
stage fright prosceniophobia, topophobia
stairs climacophobia
standing or walking basiphobia, basophobia, basistasiphobia, basostasophobia, stasibasiphobia, stasiphobia, stasobasiphobia, stasophobia
stars astrophobia, siderophobia
statues agalmaphobia
staying single anuptaphobia
stealing cleptophobia, kleptophobia
stepfather vitricophobia
stepmother novercaphobia
stillness eremophobia, hesyphobia
stings cnidophobia
stooping kyphophobia, scoliophobia
strangers xenophobia
streets agyiophobia, agryophobia; crossing~: dromophobia
string linonophobia
stuttering psellismophobia
sun heliophobia, phengophobia

surgical operations ergasiophobia, tomophobia
swallowing phagophobia
swamps paludophobia
sweating sudoriophobia
symbolism semiophobia, symbolophobia
symmetry [in Egyptian temples, Japanese art, etc.] symmetrophobia
syphilis luetiphobia, syphilidophobia, syphiliphobia, syphilophobia
talking glossophobia, laliophobia, lalophobia, phonophobia
tapeworms taeniiphobia, taeniophobia, teniophobia
taste geumaphobia, geumatophobia, geumophobia; *sour~:* acerbophobia; *sweet~:* hedisophobia
technology technophobia
teeth odontophobia
teleology teleophobia
telephones telephonophobia
termites isopterophobia
theaters theatrophobia
theology theologicophobia
thieves cleptophobia, kleptophobia, harpaxophobia
thinking phronemophobia
thirst dipsophobia
thirteen tredecaphobia, tridecaphobia, triakaidekaphobia, triskadekaphobia, triskaidekaphobia
thunder brontophobia, ceraunophobia, keraunophobia, tonitrophobia
tickling with feathers pteronophobia
ticks acarophobia
time chronophobia
toads batrachophobia, bufonophobia
tombs taphophobia; *~stones:* placophobia
tooth decay cariophobia

tornadoes lilapsophobia
touching or being touched aphephobia, chiroptophobia, haphephobia, hapnophobia, haptephobia, haptophobia, thixophobia
train travel siderodromophobia
traitors proditophobia
travel dromophobia, hodophobia
trees dendrophobia
trembling tremophobia
trichinosis trichinophobia
tuberculosis phthisiophobia, phthisophobia, tuberculophobia
Turks Turcophobia
tyrants tyrannophobia
ugliness cacophobia
ulcers helcophobia
undressing deshabillophobia
urinating urophobia
vaccinations vaccinophobia
vampires vespertiliophobia
vegetables lachanophobia
vehicles amaxophobia, ochophobia
venereal disease cyprianophobia, cypridophobia, cyprinophobia, cypriphobia, venereophobia
vermin verminophobia
vertigo illyngophobia
virginity, losing esodophobia, primeisophobia
virgins parthenophobia
vomiting emetophobia
walking ambulophobia, basiphobia, basophobia, bathmophobia
warfare polemophobia
warts verruciophobia
washing oneself ablutophobia, balneophobia
wasps spheksophobia
wasting sickness tabophobia
water aquaphobia, hydrophobia
waves cymophobia, kymophobia
wax cerophobia
weakness asthenophobia

wealth chrematophobia, chryso-
phobia, plutophobia
weapons hoplophobia
weasels galeophobia
weight, gaining obesiophobia, pro-
crescophobia
werewolves lycophobia
whirlpools dinophobia
whispering psithurophobia
white leukophobia
wickedness scelerophobia
wild animals agrizoophobia,
theriophobia
wind ancraophobia, anemiaphobia,
anemophobia
windows fenestrophobia
wine enophobia, oenophobia, oino-
phobia
winter cheimaphobia

women feminophobia, gynephobia,
gynophobia; *beautiful~:* calligy-
nephobia, venustaphobia
wood hylephobia, hylophobia, xylophobia, ylophobia
words logophobia, verbophobia;
long~: sesquipedalophobia
work ergasiophobia, ergophobia,
ponophobia
worms helminthophobia, scoleci-
phobia, vermiphobia
wounds traumatophobia
wrinkles rhytiphobia
writing graphophobia, scriptopho-
bia
x-rays radiophobia
yawning oscitophobia
young girls parthenophobia
zombies basinecrophobia

FOOD

Nonvegetarians should also see "Animals."

acorn balan- (balaniferous); gland-
(glandiferous)
almond amygdalo- (amygdala-
ceous)
apple mali- (maliform); pom-
(pomaceous)
avocado pers- (persea)
banana musa- (musaceous)
barley alphito- (alphitomancy);
crith- (crithology); horde-
(hordeaceous); ptis-(ptisan)
bean cyam- (cyamoid); fab- (fabaceous); phaseol- (phaseolous)
beer cervis- (cervisial)
belch ruct- (eructation)
berry acin- (acinaceous); baccat-
baccate; bacci- (bacciferous);
cocci- (coccigerous)

blueberry vaccin- (vaccinium)
bran furfur- (furfuraceous); pityr-
(pityroid)
bread arto- (artophagous); pan-
(panivorous)
breakfast jent- (jentacular)
butter butyro- (butyraceous)
cabbage brassic- (brassicacious)
carbohydrate -ose (fructose)
cashew anacard- (anacardic)
cereal frument- (frumentaceous)
cheese case- (casefy); tyro- (tyromancy)
cherry ceras- (cerasin)
chestnut aescul- (aesculin); castan-
(castaneous)
chew manduc- (manduction);
mastic- (mastication)

citric citro- (citron)
cook -coct- (decoction); mageir- (mageiricophobia); magir- (magiric)
corn frument- (frumentation); spici- (spiciferous)
cucumber cucumi- (cucumiform)
cultivation -ponic (hydroponics)
digest chyli- (chyliferous); chymo- (chymotrypsin)-; peps- (pepsinogen); pept- (peptic); pepto- (peptogenic)
dill aneth- (anethated)
dinner deipno- (deipnophobia); prand- (postprandial)
drink -ade (lemonade); bib- (bibulous); pino- (pinocytosis); pocul- (poculent); poto- (potomania)
eating alim- (alimentation); bromato- (bromatology); -brotic (scolecobrotic); cib- (cibarious); comest- (comestible); ed- (edible); escul- (esculent); gust- (gustatory); manduc- (manducation); mastic- (mastication); -phagous (creophagous); -phagy (anthropophagy); -sitia (asitia); sitio- (sitiophobia); -troph (heterotroph); -trophic (heterotrophic); -trophy (hypertrophy); -vora (Carnivora); -vore (herbivore); -vorous (omnivorous)
fig fici- (ficiform); syc- (sycoma)
fruit -carp (endocarp); -carpic (endocarpic); carpo- (carpophore); -carpous (monocarpous); frug- (frugivorous); pomi- (pomiform); pomo- (pomology)
garlic scoro- (scorodite)
grain farr- (confarreate); farrag- (farraginous); frument- (frumentaceous); grani- (granivorous)
grape acini- (aciniform); botry- (botryose); racem- (racemiform); rhag- (rhagite); staphylo- (staphy-

line); uvi- (uviform); uvu- (uvula); vini- (viniculture); vino- (vinosity); viti- (viticulture)
hickory cichor- (cichoraceous)
honey melli- (melliferous)
kidney bean phaseol- (phaseolous)
leek porr- (porraceous); praso- (prasophagous)
lime tilia- (tiliaceous)
lunch prand- (prandial)
meal cen- (cenatory); coen- (coenaculous); deipno- (deipnophobia); prand- (anteprandial)
meat -burger (hamburger); carni- (carnivore); carnoso- (carnosity)
mint menth- (menthaceous)
mustard sinap- (sinapistic)
nutmeg myrist- (myristic)
oats aveni- (avenaceous)
onion cep- (cepous); cromny- (cromnyomancy)
orange hesperid- (hesperidine)
parsley petrosel- (petroseline)
pea pisi- (pisiform)
peach persic- (persicaria)
peanut arach- (arachidic)
pear apio- (apiocrinite); piri- (piriform); pyri- (pyriform)
pepper piper- (piperic)
pineapple bromel- (bromeliaceous)
pomegranate balaust- (balaustine)
pumpkin pepo- (pepon)
radish raphan- (raphania)
rice oryzi- (oryzivorous); rizi- (riziform)
salad acetar- (acetarious)
salt halo- (halophile); sali- (desalination); salino- (salinometric); sals- (salsamentarious)
sandwich -burger (cheeseburger)
sausage allanto- (allantoid); botul- (botuliform)
strawberry fragar- (fragarol)
sugar gluco- (glucose); glycero- (glycerol); glyco- (glycosuria);

levul- (levulose); saccharo- (saccharometer); sucr- (sucrose)
tea thei- (theiform)
truffle hydno- (hydnocarpous)
turnip napi- (napiform)
vegetable lachan- (lachanopolist); oler- (oleraceous); olit- (olitory);

vegeti- (vegetivorous); vegeto- (vegetarian)
walnut juglan- (juglandaceous)
wheat silig- (siliginous); tritic- (triticeous)
yam dioscorea- (dioscoreaceous)

LOCATION

above ano- (anocarpous); epi- (epidermis); ob- (obliterate); over- (overhang); super- (superscript); supra- (supraliminal); sur- (surbase)
across dia- (diameter); per- (peregrinaion); trans- (transmit); transverso- (transverso-cubital)
apex -apical (periapical); apico- (apicotomy)
behind after- (afterburner); back- (backdrop); meta- (metasternum); opistho- (opisthotic); post- (postscenium); postero- (posterolateral); retro- (retrocopulant)
between/among dia- (diagnosis); enter- (entergrave); entre- (entr'acte); epi- (epidemic); inter- (interval)
distant tele- (television)
front ante- (antependium); antero- (anteroparietal); fore- (forefront); pre- (preaortic); pro- (proscenium); proso- (prosogaster)
high(er) acro- (acrocephaly); alti- (altitude); alto- (alto-relievo); hypsi- (hypsistenocephalic); hypso- (hypsometry); super- (superstructure)
inside eis- (eisegesis); em- (embedded); en- (enclose); endo- (endoskeleton); ento- (entoparasite);

eso- (esoenteritis); il- (illuminate); im- (implosion); in- (incarcerate); intero- (interoceptor); ir- (irradiate); intra- (intramural); intro- (introspection)
left laeo- (laeotropic) laevo- (laevorotatory) levo- (levogyrate) sinistro- (sinistrorse)
middle centri- (centripetal); centro- (centrolineal); -centric (heliocentric); medi- (medieval); medio- (mediodorsal); mes- (mesallantoid); mesati- (mesaticephalic); mesio- (mesio-sinistral); meso- (mesothorax); mezzo- (mezzotint); mid- (midsection)
near ad- (adjoining); by- (bystander); cis- (cismontane); epi- (epicenter); juxta- (juxtapose); para- (parametric); peri- (perigee); prox- (approximal) proximo- (proximocephalic)
outside ecto- (ectoparasite); epi- (epidermis); exo- (exoskeleton); extero- (exteroceptor); extra- (extraterritorial); extro- (extrovert); out- (outhouse); para- (paradox); preter- (preternatural)
right dexio- (dexiotropic); dextro- (dextrorse)
surrounding ambi- (ambiance); amphi- (amphithecium); be-

(beset); circum- (circumference); peri- (periotic)

through dia- (diaphanous); per- (percolate); trans- (transparent); -wide (worldwide)

under hypo- (hypodermic); infero- (inferoposterior); infra- (infrastructure); sub- (subscript); subter- (subterfluent); under- (underpinning)

upon ana- (anaclisis); epi- (epilogue); ob- (obtrude); super- (superstructure); sur- (surcharge)

with co- (coterminous); col- (colleague); com- (commingle); con- (convulse); cor- (correlate); hama- (hamadryad); inter- (intermixed); para- (parataxis); syl- (syllable); sym- (symbiosis); symphyo- (symphyogenesis); symphysio- (symphysiorrhaphy); syn- (synagogue); sys- (system)

NEGATIVES

a- *pre* not; without (atypical)

ab- *pre* away from (absorbent)

an- *pre* not; without (anorexia)

anti- *pre* opposite of; against (antidote)

apo- *pre* detached; apart (apogamy)

-atresia *comb* absence of an opening (proctatresia)

atreto- *comb* absence of an opening (atretocyst)

cata- *pre* against (catachresis)

contra- *pre* opposite; against (contravene)

counter- *comb* opposite; against (counter-clockwise)

de- *pre* deprived of; apart (devaluation)

dis- *pre* apart; opposite (disengage)

dys- *pre* badly; not correct (dysfunctional)

ectro- *comb* missing; absent (ectromelia)

ex- *pre* former; deprived of (ex-member)

il- *pre* not; opposite of (illicit)

im- *pre* not; opposite of (impartial)

in- *pre* not; opposite of (inarticulate)

ir- *pre* not; opposite of (irreverent)

-less *suf* without; unable to (restless)

lipo- *comb* lacking; leaving (lipography)

mal- *pre* poorly; not (malnutrition)

mis- *pre* wrongly; not (misalignment)

miso- *comb* antipathy; hatred (misocainea)

ne- *pre* not; opposite of (nescient)

nihil- *base* nothingness (annihilate)

no- *pre* not any (no-load)

non- *pre* not; absence of (nonallergenic)

nulli- *pre* none (nulliparous)

ob- *pre* against; inverse (obliterate)

-priv- *base* lacking; taken away (deprivation)

un- *pre* not; reversal (unimaginable)

with- *pre* apart; opposed (withstand)

NUMBERS

0   nulli- (nullipara)

⅒   decim- (decimate)

⅑   non- (nonan)

⅛   octan- (octant)

⅐   septim- (septimal)

⅙   sext- (sextant)

⅕   quint- (quintant)

¼   tetarto- (tetartohedral)

⅓   trient- (triental)

½   demi- (demitint); dicho- (dichotomize); dimid- (dimidiation); hemi- (hemisphere); mezzo- (mezzo-relievo); semi- (semicolumnar)

¾   triquadr- (triquadrantal)

1   eka- (ekaselenium); haplo- (haplopetalous); heno- (henotheism); mono- (monorail); uni- (unilateral)

1 & ½   sesqui- (sesquihoral)

2   ambi- (ambiversion); ambo- (amboceptor); amphi- (amphicarpous); ampho- (amphora); bi- (bicentennial); bin- (binaural); bis- (bissextile); deutero- (deuterogamy); deuto- (deutoplasm); di- (diplegia); dicho- (dichotomous); didym- (didymalgia); diphy-(diphyceral); diplo- (diplopia); disso- (dissogony); double- (doubleheader); du- (duplicate); duplicato- (duplicatodentate); duplici- (duplicipennate); duo- (duograph); dyo- (Dyophysite); gemelli- (gemelliparous); gemin- (geminiflorous); twi- (twinight); zygo- (zygodont)

3   ter- (tercet); -tern- (ternary); -tert- (tertiary); tri- (trifocal); triakis- (triakisoctahedron); triangulato- (triangulato-subovate); trigono- (trigonocephalic); triplo- (triploblastic); triplicato- (triplicato-pinnate); trito- (tritoencephalon)

4   quadra- (quadraphonic); quadrato- (quadrato-cubic); quadri- (quadrilateral); quadru- (quadruped); quart- (quarterly); quarti- (quartisect); quat- (quaternate); quater- (quater-centenary); quatre- (quatrefoil); tessara- (tesseraphthong); tetarto- (tetartohedral); tetra- (Tetragrammaton); tetrakis- (tetrakisdodecahedron)

5   cinque- (cinquefoil); penta- (pentacle); quin- (quinary); quinque- (quinquennium); quint- (quintuplets); quinti- (quintiped)

6   hexa- (hexahedron); hexakis- (hexakisoctahedron); seni- (senary); sex- (sexagenarian); sexi- (sexipolar); sexti- (sextisection); sise- (siseangle)

7   hebdo- (hebdomadral); hepta- (Heptateuch); septem- (September); septi- (septifolious)

8   octa- (octagon); octo- (octonary); ogdo- (ogdoastich)

9   ennea- (enneahedron); nona- (nonagon); -nov- (novena)

10   dec(a)- (decade); decem- (decempennate); deci- (decimeter); deka- (dekagram); -teen (sixteen); -ty (seventy)

11   endeca- (endecagon); hendeca- (hendecasyllabic); undec- (undecagon); undecim- (undecimal)

12   dodeca- (dodecastyle); duodec- (duodecennial); duodecim- (duodecimfid); duoden- (duodenary)

13 tredecim- (tredecimal);
triskaideka- (triskaidekaphobia)
14 quattuordec- (quattuordecillion);
tessaradeca- (tessaradecasyllabon);
tetradeca- (tetradecapod); tetra-
kaideca- (tetrakaidecahedron)
15 pentakaideca- (pentakaidecahedron); quindec- (quindecennial)
16 hexadeca- (hexadecachoron);
hexakaideca- (hexakaidecahedron); sedecim- (sedecimal)
17 heptakaideca- (heptakaidecahedron); septendecim- (septendeci-
mal)
18 duodeviginti- (duodevigintiangular); octakaideca- octakaidecahedron)
19 enneakaideca- (enneakaidecahedron); undeviginti- (undevigintiangular)
20 eico- (eicosapentaenoic: 25);
icosa- (icosandria); icosi- (icositetrahedron: 24); vicesim- (vicesimal); vigent- (vigentennial); vig-
inti- (vigintiangular)
30 triaconta- (triacontahedral);
triceni- (tricenary); triges- (trigesimal); trigint- (trigintal)
40 quadragen- (quadragenarian);
quadrages- (quadragesimal)
50 pentacosta- (pentacostaglossal);
pentecoha- (pentecontaglossal);
quinquagen- (quinquagenarian);
quinquages- (quinquagesimal)
60 hexaconta- (hexacontahedron);
sexagen- (sexagenarian); sexages-
(sexagesimal)
70 septuagen- (septuagenarian);
septuages- (septuagesimal); septu-
agint- (Septuagint)
80 octogen- (octogenarian); octo-
ges- (octogesimal)

90 enneaconta- (enneacontahedral);
nonagen- (nonagenarian);
nonages- (nonagesimal)
100 cent(i)- (centigrade); hecato-
(hecatophyllous); hecatinicosa-
(hecatinicosachoron: 120); hecto-
(hectoliter); hekto (hektogram)
200 ducen- (ducenarious)
300 trecent- (trecentene)
400 quadricent- (quadricentennial)
500 quincent- (quincentennial)
600 hexacosi- (hexacosichoron);
sexcent- (sexcentenary)
700 septingenti- (septingentenary)
800 octocent- (octocentenary)
900 enneacent- (enneacentenary)
1,000 -chili- (chiliarch); kilo- (kilogram); ~*th:* milli- (millibar)
10,000 myria- (myriameter); myrio-
(myriophyllous)
1,000,000 *one million* mega- (mega-
volt); ~*th:* micro- (microgram)
1,000,000,000 *one billion* giga-
(gigabyte); ~*th:* nano- (nanosecond); nanno- (nannoplankton)
1,000,000,000,000 *one trillion* tera-
(terahertz); ~*th:* pico- (picofarad)
1,000,000,000,000,000 *one quadrillion* peta- (petameter); ~*th:*
femto- (femtometer);
1,000,000,000,000,000,000 *one
quintillion* exa- (exameter); ~*th:*
atto- (attogram)
1,000,000,000,000,000,000,000 *one
hexillion* zetta- (zettabyte); ~*th:*
zepto- (zeptovolt)
1,000,000,000,000,000,000,000,000
one heptillion yotta- (yottameter); ~*th:* yocto- (yoctogram)

THE SENSES

Hearing

deafness -surd- (surdity)
ear auri- (auricle); auriculo-
(auriculo-temporal); ot- (othemorrhagia); oto- (otology)
hear acou- (acouasm); acoust-
(acoustical); audi- (auditory);
audio- (audiology); auri- (auricle); ecoia (dysecoia)
sound echo- (echogenic); -phone
(telephone); phono- (phono-
graph); -phony (euphony);
-phthong (diphthong); son-
(sonic); soni- (soniferous); sono-
(sonometer); sonoro- (sonorous)

RELATED PERCEPTIONS

noisy crepit- (crepitation); frem-
(fremitus); ligyr- (ligyrophobia);
strid- (strident); stridul- (stridu-
lous); strepi- (strepitus);
silent hesy- (hesychastic); tacit-
(taciturnity)

Seeing

blindness caec- (caecilian); cec-
(cecity); lusc- (eluscate); typhlo-
(typhlosis)
eye blepharo- (blepharotomy); can-
tho- (canthoplasty); cili- (ciliary);
corneo- (corneoiritis); irido-
(iridomotor); kerato- (keratotomy); oculi- (oculiform); oculo-
(oculomotor); ommat- (om-
matophore); op- (opalgia); oph-
thalmo- (ophthalmoscope); -opia
(diplopia); ophry- (ophryosis);
opsi- (opsiometer); opso- (opsoclonus); optico- (optico-papillary); opto- (optometry); retino-
(retinoschisis); sclero- (sclerotomy); tarso (tarsoplasty)

pupil core- (corelysis); coreo-
(coreoplasty); -coria (isocoria);
coro- (coroplastic); -koria
(leukokoria); pupillo- (pupillometer)
see -blep- (ablepsia); eid- (eidetic);
-opsia (hemianopsia); -opsis (synopsis); -opsy (biopsy); -scope
(telescope); -scopic (microscopic); scopo- (scopophilia);
-scopy (bioscopy); -scrut- (in-
scrutable); spec- (spectator); -
spic- (conspicuous); -vid-
(video); -vis- (vision); visuo-
(visuosensory)

RELATED PERCEPTIONS

bright fulg- (fulgurant); helio-
(helioscope); luc- (luciferous);
lumin- (luminosity)
dark amaur- (amaurosus); ambly-
(amblyopia); nyct- (nyctalopia);
scoto- (scotophobia); tenebr-
(tenebrous)

Smelling

nose nasi- (nasiform); naso- (nasol-
ogy); rhino- (rhinology)
smell bromo- (bromidrosis); fet-
(fetid); nidor- (nidorous); -odic
(euodic); odori- (odoriferous);
odoro- (odoroscope); -olent
(redolent); -olfact- (olfactory);
-osmia (anosmia); osmo- (osmodysphoria); osphresio (osphresiophobia); ozo- (ozostomia)

RELATED PERCEPTIONS

pleasant bene- (beneficial); eu- (euodic)
unpleasant cac- (cacosmia); mal-
(malodorous)

Tasting

mouth -mouthed (dry-mouthed); oro- (orolingual); stomato- (stomatalgia); -stome (cyto-stome); -stomous (monostomous)

palate palato- (palatonasal); uranisco- (uranisconitis); urano- (uranoplasty); velar- (velarize)

saliva ptyal- (ptyalagogue); sialo- (sialorrhea)

taste geum- (geumaphobia); geu-mat- (geumatophobia); -geusia (parageusia); -gust- (gustatory); sapor- (saporific)

tongue -glossia (macroglossia); glosso- (glossodynia); hyo- (hyo-glossal); lamino- (lamino-alveo-lar); ligur- (ligurition); ling- (lingible); lingui- (linguiform)

RELATED PERCEPTIONS

bitter alk- (alkaloid); picro- (picrotoxin)

salty alo- (alomancy); halo- (halophile); sal- (saline); sals- (salsamentarious)

sour acerb- (acerbity); acid- (acidulous); amar- (amarine)

sweet hedy- (hedyphane); melli- (mellifluous); dulc- (dulcify)

Touching

sensation -esthesia (myesthesia); esthesio- (esthesiometer)

skin cut(i)- (subcutaneous); derm- (dermabrasion); -derm (melano-derm); derma- (dermatherm); -derma (scleroderma); dermat- (dermatitis); dermato- (dermatol-ogy); -dermatous (xeroderma-tous); -dermis (epidermis); dermo- (dermoneural)

touch aphe- (aphephobia); -aphia (dysaphia); -apsia (parapsia); haph- (haphalgesia); hapto- (hap-tometer); -palp- (palpable); sens(i)- (sensiferous); sensori- (sensorineural); sent- (sentient); -tact- (contact); -tang- (tangible); thigmo- (thigmotaxis)

RELATED PERCEPTIONS

cold alg- (algid); cheima- (cheimaphilic); crymo- (cry-mophilic); cryo- (cryopathy); frigo- (frigorific); gelo- (gelosis); kryo- (kryometer); psychro- (psy-chroalgia); rhigo- (rhigolene)

dry -sicc- (desiccate); xero- (xero-phyte)

hard dur- (duricrust); scler- (scle-ronychia)

rough salebr- (salebrous); trachy- (trachycarpous)

smooth glabr- (glabrous); leio- (leiotrichous); levig- (levigated); lisso- (lissotrichous); lubr- (lu-bricity); psilo- (psilodermatous)

soft malac- (malacissant); malax- (malaxation); -moll- (emollient)

warm calo- (caloreceptor); calori- (calorific); caum- (caumesthesia); pyr- (pyrogenic); therm- (ther-mal); thermo- (thermosensitive); -thermy (diathermy)

wet humect- (humectant); hydro- (hydrorrhea); hygro- (hygro-scopic); madefac- (madefaction)

SHAPES

acorn-shaped glandi- (glandiform)
agate-shaped agat- (agatiform)
almond-shaped amygdal- (amygdaliform)
anchor-shaped ancry- (ancryoid)
angle -angle (quadrangle); angul- (rectangular); -gon (polygon); -gonal (polygonal); gonio- (goniometer)
antennae-shaped antenn- (antenniform)
anther-shaped anther- (antheriform)
apple-shaped pomi- (pomiform)
arch-shaped arci- (arciform)
ax-shaped securi- (securiform)
barrel-shaped dolio- (dolioform)
basket-shaped calathi- (calathiform)
beak-shaped aquil- (aquiline); corac- (coracoid); rhamph- (rhamphoid); rhyncho- (rhynchophorous); rostrato- (rostratonariform); rostri- (rostriform)
bean-shaped fabi- (fabiform)
bear-shaped urs- (ursiform)
beehive-shaped alve- (alveated)
beetle-shaped scarab- (scaraboid)
bell-shaped campan- (campaniform)
bent ancylo- (ancylostomiasis); ankylo- (ankylosis); -campsis (phallocampsis); campto- (camptocormia); campylo- (campylodactyly); -clinal (anticlinal); -clinate (proclinate); -cline (incline); -clinic (matroclinic); clino- (clinometer); -clinous (patroclinous); -clisis (pathoclisis); clit- (heteroclital); cliv- (declivity); curvi- (curvilinear); cyrto- (cyrtometer); -flect- (genuflection); flex- (flex-

ural); lechrio- (lechriodont); loxo- (loxotomy); repando- (repando-dentate); scolio- (scoliokyphosis); sinu- (sinuousity); -verge (diverge)
berry-shaped bacc- (bacciform)
boat-shaped cymb- (cymbiform); navi- (naviform); scapho- (scaphocephaly); scapulo- (scapulohumeral)
bottle-shaped ampull- (ampullaceous) *leather bottle-shaped:* utrei- (utreiform); utric- (utricular)
bowl-shaped crater- (crateriform)
branch-shaped rami- (ramiform)
breast-shaped mammi- (mammiform)
brick-shaped plinthi- (plinthiform)
bristle-shaped seti- (setiform)
broom-shaped scopi- (scopiform)
brush-shaped muscar- (muscariform)
bud-shaped gemm- (gemmiform)
bull-shaped taur- (tauriform)
canine tooth-shaped laniar- (laniariform)
cap-shaped pile- (pileiform)
caterpillar-shaped eruci- (eruciform)
catkin-shaped amenti-[2] (amentiform); juli- (juliform)
chisel-shaped scalpri- (scalpriform)
clarion-shaped litui- (lituiform)
claw-shaped ungui- (unguiform)
cleaver-shaped dolabr- (dolabriform)
cloud-shaped nubi- (nubiform)
club-shaped clav- (claviform)
cobweb-shaped arachn- (arachnoid)
coin-shaped nummi- (nummiform)

collar-shaped colli- (colliform)
column-shaped columelli- (columelliform)
comb-shaped pectin- (pectiniform)
cone-shaped coni- (coniform)
coral-shaped coralli- (coralliform)
corn-shaped grani- (graniform)
cowl-shaped cuculli- (cuculliform)
crab-shaped cancri- (cancriform)
crater-shaped crateri- (crateriform)
crescent-shaped crescenti- (crescentiform) lunul- (lunular)
cross-shaped cruc- (cruciform)
crown-shaped coron- (coroniform)
crystal-shaped crystalli- (crystalliform)
cube-shaped cubi- (cubiform)
cuckoo-shaped cuculi- (cuculiform)
cucumber-shaped cucumi- (cucumiform)
cup-shaped calath- (calathiform); cotyl- (cotyliform); crin- (crinoid); cupuli- (cupuliform); cyath- (cyathiform); pocul- (poculiform); scyphi- (scyphiform)
cylinder-shaped cylindri- (cylindriform)
dish-shaped scutel- (scutelliform)
drop-shaped gutti- (guttiform); stilli- (stilliform)
ear-shaped aur-[1] (auriform)
eel-shaped anguill- (anguilliform)
egg-shaped ov- (oviform); oval- (ovaliform)
embryo-shaped embry- (embryoniform)
eye-shaped ocul- (oculiform)
faced/faceted -hedral (hexahedral); -hedron (polyhedron)
fan-shaped flabelli- (flabelliform)
feather-shaped pinni- (pinniform); plumil- (plumiliform)
fern-shaped filici- (filiciform)

fiber-shaped fibri- (fibriform)
fibril-shaped fibrilli- (fibrilliform)
fiddle-shaped pandur- (panduriform)
fig-shaped fici- (ficiform)
finger-shaped digiti- (digitiform)
fish-shaped pisci- (pisciform)
fissure-shaped fissuri- (fissuriform)
flask-shaped ampulli- (ampulliform); lagen- (lageniform)
flat plani- (planimeter); plano- (planoconcave); platy- (platypus)
flower-shaped flor- (floriform)
foot-shaped ped-[1] (pediform)
forked -furc- (bifurcation)
fowl-shaped galli- (galliform)
frog-shaped rani- (raniform)
fruit-shaped fructi- (fructiform)
fungus-shaped fungill- (fungilliform)
funnel-shaped infundibuli- (infundibuliform)
gland-shaped aden- (adeniform)
gnat-shaped culici- (culiciform)
goat-shaped capri- (capriform)
goblet-shaped pocul- (poculiform)
grape-shaped staphylo- (staphyloma); uvi- (uviform); uvu- (uvula);~*cluster:* acini- (aciniform)
hair-shaped capilli- (capilliform)
hammer-shaped malle- (malleiform)
hand-shaped mani- (maniform)
hatchet-shaped dolabri- (dolabriform)
heart-shaped cord- (cordoform); cordato- (cordato-ovate)
helmet-shaped cassid- (cassidiform); gale- (galeate)
herring-shaped harengi- (harengiform)
hinge-shaped gingly- (ginglyform)
hood-shaped calyptri- (calyptriform)

hook-shaped hami- (hamiform);
unci- (unciform)

horn-shaped corni- (corniculate,
corniform)

horseshoe-shaped hippocrepi-
(hippocrepiform)

horsetail-shaped equiset- (equisetiform)

hull-shaped naut- (nautiform)

hydra-shaped hydr- (hydraform)

irregular poikilo- (poikilocyte)

isopod-shaped isopodi- (isopodi-
form)

ivy-shaped hederi- (hederiform)

kidney-shaped reni- (reniform)

knee-shaped genu- (genuform)

knife-shaped cultell- (cultellated);
cultri- (cultriform)

ladder-shaped scalari- (scalari-
form)

lance-shaped lanci- (lanciform)

larva-shaped larvi- (larviform)

layered -decker (double-decker);
lamelli- (lamelliform); lamin-
(lamination); -plex (cerviplex);
strat- (stratified)

leaf-shaped clad- (cladode); foli-
(foliiform); phyll- (phylliform)

leather bottle-shaped utrei-
(utreiform); utric- (utricular)

lid-shaped operculi- (operculiform)

lily-shaped lili- (liliform)

lizard-shaped lacerti- (lacerti-
form)

lyre-shaped lyri- (lyriform)

malformed -mutil- (Mutilla); pero-
(peropodous)

miter-shaped mitri- (mitriform)

moon-shaped luni- (luniform)

mummy-shaped mummi- (mum-
miform)

mushroom-shaped fungi- (fungi-
form); agar- (agariciform)

myrtle leaf-shaped myrti- (myrtiform)

necklace-shaped monili- (moniliform)

needle-shaped aci- (aciform); aci-
cul- (acicular)

nose-shaped nari- (nariform); nasi-
(nasiform)

nut-shaped caryo- (caryopsis);
karyo- (karyokinesis); nuci- (nu-
ciform); nucleo (nucleolus)

oar-shaped remi- (remiform)

oat-shaped aveni- (aveniform)

ox-shaped bov- (boviform)

oyster-shaped ostrea- (ostreiform)

pea-shaped pisi- (pisiform)

pear-shaped piri- (piriform); pyri-
(pyriform)

pen-shaped styl- (styliform)

penis-shaped pen- (peniform)

petal-shaped petuli- (petuliform)

pillar-shaped columelli- (columelliform); columni- (columniform)

pinecone-shaped strobil- (strobiliform)

pipe-shaped fistuli- (fistuliform)

placenta-shaped placenti- (placentiform)

pod-shaped siliqu- (siliquiform)

pointed aci- (acicular); acro- (acrocephaly); acu- (aculeate); acuti-
(acutifoliate); -belon- (belonophobia); cusp- (cuspid); muric-
(muricate); oxy- (oxyrhine);
-punct- (punctured); stylo- (stylograph)

pouch-shaped scroti- (scrotiform)

purse-shaped bursi- (bursiform)

rattlesnake-shaped crotali- (crotal-
iform)

reed-shaped calam- (calamiform)

rice grain-shaped rizi- (riziform)

ring-shaped annul- (annular);
circin- (circinate)

rod-shaped -bacill- (bacilliform);
bacul- (baculiform); coryn-
(coryneform); -rad- (radial);

rhabdo- (rhabdomyoma); virgul- (virgulate)

roof-shaped tecti- (tectiform)

root-shaped radic- (radiciform)

rope-shaped funil- (funiliform); resti- (restiform)

round -annul- (annulate); -anu- (anulus); -cing- (cingulum); cinct- (cincture); circin- (circinately); -circul- (recirculate); -coron- (coronation); crico- (cricoid); cyclo (cyclostomous); disco- (discoid); globo- (globosity); glomer- (glomerate); numm- (nummular); -orb- (suborbital); -rot- (rotund); -sphere (hemisphere); sphero- (spheroid); stilli- (stilliform); tereti- (tereticaudate); troch- (trochal); zon- (zonesthesia)

rush-shaped junci- (junciform)

sac-shaped bursi- (bursiform); sacc- (sacciform)

salmon-shaped salmoni- (salmoniform)

saucer-shaped acetabul- (acetabuliform)

sausage-shaped allanto- (allantoid); botul- (botuliform)

saw-shaped serrati- (serratiform)

scale-shaped lamelli- (lamelliform); squami- (squamiform)

scimitar-shaped acinaci- (acinaciform)

shell-shaped conchi- (conchiform)

shield-shaped clype- (clypeiform); pelti- (peltiform); scut- (scutiform)

sickle-shaped drepani- (drepaniform); falci- (falciform)

sieve-shaped coli- (coliform); cribri- (cribriform)

slanting loxo- (loxodromic); plagio- (plagiodont)

slug-shaped limaci- (limaciform)

snake-shaped angui- (anguiform); colubri- (colubriform); serpenti- (serpentiform)

spatula-shaped spatuli- (spatuliform)

spear-shaped hasti- (hastiform)

sphere-shaped spheri- (spheriform)

spider-shaped arene- (areneiform)

spike-shaped spic- (spiciform)

spindle-shaped fusu- (fusiform)

spine-shaped aculei- (aculeiform); spini- (spiniform)

spiral-shaped cirri- (cirriform); cochl- (cochleate); gyro- (gyroidal); helici- (heliciform); spiri- (spiriform)

spoon-shaped cochleari- (cochleariform)

square -quadr- (quadrangle)

stalactite-shaped stalacti- (stalactiform)

stalk-shaped stipiti- (stipitiform)

star-shaped aster- (asterisk); stelli- (stelliform)

straight ithy- (ithyphallic); ortho- (orthogonal)

strap-shaped liguli- (liguliform); lora- (lorate)

sword-shaped ensi- (ensiform); xiphi- (Xiphias); xipho- (xiphoid)

tea leaf-shaped thei- (theiform)

tear-shaped lachrymi- (lachrymiform)

tendril-shaped cirri- (cirriform); pampin- (pampiniform)

tentacle-shaped tentaculi- (tentaculiform)

thread-shaped fili- (filiform); nemato- (nematogen)

tongue-shaped lingui- (linguiform)

tooth-shaped denti- (dentiform)

top-shaped strombuli- (strombuliform); turbi- (turbinated)

tower-shaped pyrgo- (pyrgoidal)

trapezoid-shaped trapezi- (trapezi-
  form)
tray-shaped hypocrater- (hypocrateriform)
tree-shaped arbor- (arboriform);
  dendri- (dendriform)
triangular delt- (deltoidal); trian-
  gulato- (triangulato-subovate);
  trigon- (trigonal)
tube-shaped fistuli- (fistuliform);
  syringo- (syringotomy); tubi-
  (tubiform); tubuli- (tubuliform);
  vasi- (vasiform)
turnip-shaped napi- (napiform)
umbrella-shaped umbraculi-
  (umbraculiform)

vase-shaped urcei- (urceiform)
wart-shaped verruci- (verruciform)
wedge-shaped cune- (cuneiform);
  spheno- (sphenography)
wheel-shaped roti- (rotiform);
  troch- (trochal)
whiplash-shaped flagelli- (flagelli-
  form)
wing-shaped ala- (aliform)
wingcase-shaped elytri- (elytriform)
worm-shaped lumbric- (lumbriciform); scoleci- (scoleciform);
  vermi- (vermiform)
x-shaped decuss- (decussate)
yoke-shaped zygo- (zygomorphic)

TIME

afternoon pomerid- (pomeridian)
ancient -antiq- (antiquity);
  arch(a)eo- (archaeology);
  pal(a)eo- (Paleozoic); proto-
  (protohuman)
day -diurn- (diurnal); ephem-
  (ephemeris); hemer- (hemerine);
  -journ- (journal); quotid- (quotidian)
earlier ante- (antedate); fore- (forecast); pre- (predawn); pro- (pro-
  vision); protero- (proterotype);
  proto- (protomartyr); retro-
  (retroactive); yester- (yesteryear)
early period eo- (eolithic); paleo-
  (paleolithic)
evening crepus- (crepuscular);
  noct- (nocturnal); nocti- (noctilucent); nycto- (nyctophobia); ves-
  per- (vespertine)
hour horo- (horology)
incomplete -esce (incandesce);
  -escence (convalescence); -escent
  (incandescent)

lasting diuturn- (diuturnal); dur-
  (durable); perenn- (perennial);
  perm- (permanent); stabil- (stability)
later hystero- (hysterogenic); meta-
  (metabiosis); post (postmeridian);
  retro- (retrofit)
month -mens(i)- (mensal)
  monthly: emmen- (emmeniopathy)
morning matut- (matutinal)
new caeno- (Caenozoic); caino-
  (Cainozoic); ceno- (cenogenesis);
  neo- (neoplast); nov- (novelty);
  thalero- (thalerophagous)
night crepus- (crepuscular); noct-
  (nocturnal); nocti- (noctilucent);
  nycto- (nyctophobia); vesper-
  (vespertine)
old gerasco- (gerascophobia); gero-
  (gerodontics); geronto- (gerontology); grand- (grandfather); pres-
  byo- (presbyacusis); -sen-
  (seniority); -vet- (veteran)

recent -cene (Miocene); ceno-
(Cenozoic)

same time co- (coexist); hama-
(hamarchy); simul- (simultaneous); synchron- (synchronicity)

time chrono- (chronology) ;-temp-
(temporary)

today hodie- (hodiernal)

tomorrow crastin- (procrastinate)

twilight crepus- (crepusculine); lyg-
(lygophilia)

week -hebdom- (hebdomadal); sep-
timan- (septimanal)

year -ann- (annual); -enn- (biennial)

yesterday hestern- (hesternal);
prid- (pridian)

young juven- (juvenile)